Accession to the World Trade Organization

ELGAR INTERNATIONAL ECONOMIC LAW

Series Editors: Alan O. Sykes, *Frank and Bernice J. Greenberg Professor of Law, University of Chicago Law School, USA*, and Mary E. Footer, *Professor of International Economic Law, University of Nottingham, UK*

This monograph series is intended to provide a point of convergence for high quality, original work on various aspects of international economic and WTO law, ranging from established subject matter, such as international agricultural trade or the application of core trade disciplines such as MFN, to cross-cutting issues involving the interaction of international standards in the fields of investment, tax, competition, food safety and consumer protection with international trade law or the relationship of horizontal exceptions such as the general exception to domestic regulatory barriers. Theoretically rigorous, these books will take an analytical and discursive approach to the field, wherever possible drawing on insights from disciplines other than law, such as economics and politics, in an attempt to arrive at a genuinely inter-disciplinary perspective. Proposals are encouraged that primarily engage with new and previously under-developed themes in the field, or alternatively offer an innovative analysis of areas of uncertainty in the existing law. Bringing together work from both established authors – academics and practitioners alike – and from a new generation of scholars, the Elgar International Economic Law series aims to play an important role in the development of thinking in the field.

Titles in the series include:

International Economic Law and the Digital Divide
A New Silk Road?
Rohan Kariyawasam

The Law and Economics of Contingent Protection in the WTO
Petros C. Mavroidis, Patrick A. Messerlin and Jasper M. Wauters

International Trade and Health Protection
A Critical Assessment of the WTO's SPS Agreement
Tracey Epps

Agriculture and the WTO
Towards a New Theory of International Agricultural Trade Regulation
Fiona Smith

Reconciling Trade and Climate
How the WTO Can Help Address Climate Change
Tracey Epps and Andrew Green

International Economic Law and Monetary Measures
Limitations to States' Sovereignty and Dispute Settlement
Annamaria Viterbo

Accession to the World Trade Organization
A Legal Analysis
Dylan Geraets

Accession to the World Trade Organization

A Legal Analysis

Dylan Geraets

Associate, Mayer Brown, Brussels and Associate Fellow, Leuven Centre for Global Governance Studies, KU Leuven, Belgium

ELGAR INTERNATIONAL ECONOMIC LAW

Edward Elgar
PUBLISHING

Cheltenham, UK • Northampton, MA, USA

Published by
Edward Elgar Publishing Limited
The Lypiatts
15 Lansdown Road
Cheltenham
Glos GL50 2JA
UK

Edward Elgar Publishing, Inc.
William Pratt House
9 Dewey Court
Northampton
Massachusetts 01060
USA

A catalogue record for this book
is available from the British Library

Library of Congress Control Number: 2017953161

This book is available electronically in the **Elgar**online
Law subject collection
DOI 10.4337/9781788112598

MIX
Paper from responsible sources
FSC
www.fsc.org
FSC® C013056

ISBN 978 1 78811 258 1 (cased)
ISBN 978 1 78811 259 8 (eBook)

Typeset by Columns Design XML Ltd, Reading
Printed and bound in Great Britain by TJ International Ltd, Padstow

Contents

List of tables ix
Acknowledgements x
List of abbreviations xii
Table of cited WTO and GATT dispute settlement reports xv
Table of requests for consultations citing protocol of accession provisions xx

Introduction 1

PART I ACCESSION TO THE MULTILATERAL TRADING SYSTEM

1 The General Agreement on Tariffs and Trade 1947 (GATT 1947) and the World Trade Organization (WTO) – why join the club? 11

1.1 Introduction: the early days of the multilateral trading system 11
1.1.1 The International Trade Organization 12
1.1.2 The General Agreement on Tariffs and Trade 1947 13
1.2 The World Trade Organization 20
1.3 Rationales for accession 22
1.3.1 Economic motives for WTO accession 23
1.3.2 Political motives for WTO accession 28
1.3.3 Externalities of WTO accession 29
1.3.4 Accession in times of regionalization and the Doha Development Round 32
1.4 Conclusion 34

2 Membership of the GATT 1947 and the WTO 36

2.1 Introduction 36
2.2 Becoming a Contracting Party to the GATT 1947 37
2.2.1 Joining GATT: accession or succession? 37
2.2.2 The beginning of GATT: 23 (22) Contracting Parties 41

2.2.3 A categorization of acceding countries 47
2.3 Accession to the WTO 52
2.3.1 An overview: accessions to the WTO in numbers 52
2.3.2 Joining the WTO 56
2.4 Conclusion 69

3 The scope of the multilateral trading system 72

3.1 Introduction: the legalization of the multilateral trading system 72
3.2 Moving towards the WTO: the single undertaking 75
3.2.1 Introduction: the Punta del Este Declaration 75
3.2.2 Marrakesh Agreement Establishing the World Trade Organization 77
3.2.3 The 'accession package' 87
3.2.4 Accession commitments 90
3.3 Conclusion 94

PART II THE STATUS OF PROTOCOLS OF ACCESSION IN THE LEGAL FRAMEWORK OF THE WTO

4 The status of protocols of accession in the legal framework of the WTO 97

4.1 Introduction 97
4.2 The enforceability of GATT and WTO protocols of accession 100
4.2.1 Tracing the roots: GATT protocols of accession 100
4.2.2 WTO dispute settlement: the enforceability of WTO protocols of accession 105
4.3 The relationship between commitments in protocols of accession and the WTO Agreement 138
4.3.1 Legal basis for rules commitments 138
4.3.2 Issues in the relationship between commitments in protocols of accession and the WTO Agreement 140
4.4 Conclusion 197

PART III MAPPING EXERCISE: THE CONTENT OF PROTOCOLS OF ACCESSION

5 Mapping Exercise: Methodology and typology – commitments on specific matters 203

5.1 Introduction 203

5.2 Efforts to categorize commitments in protocols of accession 205
5.3 Scope of the mapping exercise 207
5.3.1 Numbers 207
5.3.2 Substance 211
5.4 Typology 212
5.4.1 Category 1: Transitional periods and special and differential treatment 213
5.4.2 Category 2: Ensuring conformity 214
5.4.3 Category 3: Implementing WTO obligations and bringing measures into conformity with WTO obligations 215
5.4.4 Category 4: 'Allowing other members to do something they would otherwise not be allowed to do' 224
5.4.5 Category 5: 'Prohibitions' 227
5.5 Conclusion 228

6 Mapping exercise: the results 230

6.1 Introduction: rules commitments in protocols of accession 230
6.2 Economic policies 231
6.3 Framework for making and enforcing policies 234
6.4 Policies affecting trade in goods 240
6.4.1 Transitional safeguards 240
6.4.2 Non-market economy methodologies in anti-dumping investigations 245
6.4.3 Export duties 273
6.4.4 State-owned enterprises (SOEs) 285
6.4.5 Technical Barriers to Trade (TBT) 285
6.4.6 Sanitary and Phytosanitary Measures (SPS) 287
6.5 Foreign direct investment 289
6.5.1 Investment regime 290
6.5.2 Trading rights 290
6.5.3 Trade-Related Investment Measures (TRIMs) 291
6.6 Trade-Related Intellectual Property Regime 291
6.7 Policies affecting trade in services 294
6.8 Transparency 297
6.9 Trade agreements 297
6.10 Conclusion 301

PART IV CONCLUSION

7 Concluding remarks 307

7.1 Introduction 307
7.2 Does the WTO have a multi-tiered membership? 308
7.3 Lawmaking in protocols of accession 309
7.4 Protocols of accession in WTO dispute settlement 313
7.5 Lessons for the future – towards universal membership 316
7.6 Conclusion 320

Selected bibliography 322
Index 333

Tables

2.1 Original GATT Contracting Parties 41
2.2 New GATT Contracting Parties in the 1950s 42
2.3 New GATT Contracting Parties in the 1960s 43
2.4 New GATT Contracting Parties in the 1970s 45
2.5 New GATT Contracting Parties in the 1980s 45
2.6 New GATT Contracting Parties in the 1990s 46
2.7 New WTO Members in the 1990s 53
2.8 New WTO Members in the 2000s 53
2.9 New WTO Members in the 2010s 54
2.10 Ongoing WTO accessions in 2017 54
2.11 Non-observer states (non-accessions) 55
2.12 WTO accession process 63
4.1 References to Article XX of the GATT 1994 151
5.1 Number of commitment paragraphs in working party reports on accessions 208
5.2 Groups and categories of non-original Members 210
6.1 Language used in commitments on export duties 280
6.2 Type of export duty commitment and availability of Article XX of the GATT 1994 285

Acknowledgements

This monograph is the result of a research project on the nature of the WTO accession process, carried out at KU Leuven, Belgium. The project was supervised by Prof. Dr Jan Wouters who provided indispensable guidance, advice and support. I am also indebted to a great number of other individuals, who provided feedback and input during several stages of the research. Prof. Dr Geert Van Calster provided a stimulating working environment and shared his in-depth knowledge of the law of the World Trade Organization (WTO) through commenting on subsequent drafts of this monograph. Prof. Dr Peter Van den Bossche for introducing me to the WTO and the workings of the multilateral trading system during his class on International Trade Law at Maastricht University in March 2009. Your knowledge of, and service to, the multilateral trading system continues to inspire me on a daily basis. Professors Mavroidis and Steenbergen for providing valuable comments and critical reflections on this monograph.

It has been an enormous pleasure to work with Bregt Natens, Marieke Koekkoek and Ines Willemyns as the 'trade-team' of the Leuven Centre for Global Governance Studies (GGS). Our discussions on the (future) role of the law of international trade are invaluable to me.

A special word of thanks goes out to friends and colleagues at the WTO Appellate Body Secretariat, where I had the pleasure of serving as an intern in the spring of 2016. I am also thankful to the following people for sharing their thoughts on the subject of this monograph in the course of the writing process: Prof. Dr Gabrielle Marceau, Prof. Dr Julia Ya Qin, Prof. Dr Marco Bronckers, Prof. Dr Joost Pauwelyn, Claudia Orozco, James Flett, Philippe de Baere and Arnoud Willems. A special word of thanks goes out to Paulette Vander Schueren and Nikolay Mizulin for offering me the opportunity to apply my knowledge in practice at Mayer Brown.*

* The views expressed in this volume do not express those of Mayer Brown LLP, nor those of its clients.

Finally, I am grateful to my wife, parents, family, friends and colleagues, all of whom have supported me during the past four years. Writing this book would not have been possible without you.

Dylan Geraets,
Brussels, spring 2017.

Abbreviations

AB	Appellate Body
ACDB	Accession Commitments Database
Agreement on Agriculture	Agreement on Agriculture, 15 April 1994, Marrakesh Agreement Establishing the World Trade Organization, Annex 1A, 1867 U.N.T.S. 410
Agreement on Preshipment Inspection	Agreement on Preshipment Inspection, 1868 U.N.T.S. 368
Agreement on Rules of Origin	Agreement on Rules of Origin, 1868 U.N.T.S. 397
Agreement on Safeguards	Agreement on Safeguards, 1869 U.N.T.S. 154
Agreement on Trade in Civil Aircraft	Agreement on Trade in Civil Aircraft, 1869 U.N.T.S. 508 (Text available at 1186 U.N.T.S. 170)
AMS	Aggregate Measurement of Support
Anti-Dumping Agreement	Agreement on Implementation of Article VI of the General Agreement on Tariffs and Trade 1994 (Anti-Dumping Agreement), 1868 U.N.T.S. 201
APEC	Asia-Pacific Economic Cooperation
CJEU	Court of Justice of the European Union
Customs Valuation Agreement	Agreement on Implementation of Article VII of the General Agreement on Tariffs and Trade 1994, 1868 U.N.T.S. 279
DC	Developing country
DET	Differential export tax
DSB	Dispute Settlement Body

DSU	Understanding on Rules and Procedures Governing the Settlement of Disputes
EAEU	Eurasian Economic Union
EU	European Union
FDI	Foreign direct investment
Final Act	Final Act Embodying the Results of the Uruguay Round of Multilateral Trade Negotiations, 15 April 1994, 1867 U.N.T.S. 14, 33 I.L.M. 1143 (1994)
GATS	General Agreement on Trade in Services
GATT 1947	General Agreement on Tariffs and Trade 1947
GATT 1994	General Agreement on Tariffs and Trade 1994
GDP	Gross domestic product
General Court	General Court of the European Union (formerly Court of First Instance)
GVCs	Global value chains
HS	Harmonized System
ICJ	International Court of Justice
ILC	International Law Commission
IMF	International Monetary Fund
Import Licensing Agreement	Agreement on Import Licensing Procedures
ITO	International Trade Organization
LDC	Least-Developed Country
Member	Member of the World Trade Organization
Member State	Member State of the European Union
MFN	Most-Favoured Nation
NMEs	Non-market economy(ies)
NTB	Non-tariff barrier
PEC	Planned-economy country
PPA	Protocol of Provisional Application
PTA	Preferential trade agreement
RCEP	Regional Comprehensive Economic Partnership
RTA	Regional trade agreement
Schedule	Schedule of Specific Commitments

SCM Agreement	Agreement on Subsidies and Countervailing Measures
SOE	State-owned enterprise
SPS	Sanitary and Phytosanitary Measures
SPS Agreement	Agreement on the Application of Sanitary and Phytosanitary Measures
TBT	Technical Barriers to Trade
TBT Agreement	Agreement on Technical Barriers to Trade
TDI	(EU) Trade Defence Instruments
TEU	Treaty on European Union
TFA	Agreement on Trade Facilitation
TISA	Trade in Services Agreement
TPP	Trans-Pacific Partnership
TPSSM	Transitional Product-Specific Safeguard Mechanism
TRIMS Agreement	Agreement on Trade-Related Investment Measures
TRIPS	Trade-Related Aspects of Intellectual Property Rights
TRIPS Agreement	Agreement on Trade-Related Aspects of Intellectual Property Rights
TRQ	Tariff rate quota
TTIP	Transatlantic Trade and Investment Partnership
UN	United Nations
UPOV	International Union for the Protection of New Varieties of Plants
Uruguay Round	Uruguay Round of Multilateral Trade Negotiations
USDOC	United States Department of Commerce
Vienna Convention	Vienna Convention on the Law of Treaties
WB	World Bank
WPR	Working Party Report
WTO	World Trade Organization
WTO Agreement	Marrakesh Agreement Establishing the World Trade Organization

Table of cited WTO and GATT dispute settlement reports

GATT CASES

EEC – Bananas II, GATT Panel Report, EEC – Import Regime for Bananas, DS38/R, 11 February 1994, unadopted 104
Jamaica – Margins of Preference, GATT Panel Report, Jamaica – Margins of Preference, L/3485, adopted 2 February 1971, BISD 18S, p. 183 101
Norway – Apples and Pears, GATT Panel Report, Norway – Restrictions on Imports of Apples and Pears, L/6474, adopted 22 June 1989, BISD 36S, p. 306 103–104
Spain – Soyabean Oil, GATT Panel Report, Spain – Measures Concerning Domestic Sale of Soyabean Oil – Recourse to Article XXIII:2 by the United States, L/5142, 17 June 1981, unadopted 101–102
Thailand – Cigarettes, GATT Panel Report, Thailand – Restrictions on Importation of and Internal Taxes on Cigarettes, DS10/R, adopted 7 November 1990, BISD 37S, p. 200 104
Uruguay – Recourse to Article XXIII, GATT Panel Report, Uruguayan Recourse to Article XXIII, L/1923, adopted 16 November 1962, BISD 11S, p. 95 .... 100, 101
US – Manufacturing Clause, GATT Panel Report, United States Manufacturing Clause, L/5609, adopted 15 May 1984, BISD 31S, p. 74 .... 102, 103

WTO CASES

Argentina – Footwear (EC), Appellate Body Report, Argentina – Safeguard Measures on Imports of Footwear, WT/DS121/AB/R, adopted 12 January 2000, DSR 2000:I, p. 515 129
Brazil – Desiccated Coconut, Appellate Body Report, Brazil – Measures Affecting Desiccated Coconut, WT/DS22/AB/R, adopted 20 March 1997, DSR 1997:I, p. 167 76
Brazil – Retreaded Tyres, Appellate Body Report, Brazil – Measures Affecting Imports of Retreaded Tyres, WT/DS332/AB/R, adopted 17 December 2007, DSR 2007:IV, p. 1527 .... 142, 145

Canada – Renewable Energy/Canada – Feed-In Tariff, Appellate Body Reports, Canada – Certain Measures Affecting the Renewable Energy Generation Sector/Canada – Measures Relating to the Feed-In Tariff Program, WT/DS412/AB/R/WT/DS426/AB/R, adopted 24 May 2013, DSR 2013:I, p. 7 147
Canada – Renewable Energy/Canada – Feed-In Tariff, Panel Reports, Canada – Certain Measures Affecting the Renewable Energy Generation Sector/Canada – Measures Relating to the Feed-In Tariff Program, WT/DS412/R and Add.1/WT/DS426/R and Add.1, adopted 24 May 2013, as modified by Appellate Body Reports WT/DS412/AB/R/WT/DS426/AB/R, DSR 2013:I, p. 237 147
China – Auto Parts, Appellate Body Reports, China – Measures Affecting Imports of Automobile Parts, WT/DS339/AB/R/WT/DS340/AB/R/WT/DS342/AB/R, adopted 12 January 2009, DSR 2009:I, p. 3 .... 5, 196
China – Auto Parts, Panel Reports, China – Measures Affecting Imports of Automobile Parts, WT/DS339/R, Add.1 and Add.2/WT/DS340/R, Add.1 and Add.2/WT/DS342/R, Add.1 and Add.2, adopted 12 January 2009, upheld (WT/DS339/R) and as modified (WT/DS340/R/WT/DS342/R) by Appellate Body Reports WT/DS339/AB/R/WT/DS340/AB/R/WT/DS342/AB/R, DSR 2009:I, p. 119 .... 112, 114, 120
China – Electronic Payment Services, Panel Report, China – Certain Measures Affecting Electronic Payment Services, WT/DS413/R and Add.1, adopted 31 August 2012, DSR 2012:X, p. 5305 5
China – Publications and Audiovisual Products, Appellate Body Report, China – Measures Affecting Trading Rights and Distribution Services for Certain Publications and Audiovisual Entertainment Products, WT/DS363/AB/R, adopted 19 January 2010, DSR 2010:I, p. 3 .... 5, 99, 114, 120, 141, 149, 169, 170, 171, 173, 174, 184, 185, 186, 188
China – Publications and Audiovisual Products, Panel Report, China – Measures Affecting Trading Rights and Distribution Services for Certain Publications and Audiovisual Entertainment Products, WT/DS363/R and Corr.1, adopted 19 January 2010, as modified by Appellate Body Report WT/DS363/AB/R, DSR 2010:II, p. 261 .... 64, 113, 114, 120, 168, 169, 185, 186
China – Rare Earths, Appellate Body Reports, China – Measures Related to the Exportation of Rare Earths, Tungsten, and Molybdenum, WT/DS431/AB/R/WT/DS432/AB/R/WT/DS433/AB/R, adopted 29 August 2014 .... 5, 57–58, 58, 59, 115, 122, 127, 129, 130, 135, 179–187, 203, 212, 276
China – Rare Earths, Panel Reports, China – Measures Related to the Exportation of Rare Earths, Tungsten, and Molybdenum, WT/DS431/R and Add.1/WT/DS432/R and Add.1/WT/DS433/R and Add.1, adopted 29 August 2014, upheld by Appellate Body Reports WT/DS431/AB/R/WT/DS432/AB/R/WT/DS433/AB/R 122, 176, 177–179, 186, 276, 284

China – Raw Materials, Appellate Body Reports, China – Measures Related to the Exportation of Various Raw Materials, WT/DS394/AB/R/WT/DS395/AB/R/WT/DS398/AB/R, adopted 22 February 2012, DSR 2012:VII, p. 3295 .... 5, 99, 143, 144, 174, 176, 178, 186, 212, 276, 284

China – Raw Materials, Panel Reports, China – Measures Related to the Exportation of Various Raw Materials, WT/DS394/R, Add.1 and Corr.1/WT/DS395/R, Add.1 and Corr.1/WT/DS398/R, Add.1 and Corr.1, adopted 22 February 2012, as modified by Appellate Body Reports WT/DS394/AB/R/WT/DS395/AB/R/WT/DS398/AB/R, DSR 2012:VII, p. 3501 .... 64–65, 80, 114, 115, 144, 145, 150, 173, 174, 176, 186, 218, 276

Colombia – Textiles, Panel Report, Colombia – Measures Relating to the Importation of Textiles, Apparel and Footwear, WT/DS461/R and Add.1, circulated to WTO Members 27 November 2015, p. 141 142

EC – Asbestos, Panel Report, European Communities – Measures Affecting Asbestos and Asbestos Containing Products, WT/DS135/R and Add. 1, adopted 5 April 2001, as modified by Appellate Body Report WT/DS135/AB/R 140, 285

EC – Bananas III (Article 21.5 – Ecuador II)/EC – Bananas III (Article 21.5 – US), Appellate Body Reports, European Communities – Regime for the Importation, Sale and Distribution of Bananas – Second Recourse to Article 21.5 of the DSU by Ecuador, WT/DS27/AB/RW2/ECU, adopted 11 December 2008, and Corr.1/European Communities – Regime for the Importation, Sale and Distribution of Bananas – Recourse to Article 21.5 of the DSU by the United States, WT/DS27/AB/RW/USA and Corr.1, adopted 22 December 2008, DSR 2008:XVIII, p. 7165 194

EC – Chicken Cuts, Appellate Body Report, European Communities – Customs Classification of Frozen Boneless Chicken Cuts, WT/DS269/AB/R/WT/DS286/AB/R, adopted 27 September 2005, and Corr.1, DSR 2005:XIX, 9157 196

EC – Fasteners (China), Appellate Body Report, European Communities – Definitive Anti-Dumping Measures on Certain Iron or Steel Fasteners from China, WT/DS397/AB/R, adopted 28 July 2011, DSR 2011:VII, p. 3995 .... 255–256, 257

EC – Fasteners (China), Panel Report, European Communities – Definitive Anti-Dumping Measures on Certain Iron or Steel Fasteners from China, WT/DS397/R and Corr.1, adopted 28 July 2011, as modified by Appellate Body Report WT/DS397/AB/R, DSR 2011:VIII, p. 4289 265

EC – Fasteners (China) (21.5), Appellate Body Report, European Communities – Definitive Anti-Dumping Measures on Certain Iron or Steel Fasteners from China – Recourse to Article 21.5 of the DSU by China, WT/DS397/AB/RW and Add.1, adopted 12 February 2016 258

EC – Seal Products, Appellate Body Reports, European Communities – Measures Prohibiting the Importation and Marketing of Seal Products, WT/DS400/AB/R/WT/DS401/AB/R, adopted 18 June 2014 .... 140, 141, 145

EU – Biodiesel, Appellate Body Report, European Union – Anti-Dumping Measures on Biodiesel from Argentina, WT/DS473/AB/R, adopted 26 October 2016 271
EU – Biodiesel, Panel Report, European Union – Anti-Dumping Measures on Biodiesel from Argentina, WT/DS473/R, adopted 26 October 2016, as modified by Appellate Body Report WT/DS473/AB/R 271
EU – Footwear, Panel Report, European Union – Anti-Dumping Measures on Certain Footwear from China, WT/DS405/R, adopted 22 February 2012, DSR 2012:IX, p. 4585 .... 5, 117, 258
Guatemala – Cement I, Appellate Body Report, Guatemala – Anti-Dumping Investigation Regarding Portland Cement from Mexico, WT/DS60/AB/R, adopted 25 November 1998, DSR 1998:IX, p. 3767 130
Japan – Alcoholic Beverages II, Appellate Body Report, Japan – Taxes on Alcoholic Beverages, WT/DS8/AB/R/WT/DS10/AB/R, WT/DS11/AB/R, adopted 1 November 1996, DSR 1996:I, p. 97 217
Peru – Agricultural Products, Appellate Body Report, Peru – Additional Duty on Imports of Certain Agricultural Products, WT/DS457/AB/R and Add.1, adopted 31 July 2015 194
Ukraine, Armenia – Measures Affecting the Importation and Internal Sale of Cigarettes and Alcohol Beverages, WT/DS411/2/Rev.1, 8 October 2010 110
US – Anti-Dumping and Countervailing Duties (China), Appellate Body Report, United States – Definitive Anti-Dumping and Countervailing Duties on Certain Products from China, WT/DS379/AB/R, adopted 25 March 2011, DSR 2011:V, p. 2869 .... 5, 50, 127
US – Anti-Dumping and Countervailing Duties (China), Panel Report, United States – Definitive Anti-Dumping and Countervailing Duties on Certain Products from China, WT/DS379/R, adopted 25 March 2011, as modified by Appellate Body Report WT/DS379/AB/R, DSR 2011:VI, p. 3143 127
US – Carbon Steel, Panel Report, United States – Countervailing Duties on Certain Corrosion-Resistant Carbon Steel Flat Products from Germany, WT/DS213/R and Corr.1, adopted 19 December 2002, as modified by Appellate Body Report WT/DS213/AB/R, DSR 2002:IX, p. 3833 177
US – Clove Cigarettes, Appellate Body Report, United States – Measures Affecting the Production and Sale of Clove Cigarettes, WT/DS406/AB/R, adopted 24 April 2012, DSR 2012: XI, p. 5751 134
US – Clove Cigarettes, Panel Report, United States – Measures Affecting the Production and Sale of Clove Cigarettes, WT/DS406/R, adopted 24 April 2012, as modified by Appellate Body Report WT/DS406/AB/R, DSR 2012: XI, p. 5865 285
US – COOL, Panel Reports, United States – Certain Country of Origin Labelling (COOL) Requirements, WT/DS384/R/WT/DS386/R, adopted 23 July 2012, as modified by Appellate Body Reports WT/DS384/AB/R/WT/DS386/AB/R, DSR 2012:VI, p. 2745 285

US – Countervailing and Anti-Dumping Measures (China), Appellate Body Report, United States – Countervailing and Anti-Dumping Measures on Certain Products from China, WT/DS449/AB/R and Corr.1, adopted 22 July 2014, DSR 2014:VIII, p. 3027 235
US – Gasoline, Appellate Body Report, United States – Standards for Reformulated and Conventional Gasoline, WT/DS2/AB/R, adopted 20 May 1996, DSR 1996:I, p. 3 .... 1, 109, 140, 141, 145–146
US – Shrimp, Appellate Body Report, United States – Import Prohibition of Certain Shrimp and Shrimp Products, WT/DS58/AB/R, adopted 6 November 1998, DSR 1998:VII, p. 2755 .... 143, 145
US – Shrimp II (Vietnam), Appellate Body Report, United States – Anti-Dumping Measures on Certain Shrimp from Viet Nam, WT/DS429/AB/R, adopted 22 April 2015, and Corr.1 118
US – Shrimp II (Vietnam), Panel Report, United States – Anti-Dumping Measures on Certain Shrimp from Viet Nam, WT/DS429/R and Add.1, adopted 22 April 2015, upheld by Appellate Body Report WT/DS429/AB/R 118, 150, 265, 266, 299–300
US – Shrimp (Viet Nam), Panel Report, United States – Anti-Dumping Measures on Certain Shrimp from Viet Nam, WT/DS404/R, adopted 2 September 2011, DSR 2011:X, p. 5301 110
US – Tuna II (Mexico), Appellate Body Report, United States – Measures Concerning the Importation, Marketing and Sale of Tuna and Tuna Products, WT/DS381/AB/R, adopted 13 June 2012 81
US – Tuna II (Mexico), Panel Report, United States – Measures Concerning the Importation, Marketing and Sale of Tuna and Tuna Products, WT/DS381/R, adopted 13 June 2012, modified by Appellate Body Report WT/DS381/AB/R 285
US – Tyres (China), Appellate Body Report, United States – Measures Affecting Imports of Certain Passenger Vehicle and Light Truck Tyres from China, WT/DS399/AB/R, adopted 5 October 2011, DSR 2011:IX, p. 4811 .... 5, 192, 193, 244
US – Tyres (China), Panel Report, United States – Measures Affecting Imports of Certain Passenger Vehicle and Light Truck Tyres from China, WT/DS399/R, adopted 5 October 2011, upheld by Appellate Body Report WT/DS399/AB/R, DSR 2011:IX, p. 4945 .... 191–192, 244, 245

Table of requests for consultations citing protocol of accession provisions

DS532, Russia – Measures Concerning the Importation and Transit of Certain Ukrainian Products (Complainant: Ukraine), 13 October 2017

DS525/1, Ukraine – Measures relating to Trade in Goods and Services, 1 June 2017 110

DS525, Ukraine – Measures relating to Trade in Goods and Services (Complainant: Russian Federation), 19 May 2017

DS517, China – Tariff Rate Quotas for Certain Agricultural Products (Complainant: United States), 15 December 2016 111

DS516, European Union – Measures Related to Price Comparison Methodologies (Complainant: China), 12 December 2016 .... 267, 268

DS515, United States – Measures Related to Price Comparison Methodologies (Complainant: China), 12 December 2016 267

DS512, Russian Federation – Measures Concerning Traffic in Transit (Complainant: Ukraine), 14 September 2016

DS509, China – Duties and other Measures concerning the Exportation of Certain Raw Materials (Complainant: European Union), 19 July 2016 111

DS508, China – Export Duties on Certain Raw Materials (Complainant: United States), 13 July 2016 111

DS501, China – Tax Measures Concerning Certain Domestically Produced Aircraft (Complainant: United States), 8 December 2015 111

DS451, China – Measures Relating to the Production and Exportation of Apparel and Textile Products (Complainant: Mexico), 15 October 2012 111

DS450, China – Certain Measures Affecting the Automobile and Automobile-Parts Industries (Complainant: United States), 17 September 2012 111

DS437, United States – Countervailing Duty Measures on Certain Products from China (Complainant: China), 25 May 2012 111

DS433, China – Measures Related to the Exportation of Rare Earths, Tungsten and Molybdenum (Complainant: Japan), 13 March 2012 111

DS432, China – Measures Related to the Exportation of Rare Earths, Tungsten and Molybdenum (Complainant: European Union), 13 March 2012 .... 111, 112

DS431, China – Measures Related to the Exportation of Rare Earths, Tungsten and Molybdenum (Complainant: United States), 13 March 2012 111

DS429, United States – Anti-Dumping Measures on Certain Shrimp from Viet Nam (Complainant: Viet Nam), 27 February 2012 117
DS419, China – Measures concerning Wind Power Equipment (Complainant: United States), 22 December 2010 111
DS405, European Union – Anti-Dumping Measures on Certain Footwear from China (Complainant: China), 4 February 2010 .... 111, 116
DS404, United States – Anti-Dumping Measures on Certain Shrimp from Viet Nam (Complainant: Viet Nam), 1 February 2010
DS399, United States – Measures Affecting Imports of Certain Passenger Vehicle and Light Truck Tyres from China (Complainant: China), 14 September 2009 111
DS398, China – Measures Related to the Exportation of Various Raw Materials (Complainant: Mexico), 21 August 2009 111
DS397, European Communities – Definitive Anti-Dumping Measures on Certain Iron or Steel Fasteners from China (Complainant: China), 31 July 2009 111
DS395, China – Measures Related to the Exportation of Various Raw Materials (Complainant: European Communities), 23 June 2009 111
DS394, China – Measures Related to the Exportation of Various Raw Materials (Complainant: United States), 23 June 2009 111
DS390, China – Grants, Loans and Other Incentives (Complainant: Guatemala), 19 January 2009 111
DS388, China – Grants, Loans and Other Incentives (Complainant: Mexico), 19 December 2008 111
DS387, China – Grants, Loans and Other Incentives (Complainant: United States), 19 December 2008 111
DS379, United States – Definitive Anti-Dumping and Countervailing Duties on Certain Products from China (Complainant: China), 19 September 2008 110–11
DS378, China – Measures Affecting Financial Information Services and Foreign Financial Information Suppliers (Complainant: Canada), 20 June 2008 .... 110, 111
DS373, China – Measures Affecting Financial Information Services and Foreign Financial Information Suppliers (Complainant: United States), 3 March 2008 .... 110, 111
DS363, China – Measures Affecting Trading Rights and Distribution Services for Certain Publications and Audiovisual Entertainment Products (Complainant: United States), 10 April 2007 .... 110, 113
DS359, China – Certain Measures Granting Refunds, Reductions or Exemptions from Taxes and Other Payments (Complainant: Mexico), 26 February 2007 .... 110, 111
DS358, China – Certain Measures Granting Refunds, Reductions or Exemptions from Taxes and Other Payments (Complainant: United States), 2 February 2007 .... 110, 111
DS342, China – Measures Affecting Imports of Automobile Parts (Complainant: Canada), 13 April 2006 110
DS340, China – Measures Affecting Imports of Automobile Parts (Complainant: United States), 30 March 2006 .... 110, 112

DS339, China – Measures Affecting Imports of Automobile Parts (Complainant: European Communities), 30 March 2006 .... 110, 112

EUROPEAN COURTS

Court of Justice of the European Union (CJEU), *European Commission v Rusal ZAO* (Case C-21/14 P) 261, 262, 263
General Court, *Rusal Armenal ZAO v Council of the European Union* (Case T-512/09) 2010/C 80/49 (21 December 2009) 258, 259, 260

Introduction

> Accession is a strategic priority of the WTO. To achieve universality is the ultimate goal of the WTO, because enlargement of the rules-based multilateral trading system is a key source of strength.[1]
>
> – Pascal Lamy, former European Commissioner for Trade and former Director-General of the World Trade Organization

The World Trade Organization (WTO) was founded in 1995 after the completion of the Uruguay Round of Multilateral Trade Negotiations (the Uruguay Round).[2] The organization succeeded the General Agreement on Tariffs and Trade of 1947 (GATT 1947) as the main global institution governing international trade. The WTO is founded on the Marrakesh Agreement Establishing the World Trade Organization (WTO Agreement) which sets out the organization's five main functions.[3] In succeeding GATT 1947 with its 128 Contracting Parties, the WTO has become an international organization with an almost universal membership. The multilateral trading system is firmly rooted in public international law and the legal instruments underpinning the organization are sources of international law.[4] Several events in 2016 illustrated that the organization's relevance has not reduced in the 21 years since its inception. The vote for 'Brexit' in the United Kingdom and the election of President Donald Trump in the United States placed renewed emphasis on the rules of international trade and the role of the rules-based multilateral trading system.

[1] Lamy, Pascal (2012), 26 Years of Accession Experience and Best Practices, Beijing 2012 Round Table on WTO Accession Best Practices for Least Developed Countries, 29 May. Available at http://www.wto.org/english/news_e/sppl_e/sppl231_e.htm (last accessed at 1 June 2017).

[2] Agreement Establishing the World Trade Organization (15 April 1994) 1867 U.N.T.S. 154; entered into force 1 January 1995 (WTO Agreement).

[3] Article III WTO Agreement.

[4] Appellate Body Report, *US – Gasoline*, at 17.

International trade used to be largely unregulated until the creation of the GATT 1947 shortly after the end of the Second World War.[5] Trade policy in the period leading up to the Second World War was characterized by outbursts of unbridled protectionism, which are often cited as one of the causes of the darkest period in modern history. In order to curb the hands of governments with protectionist intentions after the War, the allied governments – in particular the United States and the United Kingdom – started negotiating a commercial union. In 1946 the General Agreement on Tariffs and Trade was first negotiated in its eventual form at the London Conference.[6] The GATT was initially conceived as a tariff reduction agreement and was intended to be a part of an International Trade Organization (ITO). After this organization was stillborn, the GATT turned into a de facto international organization, which turned out to become increasingly popular in the first years of its existence.[7]

Trade liberalization continued as the GATT Contracting Parties concluded numerous negotiation rounds and the membership of GATT grew incrementally. Through these negotiation rounds the average tariff rate applied by industrialized countries on non-agricultural goods gradually dropped from between 20-30 per cent in 1947 to approximately 5.5 per cent in 2006.[8] After several decades the importance of tariffs in trade liberalization began to decrease. Non-tariff barriers (NTBs), such as product standards or origin requirements, became increasingly important. With the growing importance of NTBs, GATT Contracting Parties began to search for new ways to limit the use of these instruments for protectionist purposes. In the Uruguay Round of Multilateral Trade

---

[5] Lester, Simon, Mercurio, Bryan and Davies, Arwel (2012), *World Trade Law: Text, Materials and Commentary*, Oxford, Hart Publishing, at 56. There were of course a number of bilateral agreements that dated back to the Friendship, Commerce and Navigation (FCN) treaties. Lester, Mercurio and Davies note that these agreements 'were the first steps towards more formal trade relations based on the idea of liberalisation'.

[6] For a more detailed account of the creation of the General Agreement on Tariffs and Trade 1947, see, for example, Irwin, Douglas A., Mavroidis, Petros C. and Sykes, Alan O. (2008), *The Genesis of the GATT*, New York, Cambridge University Press.

[7] Lester, Mercurio and Davies (2012), *World Trade Law*, at 57.

[8] WTO, World Trade Report 2007, Six Decades of Multilateral Cooperation: What Have We Learnt?, at 207; WTO, Trade Profiles 2008 (simple average of applied MFN rates). See also Bown, Chad P. and Irwin, Douglas (2015), The GATT's Starting Point: Tariff Levels Circa 1947, CEPR Discussion Paper 10979, December 2015. Bown and Irwin 'debunk' the myth that average pre-GATT tariff levels were at 40% or more.

Negotiations several multilateral agreements on trade in goods – the Annex 1 Agreements – were negotiated. These agreements, such as, for example, the Agreement on Technical Barriers to Trade set out disciplines which WTO Members have to adhere to when they adopt technical regulations and standards. These agreements are a good example of the broadening scope of the multilateral trading system. The creation of the WTO thus marked the beginning of a new era in international trade law and policy. The WTO is built upon what is termed a 'single undertaking'. The WTO Agreement serves as an umbrella agreement, with annexes covering – in addition to trade in goods – services and the trade-related aspects of intellectual property. Furthermore there are agreements covering dispute settlement and the review of WTO Members' trade policy. All agreements operate as one single package.

The membership of the organization has steadily grown from 128 in 1995, to 164 in July 2016.[9] The birth of the organization did not only increase the substantive scope of the multilateral trading system, but also led to some important institutional changes. The most well-known example is the WTO's Dispute Settlement Body (DSB), which is widely heralded as one of the most successful inter-state dispute settlement mechanisms. One institutional aspect that remained unchanged, however, is the accession process that states and customs territories have to go through in order to accede to the organization. The GATT 1947 provided for the possibility of states and customs territories to accede to it 'on terms to be agreed between it and the Contracting Parties'.[10] This wording allowed for the creation of an accession process that is to a large extent power-based. Although this particular phrase is also reflected in Article XII of the WTO Agreement, the accession process has, to a certain extent, also been formalized in the first 20 years of the WTO's existence. Nevertheless, in essence, the process has remained the same. The WTO – in negotiations with the acceding state or customs territory – can demand that these states adjust their existing trade policy in order to be compliant with the WTO's obligations at the time of accession. The question that can be posed is whether this institutional aspect, combined with the broadening scope of the organization, has led to a situation in which the WTO can require states and customs territories that want to become a Member to accept an 'accession package' that includes rights and obligations, or rules commitments, that are different – or even more

---

[9] The cut-off date for this monograph is June 2017.

[10] Article XXXIII of the General Agreement on Tariffs and Trade (1994), 1867 U.N.T.S. 187, entered into force 1 January 1995 (GATT 1994).

stringent – from the rights and obligations applicable to the incumbent membership. It is important to note that the examination of the acceded states focuses on these *rules* commitments, and thus not on the *market access* commitments that these states have also had to undertake. It is evident that trade liberalization commitments in the fields of trade in goods and trade in services will differ from state to state, as a consequence of the unilateral liberalization efforts already undertaken prior to the accession bid. Whereas these differences also reflect a distinction within the membership, the extent to which states have also had to undertake different rules commitments might be the real reason for characterizing the membership of the WTO as multi-tiered. Concerns have been raised that the multi-tieredness within the WTO membership erodes the legitimacy of the organization as a whole.[11] It has been argued that 'the lack of reasoning and transparency in the accession rules is the main legitimacy problem'.[12] This contribution therefore focuses on two aspects relating to the concept of accession. First, the process of accession itself, and second, the interpretation of commitments in protocols of accession by the WTO's DSB.

The first chapters of this book address the institutional and historical aspects of the WTO accession process. Chapter 1 draws on non-legal fields of scholarship to determine the main rationales that underpin the desire to obtain membership of the multilateral trading system and the accession bids thereto. Research in the fields of economic science and international relations is examined in order to determine the main motivation for states to become a Member of the WTO. As noted, the WTO is based on the Marrakesh Agreement Establishing the World Trade Organization, which is in itself a source of international law. Chapter 2 contains an analysis of the accession process to the multilateral trading system. The ways in which states and customs territories could become Contracting Parties to the GATT 1947 are examined, followed by an

---

[11] The notion of legitimacy is broader than the notion of legality. A particular act, law or regulation may be considered legal if it complies with all the procedural steps that are required for it. However, such an act, law or regulation will only be considered as legitimate if the actors that are subject to it consider that it was taken in light of broader notions such as fairness, democracy and justice. The legitimacy of a particular act, process or outcome therefore depends on the way in which it is considered by those that will be subjected to it.

[12] Kireyev, Alexei and Sekkate, Mustapha (2015), WTO Accessions: What Does the Academic Literature Say?, in Dadush, Uri and Osakwe, Chiedu (eds) (2015), *WTO Accessions and Trade Multilateralism: Case Studies and Lessons from the WTO at Twenty*, Cambridge, Cambridge University Press, pp. 198–216, at 205.

analysis of the accession process to the WTO. This chapter also contains an overview of the evolution of the membership of the multilateral trading system. In Chapter 3 the main features of WTO accession, which is governed by Article XII of the WTO Agreement, are examined. The process of accession is examined in detail, enabling an analysis of the issue of a multi-tiered membership in subsequent chapters.

The book proceeds with an in-depth discussion of the legal status of protocols of accession within the legal framework of the WTO. These protocols are the legal instruments that together form the end result of each accession. In Chapter 4 the legal structure of the WTO is described with a view to identifying the place of protocols of accession in that structure. Questions have arisen as to the legal basis for the enforceability of the commitments contained in these protocols. The chapter addresses the case law of the WTO's DSB in order to determine how panels and the Appellate Body have dealt with protocols of accession in their reports.[13] Thirty-three requests for consultations have so far cited provisions of an accession protocol and, in several disputes, panels and the Appellate Body have dealt with the relationship between these protocols and the WTO Agreement. The interpretative approach adopted by panels and the Appellate Body in these disputes is analysed.[14] This chapter examines the relationship between the commitments contained in protocols of accession and the provisions of the WTO Agreement. To this end four important issues that arise in this respect are examined: i) the availability of the general exceptions contained in Article XX of the GATT 1994; ii) the rights or derogations that accession protocol commitments can create for other WTO Members; iii) the issue of the waiving of rights by acceding Members; and iv) the relevance of the commitments contained in protocols of accession for the interpretation of a) provisions of the

---

[13] See, inter alia, Appellate Body Reports, *China – Auto Parts*; Appellate Body Report, *China – Publications and Audiovisual Products;* Appellate Body Report, *US – Anti-Dumping and Countervailing Duties (China)*; Appellate Body Report, *US – Tyres (China)*; Appellate Body Report, *China – Raw Materials*; Panel Report, *EU – Footwear*; Panel Report, *China – Electronic Payment Services*; Appellate Body Reports, *China – Rare Earths.*

[14] Charnovitz, Steve and Hoekman, Bernard (2013), '*US – Tyres*: Upholding a WTO Accession Contract – Imposing Pain for Little Gain', *World Trade Review* (12) (2), pp. 273–96, at 286–7; Yamaoka, Tokio (2013), 'Analysis of China's Accession Commitments in the WTO: New Taxonomy of More and Less Stringent Commitments, and the Struggle for Mitigation by China', *Journal of World Trade* (47) (1), pp. 105–58; Qin, Julia Ya (2010), 'Challenges of Interpreting 'WTO-plus' Provisions', *Journal of World Trade* (44) (1), pp. 127–72.

WTO Agreement, and b) provisions of the protocols of accession of other non-original Members.

Finally, the last two chapters contain the results of a mapping exercise conducted in order to determine the prevalence and substance of so-called WTO-Plus and WTO-Minus obligations. One of the main reasons for the research has been the concern that the WTO is in fact characterized by a two-tiered – or even a multi-tiered – membership. It has been argued that, as a result of the power-based accession process, new Members have had to accept obligations that exceed the commitments that are allegedly more stringent than those undertaken by the incumbent membership.[15] Existing literature often contains assumptions over what constitutes, or does not constitute, a WTO-Plus obligation. Through a detailed mapping exercise of 36 protocols of accession, and the corresponding working party reports, an analysis is made of the type of commitments that new WTO Members have agreed to in order to be allowed to join the organization. The results of this mapping exercise, as presented in Chapters 5 and 6, allow for the definition of a typology by means of which the commitments contained in accession protocols can be compared with the existing 'baseline' obligations in the WTO Agreement, including its annexes.[16] The mapping exercise has been carried out on the basis of the accession protocols of non-original Members of the WTO. The results of the mapping exercise provide conclusions as to the prevalence of WTO-Plus and WTO-Minus obligations. Are they being negotiated more often in recent accessions? Are they merely country-specific, or is there a discernible trend? Are they negotiated in particular areas (export policies, trade remedies, subsidies, etc.) or can they be seen across the board? The mapping exercise contains detailed scrutiny of all areas in which rules obligations have been agreed upon by the new Member and the WTO. Examples of such areas include state-owned enterprises (SOEs), the domestic policy-making framework and rule of law commitments, tariff rate quotas (TRQs), quantitative restrictions, customs valuation, pre-shipment inspection, anti-dumping, countervailing duties, safeguards, subsidies, services, technical barriers to trade (TBT), sanitary and phytosanitary measures (SPS), trade-related aspects of intellectual property rights (TRIPS) and transparency obligations. Of

---

[15] It is important to note that this chapter will only address the so-called 'rules' obligations – those that lay down the material rules the incumbent Member has to adhere to – and will not address the amount of concessions required for a Member to be allowed to accede.

[16] Yamaoka (2013), Analysis of China's Accession Commitments in the WTO.

particular interest are the commitments made in respect of the elimination of export duties.[17] It will be established that there is a gap in the baseline disciplines on export restrictions, as these merely prohibit the use of quantitative export restrictions and do not focus on export taxes as a means of restricting the export of certain goods. WTO Members have sought to fill this gap by including provisions on the elimination and/or prohibition of export duties in protocols of accession. Using the results of the mapping exercise, the prevalence of this type of WTO-Plus obligation will be examined.

The final part, Chapter 7, summarizes the main findings presented in this book. Some general recommendations are proposed for countries that are not yet a Member of the WTO. The importance of, and the need for, trade-related capacity building is highlighted, especially with respect to those countries that have not yet joined the multilateral trading system. It is submitted that this is a crucial condition for achieving universal membership and maintaining the legitimacy and centrality of the WTO and the multilateral trading system in the long term.

The book adopts an integrated approach that combines a comprehensive mapping exercise with a legal analysis of the decisions by the WTO DSB involving protocols of accession. Additionally, it provides an update of the existing scholarship on WTO accession. This monograph is the first contribution that comprehensively addresses the issue of Member-specific 'WTO-Plus' commitments in protocols of accession by analysing 36 protocols of accession and their corresponding working party reports. All accessions until 2016, including those of Afghanistan, Kazakhstan and Liberia, are covered. Although it does not purport to be a comprehensive textbook on the WTO, it can nevertheless serve as a useful reference guide for those who have become interested in the workings of the organization as a result of events such as Brexit and the increase in protectionist rhetoric around the world. This book aspires to serve as a useful resource for those studying the topic of WTO accession, but also for those who are, as yet, not quite familiar with the workings of the World Trade Organization and the multilateral trading system.

---

[17] See, for example, the working party reports on the accessions of Viet Nam, para. 260, Croatia, para. 101, Tonga, para. 102, Saudi Arabia, para. 184, China, Protocol I.11, Nepal, para. 79, Russian Federation, paras. 668–9, and Ukraine, para. 255.

PART I

Accession to the multilateral trading system

1. The General Agreement on Tariffs and Trade 1947 (GATT 1947) and the World Trade Organization (WTO) – why join the club?

1.1 INTRODUCTION: THE EARLY DAYS OF THE MULTILATERAL TRADING SYSTEM

The creation of the multilateral trading system cannot be seen in isolation from the efforts to restore and preserve global peace that started to take shape in the aftermath of the Second World War.[1] Already during the Second World War, the allied powers, led by the United States, had started thinking about the future of multilateralism.[2] The Bretton Woods Conference that took place in July 1944 led to agreements on the creation of new international economic institutions. These agreements led to the creation of the World Bank (WB) and the International Monetary Fund (IMF).[3] The task of the WB can be broadly summarized as 'providing technical assistance to address development-related issues' and the 'financing of development policies' respectively.[4] The IMF was created with the aim of ensuring the stability of the international monetary system and it 'contributes to macro-economic stability primarily by providing support and advice to countries facing external payment difficulties'.[5] However, the goals of these institutions were not merely

---

[1] Lester, Simon, Mercurio, Bryan and Davies, Arwel (2012), *World Trade Law: Text, Materials and Commentary*, Oxford, Hart Publishing, at 56.

[2] Jackson, John H. (2000), *The Jurisprudence of GATT & the WTO*, Cambridge, Cambridge University Press, at 21.

[3] Wouters, Jan and De Meester, Bart (2007), *The World Trade Organization: A Legal and Institutional Analysis*, Antwerp, Intersentia, at 9.

[4] Irwin, Douglas A., Mavroidis, Petros C. and Sykes, Alan O. (2008), *The Genesis of the GATT*, New York, Cambridge University Press, at 99.

[5] Wouters, Jan and Odermatt, Jed (2014), 'Comparing the "Four Pillars" of Global Economic Governance: A Critical Analysis of the Institutional Design of

economic in nature.[6] After the establishment of the United Nations (UN) in October 1945, attention shifted towards the creation of institutions that would have to provide for global economic governance. In February 1946, the US proposed a UN Resolution aimed at the convention of a United Nations Conference on Trade and Employment.[7] It was envisaged that this Conference would serve as a forum for the negotiations on a Charter for an International Trade Organization (ITO) (also referred to as the Havana Charter).[8] The General Agreement on Tariffs and Trade 'would be an off-shoot of the broader and more ambitious ITO project'.[9]

1.1.1 The International Trade Organization

The negotiations for an international institution devoted to issues related to international trade were not part of the Bretton Woods framework. As Jackson notes, the evidence available does not support the conclusion that an eventual ITO would be placed at an equal footing with the WB and the IMF.[10] March 1948 marked the successful conclusion of the negotiations for an ITO Charter. However, due to a lack of agreement within the US Congress, it never entered into force. After the United States in 1951 decided to no longer pursue Congressional approval of the Charter for an ITO, the International Trade Organization was in fact 'stillborn'. None of the other Contracting Parties were interested in establishing an international organization governing trade-related matters, without the United States.[11] In the absence of an international organization, countries gradually turned to the GATT 1947 to 'handle problems concerning their

---

the FSB, IMF, World Bank, and WTO', *Journal of International Economic Law* (17) (1), pp. 49–76, at 52.

[6] Jackson, John H. (2000), *The Jurisprudence of GATT & the WTO*, at 21. Jackson notes that the IMF and WB were also aimed at achieving political goals. In particular he notes that 'the prevention of war and the establishment of a just system of economic relations were as important as the economic benefits that might derive from international trade and economic stability'.

[7] UN Economic and Social Council Resolution 1/13, 18 February 1946, UN Doc. E/22.

[8] Lester, Mercurio and Davies (2012), *World Trade Law*, at 56–7.

[9] Irwin, Mavroidis and Sykes (2008), *The Genesis of the GATT*, at 98.

[10] Jackson, John H. (1969), *World Trade Law and the Law of GATT: A Legal Analysis of the General Agreement on Tariffs and Trade*, Charlottesville, VA, The Michie Company/Bobbs Merill.

[11] Van den Bossche, Peter and Zdouc, Werner (2013), *The Law and Policy of the World Trade Organization*, Third Edition, Cambridge, Cambridge University Press, at 78.

trade relations'.[12] In 1955 the GATT Contracting Parties used one of the GATT review sessions that were aimed at examining the operation and functioning of the GATT to draft a new organizational protocol. The protocol was to create an Organization for Trade Co-operation, yet even though this protocol was much more concise than the proposal for an ITO, it also failed to satisfy the US Congress and hence, was also stillborn.[13]

1.1.2 The General Agreement on Tariffs and Trade 1947

The substantive negotiations for the General Agreement on Tariffs and Trade 1947 (GATT 1947) were successfully concluded on 30 October 1947. GATT 1947 entered into force on 1 January 1948, by virtue of the Protocol of Provisional Application (PPA). At the time there were 23 Contracting Parties. GATT 1947 was designed as a mechanism to guarantee the value of the tariff concessions made during the negotiations for the ITO. The working assumption had always been that it would be nothing more than an ordinary trade agreement, one that would eventually be placed within the framework offered by the ITO. Consequently, as has been observed by many, 'institutional provisions were not reflected in the GATT text'.[14] Nevertheless, 'through experimentation and trial and error', the GATT developed a set of rather elaborate procedural rules.[15] The membership of GATT 1947 was governed by Article XXXII, which stipulates that 'Contracting Parties' are 'those governments which are applying the provisions of this Agreement under Article XXVI or XXXIII or pursuant to the Protocol of Provisional Application'.

1.1.2.1 Protocol of Provisional Application

The PPA was suggested by officials at the US State Department in order to bring the GATT 1947 into effect.[16] The negotiating authority granted to the US by its legislative branch of government did not extend to many of the rules that were included in the second part of GATT 1947. Hence,

---

[12] Van den Bossche and Zdouc (2013), *The Law and Policy of the World Trade Organization*, at 78.

[13] Jackson, John H. (1997), *The World Trading System: Law and Policy of International Economic Relations*, Second Edition, Cambridge, MA, MIT Press, at 42.

[14] Irwin, Mavroidis and Sykes (2008), *The Genesis of the GATT*, at 100.

[15] Van den Bossche and Zdouc (2013), *The Law and Policy of the World Trade Organization*, at 78.

[16] Irwin, Mavroidis and Sykes (2008), *The Genesis of the GATT*, at 100.

until the US Congress approved the Charter for the ITO, these provisions would only be applied on a provisional basis. Pursuant to the PPA, the Contracting Parties undertook 'to apply provisionally as from 1 January 1948 Parts I and III of the GATT 1947 in full', and Part II 'to the fullest extent not inconsistent with existing legislation'.[17] The PPA has been described as providing for an 'existing legislation exception', or 'grandfather rights'. Legislation inconsistent with the obligations contained in Part II of the GATT 1947 could be maintained by GATT Contracting Parties. Consequently, there was no real desire on the part of the Contracting Parties to formally adopt GATT 1947 and, hence, the provisions of GATT 1947 were applied through the PPA of 30 October 1947 until 1996.[18]

1.1.2.2 The rationale underpinning GATT: reciprocity and non-discrimination

The Preamble of the General Agreement on Tariffs and Trade 1947 reads (in relevant part):

> Recognizing that their relations in the field of trade and economic endeavour should be conducted with a view to raising standards of living, ensuring full employment and a large and steadily growing volume of real income and effective demand, developing the full use of the resources of the world and expanding the production and exchange of goods,
>
> Being desirous of contributing to these objectives by entering into reciprocal and mutually advantageous arrangements directed to the substantial reduction of tariffs and other barriers to trade and to the elimination of discriminatory treatment in international commerce.

The second recital encapsulates the two main principles underpinning the multilateral trading system: reciprocity and non-discrimination. The concept of reciprocity is contained in the idea that negotiating mutual tariff reductions should ultimately lead to an economically more efficient outcome. Already during the early stages of GATT it was envisaged that the Contracting Parties would negotiate binding tariff schedules in which the relevant tariffs for a large set of products would be laid down. This principle was ultimately inscribed in Article II of the GATT 1947, in

---

[17] GATT BISD, Volume IV, 77. See also Van den Bossche and Zdouc (2013), *The Law and Policy of the World Trade Organization*, at 77.

[18] Van den Bossche and Zdouc (2013), *The Law and Policy of the World Trade Organization*, at 77.

particular subparagraphs (a) and (b) thereof. The principle of non-discrimination, on the other hand, was further refined into two distinct forms. First, the concept of Most-Favoured-Nation (MFN) treatment entails that GATT Contracting Parties would no longer provide more favourable treatment – by granting advantages, privileges or immunities – to products originating in some states, without providing that same treatment to 'like' products originating in GATT Contracting Parties. This principle is enshrined in Article I:1 of the GATT 1947, which provides:

> With respect to customs duties and charges of any kind imposed on or in connection with importation or exportation or imposed on the international transfer of payments for imports or exports, and with respect to the method of levying such duties and charges, and with respect to all rules and formalities in connection with importation and exportation, and with respect to all matters referred to in paragraphs 2 and 4 of Article III, any advantage, favour, privilege or immunity granted by any contracting party to any product originating in or destined for any other country shall be accorded immediately and unconditionally to the like product originating in or destined for the territories of all other contracting parties. [footnote omitted]

The second emanation of the concept of non-discrimination lies in the principle of National Treatment. In essence, this concept required GATT Contracting Parties to treat imported products in the same way as domestic products, both in respect of matters relating to taxation and in respect of internal regulation. The National Treatment obligation was incorporated in Article III of the GATT 1947, which reads (in relevant part):

> 1. The contracting parties recognize that internal taxes and other internal charges, and laws, regulations and requirements affecting the internal sale, offering for sale, purchase, transportation, distribution or use of products, and internal quantitative regulations requiring the mixture, processing or use of products in specified amounts or proportions, should not be applied to imported or domestic products so as to afford protection to domestic production.
>
> 2. The products of the territory of any contracting party imported into the territory of any other contracting party shall not be subject, directly or indirectly, to internal taxes or other internal charges of any kind in excess of those applied, directly or indirectly, to like domestic products. Moreover, no contracting party shall otherwise apply internal taxes or other internal charges to imported or domestic products in a manner contrary to the principles set forth in paragraph 1.
>
> [...]

> 4. The products of the territory of any contracting party imported into the territory of any other contracting party shall be accorded treatment no less favourable than that accorded to like products of national origin in respect of all laws, regulations and requirements affecting their internal sale, offering for sale, purchase, transportation, distribution or use. The provisions of this paragraph shall not prevent the application of differential internal transportation charges which are based exclusively on the economic operation of the means of transport and not on the nationality of the product. [footnotes omitted]

Although the recitals in the preamble, and the subsequent elaboration of the main principles contained therein by means of the obligations in Articles I, II and III of the GATT 1994, provide an indication of the main drivers behind the idea of creating a system aimed at governing the international trade relations of states after the Second World War, the text of the Preamble and these articles does not, as such, explain the economic theory that underpins this type of trade agreement. Why do states voluntarily restrict their sovereignty by binding themselves to a set of international rules that determine the way in which they can conduct their trade policy?[19] Three approaches that explain the rationale for international trade agreements have been identified. It has been argued that the 'avoidance of terms of trade losses', 'the establishment of economic and political commitments against domestic interests' and 'the pursuit of foreign-policy objectives related to peace and security' may all – to varying degrees – explain the existence of trade agreements such as GATT.[20] These three approaches will be discussed in this subsection. It should be noted, however, that the rationale behind the creation of the multilateral trading system as such is, in most cases, different from the motivation of individual states and customs territories to join the system at a later stage. The rationale of their accession bids will be examined in more detail in section 1.3.

1.1.2.2.1 Avoiding terms-of-trade losses The first of the three approaches that may explain the intention of the US and other original Contracting Parties in negotiating the GATT relates to the idea that a multilateral approach towards tariff liberalization is economically more efficient than a unilateral one. In a situation in which states seek the

---

[19] Ossa, Ralph (2011), 'A "New Trade" Theory of GATT/WTO Negotiations', *Journal of Political Economy* (119) (1), pp. 122–52.

[20] Van den Bossche and Zdouc (2013), *The Law and Policy of the World Trade Organization*, at 197.

unilateral liberalization of tariffs, they will face a 'prisoner's dilemma' which, as has been shown by many economists, leads to an inefficient outcome:

> Acting independently, countries may not be able to avoid the inefficient equilibrium because, if one of them were to reduce its tariffs alone, the other country would still have a unilateral incentive to maintain its duties on the tariff-reducing country.[21]

It has been argued that the principles of reciprocity and non-discrimination, as contained in Articles I, II and III of the GATT 1994, operate as 'rules that work in concert to guide governments toward efficient multilateral trade agreements'.[22] However, others have argued that, in practice, the principles of reciprocity and the principle of Most-Favoured-Nation treatment are, in fact, opposing and that the pursuit of Most-Favoured-Nation treatment, basing free trade negotiations on the idea of reciprocity, and the pursuit of a near-universal membership of GATT are fundamentally at odds with each other.[23] According to this view it would be economically more efficient if more emphasis could be placed on reciprocity, even if this would mean that the pursuit of a universal multilateral trading system would need to be abandoned. As will be explained subsequently, however, the GATT, and eventually the WTO continued in their pursuit of universal membership. The question is whether the concern expressed – that in its current form the GATT would end up as a 'seriously degenerated, nominally universal, but in practice highly unstable system, increasingly open to the use of naked power' – has become a reality.[24] In the end, it is generally considered that it is unlikely that terms-of-trade type motivations were the main – let alone the only – driver behind the creation of the GATT.

1.1.2.2.2 Establishing commitments In addition to the terms-of-trade approach, two types of commitment theories have been used to explain the creation of the GATT in the period immediately after the Second World War. Both theories operate from the idea that governments pursue

---

21 Irwin, Mavroidis and Sykes (2008), *The Genesis of the GATT*, at 178.

22 Bagwell, Kyle and Staiger, Robert W. (1999), 'An Economic Theory of GATT', *The American Economic Review* (89) (1), pp. 215–48, at 241.

23 Curzon, Gerard and Curzon, Victoria (1989), 'Non-Discrimination and the Rise of "Material" Reciprocity', *The World Economy* (12) (4), pp. 481–500, at 497.

24 Curzon and Curzon (1989), Non-Discrimination and the Rise of 'Material' Reciprocity, at 498.

trade policies that are aimed at the maximization of national welfare. From this perspective, binding the country in question to a set of international norms – in the form of trade agreements – is useful to strengthen the government's bargaining position against domestic interest groups. One can distinguish between economic commitment and political commitments.[25] At the same time, it should be recognized that neither of these two commitment theories probably fully explains states' desire to create a multilateral trading system along the lines of GATT.[26]

1.1.2.2.3 Foreign-policy objectives 'When goods don't cross borders, soldiers will.' This quote, often, yet perhaps mistakenly, attributed to French liberal economist Frédéric Bastiat, perhaps best sums up the third approach used to explain the creation of the multilateral trading system.[27] After the Second World War, governments may not only have been interested in improving the economic situation of their country, or even merely their trade balance. Nor may they have intended to create GATT in order to bind subsequent government. Rather, it is likely that more general foreign-policy objectives – such as the creation of a more stable economic climate – may have been important drivers behind the creation of the multilateral trading system. It has been stated that 'the broad objective [of the GATT] is to help to maintain international political stability by establishing rules of "good behaviour" as well as mechanisms for settling disputes'.[28] Many scholars in the field of political science have tried to explain the creation of the GATT in light of the desire of states to prevent future situations of (armed) conflict. Indeed, some accounts provide evidence for the argument that some of the driving powers during the GATT negotiations had peace, stability and security in mind when trying to develop a set of rules for the conduct of international trade. During a meeting in April 1947, US Negotiator Clair

---

[25] Irwin, Mavroidis and Sykes (2008), *The Genesis of the GATT*, at 184.

[26] Irwin, Mavroidis and Sykes (2008), *The Genesis of the GATT*, at 188.

[27] Snow, Nicolas (2010), If Goods Don't Cross Borders … , Foundation for Economic Education, 26 October. Available at http://fee.org/resources/detail/if-goods-dont-cross-borders (last accessed at 1 June 2017). Snow explains that it is unclear whether this sentence can be attributed to Bastiat. He refers to a quote by 19th century liberal Otto T. Mallery, who coined the quote 'If soldiers are not to cross international boundaries, goods must do so. Unless the Shackles can be dropped from trade, bombs will be dropped from the sky.'

[28] Robert E. Baldwin (1986), as cited by Irwin, Mavroidis and Sykes (2008), *The Genesis of the GATT*, at 188. In Baldwin's view the main rationale for establishing the GATT was a political one.

Wilcox made reference to a speech given by President of the United States Harry S. Truman, in which he stated:

> If the nations can agree to observe a code of good conduct in international trade, they will cooperate more readily in other international affairs. Such agreement will prevent the bitterness that is engendered by an economic war. It will provide an atmosphere congenial to the preservation of peace.[29]

The idea that international trade could contribute in a positive manner to establishing peace, security and stability had, however, been formulated almost a century earlier by John Stuart Mill. In his 1848 work *Principles of Political Economy*, he stated the following:

> [c]ommerce first taught nations to see with good will the wealth and prosperity of one another. Before, the patriot, unless sufficiently advanced in culture to feel the world his country, wished all countries weak, poor, and ill-governed, but his own: he now sees in their wealth and progress a direct source of wealth and progress to his own country. It is commerce which is rapidly rendering war obsolete, by strengthening and multiplying the personal interests which are in natural opposition to it. And it may be said without exaggeration that the great extent and rapid increase of international trade, in being the principal guarantee of the peace of the world, is the great permanent security for the uninterrupted progress of the ideas, the institutions, and the character of the human race.[30]

International trade as a condition for international peace and security may indeed have been one of the motivations for the negotiators of the GATT.[31] An international set of rules that governs international trade could arguably strengthen the capacity of international trade to bring about peace. Nevertheless, even though this third approach may also – to a certain extent – explain the creation of the GATT, similarly to the first and second approach, it does not in and of itself constitute the main reason for establishing the multilateral trading system. Rather, these approaches and theories should be 'understood as complementary, rather

---

[29] President of the United States of America, Harry S. Truman (1947), Address on Foreign Economic Policy, delivered at Baylor University, 6 March. Available at http://www.presidency.ucsb.edu/ws/?pid=12842 (last accessed at 1 June 2017).

[30] Mill, John Stuart (1909), *Principles of Political Economy with some of their Applications to Social Philosophy*, First Published 1848, 7th Edition, 1909, London; Longmans, Green and Co., at III.17.14.

[31] Gowa, Joanne and Hicks, Raymond (2013), 'Politics, Institutions, and Trade: Lessons of the Interwar Era', *International Organization* (67) (3), pp. 439–67.

than competing explanations for the remarkable achievements that led to the GATT in 1947'.[32]

1.2 THE WORLD TRADE ORGANIZATION

The WTO was born out of the eighth round of multilateral trade negotiations conducted in the framework of the GATT 1947. By the early 1980s, the main Contracting Parties to the GATT 1947 realized that an enhanced institutional framework was required to address the complexities posed by the globalization of the economy. GATT 1947 had provided a useful framework for the negotiation of tariff reductions, but as trade in services and international investment – two areas not regulated by GATT 1947 – began to increase, the lack of rules governing these areas became more apparent. Additionally, although the GATT 1947 did have a rules-based dispute settlement system, the attitude of some Contracting Parties towards this system became a source of concern. Non-compliance with Reports of GATT Panels was increasing, and the need for a more robust set of rules on dispute settlement was felt by many of the Contracting Parties. The Uruguay Round of Multilateral Trade Negotiations was intended to address many of the areas that had been left unregulated by GATT 1947, or which had not been regulated in sufficient detail in light of the changing nature of global commerce. After seven and a half years of intense negotiations, 123 participating governments concluded the WTO Agreement.[33] The WTO superseded GATT as an international organization, but the original rules contained in the GATT 1947 were transposed into the new legal framework. The General Agreement on Tariffs and Trade 1994 (GATT 1994) incorporates the provisions of the GATT 1947 by reference. Article 1(a) of the GATT 1994 provides that:

> 1. The General Agreement on Tariffs and Trade 1994 ('GATT 1994') shall consist of:
>
> (a) the provisions in the General Agreement on Tariffs and Trade, dated 30 October 1947, annexed to the Final Act Adopted at the Conclusion of the Second Session of the Preparatory Committee of the United Nations Conference on Trade and Employment (excluding the Protocol of Provisional Application), as rectified, amended or modified by the terms of legal

---

[32] Irwin, Mavroidis and Sykes (2008), *The Genesis of the GATT*, at 200.

[33] WTO, Understanding the WTO. Available at https://www.wto.org/english/thewto_e/whatis_e/tif_e/fact5_e.htm (last accessed at 1 June 2017).

> instruments which have entered into force before the date of entry into force of the WTO Agreement;

In addition to new rules on issues relating to anti-dumping, subsidies, technical barriers to trade, customs valuation and many others, several institutional changes were part of the results of the Uruguay Round. The dispute settlement procedures were altered fundamentally and a Dispute Settlement Body was created. Moreover, the dispute settlement rules now included a well-known 'reversed-consensus' rule, which entails that in respect of a number of provisions, a particular decision is taken, unless there is a consensus *not* to take that particular decision.[34] In the field of accession, however, there were no major changes. The main provision of the GATT 1947 on this issue, Article XXXIII, was more or less copied into the text of the WTO Agreement. Article XII of the WTO Agreement provides (in relevant part):

> 1. Any State or separate customs territory possessing full autonomy in the conduct of its external commercial relations and of the other matters provided for in this Agreement and the Multilateral Trade Agreements may accede to this Agreement, on terms to be agreed between it and the WTO. Such accession shall apply to this Agreement and the Multilateral Trade Agreements annexed thereto.
>
> 2. Decisions on accession shall be taken by the Ministerial Conference. The Ministerial Conference shall approve the agreement on the terms of accession by a two-thirds majority of the Members of the WTO.

The essence of the central phrase of Article XXXIII GATT 1947, 'on *terms to be agreed* between such government and the CONTRACTING PARTIES', remains unaltered with Article XII WTO Agreement stating 'on terms to be agreed between it [any State or separate customs territory wishing to join the WTO] and the WTO'. Subsequent chapters will discuss the different types of WTO membership (original and non-original) and the accession procedure in more detail (see in particular sections 2.3.2.2 and 4.2.2.3).

---

[34] The reversed consensus principle can, inter alia, be found in Article 6.1 DSU (on the establishment of panels), Article 16.4 DSU (on the adoption of panel reports) and Article 17.14 DSU (on the adoption of Appellate Body reports).

1.3 RATIONALES FOR ACCESSION

The rationale for the creation of the multilateral trading system has been described briefly in section 1.1.2.2. The rationale for the creation for the system as such, however, has to be distinguished from the rationales that have driven and drive the accession bids of states and customs territories looking to become part of that very system. States and customs territories historically have had a wide variety of reasons to seek accession to the multilateral trading system. Economic motives have in most cases been the primary driver behind the desire of states to join the GATT/WTO system. Since the creation of the GATT 1947, the principle of non-discrimination has provided states with an enhanced sense of security that in conducting their trade relations with other Contracting Parties their exporters would not be subject to discriminatory treatment. Moreover, the practice of binding tariff concessions multilaterally has provided producers and exporters with a more stable international playing field. Although the question of whether the GATT/WTO system has in practice led to an increase in global trade, or even an increase in global economic welfare, is subject to debate, it cannot be denied that the system has provided economic actors with more security, stability and predictability. These economic motives will be discussed in the first subsection. GATT/WTO membership has also been pursued for, what might be called, political motives. Becoming a Contracting Party to GATT or a Member to the WTO has historically signalled to the international community that the acceding state has obtained a level of 'political maturity' at the international level. Additionally, it provides a sign to potential investors that the state in question is willing and able to adhere to a set of binding international rules that will inform the way in which the state will conduct its internal trade policy. GATT/WTO membership thus makes it more attractive for a foreign investor to open up a branch in a state or customs territory. Aside from economic and political motives that underpin a state's desire to join the multilateral trading system, GATT/WTO accession also bring externalities that – although not the main driver behind an accession bid – may positively influence the economic development of the acceding state. These factors will be discussed in the third subsection. Lastly, considering the proliferation of preferential trade agreements (PTAs), regional trade agreements (RTAs) and plurilateral trade agreements, the question arises how this development impacts the desire of states who are not yet WTO Members to join the organization.[35] Does the WTO

[35] Some recent initiatives include the Transatlantic Trade and Investment Partnership (TTIP) between the European Union and the United States, the

perhaps provide for a 'safe-haven' in times of multi-polar – rather than multilateral – global economic governance?

1.3.1 Economic Motives for WTO Accession

Obtaining WTO membership comes at a cost. As will be explained further on in this contribution, the WTO accession process is often long and arduous. States are required to give up most of their existing instruments aimed at protecting domestic industries. Opening up domestic markets may come at a cost to inefficient industries which may not be able to survive foreign competition. Disruptive effects may lead to (temporary) peaks in unemployment. Why then have states continued to seek accession to the multilateral trading system, be it to the GATT 1947 or to the WTO? A first argument relates to the aforementioned 'terms of trade' theory. If states are willing to undergo, as will be established in subsequent chapters, a lengthy and sometimes costly accession process, it is to be expected that the economic gains offered by WTO membership outweigh these costs – at least to a certain extent.[36] Consequently, it might be so that membership to the GATT/WTO increases the level of trade in a former non-Member. A second explanation is derived from the fact that, at least in theory, exporters in a WTO Member benefit from non-discriminatory treatment from other WTO Members. The Most-Favoured-Nation (MFN) treatment obligation and its underlying principle may therefore still provide a ground to seek accession to the WTO.[37] Thirdly, states may have country-specific economic interests that underpin their desire to join the multilateral trading system.

1.3.1.1 Does the GATT/WTO increase trade and foreign direct investment?

Economic scholarship focusing on the effects of the creation of, and accession to, the multilateral trading system has mostly studied the

---

Trans-Pacific Partnership (TPP), the Regional Comprehensive Economic Partnership (RCEP) and the Trade in Services Agreement (TISA).

[36] Allee, Todd L. and Scalera, Jamie E. (2012), 'The Divergent Effects of Joining International Organizations: Trade Gains and the Rigors of WTO Accession', *International Organization* (66) (2), pp. 243–76; Hong, Chang (2013), 'The Political Economy of Tariff Protection in China: Evidence from the WTO Accession', *Canadian Journal of Economics* (46) (4), pp. 1295–316.

[37] Egger, Peter H. and Olarreaga, Marcelo (2014), 'Special Issue: The Political Economy of Multilateral Trade Negotiations', *The Review of International Organizations* (9) (2), pp. 135–42.

question whether being a Member to this system influences the amount of trade relative to gross domestic product (GDP) of a particular country. This section summarizes the key findings of economic research in this area.[38] One central question that has been addressed is whether the system introduced by GATT, and subsequently evolved into the WTO, increases trade.[39] One strand of scholarship has argued that the effect of the GATT/WTO on trade is limited.[40] Similarly, the argument has been made that – contrary to what one might have expected – membership of the multilateral trading system is not automatically associated with more liberal trade policy.[41] Others have argued that there is a visible effect of the GATT/WTO system on the growth of international trade.[42] Accordingly it has been found that '[t]rade among those with standing in the GATT/WTO was considerably higher than what one would predict, based purely on proximity, national income, and other non-political variables'.[43] Subsequent studies have further refined the applicable methodology by not taking into account sectors that are not within the purview

---

[38] Kohl, Tristan and Trojanowska, Sofia (2015), 'Heterogeneous Trade Agreements, WTO Membership and International Trade: An Analysis Using Matching Econometrics', *Applied Economics* (47) (33), pp. 3499–509.

[39] An expected increase in trade seems to be one of the main drivers behind accession bids. See, for example, Babetskaia-Kukharchuk, Oxana and Maurel, Mathilde (2004), 'Russia's Accession to the WTO: The Potential for Trade Increase', *Journal of Comparative Economics* (30), pp. 680–99.

[40] Rose, Andrew K. (2004), 'Do We Really Know That the WTO Increases Trade?', *The American Economic Review* (94) (1), pp. 98–113; and Rose, Andrew K. (2007), 'Do We Really Know That the WTO Increases Trade? Reply', *The American Economic Review* (97) (5), pp. 2019–25.

[41] Rose, Andrew K. (2004), 'Do WTO Members Have More Liberal Trade Policy?', *Journal of International Economics* (63) (2), pp. 209–35; see also Chandra, Piyush (2014), 'WTO Subsidy Rules and Tariff Liberalization: Evidence from Accession of China', *The Journal of International Trade & Economic Development: An International and Comparative Review* (23) (8), pp. 1170–205.

[42] Tomz, Michael, Goldstein, Judith and Rivers, Douglas (2007), 'Membership Has Its Privileges: The Impact of GATT on International Trade', *The American Economic Review* (97) (5), pp. 2005–18; Chang, Pao-Li and Lee, Myoung-Jae (2011), 'The WTO Trade Effect', *Journal of International Economics* (85), pp. 53–71, at 69, noting that 'membership in the GATT/WTO has a significant trade-promoting effect for dyads that have both chosen to be members'.

[43] Goldstein, Judith L., Rivers, Douglas and Tomz, Michael (2007), 'Institutions in International Relations: Understanding the Effects of the GATT and the WTO on World Trade', *International Organization* (61) (1), pp. 37–67, at 63.

of the WTO.[44] Since the WTO disciplines on agricultural and textiles trade are relatively weak, it has been argued that these sectors should be excluded from the analysis. Moreover, trade in oil should also be excluded given that the WTO does not address this particular type of commodity. Through this refined analysis, it has been found that the GATT/WTO system increases trade for its Members by approximately 30 per cent on average.[45] Indeed, it has been argued that 'the GATT/WTO has done a splendid job of promoting trade'.[46] However, this conclusion comes with the caveat that four identified asymmetries in the system cause an uneven distribution of the growth in trade. Most importantly, it has been found that, on average, developing countries' imports have not increased as a result of WTO membership.[47] This suggests that the effect on trade is perhaps most visible in the field of exports. In trying to reconcile these apparently conflicting findings, it has been concluded that, indeed, '[j]oining the WTO is all about exports'.[48] The question that will always be present in this context is one of attribution. To what extent can the set of rules developed in the context of the GATT/WTO, and their subsequent enforcement through its dispute settlement mechanism, be seen as the cause for the growth in trade – let alone global economic welfare?[49] In any event, the potential economic benefits of GATT/WTO membership should not be defined narrowly in terms of the size of international trade. Indeed, as has been acknowledged in the scholarship that has been referenced here, other factors such as the reducing cost of transportation and regional association have undoubtedly also contributed to the increase of international trade. One study argues that the role of GATT/WTO should not be considered merely from a numerical perspective. Rather, the multilateral trading system should be considered as a

---

[44] Kim, Myeong Hwan (2010), 'Does the WTO Promote Trade? Further Evidence', *The Journal of International Trade & Economic Development: An International and Comparative Review* (19) (3), pp. 421–37.

[45] Kim (2010), Does the WTO Promote Trade? Further Evidence, at 430.

[46] Subramanian, Arvind and Wei, Shang-Jin (2007), 'The WTO Promotes Trade, Strongly but Unevenly', *Journal of International Economics* (72), pp. 151–75, at 173; see also Chang and Lee (2011), The WTO Trade Effect, at 69.

[47] Subramanian and Wei (2007), The WTO Promotes Trade, Strongly but Unevenly, at 173.

[48] Balding, Christopher (2010), 'Joining the World Trade Organization: What Is the Impact?', *Review of International Economics* (18) (1), pp. 193–206.

[49] Anderson, Kym (2014), 'Contributions of the GATT/WTO to Global Economic Welfare: Empirical Evidence', *Journal of Economic Surveys* (30) (1), pp. 56–92.

forum that fosters coordination between countries. It has been suggested that '[b]y being part of the negotiating structure, countries form relationships and put their policies and priorities transparently on the table. In a word, they build trust, which is fundamental to facilitating international trade.'[50] Looking more broadly at the question of how GATT/WTO accession influences growth and investment, it has been found that if a country is required to undertake substantial domestic reforms in order to be accepted by the WTO, this is associated with 'significant increases in growth and investment'.[51] More specific findings on the relationship between WTO accession and foreign direct investment have been made with regard to Viet Nam. In a case study, it was found that the country's WTO accession in 2006 has had a 'strong and positive impact on Vietnam's imports and inward FDI [foreign direct investment]'.[52] It has been observed that, more generally, FDI increases with GATT/WTO membership.[53] The positive impact of WTO accession on a country's investment climate has also been revealed in the context of the accession of Least-Developed Countries (LDCs). WTO accession will require these countries to implement domestic reforms, also related to rule of law issues, which will make them more attractive as a potential host-state for FDI.[54] Nevertheless, although WTO accession may have a positive influence on FDI because of the fact that WTO accession requires certain domestic reforms, the causality remains precisely between these domestic reforms and an increase in FDI. Consequently, where a country decides

---

[50] Grant, Jason H. and Boys, Kathryn A. (2012), 'Agricultural Trade and the GATT/WTO: Does Membership Make a Difference?', *American Journal of Agricultural Economics* (94) (1), pp. 1–24, at 20.

[51] Tang, Man-Keung and Wei, Shang-Jin (2006), Is Bitter Medicine Good for You? The Economic Consequences of WTO/GATT Accessions, paper presented at the Trade Conference, Research Department hosted by the International Monetary Fund, 13 April 2006, at 22; Tang, Man-Keung and Wei, Shang-Jin (2009), 'The Value of Making Commitments Externally: Evidence from WTO Accessions', *Journal of International Economics* (78) (2), pp. 216–29.

[52] Pham, Thi Hong Hanh (2011), 'Does WTO Accession Matter for the Dynamics of Foreign Investment and Trade? Vietnam's New Evidence', *Economics of Transition* (19) (2), pp. 255–85, at 282.

[53] Dreher, Axel, Mikosh, Heiner and Voigt, Stefan (2015), 'Membership Has Its Privileges: The Effect of Membership in International Organizations on FDI', *World Development* (66), pp. 346–58, at 354.

[54] Chekol, Abebe Abebayehu (2008), Accession to the WTO: Brightening the Prospect for Attraction of Investment? A Least-Developed Country's Perspective, CEPMLP Annual Review, Volume 12 (2007–08). Available at http://www.dundee.ac.uk/cepmlp/gateway/index.php?news=29870 (last accessed at 1 June 2017).

to implement the necessary policy changes at an earlier stage, FDI in the affected sectors may already increase prior to WTO accession.[55] Economic scholarship does not seem to support the conclusion that WTO membership in itself is enough to trigger domestic reform. Nevertheless, WTO accession aspirations will, inevitably, often coincide with a drive towards more market-oriented policies and an improved system of governance.

1.3.1.2 The benefits of non-discrimination

The principle of non-discrimination has always been one of the cornerstones of the multilateral trading system. As explained, the MFN-treatment obligation and the National Treatment obligation required GATT Contracting Parties not to discriminate between and against imported products. Those states and customs territories that were not a Contracting Party to the GATT or are not a Member of the WTO did not, and do not, benefit from the treatment prescribed by these two obligations. There is no obligation on WTO Members to extend MFN-treatment or National Treatment to the products from non-WTO Members. Consequently, the protection afforded by the MFN-treatment obligation and the National Treatment obligation is an incentive for states and customs territories to seek accession to the multilateral trading system. Historically, this has been the driver behind many of the GATT-accession bids from smaller economies. As has been noted, these countries began to 'appreciate multilateralism in trade as a shield of protection against bilateral pressures from trading powers, assuring non-discriminatory treatment and fair procedures'.[56] Similarly, planned-economy countries, such as Yugoslavia, Poland, Romania and Hungary saw the benefit of the protection offered by these principles and consequently acceded to the GATT in the late 1960s and early 1970s.

1.3.1.3 Country-specific and sector-specific impacts of accession

In a number of accessions, certain country-specific or sector-specific interests influenced the desire of the state in question to join the multilateral trading system. In a study on agricultural trade and the GATT/WTO, mentioned in the previous subsection, it was found that

[55] Desta, Melaku Geboye (2009), 'Accession for What? An Examination of Ethiopia's Decision to Join the WTO', *Journal of World Trade* (43) (2), pp. 339–62, at 357.

[56] Benedek, Wolfgang and Ginther, Konrad (1988), Planned-Economy Countries and GATT: Legal Issues of Accession, in *German Yearbook of International Law/Jahrbuch für Internationales Recht* (31), pp. 70–106, at 72.

accession 'generates sizable trade flow gains and establishes an atmosphere conducive to commercial exchange'.[57] These findings are consistent with studies carried out with respect to agricultural trade and food security in China. It has been observed that WTO accession has been beneficial to China's agricultural sector, yet it has also been noted that, again, additional steps are necessary to 'improve transparency, information, quality, sanitary measures and other measures in order to benefit fully from opportunities'.[58] Turning to more country-specific findings, one study revealed that accession may also have a positive impact on the reduction of household poverty.[59] Some studies have also addressed the impact of WTO accession at the firm-level or within specific sectors.[60]

1.3.2 Political Motives for WTO Accession

In addition to the economic rationale for WTO accession, political considerations may also play an important role in the desire of states to become part of the multilateral trading system.[61] It has been shown that 'geopolitical factors attract some countries to the regime while making others hesitant to join'. These findings have been explained by referencing the example of the accession of formerly communist states in the second half of the 20th century. The GATT 'enticed new members with

---

[57] Grant and Boys (2012), Agricultural Trade and the GATT/WTO: Does Membership Make a Difference?, at 20; Li, David L. and Wu, Changqi (2004), GATT/WTO Accession and Productivity, in Ito, Takatoshi and Rose, Andrew K. (eds) (2004), *Growth and Productivity in East Asia, NBER-East Asia Seminar on Economics*, vol. 13, Chicago, University of Chicago Press.

[58] Palma, Carolina (2015), 'WTO Implications of China's Food Security Policy', *Global Trade and Customs Journal* (10) (6), pp. 217–27, at 224.

[59] Rutherford, Thomas F. and Tarr, David G. (2008), 'Poverty Effects of Russia's WTO Accession: Modeling "Real" Households with Endogenous Productivity Effects', *Journal of International Economics* (75), pp. 131–50, at 149; Tarr, David G. (2007), 'Russian Accession to the WTO: An Assessment', *Euroasian Geography and Economics* (48) (3), pp. 306–19.

[60] Jiang, Neng and Kattuman, Paul A. (2012), 'China's WTO Accession and Long-Term Profitability of Chinese Firms', *International Journal of the Economics of Business* (19) (1), pp. 53–73; Mattoo, Aaditya (2003), 'China's Accession to the WTO: The Services Dimension', *Journal of International Economic Law* (6) (2), pp. 299–339; Li, Shanshan and Xu, Ningxiang (2015), 'The Influences of WTO Accession on China's State-Owned Enterprises', *Open Journal of Business and Management* (3), pp. 192–8.

[61] McKenzie, Francine (2008), 'GATT and the Cold War: Accession Debates, Institutional Development and the Western Alliance, 1947–1959', *Journal of Cold War Studies* (10) (3), pp. 78–109.

lenient conditions when engaged in rivalry with the Soviet bloc, and only began to impose strict conditions when the end of Cold War reduced the salience of foreign policy in the domain of economic decision-making'.[62] Another example is formed by the applications for accession to the WTO from Iraq and Afghanistan in the aftermath of US-led military interventions in these countries. Whereas these political motives stem, to a large extent, from geopolitical considerations, domestic politics may also serve as the basis for a WTO accession bid. Such political considerations have also been mentioned as the driver behind China's accession bid to the WTO in 2001.[63] It has been argued that China's desire to join the WTO did not only stem from 'a desire to protect itself from potential economic blackmail by the United States', but also reflects the realization that China's economic institutions have to be aligned 'with the economic institutions of modern capitalist economies'.[64] Moreover, it has been suggested that China's leadership 'is confident that its explicit embrace of capitalist institutions under WTO auspices would be seen by the general Chinese public (and the Chinese elite) as a step forward in the reform process rather than as surrender of China's sovereignty in economic experimentation'.[65]

1.3.3 Externalities of WTO Accession

In addition to the expected or desired effects of WTO accession that have been discussed in previous sections, states may experience societal changes that had not been expected, or were not the main reason for the accession. These externalities, or unexpected and unintended consequences, of WTO accession are the subject of this subsection. One of the main externalities brought about by WTO accession and highlighted in

---

[62] Davis, Christina L. and Wilf, Meredith (2013), 'Joining the Club: Accession to the GATT/WTO', *The Journal of Politics* (79) (3), pp. 964–78; see also Davis, Christina and Wilf, Meredith (2015), WTO Membership, in Martin, Lisa L. (ed.), *The Oxford Handbook of the Political Economy of International Trade*, New York, Oxford University Press, at 392.

[63] In this respect note the political sensitivities surrounding the WTO accession of Chinese Taipei (or Taiwan). See Charnovitz, Steve (2006), 'Taiwan's WTO Membership and Its International Implications', *Asian Journal of WTO and International Health Law and Policy* (1), pp. 401–31.

[64] Sachs, Jeffrey D. and Woo, Wing Thye (2003), 'China's Economic Growth after WTO Membership', *Journal of Chinese Economic and Business Studies* (1) (1), pp. 1–31, at 25.

[65] Sachs and Woo (2003), China's Economic Growth after WTO Membership, at 26.

academic literature is the impact it has on, what will be called, the system of governance and the rule of law in the acceding state.[66] Similarly, it may also impact the legal culture in the acceding state.[67] As will be explained in subsequent chapters, accession to the WTO does not only require states to liberalize their markets, lower their tariffs and grant

---

[66] Elgindi, Ali Ibn Abi Talib A. and Lunenborg, Peter (2012), 'The WTO Accession Process and Non-Economic Considerations', *Global Trade and Customs Journal* (7) (11–12), pp. 461–5; Shaffer, Gregory (2015), 'How The World Trade Organization Shapes Regulatory Governance', *Regulation and Governance* (9) (1), pp. 1–15, at 8; Guohua, Yang and Jin, Cheng (2001), 'The Process of China's Accession to the WTO', *Journal of International Economic Law* (4) (2), pp. 297–328.

[67] See, in respect of China, Gao, Henry (2007), 'Taming The Dragon: China's Experience in the WTO Dispute Settlement System', *Legal Issues of Economic Integration* (34) (4), pp. 369–92; Qin, Julia Ya (2007), 'Trade, Investment and Beyond: The Impact of WTO Accession on China's Legal System', *The China Quarterly* (191), pp. 720–41; Don Harpaz, Marcia (2010), 'Sense and Sensibilities of China and WTO Dispute Settlement', *Journal of World Trade* (44) (6), pp. 1155–86, at 1178; Don Harpaz, Marcia (2011), 'China's WTO Compliance-Plus Anti-Dumping Policy', *Journal of World Trade* (45) (4), pp. 726–66; Toohey, Lisa (2011), 'China and the World Trade Organization: The First Decade', *International and Comparative Law Quarterly* (60) (3), pp. 788–98; Zhuang, Wei (2011), 'An Empirical Study of China's Participation in the WTO Dispute Settlement Mechanism: 2001–2010', *The Law and Development Review* (4) (1), pp. 217–46; Kennedy, Matthew (2012), 'China's Role in WTO Dispute Settlement', *World Trade Review* (11) (4), pp. 555–89; Chi, Manjiao (2012), 'China's Participation in WTO Dispute Settlement over the Past Decade: Experiences and Impacts', *Journal of International Economic Law* (15) (1), pp. 29–49; Mercurio, Bryan and Tyagi, Mitali (2012), China's Evolving Role in WTO Dispute Settlement: Acceptance, Consolidation and Activation, in Herrmann, Christoph and Terhechte, Jörg Philipp (eds) (2012), *European Yearbook of International Economic Law*, vol. 3, Heidelberg, Springer; Guohua, Yang (2015), 'China in the WTO Dispute Settlement: A Memoir', *Journal of World Trade* (49) (1), pp. 1–18; Li, Liao and Minyou, Yu (2015), 'Impact of the WTO on China's Rule of Law in Trade: Twentieth Anniversary of the WTO', *Journal of World Trade* (49) (5), pp. 837–72, at 872. Li and Minyou note that '[i]t is another long march that establishment of the rule of law in China, which could not be realized without cultivating the rule of law in trade within China. As the first major power of trade in goods and the second largest economy, China still has considerable progress to make for the rule of law in trade.' Burnay, Matthieu and Wouters, Jan (2015), The EU and China in the WTO: What Contribution to the International Rule of Law? Reflections in Light of the Raw Materials and Rare Earths Disputes, in Wang, Jianwei and Song, Weiqing (eds), *China, the European Union, and International Politics of Global Governance*, London, Palgrave MacMillan (forthcoming).

non-discriminatory treatment to imported products. Rather, the obligations that are contained in the WTO agreements require WTO Members to establish – albeit to a limited extent – a system of governance that provides for access to an independent court of law.[68] Additionally, the transparency obligations contained in some of the WTO agreements force WTO Members to establish policies that allow for the publication of official documents.[69] Interestingly, as will be established in Part III of this monograph, the WTO's accession process sometimes leads to a situation in which the acceding state agrees to more extensive transparency and 'rule of law' obligations.[70] This finding has led some authors to conclude that the WTO may have a positive impact on the establishment of 'some democratic rights' in countries where this might – absent WTO accession – not have been the case.[71] The same literature has also found that the length of GATT/WTO membership is also positively correlated with the level of political participation and the existence of due process rights in a given GATT/WTO Member.[72] More recent research on the issue of whether the WTO contributes in a positive way to governance in recently acceded Members is more ambivalent.[73] Although it appears that WTO accession may have some positive influence on the creation of accountable and inclusive institutions in acceded Members, quantitative analyses carried out do not provide evidence of a consistent pattern on this issue.[74] It is also important to keep in mind that the WTO as an institution is focused on establishing a legal regime that is aimed at

---

[68] See, for example, Article X:3 of the GATT 1994.

[69] See, for example, Article X:1 of the GATT 1994; Article 63 of the Agreement on Trade-Related Aspects of Intellectual Property Rights, 1869 U.N.T.S. 299, entered into force 1 January 1995 (TRIPs Agreement); and Article 2(g) of the Agreement on Rules of Origin, 1868 U.N.T.S. 397, entered into force 1 January 1995 (Agreement on Rules of Origin).

[70] Shaffer (2015), How The World Trade Organization Shapes Regulatory Governance, at 10.

[71] Aaronson, Susan Ariel and Abouharb, M. Rodwan (2011), 'Unexpected Bedfellows: The GATT, the WTO and *Some* Democratic Rights', *International Studies Quarterly* (55) (2), pp. 379–408, at 404. See also Desta (2009), Accession for What? An Examination of Ethiopia's Decision to Join the WTO, at 361.

[72] Aaronson and Abouharb (2011), Unexpected Bedfellows: The GATT, the WTO and *Some* Democratic Rights, at 404.

[73] See, for example, Copelovitch, Mark S. and Ohls, David (2012), 'Trade, Institutions, and the Timing of GATT/WTO Accession in Post-Colonial States', *Review of International Organizations* (7) (1), pp. 81–107, at 104.

[74] Elsig, Manfred (2013), 'The Democratizing Effects of Multilateral Organizations: A Cautionary Note on the WTO', *World Trade Review* (12) (3), pp. 487–507, at 504.

facilitating the rules-based liberalization of international trade. Any positive effect that the organization has on the pursuit of other universal values such as democracy and human rights is to be welcomed, but one should remember that the main purpose of the institution was to establish a rules-based multilateral trading system. Nevertheless, accession to the WTO can contribute to economic development and the establishment of good governance in acceded Members, since the 'norms of good governance promoted by the WTO gradually filter into the polity as a whole'.[75]

1.3.4 Accession in Times of Regionalization and the Doha Development Round

The negotiating arm of the WTO is often criticized for the lack of progress that has been made during the Doha Development Round, which was launched in 2001. Indeed, when put in contrast with the highly effective and successful dispute settlement mechanism, the negotiating function of the WTO may seem to be underperforming. In parallel with the slow progress of multilateral negotiations, recent decades have seen a proliferation of bi- and plurilateral liberalization initiatives, prompting some to ask the question whether the WTO 'has become passé?'[76] In some instances these initiatives have led to the formation of what are termed regional trade agreements (RTAs). Nevertheless, even in times of what has been termed '(mega-)regionalisation', the WTO does not seem to have lost its appeal to states.[77] Since the launch of the Doha Round in November 2001, 22 countries have acceded to the WTO. In the past four years alone, nine states have joined the organization.[78] There are 19 states that have applied for WTO membership and which are currently in the accession phase.[79] Consequently, it is safe to argue that the organization

---

[75] Aaronson, Susan Ariel and Abouharb, M. Rodwan (2013), 'Does the WTO Help Member States Improve Governance', *World Trade Review* (13) (3), pp. 547–82, at 578.

[76] Bagwell, Kyle, Bown, Chad P. and Staiger, Robert W. (2015), Is the WTO Passé?, World Bank Policy Research Paper No. 7304, Washington, D.C.

[77] Hoekman, Bernard (2014), 'Sustaining Multilateral Trade Cooperation in a Multipolar World Economy', *The Review of International Organizations* (9) (2), pp. 241–60, at 258.

[78] Montenegro, Samoa, Russian Federation, Vanuatu, Lao PDR, Tajikistan, Yemen, Seychelles and Kazakhstan.

[79] Algeria, Andorra, Azerbaijan, Bahamas, Belarus, Bhutan, Bosnia and Herzegovina, Comoros, Equatorial Guinea, Ethiopia, Iran, Iraq, Lebanese Republic, Libya, São Tomé and Principe, Serbia, Sudan, Syrian Arab Republic and Uzbekistan.

is slowly heading in the direction of universal membership. Nevertheless, there are still 15 UN Member States and UN Observer States which are neither Members nor observer-Members to the WTO.[80] The reasons behind the 'non-accession' of these states have also been researched.[81] Capacity constraints, the lack of a trade-supporting domestic constituency and the lack of external pressure and/or the lack of political will have been found to explain why these countries have so far not applied for WTO membership.[82] Moving forward, the pursuit of the completion of the 'shallow integration approach of traditional GATT/WTO disciplines' should be combined with new modalities aimed at tackling more novel issues in international trade. It has been argued that the WTO has not kept track with developments such as the emergence of international production networks and the associated 'supply-chain-trade'.[83] The pursuit of 'critical mass agreements' or plurilateral agreements that aim to address these new realities of international commerce has been suggested as a way forward. Issues not (sufficiently) addressed by current WTO disciplines include 'tangible and intangible property rights and assurances on the free-flow of goods, services, capital, and people involved in international production networks'.[84] These novel developments and the future of the multilateral trading system are important. As such, they will feature in certain chapters of this monograph. Nevertheless, this contribution deals with the legal framework of the WTO as it stands. It assesses the obligations that new Members have entered into upon accession to the organization. As will be established, some of these obligations might prove to be exemplary for future disciplines that will eventually govern new generations of the multilateral trading system. However, for now, the

---

80 These are Eritrea, Kiribati, Marshall Islands, Federated States of Micronesia, Monaco, Nauru, North Korea, Palau, Palestine, San Marino, Somalia, South Sudan, Timor-Leste, Turkmenistan and Tuvalu.

81 Brazys, Samuel (2014), 'Outside Looking In: Non-Accession to the WTO', *Cambridge Review of International Affairs* (27) (4), pp. 644–65.

82 Brazys (2014), Outside Looking In: Non-Accession to the WTO, at 659.

83 Baldwin, Richard (2014), 'WTO 2.0: Governance of 21st Century Trade', *The Review of International Organizations* (9) (2), pp. 261–83, at 261; Hufbauer, Gary Clyde and Cimino, Cathleen (2013), 'What Future for the WTO?', *The International Trade Journal* (27) (5), pp. 394–410, at 407; Lamy, Pascal (2014), 'Is Trade Multilateralism Being Threatened by Regionalism?', *Adelphi Series* (54) (450), pp. 61–78, at 67.

84 Baldwin (2014), WTO 2.0: Governance of 21st Century Trade, at 280; MacMillan, Euan (2014), 'Explaining Rising Regionalism and Failing Multilateralism: Consensus Decision-Making and Expanding WTO Membership', *International Economics and Economic Policy* (11) (4), pp. 599–617.

main focus lies on the creation of these new rules in the context of accession negotiations.

1.4 CONCLUSION

In this first chapter the rationale for the creation of a multilateral trading system in the aftermath of the Second World War has been explored. Initially intended to complement the Bretton Woods institutions, the ITO was in fact stillborn. The Contracting Parties to the GATT nevertheless decided to apply the tariff reduction agreement through a PPA. In the decades after the inception of the GATT, the agreement transformed into a de facto international organization with its own secretariat. Three main theories have been used to explain the creation of the GATT; however, it has been pointed out that none of these theories in and of itself fully explains the inception of the multilateral trading system. The terms-of-trade approach, the commitment theory and the foreign-policy theory should rather be seen as complementary. GATT was created as an institution with an open-door policy. Since the beginning of GATT, states and customs territories have been invited to negotiate their accession with the existing Contracting Parties. From the initial 23 Contracting Parties, GATT membership grew to 123 Contracting Parties at the end of the Uruguay Round. When the WTO was established in 1995, it had 128 Members, and over the first 20 years of its existence, this number has grown to 162. Economic considerations have been the main driver behind most accession bids. Although there has been considerable debate as to the question whether WTO membership increases trade or even welfare, the conclusion that it contributes positively to a country's economic development seems warranted. Membership of the multilateral trading system is associated with increasing levels of FDI and it is considered to contribute to good governance. Finally, it is worth recalling that the latest major update of the rules governing international trade dates back to 1995. The disciplines that govern the economic relations between countries are more than 20 years old. Multilateral negotiations towards an updated set of rules in the context of the Doha Development Round are gridlocked. Considering that the agenda for this particular round of multilateral trade negotiations was drafted in 2001, the current multilateral negotiating mandate does not seem to reflect the realities of 21st century 'supply-chain' trade. Numerous scholars, academics and practitioners have recognized this reality and have suggested ways of moving forward. A gradual consensus appears to be emerging that highlights the importance of so-called 'critical mass agreements' and plurilateral agreements. Although one can express hope that these initiatives can eventually be multilateralized in the context of the World Trade Organization, some scholars have argued that whereas the GATT/WTO multilateral trading system is based on ideas of reciprocity and the pursuit of a universal membership, according to some these concepts are fundamentally at odds with the realities of 'supply-chain' trade. As such: 'the basic deal in supply-chain cooperation is not "I'll keep my market open if you keep yours open" – as in WTO 1.0. It is "I'll offshore my factories and technologies if you assure my tangible and intangible assets are protected."'[85] Some of the additional rules obligations negotiated in the context of WTO protocols of accession might prove to be initial attempts to address the realities posed by 21st century trade. Therefore, this monograph provides an answer to the question of whether negotiations in the context of WTO accession sometimes have served as 'rule-making laboratories' in which the WTO has attempted to gradually reform some of the disciplines that currently underpin the organization.

[85] Baldwin (2014), WTO 2.0: Governance of 21st Century Trade, at 280.

2. Membership of the GATT 1947 and the WTO

2.1 INTRODUCTION

This chapter examines the process of accession to the multilateral system as formed initially by the General Agreement on Tariffs and Trade and subsequently by the World Trade Organization (WTO). By conducting an analysis of the relevant legal provisions in both the GATT 1947 and the WTO Agreement, a comparison is made between the accession processes to both institutions. The purpose of the chapter is to find an answer to the question why the process of accession remained unaltered in the course of the Uruguay Round. It will be established that, contrary to many of the other institutional features of the multilateral trading system, such as dispute settlement, the process of accession was not formally 'legalized'.[1] Rather, as will be shown in section 2.3, the WTO's accession process remains relatively informal and political in nature. In section 2.2, the manner in which GATT membership could be obtained will be explored by discussing the evolution of GATT membership at the beginning of this section. A similar approach is adopted with respect to the WTO's accession process in section 2.3. After a descriptive exercise in which the evolution of the WTO membership is provided, attention turns towards the process of accession itself.

---

[1] Jones, Kent (2009), 'The Political Economy of WTO Accession: The Unfinished Business of Universal Membership', *World Trade Review* (8) (2), pp. 279–314, at 290. Jones argues that although Article XII WTO Agreement is still very much similar to Article XXXIII of the GATT 1994, the accession negotiations under the WTO system are much more formal than those under the GATT. Although indeed, the WTO has developed a more institutionalized accession process, it is submitted that through this process, power politics still play an important role.

2.2 BECOMING A CONTRACTING PARTY TO THE GATT 1947

2.2.1 Joining GATT: Accession or Succession?

As mentioned above, the GATT 1947 as such was never designed to serve as the basis for an international organization. At the New York Conference, which took place in January and February 1947, a Drafting Committee began to work on a first draft of the GATT 1947. During the negotiations it became apparent that the GATT 1947 would probably enter into force prior to the ITO Charter. This prompted the negotiators to 'introduce in the GATT text some institutional provisions that would help administer the tariff bargain and the various other commitments'.[2] In addition to provisions on dispute settlement (Article XXIV:2), revision, amendment and termination (Article XXIII) and entry into force and withdrawal (Article XXV), a provision regarding accession was added in the form of Article XXVI. The Second Preparatory Meeting that took place in Geneva, Switzerland from April to November 1947 was actually an elaborate conference in three major parts.[3] The institutional provisions that were negotiated during the New York Conference were confirmed during this meeting. GATT 1947 provided states wishing to join the 'organization' with two options. The first was the possibility to 'accede' to GATT.[4] The second way to become a Contracting Party to the GATT 1947 dealt specifically with (former) colonies of GATT Contracting Parties, and can be found in Article XXVI:5(c) of the GATT 1947.

2.2.1.1 Article XXXIII GATT 1947

Article XXVI:2 GATT 1947 opened the possibility for Contracting Parties and Contracting Parties negotiating 'accession' to join the GATT, whereas Article XXXIII GATT deals with the issue of accession and provides:

---

[2] Irwin, Douglas A., Mavroidis, Petros C. and Sykes, Alan O. (2008), *The Genesis of the GATT*, New York, Cambridge University Press, at 168.

[3] Van den Bossche, Peter and Zdouc, Werner (2013), *The Law and Policy of the World Trade Organization*, Third Edition, Cambridge, Cambridge University Press, at 76, quoting Jackson, John (1998), *The World Trade Organization: Constitution and Jurisprudence*, London, Royal Institute of International Affairs, at 16.

[4] Article XXVI GATT 1947. See also Irwin, Mavroidis and Sykes (2008), *The Genesis of the GATT*, at 169.

> A government not party to this Agreement, or a government acting on behalf of a separate customs territory possessing full autonomy in the conduct of its external commercial relations and of the other matters provided for in this Agreement, may accede to this Agreement, on its own behalf or on behalf of that territory, on *terms to be agreed* between such government and the CONTRACTING PARTIES. Decisions of the CONTRACTING PARTIES under this paragraph shall be taken by a two-thirds majority. [emphasis added]

The phrase 'terms to be agreed between such government and the Contracting Parties' dates back to the language used in the context of the Annecy Protocol. In June 1949 the Working Party on Accession drafted a report in which the methods of joining the GATT were discussed.[5] The drafters decided that governments seeking to join the GATT should accede to the agreement. Thereto the Draft Annecy Protocol of Terms of Accession to the General Agreement on Tariffs and Trade was drawn up. The third recital of the preamble of the Draft Protocol reads: '[...] Hereby Agree upon the terms on which the acceding governments may so accede, which terms are embodied in this Protocol [...]'[6] This language has been used in almost all protocols of accession since the Annecy Protocol.[7] The provision exemplifies the political nature of the accession process to the GATT. GATT accession was characterized by reciprocal bargaining between the government wishing to accede to the Agreement and the incumbent GATT Contracting Parties. The outcome of these accession tariff negotiations was an accession schedule of commitments.[8] The drafting history of this article indicates that the negotiators had a rather flexible nature of the accession process in mind. The chairman of the Ad-Hoc Tariff Procedures Sub-committee, Mr Adarkar, noted in his report to the Tariff Agreement Committee that dates concerning the elimination of certain transitional measures that were in force in countries seeking to accede to the International Trade Organization after the signing of the original treaty could be included in the terms of accession:

> On the whole, the Sub-committee considered the problem could best be solved under Article XXXIII, the Article about Accession, which enables the other Contracting Parties to stipulate terms on which new Members would be permitted to accede to the Agreement. In fixing those terms, the other

---

5 GATT, Working Party on Accession, GATT/CP.3/37, 2 June 1949.

6 GATT, Working Party on Accession, GATT/CP.3/37, 2 June 1949, at 13.

7 WTO, Analytical Index, Article XXXIII – Accession.

8 Jackson, John H. (1969), *World Trade Law and the Law of GATT: A Legal Analysis of the General Agreement on Tariffs and Trade*, Charlottesville, VA, The Michie Company/Bobbs Merill, at 92.

> Contracting Parties could, if necessary, indicate a date before which the new Members will have to notify the restrictions in force in their countries.[9]

The Sub-committee further noted that:

> In the Charter there is nothing to prevent separate customs territories from adhering to the Charter on the same conditions as the other States, but when we considered the General Agreement we found that the separate customs territories would not have negotiated here in Geneva. Therefore, if they were to adhere in a kind of unilateral way to the General Agreement they would acquire the benefits of the concessions made here without negotiation.[10]

Despite the bargaining required to be admitted to the GATT 1947, the procedure of accession seemed biased in favour of newcomers: 'established members of GATT do not normally try to drive too hard a bargain in payment of concessions which they made to third countries many years before. Rather they encourage new countries in the hope that overall adherence to the GATT trade rules will pay off in the long run.'[11] The founding Contracting Parties of GATT, in particular the United States, accommodated the demands for exceptions or weaker language at various points in the GATT negotiations to ensure the continued participation of other countries. During the early years of the multilateral trading system there was a clear desire on behalf of the Contracting Parties to ensure that this system would attain a truly multilateral status. Rather than driving hard bargains with states or customs territories seeking to accede to the GATT 1947, the Contracting Parties aimed at

---

[9] United Nations Economic and Social Council, Second Session of the Preparatory Committee of the United Nations Conference on Trade and Employment: Verbatim Report. Twenty-Second Meeting of the Tariff Agreement Committee held on Wednesday, 17 September 1947 at 2.30 p.m. in the Palais des Nations, Geneva, E/PC/T/TAC/PV/22, at 6.

[10] United Nations Economic and Social Council, Second Session of the Preparatory Committee of the United Nations Conference on Trade and Employment: Verbatim Report. Twenty-Second Meeting of the Tariff Agreement Committee held on Wednesday, 17 September 1947 at 2.30 p.m. in the Palais des Nations, Geneva, E/PC/T/TAC/PV/22, at 20.

[11] Curzon, Gerard (1965), *Multilateral Commercial Diplomacy: The General Agreement on Tariffs and Trade and Its Impact on National Commercial Politics and Techniques*, London, Joseph, 1965, at 36.

facilitating their accession, even though they were aware of the potential of 'free-riding' on the back of tariff concessions that had already been made.[12]

2.2.1.2 Article XXVI:5(c) GATT 1947

The second method of becoming a Contracting Party to GATT can be found in Article XXVI:5(c) of the GATT 1947. This article deals with the relationship between (former) colonies and their 'parent' countries. It provides that:

> If any of the customs territories, in respect of which a contracting party has accepted this Agreement, possesses or acquires full autonomy in the conduct of its external commercial relations and of the other matters provided for in this Agreement, such territory shall, upon sponsorship through a declaration by the responsible contracting party establishing the abovementioned fact, be deemed to be a contracting party.

Consequently, this article provided many former colonies with a relatively straightforward way of becoming a Contracting Party to GATT 1947. In fact, over 50 newly independent countries became Contracting Parties in this particular way.[13] Indonesia was the first country to become a Contracting Party under the procedure stipulated by Article XXVI:5(c) GATT 1947. It took until 1957 for the next former colony to join the GATT under this article.

---

[12] Náray, Péter (2001), *Russia and the World Trade Organization*, Basingstoke, Palgrave, at 11–14. Náray notes, inter alia, '[i]n the 1960s and 1970s, as it has been indicated above, the flexibility and ingenuity of GATT contracting parties in integrating centrally planned economies into the market-based GATT system was remarkable. One wonders why all these efforts were made to integrate into a market-based trade institution countries with fundamentally different economic systems.' Moreover, '[t]he much admired flexibility of the GATT in developing devices to bridge the gap between its market based rules and centrally planned economies was the product of the cold war. Contracting parties accepted certain centrally planned economies in the GATT system for political reasons under the policy of differentiation. If a centrally planned country indicated some signs of independence from the Soviet Union, either in domestic or foreign policy, and there was some hope that the participation of that country in the GATT could contribute to the loosening of the enemy's cohesion, the request for accession was received favourably. In those cases, basic philosophical differences did not constitute insurmountable barriers, as the accession conditions of Poland and Romania demonstrated.'

[13] Jackson, John H. (1997), *The World Trading System: Law and Policy of International Economic Relations*, Second Edition, Cambridge, MA, MIT Press, at 60.

2.2.2 The Beginning of GATT: 23 (22) Contracting Parties

The beginning of GATT is marked by the signature of the Final Act after the Second Session of the Preparatory Committee of the United Nations Conference on Trade and Employment in October 1947. Twenty-three states signed up to this Final Act.[14] Recall that GATT was applied through the Protocol of Provisional Application, see Chapter 1. All countries, except Chile, signed the Protocol of Provisional Application prior to the cut-off date of 30 June 1948. In order to accommodate Chile's wish to join the GATT after the cut-off date, the Contracting Parties prepared a Protocol of Accession that would allow it to accede under Article XXXIII of the GATT 1947.[15] Table 2.1 lists the original Contracting Parties to the GATT 1947 and the date of their membership.

Table 2.1 Original GATT Contracting Parties

Country	Date
Australia	1 January 1948
Belgium	1 January 1948
Canada	1 January 1948
Cuba	1 January 1948
France	1 January 1948
Luxembourg	1 January 1948
The Netherlands	1 January 1948
United Kingdom	1 January 1948
United States of America	1 January 1948
South Africa	13 June 1948
India	8 July 1948
Norway	10 July 1948
Rhodesia (Zimbabwe)	11 July 1948
Myanmar (Burma)	29 July 1948
Sri Lanka	29 July 1948
Brazil	30 July 1948
New Zealand	30 July 1948
Pakistan	30 July 1948
Chile	16 March 1949

[14] In alphabetical order: Australia, Belgium, Brazil, Burma, Canada, Ceylon, Chile, China, Cuba, Czechoslovak Republic, France, India, Lebanon, Luxemburg, The Netherlands, New Zealand, Norway, Pakistan, Southern Rhodesia, Syria, South Africa, United Kingdom, United States of America.

[15] Jackson (1969), *World Trade Law and the Law of GATT: A Legal Analysis of the General Agreement on Tariffs and Trade*, at 91.

Chile was the first state to accede to the GATT under the procedure prescribed by Article XXXIII of the GATT 1994. In subsequent years, states and customs territories either joined the multilateral trading system through the same procedure (accession), or they joined through the procedure laid down by Article XXVI:5(c) GATT 1994. This provision was designed for former colonies that, after gaining independence, intended to remain bound by the provisions of the GATT. In cases where the colony had previously been treated as a customs territory under the rules of the GATT, it was allowed to join the system under the sponsorship of the colonial power.[16]

2.2.2.1 1950s

In the 1950s, 17 Countries joined the GATT. Three of the countries listed in Table 2.2 were former colonies that became a Contracting Party under sponsorship. These are Indonesia, Ghana and Malaysia.

Table 2.2 New GATT Contracting Parties in the 1950s

Country	Date	Article XXVI:5(c) or Article XXXIII GATT 1947?
Haiti[17]	1 January 1950	Article XXXIII GATT 1947
Indonesia	24 February 1950	Article XXVI:5(c) GATT 1947
Greece	1 March 1950	Article XXXIII GATT 1947
Sweden	30 April 1950	Article XXXIII GATT 1947
Dominican Republic	19 May 1950	Article XXXIII GATT 1947
Finland	25 May 1950	Article XXXIII GATT 1947
Denmark	28 May 1950	Article XXXIII GATT 1947
Nicaragua	28 May 1950	Article XXXIII GATT 1947
Italy	30 May 1950	Article XXXIII GATT 1947
Germany	1 October 1951	Article XXXIII GATT 1947
Peru	7 October 1951	Article XXXIII GATT 1947
Turkey	17 October 1951	Article XXXIII GATT 1947
Austria	19 October 1951	Article XXXIII GATT 1947

[16] Jones (2009), The Political Economy of WTO Accession: The Unfinished Business of Universal Membership, at 289.

[17] Haiti subsequently accepted the GATT itself directly, pursuant to Article XXVI:2 of the GATT 1947, L/2375/Add.1. See also Jackson, John H. (2000), *The Jurisprudence of GATT & the WTO*, Cambridge, Cambridge University Press, at 30.

Country	Date	Article XXVI:5(c) or Article XXXIII GATT 1947?
Uruguay	6 December 1953	Article XXXIII GATT 1947
Japan	10 September 1955	Article XXXIII GATT 1947
Ghana	17 October 1957	Article XXVI:5(c) GATT 1947
Malaysia	24 October 1957	Article XXVI:5(c) GATT 1947

2.2.2.2 1960s

The 1960s were characterized by a period of decolonization in which many former colonies obtained independence. Rather than having to accede through Article XXXIII GATT 1947, these countries were able to resume their status of GATT Contracting Party under Article XXVI:5(c) GATT 1947. Only a handful of non-colonies – and mainly European states – joined the GATT system in the 1960s: Portugal, Israel, Spain, Switzerland, Yugoslavia, Korea, Argentina, Poland, Ireland and Iceland (Table 2.3).

Table 2.3 New GATT Contracting Parties in the 1960s

Country	Date	Article XXVI:5(c) or Article XXXIII GATT 1947?
Nigeria	18 November 1960	Article XXVI:5(c) GATT 1947
Sierra Leone	19 May 1961	Article XXVI:5(c) GATT 1947
Tanzania	9 December 1961	Article XXVI:5(c) GATT 1947
Portugal	6 May 1962	Article XXXIII GATT 1947
Israel	5 July 1962	Article XXXIII GATT 1947
Trinidad and Tobago	23 October 1962	Article XXVI:5(c) GATT 1947
Uganda	23 October 1962	Article XXVI:5(c) GATT 1947
Burkina Faso	3 May 1963	Article XXVI:5(c) GATT 1947
Cameroon	3 May 1963	Article XXVI:5(c) GATT 1947
Central African Republic	3 May 1963	Article XXVI:5(c) GATT 1947
Congo, Republic of	3 May 1963	Article XXVI:5(c) GATT 1947
Gabon	3 May 1963	Article XXVI:5(c) GATT 1947
Kuwait	3 May 1963	Article XXVI:5(c) GATT 1947
Chad	12 July 1963	Article XXVI:5(c) GATT 1947
Cyprus	15 July 1963	Article XXVI:5(c) GATT 1947
Spain	29 August 1963	Article XXXIII GATT 1947

Table 2.3 (continued)

Country	Date	Article XXVI:5(c) or Article XXXIII GATT 1947?
Benin	12 September 1963	Article XXVI:5(c) GATT 1947
Senegal	27 September 1963	Article XXVI:5(c) GATT 1947
Madagascar	30 September 1963	Article XXVI:5(c) GATT 1947
Mauritania	30 September 1963	Article XXVI:5(c) GATT 1947
Côte d'Ivoire	31 December 1963	Article XXVI:5(c) GATT 1947
Jamaica	31 December 1963	Article XXVI:5(c) GATT 1947
Niger	31 December 1963	Article XXVI:5(c) GATT 1947
Kenya	5 February 1964	Article XXVI:5(c) GATT 1947
Togo	20 March 1964	Article XXVI:5(c) GATT 1947
Malawi	28 August 1964	Article XXVI:5(c) GATT 1947
Malta	17 November 1964	Article XXVI:5(c) GATT 1947
Gambia	22 February 1965	Article XXVI:5(c) GATT 1947
Burundi	13 March 1965	Article XXVI:5(c) GATT 1947
Rwanda	1 January 1966	Article XXVI:5(c) GATT 1947
Guyana	5 July 1966	Article XXVI:5(c) GATT 1947
Switzerland	1 August 1966	Article XXXIII GATT 1947
Yugoslavia	25 August 1966	Article XXXIII GATT 1947
Barbados	15 February 1967	Article XXVI:5(c) GATT 1947
Korea, Republic of	14 April 1967	Article XXXIII GATT 1947
Argentina	11 October 1967	Article XXXIII GATT 1947
Poland	18 October 1967	Article XXXIII GATT 1947
Iceland	22 December 1967	Article XXXIII GATT 1947
Ireland	21 April 1968	Article XXXIII GATT 1947

2.2.2.3 1970s

Only nine countries became Contracting Parties in the 1970s (Table 2.4). Three former colonies (Mauritius, Singapore and Suriname) acquired GATT membership through Article XXVI:5(c) GATT 1947.

Table 2.4 New GATT Contracting Parties in the 1970s

Country	Date	Article XXVI:5(c) or Article XXXIII GATT 1947?
Egypt	9 May 1970	Article XXXIII GATT 1947
Mauritius	2 September 1970	Article XXVI:5(c) GATT 1947
Zaire	11 September 1971	Article XXXIII GATT 1947
Romania	14 November 1971	Article XXXIII GATT 1947
Bangladesh	16 December 1972	Article XXXIII GATT 1947
Singapore	20 August 1973	Article XXVI:5(c) GATT 1947
Hungary	9 September 1973	Article XXXIII GATT 1947
Suriname	22 March 1978	Article XXVI:5(c) GATT 1947
Philippines	27 December 1979	Article XXXIII GATT 1947

2.2.2.4 1980s

In the 1980s GATT membership grew slowly with the accession of Colombia, Thailand, Mexico and Morocco. Zambia, Maldives, Belize, Hong Kong, Antigua and Barbuda, Botswana and Lesotho became Contracting Parties under sponsorship, through the procedure established by Article XXVI:5(c) of the GATT 1947 (Table 2.5).

Table 2.5 New GATT Contracting Parties in the 1980s

Country	Date	Article XXVI:5(c) or Article XXXIII GATT 1947?
Colombia	3 October 1981	Article XXXIII GATT 1947
Zambia	10 February 1982	Article XXVI:5(c) GATT 1947
Thailand	20 November 1982	Article XXXIII GATT 1947
Maldives	18 April 1983	Article XXVI:5(c) GATT 1947
Belize	7 October 1983	Article XXVI:5(c) GATT 1947
Hong Kong	23 April 1986	Article XXVI:5(c) GATT 1947
Mexico	24 August 1986	Article XXXIII GATT 1947
Antigua and Barbuda	30 March 1987	Article XXVI:5(c) GATT 1947
Morocco	17 June 1987	Article XXXIII GATT 1947
Botswana	28 August 1988	Article XXVI:5(c) GATT 1947
Lesotho	8 January 1988	Article XXVI:5(c) GATT 1947

2.2.2.5 1990s

With the end of the Uruguay Round in sight, the 1990s saw an increase in the applications for GATT membership. Many countries and former colonies decided to submit their application for GATT membership in order to ensure that they could still benefit from the procedures available under GATT 1947. With the establishment of the WTO on the horizon, 24 countries joined the GATT in the last two years of its existence (Table 2.6).

Table 2.6 New GATT Contracting Parties in the 1990s

Country	Date	Article XXVI:5(c) or Article XXXIII GATT 1947?
Tunisia	29 August 1990	Article XXXIII GATT 1947
Venezuela	31 August 1990	Article XXXIII GATT 1947
Bolivia	8 September 1990	Article XXXIII GATT 1947
Costa Rica	24 November 1990	Article XXXIII GATT 1947
Macao	11 January 1991	Article XXVI:5(c) GATT 1947
El Salvador	22 May 1991	Article XXXIII GATT 1947
Guatemala	10 October 1991	Article XXXIII GATT 1947
Mozambique	27 July 1992	Article XXVI:5(c) GATT 1947
Namibia	15 September 1992	Article XXVI:5(c) GATT 1947
Mali	11 January 1993	Article XXVI:5(c) GATT 1947
Swaziland, Kingdom of	8 February 1993	Article XXVI:5(c) GATT 1947
Saint Lucia	13 April 1993	Article XXVI:5(c) GATT 1947
Czech Republic	15 April 1993	Article XXXIII GATT 1947
Slovak Republic	15 April 1993	Article XXXIII GATT 1947
Dominica	20 April 1993	Article XXVI:5(c) GATT 1947
Saint Vincent and the Grenadines	18 May 1993	Article XXVI:5(c) GATT 1947
Fiji	16 November 1993	Article XXVI:5(c) GATT 1947
Brunei Darussalam	9 December 1993	Article XXVI:5(c) GATT 1947
Bahrain	13 December 1993	Article XXVI:5(c) GATT 1947
Paraguay	6 January 1994	Article XXXIII GATT 1947
Grenada	9 February 1994	Article XXVI:5(c) GATT 1947
United Arab Emirates	8 March 1994	Article XXVI:5(c) GATT 1947
Guinea Bissau	17 March 1994	Article XXVI:5(c) GATT 1947

Country	Date	Article XXVI:5(c) or Article XXXIII GATT 1947?
Saint Kitts and Nevis	24 March 1994	Article XXVI:5(c) GATT 1947
Liechtenstein	29 March 1994	Article XXVI:5(c) GATT 1947
Qatar	7 April 1994	Article XXVI:5(c) GATT 1947
Angola	8 April 1994	Article XXVI:5(c) GATT 1947
Honduras	10 April 1994	Article XXXIII GATT 1947
Slovenia	30 October 1994	Article XXXIII GATT 1947
Guinea	8 December 1994	Article XXVI:5(c) GATT 1947
Djibouti	16 December 1994	Article XXVI:5(c) GATT 1947
Papua New Guinea	16 December 1994	Article XXVI:5(c) GATT 1947
Solomon Islands	28 December 1994	Article XXVI:5(c) GATT 1947

2.2.3 A Categorization of Acceding Countries

2.2.3.1 Former colonies

As described in the previous subparagraphs, Article XXVI:5(c) GATT 1947 enabled former colonies to join the GATT system under sponsorship of the colonial power, after obtaining independence.

2.2.3.2 Non-market (planned) economies

If the accession process to the GATT is compared with accession to, for example, the United Nations or the European Union, it is notable that the GATT did not prescribe any characteristics that the acceding country or customs territory should possess in order to be eligible for GATT membership.[18] The United Nations merely requires states wishing to acquire membership to accept the obligations of its charter and *to be able* and *willing* to carry out these obligations.[19] Article 4 of the Charter of the United Nations attaches the precondition 'peace-loving' to the term 'state'. In practice, however, this precondition has been ignored, and Article 4 has been considered as 'endowing any formally independent state with a right to membership in the United Nations'.[20] In the First Admission Case the International Court of Justice (ICJ) dealt with the

[18] Náray (2001), *Russia and the World Trade Organization*, at 11–14.

[19] Article 4.1 Charter of the United Nations.

[20] Benedek, Wolfgang and Ginther, Konrad (1988), Planned-Economy Countries and GATT: Legal Issues of Accession, in *German Yearbook of International Law/Jahrbuch für Internationales Recht* (31), pp. 70–106, at 73–4.

question whether under Article 4 of the UN Charter 'a Member of the United Nations [...] is entitled juridically to make its consent to the admission dependent on conditions not expressly provided by paragraph 1 of the said Article'.[21] This Advisory Opinion has been interpreted as meaning that the accession of a given country cannot be made dependent on conditions other than those specified in the Charter. This would mean that an acceding country is entitled to an examination by the existing Members upon the question of whether it meets the conditions requested.[22] European states that want to accede to the European Union need to have established the 'stability of institutions guaranteeing the existence of a functioning market economy'.[23] EU accession is governed by Article 49 of the Treaty on the European Union (TEU).[24] The procedure requires the applicant-state to conclude an agreement with the

---

[21] ICJ, 'Admission of a State to the United Nations (Charter, Article 4), Advisory Opinion: I.C.J. Reports 1948, at 57. In defining the scope of the question, the ICJ held that this question merely required it to examine whether the conditions listed in Article 4 are exhaustive. One of the parties made the argument that 'the conditions enumerated represent only an indispensable minimum, in the sense that political considerations could be superimposed upon them, and prevent the admission of an applicant which fulfils them'. The Court held that such an interpretation would be inconsistent with the terms of paragraph 2 of Article 4, which provide for the admission of *'tout Etat* remplissant ces conditions' – 'any *such* State'. Consequently, it 'would lead to conferring upon Members an indefinite and practically unlimited power of discretion in the imposition of new conditions'.

[22] Parenti, Antonio (2000), 'Accession to the World Trade Organization: A Legal Analysis', *Legal Issues of Economic Integration* (27) (2), pp. 141–57, 143. Parenti further notes, in footnote 10, that 'It should be recalled, in fact, that the ICJ opinion was a contested one with a dissenting opinion expressed by six judges. In addition, the then Soviet Union and also the US never accepted the opinion of the Court.'; see also Magliveras, Konstantinos D. (2011), Membership in International Organizations, in Klabbers, Jan and Wallendahl, Åsa (2011), *Research Handbook on the Law of International Organizations*, Cheltenham, UK and Northampton, MA, USA, Edward Elgar, 84–107, at 88.

[23] This term appears to have been introduced as part of the Copenhagen Criteria that govern accession to the European Union.

[24] Article 49 TEU provides: 'Any European State which respects the principles set out in Article 6(1) may apply to become a member of the Union. It shall address its application to the Council, which shall act unanimously after consulting the Commission and after receiving the assent of the European Parliament, which shall act by an absolute majority of its component members. The conditions of admission and the adjustments to the Treaties on which the Union is founded, which such admission entails, shall be the subject of an agreement between the Member States and the applicant State. This agreement

incumbent Member States of the European Union (Member States).[25] In practice, therefore, the accession process to the EU requires applicant states to amend their domestic legislation and policies to a far larger extent than what would be required for accession to a more intergovernmental organization. The accession process is characterized by a number of conditions set out by respective European Councils, which are subsequently elaborated upon by the European Commission.[26] As such it may seem as if concrete accession guidelines and requirements exist within the EU. This conclusion has, however, been disputed since 'virtually all formal, less formal and tacit conditions for accession are very fluid and fuzzy'.[27] In addition to requiring that the state seeking to accede is a 'European state', this provision makes accession conditional upon respect for the principles laid down in Article 2 TEU. In the context of the potential accession of Central and Eastern European countries to the EU, the European Council in 1993 laid down a set of criteria (the 'Copenhagen Criteria') that such states would have to fulfil. The criteria stipulate [in relevant part]: 'Membership requires that the candidate country has achieved stability of institutions guaranteeing democracy, the rule of law, human rights and respect for and protection of minorities, *the existence of a functioning market economy* as well as *the capacity to cope with competitive pressure and market forces within the Union*.'[28] The EU thus requires applicant states to establish a market economy. Although both the GATT (and the WTO) and the EU are based on the concepts of trade liberalization, reference to such explicit 'market economy' terminology is missing from both the GATT 1947 and from the WTO Agreement. This is not to say that the GATT 1947 is completely silent on states that are characterized by a large degree of governmental involvement in the operation of its economy. First, the Havana Charter – which was used as the basis for drafting GATT 1947 – in fact already envisaged

shall be submitted for ratification by all the contracting States in accordance with their respective constitutional requirements.'

[25] Hoffmeister, Frank (2012), Article 15: Consent to be Bound by a Treaty Expressed by Accession, in Dörr, Oliver and Schmalenbach, Kirsten (eds) (2012), *Vienna Convention on the Law of Treaties: A Commentary*, Berlin-Heidelberg, Springer Verlag, 196–208, at 207.

[26] Athanassiou, Phoebus and Laulhé Shaelou, Stéphanie (2014), 'EU Accession from Within? – An Introduction', *Yearbook of European Law* (33) (1), pp. 335–84.

[27] Lavigne, Marie (1998), 'Conditions for Accession to the EU', *Comparative Economic Studies* (40) (3), pp. 38–57, 54.

[28] European Council, European Council in Copenhagen 21–22 June 1993, Conclusions of the Presidency, SN180/1/93 REV 1 (emphasis added).

the participation of 'Non-Market Economies' (NMEs) in the multilateral trading system. Referencing Clair Wilcox (Deputy Head of the US delegation in Havana), Benedek and Ginther provide a detailed account of the negotiations. Wilcox stated that:

> [t]he solution must be found, rather, in an arrangement, which will enable the *free market economies* and the *controlled economies* to trade with one another on the basis of fair dealing and mutual advantage. The rules that govern international commerce should be so drafted that they will apply to the two systems with equal justice and with equal force.[29]

Second, the second *Ad* Note to Article VI:1 GATT 1994 further stipulates that in the context of anti-dumping investigations concerning imports originating in such NMEs, it might not 'be appropriate' to rely on a strict comparison with domestic prices. The second *Ad* Note was added in the context of the accession of Czechoslovakia to the GATT in 1955.[30] Reference is made to countries that are characterized by 'a complete or substantially complete monopoly of its trade and where all domestic prices are fixed by the State [...]'. Indeed, in the context of anti-dumping proceedings, the economic characterization of a state may be of particular relevance. In 2011 the Appellate Body held in *US – Anti-Dumping and Countervailing Duties (China)* that this provision allows 'for the use of surrogate values for NMEs in anti-dumping investigations' and allows investigating authorities to have recourse to 'exceptional methods' for the calculation of normal value when investigating imports from NMEs.[31]

---

[29] Benedek and Ginther (1988), Planned-Economy Countries and GATT: Legal Issues of Accession, at 74, referencing Wilcox, Clair (1949), *A Charter for World Trade*, reprint New York, Arno Press, 1972, at 164; see also Kennedy, Kevin C. (1987), 'The Accession of the Soviet Union to GATT', *Journal of World Trade* (21), pp. 23–39; Laczkowski, Bohdan (1971), 'Poland's Accession to GATT', *Journal of World Trade* (5) (1), pp. 110–19; Lücke, Matthias (1995), 'The Impact of Accession to GATT on the Trade-Related Policies of CIS Countries', *Journal of World Trade* (29) (4), pp. 165–92.

[30] GATT Document, L/334, circulated 1 March 1955. For a more detailed account of the negotiating history of the second *Ad* Note to Article VI GATT 1994, see Miranda, Jorge (2014), 'Interpreting Paragraph 15 of China's Protocol of Accession', *Global Trade and Customs Journal* (9) (3), pp. 94–103, at 95.

[31] Appellate Body Report, *US – Anti-Dumping and Countervailing Duties (China).* See also, Benedek and Ginther (1988), Planned-Economy Countries and GATT: Legal Issues of Accession. It has been argued that the term 'Non-Market Economies' is misleading and that the term 'planned-economy countries' (PECs) should be used instead. Their critique was based on the fact that the term NMEs originates in US trade legislation which defines an NME as 'any foreign country

Although the drafters of GATT were aware of the differences in economic systems between the non-market economy countries and the market economy countries, this did not result in a set of criteria a country would have to fulfil in order to be allowed to join the multilateral trading system. The absence of such general requirements and the phrase 'on *terms to be agreed* between such government and the CONTRACTING PARTIES' contained in Article XXXIII of the GATT 1994 led to a situation in which the accession procedures to the General Agreement on Tariffs and Trade were conducted largely on an ad hoc basis. The informal nature of the accession process enabled the incumbent membership to exert considerable political influence in the course of the accession process in order to obtain concessions from states and customs territories desiring to become part of the club. GATT 1947 started with 23 Contracting Parties, including Czechoslovakia and Cuba. When trade between Eastern European countries on the one hand and Western European countries and the United States on the other began to increase in the mid-1950s, Czechoslovakia raised the issue of the trade relationships between these two groups of differently organized economies. It was in this context that the second *Ad* Note to Article VI:1 GATT 1947 was added. However, it was Poland that was the first planned economy to actually accede to GATT through the procedure laid down in Article XXXIII GATT 1947.[32] Yugoslavia, Romania and Hungary were also NMEs that acceded to GATT. In the GATT days there was a willingness to meet this group of countries 'halfway'. Although GATT was originally

---

that the administering authority determines does not operate on market principles of cost or pricing structures, so that sales of merchandise in such country do not reflect the fair value of the merchandise'. It has been suggested that this term is misleading since it suggests that markets did not play any role whatsoever in these economies. Moreover, it has been argued, the agricultural policy in, for example, the European Union, is also characterized by substantial governmental interventions. In sum, therefore, although the theoretical underpinnings of the multilateral trading system can be considered rooted in the ideas of liberalization, comparative advantage and free markets, these underpinnings did not translate themselves into assumptions concerning the types of economies that would ultimately be able to join the system.

[32] For a more detailed account see Huang, Chieh (2009), 'Non-Market Economies' Accessions to the WTO: Evolution of the Approach and Implications for the Organization', *The Hague Journal of Diplomacy* (4), pp. 61–81, at 66, referencing Van Brabant, Jozef M. (1991), *The Planned Economies and International Economic Organizations*, Cambridge, Cambridge University Press, and Kostecki, M.M. (1979), *East–West Trade and the GATT System*, New York, St Martin's, 1979.

envisaged for market economies, NMEs were still allowed to join, albeit under certain conditions.[33] This 'flexibility and ingenuity of GATT Contracting Parties in integrating centrally planned economies into the market-based GATT system was remarkable'.[34] Poland and Romania, for example, agreed to increase the value of imports from GATT Contracting Parties in the years after accession. Hungary did not undertake a similar commitment, but it accepted a selective safeguard clause.[35] After the 1960s the scope of GATT started to broaden substantially. The limitations on international trade caused by Non-Tariff Measures began to overtake customs tariffs as the main area of negotiations. The Tokyo Round Codes on, for example, subsidies, anti-dumping and technical barriers to trade are prime examples of this development. With the broadening scope of GATT, the content of the negotiations for accession to GATT also began to change. The establishment of the WTO at the end of the Uruguay Round meant that joining the multilateral trading system required far more than simply negotiating an agreement on concessions relating to market access.

2.3 ACCESSION TO THE WTO

2.3.1 An Overview: Accessions to the WTO in Numbers

The WTO started off in 1995 with 123 Original Members. Soon after the creation of the WTO, a number of accessions were completed in the 1990s. Meanwhile, the number of WTO Members has grown to over 160. At the same time, more than 20 countries are currently in the process of accession to the WTO. The development of the WTO membership can be seen in Tables 2.7 to 2.10 in the sections below.

---

[33] See for a case study on the Bulgarian accession bid Breskovski, Vassil (1993), 'Bulgaria and the GATT: A Case Study for Accession', *World Competition* (17) (2), pp. 45–67.

[34] Náray (2001), *Russia and the World Trade Organization*, at 11.

[35] VanGrasstek, Craig (2001), Why Demands on Acceding Countries Increase over Time: A Three-Dimensional Analysis of Multilateral Trade Diplomacy, in United Nations Conference on Trade and Development (2001), *WTO Accessions and Development Policies*, Geneva, United Nations, UNCTAD/DITC/TNCD/11, at 84.

2.3.1.1 1990s

Table 2.7 New WTO Members in the 1990s

Country	Date	Developed, Developing (DC) or Least-Developed Country (LDC)
Ecuador	21 January 1996	DC
Bulgaria	1 December 1996	Developed
Mongolia	29 January 1997	DC
Panama	6 September 1997	DC
Kyrgyz Republic	20 December 1998	DC
Latvia	10 February 1999	Developed
Estonia	13 November 1999	Developed

2.3.1.2 2000s

Table 2.8 New WTO Members in the 2000s

Country	Date	Developed, Developing (DC) or Least-Developed Country (LDC)
Jordan	11 April 2000	DC
Georgia	14 June 2000	DC
Albania	8 September 2000	DC
Oman	9 November 2000	DC
Croatia	30 November 2000	Developed
Lithuania	31 May 2001	Developed
Moldova	26 July 2001	DC
China	11 December 2001	DC
Chinese Taipei	1 January 2002	DC
Armenia	5 February 2003	DC
FYR Macedonia	4 April 2003	DC
Nepal	23 April 2004	LDC
Cambodia	13 October 2004	LDC
Saudi Arabia	11 December 2005	DC
Viet Nam	11 January 2007	DC
Tonga	27 July 2007	DC
Ukraine	16 May 2008	DC
Cape Verde	23 July 2008	DC

2.3.1.3 2010s and beyond

Table 2.9 New WTO Members in the 2010s

Country	Date	Developed, Developing (DC) or Least-Developed Country (LDC)
Montenegro	29 April 2012	DC
Samoa	10 May 2012	LDC
Russian Federation	22 August 2012	DC
Vanuatu	24 August 2012	LDC
Lao PDR	2 February 2013	LDC
Tajikistan	2 March 2013	DC
Yemen	26 June 2014	LDC
Seychelles	26 April 2015	DC
Kazakhstan	30 November 2016	DC
Liberia	14 July 2016	DC
Afghanistan	29 July 2016	DC

Table 2.10 Ongoing WTO accessions in 2017

Country	Date of Application	Developed, Developing (DC) or Least-Developed Country (LDC)
Algeria	June 1987	DC
Andorra	October 1997	Developed
Azerbaijan	July 1997	DC
Bahamas	May 2001	DC
Belarus	September 1993	DC
Bhutan	September 1999	LDC
Bosnia and Herzegovina	May 1999	DC
Comoros	February 2007	LDC
Equatorial Guinea	February 2007	LDC
Ethiopia	January 2003	LDC
Iran	July 1996	DC
Iraq	September 2004	DC
Lebanese Republic	January 1999	DC
Libya	June 2004	DC

Country	Date of Application	Developed, Developing (DC) or Least-Developed Country (LDC)
São Tomé and Principe	January 2005	LDC
Serbia	December 2004	DC
Sudan	October 1994	LDC
Syrian Arab Republic	October 2001	DC
Uzbekistan	December 1994	DC

Table 2.11 Non-observer states (non-accessions)

Country	Developed, Developing (DC) or Least-Developed Country (LDC)
Eritrea	LDC
Federated States of Micronesia	DC
Kiribati	LDC
Marshall Islands	DC
North Korea	DC
Monaco	Developed
Nauru	DC
Palau	DC
San Marino	Developed
Somalia	LDC
South Sudan	LDC
Timor-Leste	LDC
Turkmenistan	DC
Tuvalu	LDC

In 2016 there were only 14 states who had not yet sought accession to the WTO (Table 2.11). Among these states are some of the world's smallest and poorest countries. In 2014 they accounted for 0.05 per cent of world trade, 0.03 per cent of world GDP and 0.70 per cent of world population.[36] The non-accession of these states is caused by capacity

[36] Williams, Peter John (2008), *A Handbook on Accession to the WTO*, Cambridge, Cambridge University Press, at 11.

constraints, a lack of a trade-supporting domestic constituency, the absence of political pressure and/or the absence of political will.[37] Levels of trade or levels of democracy appear, contrary to what previous research may have indicated, not to influence the decisions of states to not accede to the WTO.

2.3.2 Joining the WTO

Accession to the WTO is governed by Articles XI and XII of the WTO Agreement. The former distinguishes two types of Members, whereas the latter stipulates in brief terminology under which conditions a state or customs territory may become a Member of the organization. Article XII WTO Agreement stipulates (in relevant part) that states or customs territories may accede to that Agreement 'on terms between it [the acceding State or customs territory]' and that the accession will apply to this Agreement (the WTO Agreement) and the Multilateral Trade Agreements annexed to it. As such it mirrors Article XXXIII GATT 1947. Although the term 'government' has been changed to the term 'state', there is no substantial difference between the accession provisions in both agreements. Article XII WTO Agreement does not stipulate anything concerning the procedure of accession, the outcome of this process or on the exact meaning of the 'terms to be agreed' between the acceding Member and the WTO.

2.3.2.1 Article XI WTO Agreement

At the conclusion of the Uruguay Round of Multilateral Trade Negotiations, 123 GATT Contracting Parties and the European Communities obtained 'original' WTO membership by virtue of Article XI WTO Agreement.[38] This provision stipulates that:

> 1. The contracting parties to GATT 1947 as of the date of entry into force of this Agreement, and the European Communities, which accept this Agreement and the Multilateral Trade Agreements and for which Schedules of Concessions and Commitments are annexed to GATT 1994 and for which Schedules

---

[37] Brazys, Samuel (2014), 'Outside Looking In: Non-Accession to the WTO', *Cambridge Review of International Affairs* (27) (4), pp. 644–65, at 659.

[38] Van den Bossche and Zdouc (2013), *The Law and Policy of the World Trade Organization*, at 109. Schorkopf, Frank (2006), Article XI WTO Agreement, in Wolfrum, Rüdiger, Stoll, Peter-Tobias and Kaiser, Karen (eds), *Max Planck Commentaries on World Trade Law: WTO – Institutions and Dispute Settlement*, Leiden, Martinus Nijhoff Publishers, 137–43.

of Specific Commitments are annexed to GATS [General Agreement on Trade in Services] shall become original Members of the WTO.

2. The least-developed countries recognized as such by the United Nations will only be required to undertake commitments and concessions to the extent consistent with their individual development, financial and trade needs or their administrative and institutional capabilities.

Countries and customs territories that were not yet GATT Contracting Parties at the time of the establishment of the WTO had to apply for WTO membership through the procedure of accession, provided for in Article XII of the WTO Agreement.

2.3.2.2 Article XII WTO Agreement

In addition to 'original' membership, the WTO leaves open the possibility for states and customs territories to obtain 'non-original' membership by means of accession.[39] Article XII of the WTO Agreement stipulates:

1. Any State or separate customs territory possessing full autonomy in the conduct of its external commercial relations and of the other matters provided for in this Agreement and the Multilateral Trade Agreements may accede to this Agreement, on terms to be agreed between it and the WTO. Such accession shall apply to this Agreement and the Multilateral Trade Agreements annexed thereto.

2. Decisions on accession shall be taken by the Ministerial Conference. The Ministerial Conference shall approve the agreement on the terms of accession by a two-thirds majority of the Members of the WTO.

3. Accession to a Plurilateral Trade Agreement shall be governed by the provisions of that Agreement.

Most of the disputes that have involved a protocol of accession contain a discussion on the role of Article XII of the WTO Agreement.[40] At this stage it is warranted to already highlight one of the main findings of the Appellate Body in *China – Rare Earths* concerning the scope of the accession process.[41] The Appellate Body noted that the 'terms of accession' to which Article XII:1 of the WTO Agreement refers are not

---

[39] Schorkopf, Frank (2006), Article XII WTO Agreement, in Wolfrum, Rüdiger, Stoll, Peter-Tobias and Kaiser, Karen (eds), *Max Planck Commentaries on World Trade Law: WTO – Institutions and Dispute Settlement*, Leiden, Martinus Nijhoff Publishers, 144–52.

[40] For an overview of the relevant case law, see in particular section 4.2.2.3.

[41] Appellate Body Reports, *China – Rare Earths*, para. 5.27.

defined.[42] Consequently, it concluded that 'apart from the stipulation in the second sentence of Article XII […] this provision does not spell out the content of, or impose limitations on, such "terms"'.[43] This finding is important as it clarifies that these terms are to be 'agreed' upon by the WTO and the state or customs territory seeking accession in the context of a specific accession process. It also confirms that the practice of the WTO to negotiate 'additional', 'more stringent', or 'WTO-plus' rules commitments is not inconsistent with the text of Article XII of the WTO Agreement. In fact, it has been observed that 'the WTO accession regime is unique among international organisations in that it permits the conclusion of Accession Protocols to alter the rights and obligations of its members under the underlying treaties of the WTO, all without going through the formal procedures for amendment'.[44] The Appellate Body further emphasized the importance of the second sentence of Article XII:1 WTO Agreement as it reflects that the terms mentioned in the *first* sentence of that article indicate 'that an acceding Member is subject to the rights and obligations in *all* of the Multilateral Trade Agreements'.[45] Consequently, it has been clarified that Article XII governs the entirety of the WTO accession process – that is the accession to the WTO as an international organization – and not merely the accession to the multilateral treaty that is the WTO Agreement. The Appellate Body also found support for this position by comparing Article II and Article XII of the WTO Agreement, both of which reflect the importance of the single undertaking. It held that:

> [a]rticle II:2 […] stipulates the requirement on existing WTO Members to abide by the obligations under all of the agreements in this package. Article XII:1, which concerns accession, extends the same requirement to acceding Members. […] These two provisions […] serve closely related, albeit distinct, functions; they are not merely duplicative of each other. Read together, they

---

42 Appellate Body Reports, *China – Rare Earths*, para. 5.27.

43 Appellate Body Reports, *China – Rare Earths*, para. 5.27. It should be noted that this phrase should have referred to the second sentence of Article XII:1, and not merely the second sentence of Article XII of the WTO Agreement.

44 Kireyev, Alexei and Sekkate, Mustapha (2015), WTO Accessions: What Does the Academic Literature Say?, in Dadush, Uri and Osakwe, Chiedu (eds) (2015), *WTO Accessions and Trade Multilateralism: Case Studies and Lessons from the WTO at Twenty*, Cambridge, Cambridge University Press, pp. 198–216, at 204.

45 Appellate Body Reports, *China – Rare Earths*, para. 5.28 (emphasis added).

ensure that the fundamental principle of the single undertaking applies to both *existing* and *newly acceded* Members of the WTO.[46]

Qin questions the Appellate Body finding that Article XII of the WTO Agreement does not place any limits on the 'terms of accession'.[47] She maintains that the 'context' of Article XII of the WTO Agreement makes clear that the substantive conditions for membership of original and non-original membership should be the same and that, therefore, the acceptance of the rules contained in the WTO Agreement and the Multilateral Trade Agreements, and the acceptance of specific commitments in the fields of trade in goods and trade in services are sufficient to obtain membership.[48] At the same time she concedes that country-specific rules can be made in the context of an accession; however, she submits that where these rules derogate from the generally applicable rules they should be transitional in nature and 'should not exceed the scope of the existing provisions of the WTO Agreement'.[49] It has been submitted that the legal basis for such country-specific rule-making can be found in the subsequent practice of the WTO, which has been accepted by its Members. Qin submits that this practice results in 'the dismantling of the uniformity of WTO rules' and that it 'damages the legitimacy of the WTO'.[50] This criticism is addressed in more detail in subsequent sections of this contribution.

2.3.2.3 The four-step accession process

One of the most remarkable features of the articles in the WTO Agreement that cover WTO membership is their simplicity.[51] Article XI:1 WTO Agreement creates a distinction between 'original Members of the

---

[46] Appellate Body Reports, *China – Rare Earths*, para. 5.30 (emphasis added) (footnoted omitted).

[47] Qin, Julia Ya (2017), Mind the Gap: Navigating Between the WTO Agreement and Its Accession Protocols, in Elsig, Manfred, Hoekman, Bernard and Pauwelyn, Joost (2017), *Assessing the World Trade Organization: Fit for Purpose?*, Cambridge, Cambridge University Press, pp. 223–75, at 232–3.

[48] Qin (2017), Mind the Gap: Navigating Between the WTO Agreement and Its Accession Protocols, at 233.

[49] Qin (2017), Mind the Gap: Navigating Between the WTO Agreement and Its Accession Protocols, at 234.

[50] Qin (2017), Mind the Gap: Navigating Between the WTO Agreement and Its Accession Protocols, at 235.

[51] Lanoszka, Anna (2001), 'The World Trade Organization Accession Process: Negotiating Participation in a Globalizing Economy', *Journal of World Trade* (35) (4), pp. 575–602.

WTO' and non-original Members. Original Members are those Members that were Contracting Parties to the GATT 1947 as well as the European Communities. Non-original Members are those Members that joined the WTO through the accession process laid down in Article XII:1 WTO Agreement. This article merely provides that accession to the WTO will take place 'on terms between it [the acceding State or customs territory]' and that the accession will apply to this Agreement (the WTO Agreement) and the Multilateral Trade Agreements annexed to it. As such it mirrors Article XXXIII GATT 1947. Article XII WTO Agreement does not stipulate anything concerning the procedure of accession, the outcome of this process or on the exact meaning of the 'terms to be agreed' between the acceding Member and the WTO. The text of the provision does not reveal how decentralized the WTO accession process actually is.[52] It has been put forward that the reason the drafters of Article XII WTO Agreement chose not to draft universally applicable terms of accession was that these 'terms are to a large extent decided in negotiations on a case-by-case basis, in relation to each applicant's measures'.[53] Strikingly, in spite of the criticism – addressed in more detail in Chapters 3 and 4 – in respect of this 'vague' language, similar terminology has been used in the drafting of more recent regional trade agreements. Article 30.4 of the Trans-Pacific Partnership (TPP), for example, stipulates that the agreement is open to accession by members of Asia-Pacific Economic Cooperation (APEC) and any other state or customs territory, provided that they are:

> prepared to comply with the obligations in this Agreement, subject to such *terms and conditions as may be agreed* between the State or separate customs territory and the Parties, and following approval in accordance with the applicable legal procedures of each Party and acceding State or separate customs territory (accession candidate).

This indicates that even for more recent regional trade agreements (RTAs), parties do not appear to oppose an accession process that may involve the negotiation of specific conditions.

Compared to other competences of the WTO, such as its legislative or dispute settlement function, the accession process is characterized by a lack of rules. As such it remains a highly political process. This finding is

---

[52] Schneider, Christina J. and Urpelainen, Johannes (2012), 'Accession Rules for International Institutions: A Legitimacy-Efficacy Trade-Off?', *Journal of Conflict Resolution* (56) (2), pp. 290–312.

[53] Williams (2008), *A Handbook on Accession to the WTO*, at 12.

important since, as will be illustrated below, protocols of accession may contain rules that go beyond the rights and obligations that original Members have committed to. Some have argued that Article XII WTO Agreement 'allows existing Members a carte blanche to impose unreasonable conditions'.[54] It has also been submitted that 'country-specific rulemaking has become a standard practice in WTO accessions'.[55] Despite the fact that Article XII WTO Agreement does not contain any rules of procedure for the accession process, the WTO Secretariat, in consultation with the Members, has developed a fairly well-defined standard accession procedure.[56] The Secretariat has compiled several technical notes on the accession process and notes on procedures for negotiations under Article XII WTO Agreement that outline in broad terms the steps that are followed in the course of accession negotiations.[57] Accession is a four stage process.[58] In the first phase, a working party is established which oversees the whole process. The acceding Member drafts a memorandum in which it lists all aspects of its trade and economic policy. The accession negotiations take place on a bilateral

---

[54] Basra, Hardeep (2012), 'Increased Legalization or Politicalization? A Comparison of Accession under the GATT and WTO', *Journal of World Trade* (46) (4), pp. 937–60, at 948.

[55] Qin (2017), Mind the Gap: Navigating Between the WTO Agreement and Its Accession Protocols, at 12.

[56] Williams (2008), *A Handbook on Accession to the WTO*, at 13.

[57] See, for example, WTO, Accession to the World Trade Organization, Note by the Secretariat, WT/ACC/1, 24 March 1995. The most recent version of this document is WTO, Accession to the World Trade Organization, Procedures for Negotiations under Article XII, Note by the Secretariat, WT/ACC/22/Rev.1, 5 April 2016. This document indeed specifies in paragraph 18 that '[i]n parallel to the examination of the foreign trade regime, interested Working Party members may initiate bilateral market access negotiations on goods and services *and on other terms to be agreed*' (emphasis added). See also WTO, Technical Note on the Accession Process, Note by the Secretariat, WT/ACC/10/Rev.4/Add.1, 25 May 2010.

[58] See for a description of this process, inter alia, Beslać, Petra and Osakwe, Chiedu (2015), The Evolution of the GATT/WTO Accession Protocol: Legal Tightening and Domestic Ratification, in Dadush, Uri and Osakwe, Chiedu (eds) (2015), *WTO Accessions and Trade Multilateralism: Case Studies and Lessons from the WTO at Twenty*, Cambridge, Cambridge University Press, pp. 348–93, at 355–9 and Wouters, Jan and De Meester, Bart (2007), *The World Trade Organization: A Legal and Institutional Analysis*, Antwerp, Intersentia, at 153–60.

basis in the second phase.[59] After every interested WTO Member has completed its bilateral discussions with the state or customs territory wanting to accede, the working party finalizes the outcomes of the negotiations in the third phase. The 'terms agreed upon' between the acceding Member and the WTO are contained in a 'Protocol of Accession' and schedules of commitments. In the fourth and final phase, the Working Party Report, the Protocol of Accession and the Schedules of Commitments are presented to the WTO's General Council or Ministerial Conference. The accession process has been compared with several 'train tracks' that run in parallel with each other, before they converge into one (Table 2.12).[60]

Decisions on accession are taken by consensus, unless a consensus cannot be arrived at. Compared with the GATT accession process, which essentially revolved around the negotiation of tariff concessions, the procedure of accession to the WTO is more complicated because of the additional subject areas involved.[61] In addition to a schedule of tariff concessions, accession working party reports now list additional commitments such as publication of trade regulations, elimination of quantitative restrictions (on imports and exports), elimination of discrimination in international taxation or of import charges in excess of bound duty rates and various notification requirements. These additional commitments may go well beyond the obligations incumbent (original) WTO Members are under. They are subject to the obligations contained in the annexes to the WTO Agreement, which serves as an umbrella agreement. The result of the accession negotiations is known as 'the accession package', which consists of the Protocol of Accession, the Working Party Report and Schedules of Concessions for both trade in goods and trade in services. The differences between the accession process to the GATT and that to the WTO have also been explained from the perspective of historical institutionalism. It has been suggested that the creation of the WTO 'has not diminished the role and impact of power politics; instead the asymmetry this produces has become more ingrained in the WTO and

[59] Wouters and De Meester (2007), *The World Trade Organization: A Legal and Institutional Analysis*, at 154.

[60] Beslać and Osakwe (2015), The Evolution of the GATT/WTO Accession Protocol: Legal Tightening and Domestic Ratification, at 356.

[61] Jones (2009), The Political Economy of WTO Accession: The Unfinished Business of Universal Membership, at 290.

Table 2.12 WTO accession process[62]

<table>
<tr><td rowspan="7">Working Party established</td><td colspan="4">Multilateral Process</td><td rowspan="7">Draft accession package adopted, ad referendum, by the working party</td><td rowspan="7">Formal action by General Council/ Ministerial Conference</td><td rowspan="7">Acceptance by acceding government</td><td rowspan="7">Notification of acceptance</td><td rowspan="7">Membership</td></tr>
<tr><td>Memorandum on the foreign trade regime</td><td>Factual Summary</td><td>Elements of a draft working party report (DWPR)</td><td>DWPR</td></tr>
<tr><td colspan="4">Plurilateral Process</td></tr>
<tr><td>Agriculture</td><td>Any other area of rules, as necessary (e.g. SPS)</td><td>Technical verification of schedules</td><td>Agreed elements are reflected in the DWPR</td></tr>
<tr><td colspan="4">Bilateral Process</td></tr>
<tr><td>Initial goods offer</td><td>Negotiations on goods</td><td colspan="2">Draft Goods Schedule</td></tr>
<tr><td>Initial services offer</td><td>Negotiations on services</td><td colspan="2">Draft Services Schedule</td></tr>
</table>

[62] Table taken from Beslać and Osakwe (2015), The Evolution of the GATT/WTO Accession Protocol: Legal Tightening and Domestic Ratification, at 357.

further protracted during accession'.[63] In Part II the relationship between protocols of accession to the World Trade Organization and the WTO Agreement, including all of its annexes will be discussed in more detail. Article XII WTO Agreement does not provide any clarification on the status of protocols of accession, nor does it explain whether there is a certain hierarchy between the WTO Agreement itself and these protocols. On this particular issue, for now, it suffices to mention that Article XII WTO Agreement has been mentioned in a number of panel reports and in one Appellate Body report. In *China – Publications and Audiovisual Products* the Panel had to examine the evidentiary question as to whether certain bilateral agreements concluded between the United States and China (as part of the China-US accession negotiations) could be considered to be 'agreements with the WTO'. Noting that Article XII of the WTO Agreement provides that 'a State may accede to the WTO "on terms to be agreed between it and the WTO" – not terms agreed between it and individual WTO Members', the Panel found that this was not the case.[64]

The Panel in *China – Raw Materials* held in paragraph 7.112 that:

> Accession to the WTO is achieved through negotiation with other WTO Members. Pursuant to Article XII of the Marrakesh Agreement, accessions take place 'on terms to be agreed' between the acceding Member and the WTO membership. Most accession processes take several years to complete and lead to detailed negotiated provisions. The terms of each WTO Member's accession are set out in its Accession Protocol and accompanying Working Party Report. The negotiated agreement between the WTO membership and the acceding Member results in a delicate balance of rights and obligations, which are reflected in the specific wording of each commitment set out in these documents. Ultimately, the acceding Member and the WTO membership recognize that the intensively negotiated content of an accession package is the 'entry fee' to the WTO system.[65]

This finding was not appealed by either of the parties to the dispute. The second part of this contribution will elaborate on the legal status of protocols of accession in the framework of the WTO, taking into account the relevant reports of panels and the Appellate Body. In that part

---

[63] Basra (2012), Increased Legalization or Politicalization? A Comparison of Accession under the GATT and WTO, at 948.

[64] Panel Report, *China – Publications and Audiovisual Products*, para. 7.1238.

[65] Panel Reports, *China – Raw Materials*, para. 7.112.

questions concerning the enforceability of protocols of accession and the jurisdiction over these instruments will be addressed in more detail.

2.3.2.4 Proposals to reform the WTO accession process

Accession has been a recurring theme at the WTO's Ministerial Conferences. The organization is keen on enlarging its membership and moving in the direction of universal membership.[66] In December 2017 the 11th WTO Ministerial Conference will be organized in Buenos Aires, Argentina. Previous Ministerial Conferences have taken place in Singapore (December 1996), Geneva (May 1998), Seattle (November-December 1999), Doha (November 2001), Cancún (September 2003), Hong Kong (December 2005), Geneva (December 2009), Geneva (December 2011) and Bali (December 2013). The tenth WTO Ministerial Conference was held in Nairobi in December 2015.

Singapore (December 1996) The first WTO Ministerial Conference in Singapore resulted in a Ministerial Declaration which emphasized the importance of an expeditious accession process.[67] Members expressed their concern about the length of the accession process.

Geneva (May 1998) The Geneva Ministerial Declaration of 1998 addressed the issue of accession in brief, stating that the WTO Members:

> welcome the WTO Members who have joined since we met in Singapore: Congo, Democratic Republic of Congo, Mongolia, Niger and Panama. We welcome the progress made with 31 applicants currently negotiating their accession and renew our resolution to ensure that the accession processes proceed as rapidly as possible. We recall that accession to the WTO requires full respect of WTO rules and disciplines as well as meaningful market access commitments on the part of acceding candidates.[68]

Seattle (November–December 1999) Accessions were not on the agenda of the Seattle Ministerial Conference.

---

[66] Hoekman, Bernard (2005), 'Expanding WTO Membership and Heterogeneous Interests', *World Trade Review* (5) (3), pp. 401–8.

[67] WTO, Singapore WTO Ministerial 1996, Ministerial Declaration, 9–13 December 1996, WT/MIN(96)/DEC/, adopted on 13 December 1996.

[68] WTO, Ministerial Declaration, Second Session, Geneva, 18 and 20 May 1998, WT/MIN(98)/DEC/1, adopted on 20 May 1998.

Doha (November 2001) The Doha Ministerial Declaration marks the start of the Doha Round of Multilateral Trade Negotiations.[69] The Declaration also marks the entry of China and Chinese Taipei to the multilateral trading system. Members again emphasized the importance of accelerating the accession process, in particular that of Least-Developed Countries (LDCs). The membership thereto instructed the Secretariat to 'reflect the priority we attach to LDC's accessions in the annual plans for technical assistance'.[70]

Cancún (September 2003) The Cancún Ministerial Conference is considered to be a dismal failure, where nothing was agreed upon.[71] The Draft Ministerial Text states that Cambodia and Nepal were welcomed as first LDCs to accede to the WTO.[72] It further expresses the intention of Members to conclude ongoing accessions as quickly as possible.[73]

Hong Kong (December 2005) The Hong Kong Ministerial Declaration was adopted on 18 December 2005 in light of the Doha Work Programme.[74] In this Ministerial Declaration the WTO Membership expressed its intention to make the WTO truly global in scope and membership, noting that recent accessions further strengthened the rules-based multilateral trading system.[75] Interestingly, the WTO membership also recognized the special situation of recently acceded Members who had undertaken extensive market access commitments as part of their accession package, noting that this situation would be taken into account in the negotiations.[76] The Ministerial Declaration also explicitly recognized the problems LDCs face when trying to accede to the WTO. To this

---

69 WTO, Ministerial Declaration, Fourth Session, Doha, 9–14 November 2001, WT/MIN(01)/DEC/1, adopted on 14 November 2001.

70 WTO, Ministerial Declaration, Fourth Session, Doha, 9–14 November 2001, WT/MIN(01)/DEC/1, adopted on 14 November 2001, para. 42.

71 Van den Bossche and Zdouc (2013), *The Law and Policy of the World Trade Organization*, at 89.

72 WTO, Ministerial Declaration, Draft Cancún Ministerial Text, 13 September 2003, JOB(03)/150/Rev.2, para. 30

73 WTO, Ministerial Declaration, Draft Cancún Ministerial Text, 13 September 2003, JOB(03)/150/Rev.2, para. 30

74 WTO, Ministerial Declaration, Doha Work Programme, adopted on 18 December 2005, WT/MIN(05)/DEC.

75 WTO, Ministerial Declaration, Doha Work Programme, adopted on 18 December 2005, WT/MIN(05)/DEC, para. 59.

76 WTO, Ministerial Declaration, Doha Work Programme, adopted on 18 December 2005, WT/MIN(05)/DEC, para. 58.

end the Declaration stipulates that the Members 'agree to facilitate and accelerate negotiations with acceding LDCs based on the accession guidelines adopted by the General Council in December 2002'.[77]

Geneva (December 2009) The 2009 Geneva Ministerial Conference did not produce any concrete results in terms of accession. Cambodia reported on a roundtable it had organized jointly with Tanzania on the issue of LDC Accession. The statement reiterated the need to take into account the interests of LDCs in the accession process to the WTO.

Geneva (December 2011) The 2011 Geneva Ministerial Conference was considered another failure in terms of attempting to conclude the Doha Round. On the issue of accessions, however, Members issued a decision on the accession of LDCs in which the LDC Accession guidelines adopted in 2002 were reaffirmed. Members further recognized the need for increased transparency in the accession process, as well as transitional periods for LDCs, increased technical assistance and capacity building.[78]

Bali (December 2013) In the first few months of 2013 Laos and Tajikistan were welcomed to the WTO. Other accessions such as those of Yemen, Kazakhstan, Afghanistan, Serbia and Seychelles moved into the final stages.

Nairobi (2015) The 10th Ministerial Conference in Nairobi in December 2015 saw the conclusion of the accessions of Afghanistan and Liberia. The Ministerial Declaration that was adopted at the Conference makes extensive reference to the issue of accession. Paragraph 18 stipulates:

> We celebrate the enlargement of the Organization by accessions in accordance with Article XII of the Marrakesh Agreement. We note that the accessions of the Republic of Yemen, the Republic of Seychelles and the Republic of Kazakhstan to the WTO have been completed since our last Session. In particular, we note with satisfaction that this Conference has completed the accession procedures for two least-developed countries, the Republic of Liberia and the Islamic Republic of Afghanistan. We recognize the extensive commitments and the contribution of the Article XII Members resulting from

---

[77] WTO, Ministerial Declaration, Doha Work Programme, adopted on 18 December 2005, WT/MIN(05)/DEC, para. 47. This commitment is reiterated in the final paragraph (59).

[78] WTO, Ministerial Decision on the Accession of Least-Developed Countries, 17 December 2011, WT/L/846.

> their accessions to the strengthening of the multilateral trading system. We will work jointly on the expeditious completion of current accessions. We remain committed to efforts to facilitate accessions and provide technical assistance to acceding countries, including in the post-accession phase.[79]

Interestingly, at the Nairobi Ministerial Conference, WTO Members also acknowledged that non-original Members often have had to make extensive market access commitments in order to obtain membership:

> We recognize the special situation of the Members acceded in accordance with Article XII of the Agreement Establishing the World Trade Organization who have undertaken extensive market access commitments at the time of accession. This situation shall be taken into account in the negotiations.[80]

Although the issue has been on the agenda of a number of Ministerial Conferences, none of these conferences have led to an agreement on a more simplified accession procedure or changes in the text of Article XII of the WTO Agreement. Members have emphasized the importance of a swift accession procedure. In the first decade of the WTO's existence, LDCs experienced a lot of difficulties in meeting the requirements set forth as part of the WTO's accession process.[81] This has led to the adoption of Guidelines for the Accession of LDCs. The Guidelines contain four subsections that deal with Market Access, WTO Rules, the Process of Accession and Trade-Related Technical Assistance and Capacity Building. WTO Members agreed to 'exercise restraint' in seeking concessions and commitments on trade in goods and services from acceding LDCs.[82] In terms of WTO Rules, WTO Members agreed to apply the provisions on Special and Differential Treatment as contained in the Multilateral Trade Agreements, Ministerial Decisions and other relevant WTO legal instruments to all acceding LDCs. Moreover, it was agreed that acceding LDCs would be able to benefit from the transitional periods as foreseen in the specific WTO agreements. Perhaps most importantly, especially in light of the capacity constraints that have been

---

[79] WTO, Nairobi Ministerial Declaration, 19 December 2015, WT/MIN(15)/DEC, para. 18.

[80] WTO, Nairobi Ministerial Declaration, 19 December 2015, WT/MIN(15)/DEC, para. 27.

[81] Hawthorne, Helen (2009), 'Acceding to the Norm: The Accession of LDCs to the WTO', *The Hague Journal of Diplomacy* (4), pp. 7–35, at 20.

[82] Nguyen, Nhan (2008), 'WTO Accession at Any Cost? Examining the Use of WTO-Plus and WTO-Minus Obligations for Least-Developed Country Applicants', *Temple International & Comparative Law Journal* (22), pp. 243–77.

signalled, the WTO Members agreed to provide targeted and coordinated technical assistance and capacity building to acceding LDCs. Since the creation of the WTO in 1995, six LDCs have joined the organization. Nepal and Cambodia in 2004, shortly after the adoption of the first version of the LDC Accession guidelines, and Samoa, Vanuatu, Lao PDR and Yemen between 2012 and 2014.

2.4 CONCLUSION

Accession to the multilateral trading system is relatively different from the accession to other international organizations. Whereas organizations such as the UN, the IMF and the World Bank set conditions for the eligibility of actors to join these organizations in their founding documents, the WTO Agreement merely states that these conditions have to be agreed upon by the acceding state or customs territory and the WTO. The difference can be logically explained by the fact that the WTO system exists of a broad range of legal obligations that are aimed at curtailing the trade restrictive effects that domestic legislation can have. The roots for the difference lie in the idea of reciprocity that is prevalent in trade negotiations. WTO Members that had already opened their markets as part of their own tariff or accession negotiations were reluctant to let new Members free-ride into the system without having to 'pay their entrance fee'. In order to ensure that new Members will also adhere to these obligations, the organization carefully scrutinizes the existing trade policy of the acceding state. Where inconsistencies are found, the acceding state is asked to alter its laws and regulations. Part III of this monograph will discuss the commitments that acceding states enter into in detail as part of a mapping exercise. This detailed scrutiny of potential Members' trade policy as part of their accession to the WTO stands in contrast with the accession process to the GATT. Between the early 1950s and 1994 states and customs territories were able to join GATT through two distinct procedures. For newly independent states that wanted to subsume the obligations entered into by their former colonial powers, it was possible to join GATT under sponsorship of that power. Sixty-four Contracting Parties to GATT 1947, such as Indonesia, Ghana, Malaysia and Suriname, obtained their membership through this procedure laid down by Article XXVI:5(c) GATT 1947. Alternatively, states that were not among the original Contracting Parties of GATT were provided with the opportunity to accede to the agreement through the procedure stipulated in Article XXXIII GATT 1947. It is important to note that the GATT operated an 'open-door' policy. Especially in the early days of the multilateral trading system the Contracting Parties attempted to enlarge the membership to the agreement. Creative solutions were designed in order to enable the accession of states that did not have a strict market economy.[83] States such as Yugoslavia, Romania and Hungary acceded to GATT, accepting obligations to increase their imports from GATT Contracting Parties (Yugoslavia and Romania) or 'selective safeguards clauses' (Hungary) that allowed GATT Contracting Parties to temporarily suspend imports from these countries. WTO accession is in essence similar to GATT accession. Article XII of the WTO Agreement contains the same wording as Article XXXIII GATT 1994. One fundamental difference, however, is that the scope of the WTO is far bigger than that of GATT. Whereas the latter merely dealt with tariffs and a limited number of certain 'non-tariff barriers', the WTO Agreement now contains annexes on, inter alia, technical barriers to trade, anti-dumping, rules of origin and customs valuation.[84] The accession procedure of new Members reflects this enlarged scope. Acceding states are asked to report on their trade and economic policies. Essentially, the working party that governs the accession of new Members carefully scrutinizes whether these policies are consistent with the WTO obligations that the new Member will be bound to undertake. Applicants are requested to implement legislative reforms where necessary. In some cases, where the WTO has reservations about the applicant's ability or willingness to adhere to certain obligations, additional requirements and obligations are asked from the new Member. The results of the accession negotiations are called the 'accession package', and are generally considered to constitute the 'entry fee' to the WTO system. The following chapter of this monograph analyses the scope of the WTO system in more detail. Considering the scope of the WTO Agreement and the amount of detail that is required in the reporting on the applicant's trade policy, accession negotiations can be costly. Especially for LDCs lacking the required

[83] Carroll, Peter (2014), 'Policy Transfer and Accession: A Comparison of Three International Governmental Organizations', *Journal of Comparative Policy Analysis: Research and Practice* (16) (3), pp. 280–96, at 286.

[84] There are several other institutional differences between the GATT 1947 and the WTO Agreement. One example is that the legal personality of the WTO is explicitly conferred to the organization by Article VIII:1, whereas the GATT 1947 obtained legal personality through subsequent state practice. See Minnerop, Petra (2006), Article VIII WTO Agreement, in Wolfrum, Rüdiger, Stoll, Peter-Tobias and Kaiser, Karen (eds), *Max Planck Commentaries on World Trade Law: WTO – Institutions and Dispute Settlement*, Leiden, Martinus Nijhoff Publishers, 90–105, at 93.

infrastructure, the accession process can be cumbersome. To this end, WTO Members have adopted Guidelines on the Accession of LDCs in order to streamline their accession bids to the multilateral trading system. Moreover, on numerous occasions, the WTO has emphasized the importance of a swift accession process. In the following chapter the institutional framework of the WTO will be discussed in order to obtain a better understanding of the obligations that new Members will have to undertake. Furthermore, the commitments that new Members enter into in their 'accession package' will be examined in more detail. New Members do not only have to ensure that their trade and economic policy is in conformity with their WTO obligations, they also have to offer market access concessions in the fields of trade in goods and trade in services.

3. The scope of the multilateral trading system

3.1 INTRODUCTION: THE LEGALIZATION OF THE MULTILATERAL TRADING SYSTEM

The second chapter of this contribution dealt with the ways in which states and customs territories have been able to become a member of the multilateral trading system. During the GATT it was possible for former colonies to succeed their colonial power as a GATT Contracting Party under the provision laid down by Article XXVI:5(c) GATT 1947.[1] Moreover, states and customs territories could apply for accession using the procedure laid down by Article XXXIII GATT 1947. The WTO accession process as stipulated by Article XII of the WTO Agreement in essence reflects the core characteristics of GATT accession. However, as prior observations already revealed, whereas the GATT-era was characterized by a desire on the part of the original Contracting Parties to achieve the broadest possible scope in terms of members fuelled by an aspiration for universalism, the concessions that were required of new applicant states began to increase in the second half of the 1960s. With the increasing scope of GATT and the addition of new subject areas such as standards, anti-dumping and subsidies, the accession negotiations also began to include more than just talks on tariff concessions. The establishment of the World Trade Organization in 1995 further cemented this development. Where the GATT system was lacking severely in terms of institutional provisions, the conclusion of the Uruguay Round of Multilateral Trade Negotiations saw the emergence of a true intergovernmental organization with strong institutional foundations. The establishment of a true rules-based multilateral trading system meant that several institutional aspects of the GATT system underwent a process of legalization. Although the provision governing the procedure of accession was not

[1] Jackson, John H. (1969), *World Trade Law and the Law of GATT: A Legal Analysis of the General Agreement on Tariffs and Trade*, Charlottesville, VA, The Michie Company/Bobbs Merill, at 87–90.

changed textually, the accession process has become more and more standardized since the creation of the WTO. Undoubtedly the WTO Secretariat has played a substantial role in this process of standardization.[2] Moreover, the Secretariat tries to ensure that applicants are aware of the consequences of accession and the potential outcome of the negotiations.[3] In addition to the standardization of the process of accession, the contents of the accession negotiations have also changed dramatically when compared to the GATT system. Whereas GATT accession negotiations centred around the issue of tariff concessions, with the incumbent members trying to ensure that new Contracting Parties would not 'free ride' on their earlier commitment, the accession negotiations to the WTO are far broader in scope. Similar to the GATT accession negotiations, they include negotiations on tariff concessions for trade in goods. Additionally, however, the creation and adoption of the General Agreement on Trade in Services (Annex 1B to the WTO Agreement) has led to the situation in which acceding states and customs territories are also required to table an offer for concessions relating to the liberalization of trade in services. Inevitably, the demands made will differ from accession to accession. In addition to negotiations on 'market access', accession negotiations now typically also include detailed discussions on, what will be called, 'rules' commitments.

As will be explained in more detail in the relevant subparagraphs, the importance of tariff barriers to trade in goods has been declining steadily in the past decades. This trend started in the last quarter of the 20th century and has continued ever since. In the meantime the relative importance of NTBs has increased exponentially. The establishment of the WTO and the negotiation of a number of multilateral trade agreements on trade in goods, an agreement on trade in services, an agreement on the trade-related aspects of intellectual property, and several plurilateral agreements, can be seen as attempts by the international community to regulate the changing nature of global commerce. These attempts reflect the increased scope of the multilateral trading system. The scope of the accession negotiations to the WTO has changed accordingly with the expanding scope of the multilateral trading system. The WTO seeks to ensure that new Members of the organization adhere to their obligations under the WTO's legal system. To this end, the accession negotiations not only focus on 'market access' commitments, but also entail

---

[2] Williams, Peter John (2008), *A Handbook on Accession to the WTO*, Cambridge, Cambridge University Press, at 17.

[3] See also Milthorp, Peter (2009), 'WTO Accessions: The Story so Far', *The Hague Journal of Diplomacy* (4) (1), pp. 103–12, at 110.

detailed scrutiny of the applicant state's trade and economic policy. The WTO will require applicant states to alter their regulatory framework where it is found that aspects of it are inconsistent with the obligations the state is about to undertake as a Member of the WTO. Moreover, in some instances, the WTO has required certain states to sign up to additional 'rules' commitments that are supposed to guarantee the applicant state's long-term intention to abide by the rules of the organization. As a result of these features of the WTO accession process, some authors have spoken of a two-tiered membership of the WTO.[4] In their view, one category of Members consists of those Members that are 'original members' who became part of the organization by virtue of their GATT membership.[5] The second category of Members consists of those Members that joined the WTO through the procedure of accession as stipulated by Article XII WTO Agreement. These Members have to adhere to the commitments made in their protocols of accession, in addition to the obligations contained in the WTO Agreement.[6] Others have disputed this characterization of the membership of the WTO and have argued that, instead, we should speak of a *multi*-tiered membership, with differing levels of commitments that reflect each Member's level of economic development.[7] This chapter explores the scope of the multilateral trading system in more detail in order to establish the 'baseline'

---

[4] Polouektov, Alexander (2002), 'Non-Market Economy Issues in the WTO Anti-Dumping Law and Accession Negotiations: Revival of a Two-Tier Membership', *Journal of World Trade* (36) (1), pp. 1–37.

[5] Tyagi, Mitali (2012), 'Flesh on a Legal Fiction: Early Practice in the WTO on Accession Protocols', *Journal of International Economic Law* (15) (2), pp. 391–441, at 396. Tyagi cites Maxim Medvedkov, then Head of Delegation of the Russian Federation on WTO Accession, as stating (in relevant part): 'Acceding countries are required to make commitments which go beyond the standard WTO package [...] Another dangerous development is connected with the denial to some acceding countries of members' rights established by respective WTO Agreements, like those on antidumping or safeguards. All these additional requirements are not based on the legal norms of the WTO, and they do not take into account the actual situation in acceding countries. Furthermore, acceding countries are required to make bigger commitments than the original members were. This creates a *two-tiered system of rights and obligations* for different members, thus substantially damaging the main principles of the WTO: non-discrimination, equal rights and transparency.'

[6] Van den Bossche, Peter and Zdouc, Werner (2013), *The Law and Policy of the World Trade Organization*, Third Edition, Cambridge, Cambridge University Press, at 109–13.

[7] Discussion with a staff member of the WTO Secretariat's Legal Affairs Division.

with which rules commitments made in the context of the accession process have to be compared.[8] What the baseline for a particular accession protocol commitment is will depend on the area in which the commitment is undertaken. At the outset it is important to note that the two- or multi-tieredness of the membership in the context of this monograph does not refer to the level of trade liberalization that is undertaken by acceding states and customs territories. Inevitably, different states negotiate different levels of market access commitments in the areas of trade in goods and trade in services. The liberalization effort required by the WTO is, logically, largely dependent on the extent to which the state in question has already liberalized its trade regime unilaterally. Rather, when referring to the notion of a multi-tiered membership, this monograph points at the situation in which different Members of the same organization are under different types of rules obligations that determine the way in which they can conduct their trade policy.

3.2 MOVING TOWARDS THE WTO: THE SINGLE UNDERTAKING

3.2.1 Introduction: The Punta del Este Declaration

The GATT 1947 was initially envisaged to be administered under the auspices of an International Trade Organization (ITO). As a result of the stillbirth of this organization, the GATT Contracting Parties were required to adopt a pragmatic approach. Eventually, the GATT – as the basis of the multilateral trading system – transformed in a 'de facto' international organization.[9] As noted, GATT was successful in reducing tariff barriers to trade in goods. As a forum for dealing with non-tariff barriers, the picture was less positive. In this respect the absence of a proper institutional framework was, for a large part, to blame. Although the issue of non-tariff barriers (or non-tariff measures) was on the agenda

---

[8] Charnovitz, Steve (2008), 'Mapping the Law of WTO Accession', in Janow, Merit E., Donaldson, Victoria and Yanovich, Alan (eds), *The WTO: Governance, Dispute Settlement and Developing Countries*, Huntington, NY, Juris Publishing, pp. 855–920, at 868. Charnovitz was one of the first to advocate a comparison between accession protocol commitments and the WTO Agreement as the baseline.

[9] Van den Bossche and Zdouc (2013), *The Law and Policy of the World Trade Organization*, at 78.

for several negotiating rounds, the implementation of the agreements that were reached was often less than satisfactory. The Kennedy Round only resulted in the 1967 Antidumping (AD) Code.[10] The Tokyo Round was more successful. However, since many of the agreements that were concluded were plurilateral rather than multilateral in nature, it did not address the issue of the proliferation of NTBs in a satisfactory manner.[11] It took a few more years for the Contracting Parties to the GATT to reach agreement on the start of a new round of multilateral trade negotiations. Although not all Contracting Parties were keen on the idea of launching a new round of multilateral trade negotiations, agreement was found eventually in September 1986 at Punta del Este.[12] The 1986 Punta del Este Ministerial Declaration formally launched the Uruguay Round of Multilateral Trade Negotiations. The Round would eventually take eight years to conclude and resulted in the establishment of the World Trade Organization.[13] The Contracting Parties aimed to remedy the major institutional flaws that were present in the GATT system. However, this was not one of the initial objectives of the negotiations. Rather, the GATT Contracting Parties tried to find agreement on new disciplines that would govern NTBs. This subsection discusses the results of the Uruguay Round and the institutional changes it brought about in the multilateral trading system.[14] Additionally, it discusses the approach of the single undertaking that was used as the basis for the negotiations.[15] Ultimately, the outcome of the Uruguay Round contains the rights and obligations

---

[10] Jackson, John H. (1997), *The World Trading System: Law and Policy of International Economic Relations*, Second Edition, Cambridge, MA, MIT Press, at 75.

[11] Van den Bossche and Zdouc (2013), *The Law and Policy of the World Trade Organization*, at 79; Jackson (1997), *The World Trading System: Law and Policy of International Economic Relations*, at 76–7.

[12] GATT, Ministerial Declaration on the Uruguay Round, MIN.DEC, 20 September 1986.

[13] Article I of the WTO Agreement; see also Final Act Embodying the Results of the Uruguay Round of Multilateral Trade Negotiations (15 April 1994) 1867 U.N.T.S. 14 (Final Act).

[14] GATT, Ministerial Declaration on the Uruguay Round, MIN.DEC, 20 September 1986, at 7–8.

[15] Appellate Body Report, *Brazil – Desiccated Coconut*, at 12–13. The Appellate Body noted that: 'The single undertaking is further reflected in the provisions of the *WTO Agreement* dealing with original membership, accession, non-application of the Multilateral Trade Agreements between particular Members, acceptance of the *WTO Agreement*, and withdrawal from it. Within this framework, all WTO Members are bound by all the rights and obligations in the *WTO Agreement* and its Annexes 1, 2 and 3' (footnote omitted).

that all Members, including non-original Members, have to adhere to. However, as has been explained, acceding Members have, in some cases, been asked by the WTO to make additional commitments on issues that are included in the WTO Agreement. Hence, the purpose of this chapter is to determine the baseline rights and obligations that all WTO Members have to adhere to, in order to establish which accession commitments exceed the baseline obligations. The Punta del Este Declaration signalled that the Uruguay Round negotiations would, for the first time, not only cover trade in goods, but also trade in services.[16] Before going into the negotiations on new disciplines to address NTBs, attention will be paid to the institutional changes that were ultimately realized at the end of the Uruguay Round.

3.2.2 Marrakesh Agreement Establishing the World Trade Organization

The WTO Agreement was signed in Marrakesh on 15 April 1994.[17] The Agreement entered into force on 1 January 1995. The Preamble of the WTO Agreement lists the main objectives of the WTO. It provides (in relevant part):

> Recognizing that their relations in the field of trade and economic endeavour should be conducted with a view to raising standards of living, ensuring full employment and a large and steadily growing volume of real income and effective demand, and expanding the production of and trade in goods and services, while allowing for the optimal use of the world's resources in accordance with the objective of sustainable development, seeking both to protect and preserve the environment and to enhance the means for doing so in a manner consistent with their respective needs and concerns at different levels of economic development,
>
> *Recognizing* further that there is need for positive efforts designed to ensure that developing countries, and especially the least developed among them, secure a share in the growth in international trade commensurate with the needs of their economic development.

---

[16] GATT, Ministerial Declaration on the Uruguay Round, MIN.DEC, 20 September 1986, Part II, at 10.

[17] Agreement Establishing the World Trade Organization (15 April 1994) 1867 U.N.T.S. 154; entered into force 1 January 1995 (WTO Agreement); see also Final Act Embodying the Results of the Uruguay Round of Multilateral Trade Negotiations (15 April 1994) 1867 U.N.T.S. 14 (Final Act).

Based on the text of the preamble, the objectives of the WTO have been summarized as follows: i) the increase of standards of living; ii) the attainment of full employment; iii) the growth of real income and effective demand; and iv) the expansion of production of, and trade in, goods and services. Nevertheless, in the pursuit of these objectives, the organization must take due account of the principles of sustainable development and the need to ensure the integration of developing countries, in particular 'Least-Developed Countries' in the multilateral trading system.[18] The means through which these objectives are to be achieved are laid down by the third recital of the preamble:

> *Being desirous* of contributing to these objectives by entering into reciprocal and mutually advantageous arrangements directed to the substantial reduction of tariffs and other barriers to trade and to the elimination of discriminatory treatment in international trade relations [...]

Further reducing tariff barriers and trying to eliminate discriminatory treatment in international trade relations are thus the two means through which WTO Members are supposed to ensure the attainment of the four objectives outlined above.[19] In addition to the objectives of the WTO contained in the preamble, the WTO Agreement also lays down the tools that are available to WTO Members to work towards the attainment of these objectives. In broad terms, Article II:1 of the WTO Agreement provides that:

> The WTO shall provide the common institutional framework for the conduct of trade relations among its Members in matters related to the agreements and associated legal instruments included in the Annexes to this Agreement.

This statement is further specified in Article III of the WTO Agreement, which lays down five of the six widely defined functions of the WTO:

> 1. The WTO shall facilitate the implementation, administration and operation, and further the objectives, of this Agreement and of the Multilateral Trade Agreements, and shall also provide the framework for the implementation, administration and operation of the Plurilateral Trade Agreements.

---

[18] Van den Bossche and Zdouc (2013), *The Law and Policy of the World Trade Organization*, at 83.

[19] Lester, Simon, Mercurio, Bryan and Davies, Arwel (2012), *World Trade Law: Text, Materials and Commentary*, Oxford, Hart Publishing, at 65.

2. The WTO shall provide the forum for negotiations among its Members concerning their multilateral trade relations in matters dealt with under the agreements in the Annexes to this Agreement. The WTO may also provide a forum for further negotiations among its Members concerning their multilateral trade relations, and a framework for the implementation of the results of such negotiations, as may be decided by the Ministerial Conference.
3. The WTO shall administer the Understanding on Rules and Procedures Governing the Settlement of Disputes (hereinafter referred to as the 'Dispute Settlement Understanding' or 'DSU') in Annex 2 to this Agreement.
4. The WTO shall administer the Trade Policy Review Mechanism (hereinafter referred to as the 'TPRM') provided for in Annex 3 to this Agreement.
5. With a view to achieving greater coherence in global economic policy-making, the WTO shall cooperate, as appropriate, with the International Monetary Fund and with the International Bank for Reconstruction and Development and its affiliated agencies.

The provision of technical assistance to developing-country Members, to allow the latter to integrate into the world trading system, is, undisputedly, also an important sixth function of the WTO.[20] Clearly, the importance of facilitating the accession of developing countries and LDCs to the WTO can also be linked to this sixth objective.[21]

3.2.2.1 The institutional structure

The basic institutional structure of the WTO is described in Article IV of the WTO Agreement. At the top of the institutional pyramid is the Ministerial Conference, which meets at least once every two years.[22] The WTO's General Council is in charge of the day-to-day operation of the organization. According to Article IV:2 of the WTO Agreement, it shall 'meet as appropriate'. The General Council can meet in its own capacity, but usually it meets in the context of three of the tasks that have been bestowed upon it. Article IV:3 of the WTO Agreement provides that the General Council may convene as the Dispute Settlement Body in order to discharge the functions provided in the Understanding on Rules and Procedures Governing the Settlement of Disputes (DSU). Moreover,

---

[20] Van den Bossche and Zdouc (2013), *The Law and Policy of the World Trade Organization*, at 85. They refer to Paragraph 38 of the Doha Ministerial Declaration.

[21] In 20 years of WTO accession practice 23 developing countries and 8 LDCs have acceded under the provision of Article XII WTO Agreement.

[22] Lester, Mercurio and Davies (2012), *World Trade Law*, at 74.

the General Council may convene as the Trade Policy Review Body based on Article IV:4 of the WTO Agreement. The General Council also has the mandate to set up accession working parties. When it does so, 'it delegates the examination of the request for accession to that body.' When the Working Party concludes the accession negotiations and finalizes its report, the report is then brought before the General Council. The procedure of the adoption of the Working Party Report has been as follows:

> At the invitation of its Chairperson, the General Council/Ministerial Conference then:
>
> - approves the text of the draft Protocol of Accession and the text of the draft Decision on the Accession of [X];
> - in accordance with the Decision-Making Procedures under Articles IX and XII of the WTO Agreement agreed in November 1995, adopts the draft Decision on the Accession of [X]; and
> - adopts the Report of the Working Party as a whole, including the Schedule on Goods in its Addendum 1 and the Schedule on Services in its Addendum 2.[23]

The Protocol of Accession, including the Working Party Report and the Schedules of Concessions are known as the 'Accession Package' which is the 'entry fee' to the WTO system.[24]

3.2.2.2 Negotiations

The second function of the WTO is to provide a 'forum for negotiations among its Members concerning their multilateral trade relations', according to Article III:2 of the WTO Agreement. Six years after the creation of the WTO, the Doha Round of Multilateral Trade Negotiations was launched at the Doha Ministerial Conference in November 2001. The Doha Ministerial Declaration stipulated 1 January 2005 as the deadline for negotiations, but 11 years and several missed deadlines later, the negotiations are still ongoing. This does, however, not mean that the negotiating arm of the WTO has not delivered any concrete results. Agreements have been reached, for example, on further market access commitments for trade in services, the liberalization of information

---

[23] Williams (2008), *A Handbook on Accession to the WTO*, at 46 (footnote omitted).

[24] Panel Reports, *China – Raw Materials*, para. 7.112.

technology products, and the amendment of the Agreement on Government Procurement.[25] At the 2013 Ministerial Conference in Bali, WTO Members reached agreement on some aspects of the Doha Round. The Trade Facilitation Agreement, which aims at reducing barriers to trade caused by lengthy customs-procedures, was concluded there. Moreover, the negotiations in WTO bodies such as the TBT Committee and the SPS Committee have resulted in agreement among Members.[26] As noted in section 1.3.4, the proliferation of RTAs and plurilateral trade liberalization initiatives reflect the desire of some Members to further liberalize trade. It appears that, to some extent at least, the multilateral track does not produce the desired results. Despite all of this, the benefits of WTO membership should not be underestimated, as evidenced by the fact that 36 accession negotiations have been successfully completed to this date.

3.2.2.3 Dispute settlement

The dispute settlement function bestowed upon the WTO through Article III:3 of the WTO Agreement is governed by the DSU. Some aspects of the dispute settlement procedure are reminiscent of the GATT era, but it is generally accepted that dispute settlement in the multilateral trading system has moved from a diplomatic system to a quasi-judicial system in the WTO.[27] In fact, dispute settlement is one of the areas in which the legalization of the multilateral trading system can be most clearly observed.[28]

---

[25] WTO (2015), Information Technology Agreement press conference: Remarks by Director-General Roberto Azevêdo, 16 December; see also the Revised Agreement on Government Procurement. Available at https://www.wto.org/english/docs_e/legal_e/rev-gpr-94_01_e.pdf (last accessed at 1 June 2017).

[26] See, for example, Decision of the Committee on Principles for the Development of International Standards, Guides and Recommendations with relation to Articles 2, 5 and Annex 3 of the Agreement, in WTO document G/TBT/1/Rev.10, Decisions and Recommendations adopted by the WTO Committee on Technical Barriers to Trade since 1 January 1995, 9 June 2011, pp. 46–8. Interestingly, and perhaps even controversially, these decisions have also been used in WTO dispute settlement proceedings: see Appellate Body Report, *US – Tuna II (Mexico)*.

[27] Van den Bossche and Zdouc (2013), *The Law and Policy of the World Trade Organization*, at 159.

[28] Petersmann, Ernst-Ulrich (1997), 'Constitutionalism and International Organizations', *Northwestern Journal of International Law & Business* (17) (1), pp. 398–469, at 468.

3.2.2.4 Membership of the WTO

Article XI of the WTO Agreement distinguishes between original Members of the WTO and non-original Members. Original membership was available for Contracting Parties to the GATT 1947 and the European Communities. It could be obtained by accepting the WTO Agreement and the Multilateral Trade Agreements, and by making concessions and commitments for both trade in goods and services. All GATT Contracting Parties, except Yugoslavia, became original Members of the WTO on the date of the entry into force of the WTO Agreement. The European Communities also became an original Member of the WTO. Original membership was open until March 1997. The second way of obtaining WTO membership is through accession. This option, as provided for in Article XII of the WTO Agreement is open indefinitely. In July 2016, 36 states or customs territories had completed their accession to the WTO through the procedure laid down in this article. Another 19 accessions were still ongoing. The first condition to become a Member through accession is to accept the terms of the WTO Agreement and those contained in the Multilateral Trade Agreements. In this respect, therefore, membership through accession is not different from original membership under Article XI of the WTO Agreement. The terms of the WTO agreements and the Multilateral Trade Agreements annexed thereto are succinctly described in the subsequent paragraphs of this chapter. In addition to accepting these core principles and obligations, however, states and customs territories that want to become a Member of the WTO have to negotiate 'a ticket of admission' or an 'entry fee'. During the four-step accession procedure (2.3.2.3), acceding states will be asked to negotiate market access commitments and concessions in both trade in goods and trade in services.[29] Moreover, the accession negotiations always involve negotiations on rules.[30] These negotiations focus, typically, on the regulatory framework of the acceding state and aim to ensure that the laws and regulations are in compliance with the WTO obligations the acceding state is about to undertake as a Member of the WTO. The substance of the accession negotiations will be discussed in more detail in section 3.2.4.

---

[29] Lester, Mercurio, and Davies (2012), *World Trade Law*, at 86.

[30] Qin has questioned this practice. See Qin, Julia Ya (2017), Mind the Gap: Navigating Between the WTO Agreement and Its Accession Protocols, in Elsig, Manfred, Hoekman, Bernard and Pauwelyn, Joost (2017), *Assessing the World Trade Organization: Fit for Purpose?*, Cambridge, Cambridge University Press, pp. 223–75.

3.2.2.5 The scope of the WTO

One of the main drivers behind the decision to start the Uruguay Round of Multilateral Trade Negotiations was the realization on the part of GATT Contracting Parties that the rules contained in the GATT 1947 were no longer sufficient to address the changing realities of global commerce.[31] Whereas tariff barriers had been the most important barrier to trade in the 1940s, 1950s and the first half of the 1960s, this began to change gradually. Instead of tariff barriers, NTBs, such as standards, subsidies and discriminatory regulations increasingly began to operate as barriers to international trade. After moderately successful attempts to address the proliferation of NTBs in the course of the Kennedy Round and the Tokyo Round, the negotiation of new disciplines on these matters became one of the central pillars of the Uruguay Round. Eventually this led to the conclusion of the WTO Agreement and its numerous annexes. From a multilateral trading system that was based entirely upon the GATT 1947 and codes on standards, anti-dumping and subsidies, the system of international trade governance transformed into the WTO Agreement with annexes containing agreements and understandings that deal with issues ranging from technical barriers to trade, sanitary and phytosanitary measures, subsidies and countervailing measures, anti-dumping, rules of origin and customs valuation.

3.2.2.6 References to protocols of accession

3.2.2.6.1 References in the WTO Agreement As was mentioned above, the WTO Agreement operates as an 'umbrella agreement' which consists of a relatively short 'basic agreement' and several annexes containing other agreements and understandings. Article II:2 of the WTO Agreement provides that:

> 2. The agreements and associated legal instruments included in Annexes 1, 2 and 3 (hereinafter referred to as 'Multilateral Trade Agreements') are integral parts of this Agreement, binding on all Members.

The 16 articles of the WTO Agreement do not expressly stipulate anything relating to the legal status of protocols of accession. Article XII WTO Agreement, the provision that deals with accession, is characterized by its brevity. It does neither stipulate anything concerning the procedure that is to be followed during accession negotiations, nor does it expressly

---

[31] GATT, Ministerial Declaration on the Uruguay Round, MIN.DEC, 20 September 1986, at 2.

state that protocols of accession shall be included as an annex to the WTO Agreement.

During the meeting of the Trade Negotiations Committee in Marrakesh on 14 April 1994 a Ministerial Decision on Acceptance of and Accession to the Agreement Establishing the World Trade Organization was adopted. This decision provides further information on how the Ministerial Conference would deal with requests for acceptance of and accession to the WTO Agreement. The seventh recital of the preamble to the decision provides:

> Recognizing that the WTO Agreement does not distinguish in any way between WTO Members which accepted that Agreement in accordance with Articles XI and XIV and WTO Members which acceded to it in accordance with its Article XII and wishing to ensure that the procedures for accession of the States and separate customs territories which have not become contracting parties to the GATT 1947 as of the date of entry into force of the WTO Agreement are such as to avoid any unnecessary disadvantage or delay for these States and separate customs territories.[32]

It has been suggested that the text of this recital means that 'the terms to be agreed' in Article XII of the WTO Agreement would not allow for the adoption of specific or additional rules commitments in the context of accession negotiations.[33] However, although the recital reiterates that the WTO Agreement itself does not distinguish between original and non-original Members, it also stipulates that there are 'Members which acceded to [the WTO Agreement] *in accordance with its Article XII*'. That provision stipulates, as stated above, that accession may take place 'on the terms to be agreed' between any state or separate customs territory and the WTO. Therefore, neither the text of the article, nor the text of this particular recital should be viewed as imposing any limitation on what these 'terms' may encompass.

3.2.2.6.2 References in the GATT 1994 The General Agreement on Tariffs and Trade 1994 (GATT 1994) sets out the main rules for trade in

---

[32] Decision on Acceptance of and Accession to the Agreement Establishing the World Trade Organization, LT/UR/D-6/1, 15 April 1995.

[33] Qin, Julia Ya (2015), 'The Conundrum of WTO Accession Protocols: In Search of Legality and Legitimacy', *Virginia Journal of International Law* (55) (2), pp. 370–450, at 390 and 443; and Qin (2017), Mind the Gap: Navigating Between the WTO Agreement and Its Accession Protocols.

goods. Its structure is, however, not straightforward.[34] During the Uruguay Round the negotiators did not negotiate an entirely new text containing the basic obligations and main principles that were contained in the General Agreement on Tariffs and Trade 1947 (GATT 1947). Rather they chose to incorporate the provisions of the GATT 1947 by reference into the legal structure of the WTO. Thereto, Paragraph 1 of the Introductory Text of the GATT 1994 states (in relevant part):

> 1. The General Agreement on Tariffs and Trade 1994 ('GATT 1994') shall consist of:
>
> (a) the provisions in the General Agreement on Tariffs and Trade, dated 30 October 1947, annexed to the Final Act Adopted at the Conclusion of the Second Session of the Preparatory Committee of the United Nations Conference on Trade and Employment (excluding the Protocol of Provisional Application), as rectified, amended or modified by the terms of legal instruments which have entered into force before the date of entry into force of the WTO Agreement.

The provisions of the GATT 1947 therefore continue to be used. The Agreement itself, however, was terminated in 1996. It is noteworthy that the drafters of the WTO Agreement deemed it necessary to include a paragraph that explicitly states that the GATT 1994 is legally distinct from the GATT 1947. Article II:4 of the WTO Agreement provides:

> 4. The General Agreement on Tariffs and Trade 1994 as specified in Annex 1A (hereinafter referred to as 'GATT 1994') is legally distinct from the General Agreement on Tariffs and Trade, dated 30 October 1947, annexed to the Final Act Adopted at the Conclusion of the Second Session of the Preparatory Committee of the United Nations Conference on Trade and Employment, as subsequently rectified, amended or modified (hereinafter referred to as 'GATT 1947').

Importantly, the GATT 1994 also refers to protocols of accession. Paragraph 1(b)(ii) of the Introductory Text of the GATT 1994 provides that:

> 1. The General Agreement on Tariffs and Trade 1994 ('GATT 1994') shall consist of:
>
> [...]

---

[34] Van den Bossche and Zdouc (2013), *The Law and Policy of the World Trade Organization*, at 42.

> b) the provisions of the legal instruments set forth below that have entered into force under the GATT 1947 before the date of entry into force of the WTO Agreement:
>
> [...]
>
> (ii) protocols of accession (excluding the provisions (a) concerning provisional application and withdrawal of provisional application and (b) providing that Part II of GATT 1947 shall be applied provisionally to the fullest extent not inconsistent with legislation existing on the date of the Protocol).

It should be noted that the term 'protocols of accession' in Paragraph 1(b)(ii) of the Introductory Text of the GATT 1994 refers to *GATT 1947 protocols of accession*. Through this provision, these instruments have become part of the legal framework of the WTO and they therefore fall within the scope of the WTO Agreement.

3.2.2.6.3 References in the DSU The terms 'protocols of accession' or 'accession protocol' cannot be found in the Understanding on Rules and Procedures Governing the Settlement of Disputes (DSU). There is therefore no unequivocal statement in the DSU that stipulates that protocols of accession or working party reports shall fall under the jurisdiction of the WTO's Dispute Settlement Body (DSB). Rather, Article 1.1 of the DSU provides that:

> The rules and procedures of this Understanding shall apply to disputes brought pursuant to the consultation and dispute settlement provisions of the agreements listed in Appendix 1 to this Understanding (referred to in this Understanding as the 'covered agreements'). The rules and procedures of this Understanding shall also apply to consultations and the settlement of disputes between Members concerning their rights and obligations under the provisions of the Agreement Establishing the World Trade Organization (referred to in this Understanding as the 'WTO Agreement') and of this Understanding taken in isolation or in combination with any other covered agreement.

Appendix 1 of the DSU then lists the covered agreements:

- (A) Agreement Establishing the World Trade Organization
- (B) Multilateral Trade Agreements
- Annex 1A: Multilateral Agreements on Trade in Goods
- Annex 1B: General Agreement on Trade in Services
- Annex 1C: Agreement on Trade-Related Aspects of Intellectual Property Rights
- Annex 2: Understanding on Rules and Procedures Governing the Settlement of Disputes
- (C) Plurilateral Trade Agreements

- Annex 4: Agreement on Trade in Civil Aircraft
- Agreement on Government Procurement
- International Dairy Agreement
- International Bovine Meat Agreement

The applicability of this Understanding to the Plurilateral Trade Agreements shall be subject to the adoption of a decision by the parties to each agreement setting out the terms for the application of the Understanding to the individual agreement, including any special or additional rules or procedures for inclusion in Appendix 2, as notified to the DSB.

Notably, protocols of accession were not explicitly mentioned by the drafters of the DSU as legal texts that would be enforceable by the DSB.[35] The next part of this monograph addresses the question of jurisdiction over, and enforceability of, protocols of accession in more detail.[36]

3.2.3 The 'Accession Package'

The 'Accession Package' consists of the Protocol of Accession, the Working Party Report and the Schedules of Concessions for both trade in goods and trade in services.[37] This section describes the contents and role of these elements in more detail.

3.2.3.1 The Protocol of Accession

The Protocol of Accession is the legal document through which an applicant state formally becomes part of the WTO. According to Article XII:2 WTO Agreement, ultimately it is the General Council/Ministerial Conference that decides upon the issue of accession. The article stipulates that an agreement on the terms of accession shall be approved by a two-thirds majority; however, in practice these decisions have been taken by consensus.[38] The Protocol of Accession is annexed to the decision by the General Council/Ministerial Conference. Williams notes that, 'in adopting the Decision, WTO Members offer terms of accession to the

---

[35] Kennedy, Matthew (2013), 'The Integration of Accession Protocols into the WTO Agreement', *Journal of World Trade* (47) (1), pp. 45–76, at 51.

[36] See below Chapters 4 and 5.

[37] Bhala, Raj K. (2005), *Modern GATT Law: A Treatise on the General Agreement on Tariffs and Trade and Other World Trade Organization Agreements*, First Edition, London, Sweet and Maxwell, Thomson Reuters, at 1118.

[38] On the occasion of Ecuador's accession in 1995, the decision was subject to a vote by postal ballot. See WTO document WT/GC/M/6 of 20 September 1995, Minutes of General Council Meeting held on 31 July 1995, pp. 2–5.

applicant. The applicant also accepts those terms by accepting the Protocol. WTO Members do not, therefore, need to sign the Protocol.'[39] The Protocol of Accession typically consists of three parts. Part I (General) confirms that the applicant will become a Member of the WTO upon the entry into force of the Protocol. More importantly, it stipulates that the applicant will accede to the WTO Agreement as 'rectified, amended or otherwise modified by such legal instruments as may have entered into force before the date of entry into force of this Protocol'. Finally, and crucially for the relationship between the Protocol of Accession and the WTO Agreement, this section stipulates that the Protocol, which shall include the commitments referred to in one of the concluding paragraphs of the Working Party Report (WPR), 'shall be an integral part of the WTO Agreement'. One notable exception to the otherwise generally applicable provisions in Part I of the Protocol of Accession is China.[40] Part I of China's Protocol of Accession contains 18 paragraphs in total. In addition to the general provisions in Paragraph 1, there are 17 paragraphs containing obligations that China agreed to as a condition for its accession to the WTO. Most of these paragraphs begin with the phrase 'China shall', indicating that these obligations require China to act in a particular manner upon accession to the WTO. None of

---

[39] Williams (2008), *A Handbook on Accession to the WTO*, at 47 (footnote omitted).

[40] WTO, Protocol on the Accession of the People's Republic of China, WT/L/432, 23 November 2001. China's accession was a very complex exercise in general. See, for example, Yu-shu, Feng (1988), 'China's Membership of GATT: A Practical Proposal', *Journal of World Trade* (22) (6), pp. 53–70; Qin, Julia Ya (1993), 'China and GATT: Accession Instead of Resumption', *Journal of World Trade* (27) (2), pp. 77–98; Anderson, Kym (1997), 'On the Complexities of China's WTO Accession', *The World Economy* (20) (6), pp. 749–72; Bhala, Raj (2000), 'Enter the Dragon: An Essay on China's WTO Accession Saga', *American University International Law Review* (15) (6), pp. 1469–538; Kong, Qingjiang (2000), 'China's WTO Accession: Commitments and Implications', *Journal of International Economic Law* (3) (4), pp. 655–90; Cai, Wenguo (1992), 'China's GATT Membership: Selected Legal and Political Issues', *Journal of World Trade* (26) (1), pp. 35–61; Clarke, Donald C. (1994), 'GATT Membership for China?', *University of Puget Sound Law Review* (17) (3), pp. 517–31; Clarke, Donald C. (2003), 'China's Legal System and the WTO: Prospects for Compliance', *Washington University Global Studies Law Review* (2), pp. 97–118; Halverson, Karen (2004), 'China's WTO Accession: Economic, Legal and Political Implications', *Boston College International & Comparative Law Review* (27), pp. 319–70; He, Ling-Ling and Sappideen, Razeen (2009), 'Reflections on China's WTO Accession Commitments and Their Observance', *Journal of World Trade* (43) (4), pp. 847–71.

the other 35 protocols of accession contain the same approach. Rather, the obligations that China agreed to in the context of its Protocol of Accession are usually contained in the WPR and then, as outlined earlier, incorporated by reference. In the reports of accession working parties, the obligation the applicant has agreed to is usually followed by the phrase 'the Working Party took note of this (these) commitment(s)'. Part II (Schedules) indicates that the Schedules annexed to the Protocol shall be the relevant Schedule of Concessions and Commitments annexed to the General Agreement on Tariffs and Trade 1994 (GATT 1994) and the Schedule of Specific Commitments annexed to the General Agreement on Trade in Services (GATS). Finally, Part III (Final Provisions) states the date from which the Protocol will be open for acceptance.

3.2.3.2 The Working Party Report

Reports of accession working parties contain the results of the negotiations conducted between the incumbent Members that were part of the working party and the applicant. WPRs are typically structured as follows:

1. Introduction
2. Economic Policies
3. Framework for Making and Enforcing Policies
4. Policies Affecting Trade in Goods
5. Trade-Related Intellectual Property Regime
6. Policies Affecting Trade in Services
7. Transparency
8. Trade Agreements
9. Conclusions

Applicants have made commitments in all of the sections, apart from the introduction and conclusion. The first paragraph of the conclusion lists the paragraphs containing commitments given by the applicant in relation to certain specific matters. This paragraph is referenced in the first Part of the Protocol of Accession. In the third part of this monograph the results of a mapping exercise of all 1520 paragraphs containing 'commitments on certain specific matters' are presented.[41]

---

[41] See below Chapters 5 and 6.

3.2.3.3 Schedules of Concessions

In addition to the Protocol of Accession itself and the WPR, the 'accession package' includes the schedules of concessions for goods and services of the acceding Member. The Schedules are annexed to the Protocol of Accession. These schedules contain the market access commitments that the Member in question has agreed to.

3.2.4 Accession Commitments

In order to arrive at the stage of the accession package, negotiations are held to determine the terms on which the applicant will accede to the WTO.[42] These negotiations take place in four main parts.[43] The negotiations on the commitments to be made in trade in goods and services take place at the bilateral level between the applicant and interested WTO Members.[44] The negotiations on agricultural domestic support and export subsidies take place at the plurilateral level, between the applicant and interested WTO Members.[45] Commitments on Rules are held at the multilateral level between the applicant and the members of the Working Party.[46]

3.2.4.1 Goods commitments

The negotiations on the commitments to be made in the area of trade in goods can be distinguished into i) negotiations on tariff concessions; and ii) negotiations on agricultural support and export subsidies.

---

[42] VanGrasstek, Craig (2014), *The History and Future of the World Trade Organization*, World Trade Organization, WTO Publications, at 122.

[43] Williams (2008), *A Handbook on Accession to the WTO*, at 38.

[44] It should be noted that the scope and depth of the market access commitments made by applicants in the course of their WTO accession negotiations is beyond the scope of this monograph. Inevitably, the level of market access commitments made will depend on the characteristics of the applicant's economy and will be the result of intense negotiations between the applicant and the interested members of the Working Party.

[45] For a detailed discussion on this issue, see Guivarra, Julie-Ann (2015), WTO Accession Negotiations: Trends and Results in Agriculture Plurilaterals, in Dadush, Uri and Osakwe, Chiedu (eds) (2015), *WTO Accessions and Trade Multilateralism: Case Studies and Lessons from the WTO at Twenty*, Cambridge, Cambridge University Press, at 425–38.

[46] Williams (2008), *A Handbook on Accession to the WTO*, at 38–9 (footnote omitted).

3.2.4.1.1 Tariff concessions The negotiations on tariff concessions are in essence a continuation of the accession practice under the GATT 1947. They are conducted in a bilateral setting on the basis of an offer by the applicant and requests from the interested members of the Working Party.

3.2.4.1.2 Agricultural support and export subsidies Agricultural support and export subsidies are among the most contentious issues in WTO law. As part of the application procedure, applicants are required to provide information on the levels of their domestic support measures and of their export subsidies. This information has to be supplied based on the format laid down in the technical note by the Secretariat on 'Information to be Provided on Domestic Support and Export Subsidies in Agriculture'. The note is aimed at helping applicants comply with the relevant notification agreements of the Agreement on Agriculture. Articles 3.2 and 6 of the Agreement prohibit the use of domestic support in favour of agricultural producers in excess of commitment levels specified in schedules. There are three exceptions to this rule:

1. Measures that have no, or at most minimal, trade distortion effects or effects on production and which meet basic and policy-specific criteria and other conditions as set out in Annex 2 of the Agreement on Agriculture; these are known as 'green box' measures;
2. Some measures of assistance, whether direct or indirect, to encourage agricultural and rural development and which are an integral part of the development programmes of developing countries (Article 6.2 Agreement on Agriculture); and
3. Direct payments under production-limiting programmes (Article 6.5 Agreement on Agriculture).

Under the Agreement on Agriculture, the commitments are to be made on the basis of a total Aggregate Measurement of Support (AMS), which is an aggregation of support measures provided on a product-specific basis for those measures that affect only one or a limited number of products, and support measures provided on a non-product-specific basis for other measures.[47] The AMS is defined in Article 1(a) of the Agreement on Agriculture and the Total AMS is defined in Article 1(h). Export subsidies are in principle prohibited under WTO law. Article 3.1(a) of the

[47] Guivarra (2015), WTO Accession Negotiations: Trends and Results in Agriculture Plurilaterals, at 426.

Agreement on Subsidies and Countervailing Measures prohibits 'subsidies contingent, in law or in fact, [...] upon export performance'.[48] Similarly, Article 9.1 of the Agreement on Agriculture provides examples of export subsidies that are subject to reduction commitments.

3.2.4.2 Services commitments

Similarly to the negotiations on tariff concessions, negotiations on services are conducted on the basis of an offer and request approach.[49] It is for the applicant to table an initial services offer that will serve as the basis for negotiations with the interested members of the Working Party. Negotiations are conducted on a bilateral basis. Where concessions have been agreed upon with two or more Members, the WTO Secretariat 'will take the least restrictive of these into the draft schedule', by virtue of the MFN-treatment obligation that is contained in Article II of the GATS.[50] It has been observed that, generally, the more a country has to offer, the more substantial the concessions that will be asked from it.[51]

3.2.4.3 Commitments on rules

In addition to the negotiations on the concessions to be made relating to trade in goods and trade in services, and the reductions of agricultural domestic support and export subsidies to be made by the applicant, the accession negotiations include detailed scrutiny of the applicant's regulatory framework relating to its trade policy. Applicants typically provide 'legislative action plans' that outline the changes that are to be made in order to bring its legislation in conformity with the WTO obligations it is about to undertake. It has now become common practice for applicants to present draft legislation to the Working Party in order to ensure the WTO-consistency of such legislation. The text of the WPR often contains commitments that refer to such legislative action plans. Often these legislative action plans are drawn up to assist applicants in drafting legislation that is compatible with the requirements set out by WTO agreements such as the Agreement on Technical Barriers to Trade (TBT

---

[48] Footnote omitted.

[49] Carzaniga, Antonia, Lim, Aik Hoe and Lee, Juneyoung (2015), Services Market Opening: Salience, Results and Meaning, in Dadush, Uri and Osakwe, Chiedu (eds) (2015), *WTO Accessions and Trade Multilateralism: Case Studies and Lessons from the WTO at Twenty*, Cambridge, Cambridge University Press, at 641–63.

[50] Williams (2008), *A Handbook on Accession to the WTO*, at 44.

[51] Pelc, Krzysztof J. (2011), 'Why Do Some Countries Get Better WTO Accession Terms than Others?', *International Organization* (65) (4), pp. 639–72.

Agreement), the Agreement on the Application of Sanitary and Phytosanitary Measures (SPS Agreement) or the Agreement on the Trade-Related Aspects of Intellectual Property Rights (TRIPS Agreement).

In addition to the legislative action plans that are aimed at ensuring the compatibility of domestic legislation with the WTO agreements, some accession negotiations have sometimes resulted in rules commitments that go beyond the scope of these agreements. Where the WTO agreements do not discipline a certain type of governmental behaviour, in principle WTO Members are free to adopt measures as they deem necessary. However, in some accession negotiations additional rules commitments have been agreed upon that exceed the scope of the WTO Agreement. Consequently, the results of the negotiations on rules commitments have been the most controversial in the academic debate concerning the WTO accession process. The fact that some applicants have had to accept more 'stringent' terms than others in order to be allowed access to the organization has led some practitioners and commentators to argue that the WTO has a two-tiered membership. It cannot be denied that, indeed, the commitments entered into by various applicants sometimes differ. Some acceded Members have accepted rules commitments that are not applicable to original WTO Members, or even to other acceded Members. Ultimately, this fact is the logical outcome of an accession process that grants the freedom to the organization and the applicant to determine 'the terms on which' the latter may accede to the organization. Inevitably the power balance between the organization and most applicants weighs heavily in favour of the organization.[52] Since the applicant is the party that has, in most cases, the most to gain from obtaining membership, it is often willing to accept conditions that are not applicable to other members. So far, however, no study has examined in detail the prevalence and content of these additional 'rule commitments' by applicants.

---

[52] Such commitments have, however, remained confined to the area of trade, and have not expanded to other fields. See Charnovitz, Steve (2007), 'The WTO's Environmental Progress', *Journal of International Economic Law* (10) (3), pp. 685–706, at 691–2, noting that '[t]he accession negotiations routinely demand WTO-plus commitments from applicant countries, but the WTO has not used its bargaining leverage to seek improvements in sustainable development'.

3.3 CONCLUSION

This chapter has explored the institutional characteristics of the WTO and the scope of the WTO Agreement. In the 1980s the Contracting Parties to the GATT 1947 realized that the rules contained in that agreement were no longer sufficient to adequately address the changing nature of international commerce. Moreover, the lack of a proper institutional framework and, in particular, the lack of a (more) formalized form of dispute settlement started to cast its shadow over the multilateral trading system. The Uruguay Round of Multilateral Trade Negotiations eventually led to the establishment of the WTO. The WTO Agreement and its annexes provided for a more elaborate set of rules and laid down a new institutional structure. The enlarged scope of the WTO, as compared to the GATT 1947, meant that states that were still outside of the multilateral trading system during the mid-1990s – and who had the intention of becoming a part of it – had to enter into an accession process that involved more than the simple negotiation of tariff concessions. Applicants now not only have to accept the basic obligations contained in the WTO Agreement, but also have to negotiate tariff concessions for trade in goods and trade in services, commitments on the reduction of domestic agricultural support and export subsidies, as well as rules commitments that determine the way in which domestic legislation has to be amended in order to conform to the obligations laid down by the WTO Agreement. The obligations that are contained in the WTO Agreement and its annexes will, from this point onwards, be referred to as the 'baseline obligations' that all Members of the WTO are bound by. As a result of the accession process as described in Chapter 2 and this chapter, WTO Members that have joined the organization through the procedure as described by Article XII of the WTO Agreement have, in some instances, made commitments in their protocols of accession that exceed (or are more stringent than) the obligations laid down in the WTO Agreement. In Part III of this contribution the results of a detailed mapping exercise of this phenomenon are presented. First, however, the next chapter of this monograph addresses the exact location of protocols of accession in the WTO legal framework.

PART II

The status of protocols of accession in the legal framework of the WTO

4. The status of protocols of accession in the legal framework of the WTO

4.1 INTRODUCTION

In Chapter 2 it was explained that there were two methods of becoming a GATT Contracting Party in the GATT era: first, former colonies could succeed their colonial power as GATT Contracting Party through the procedure laid down by Article XXVI:5(c) GATT 1947; second, states and customs territories could seek to 'accede' to the GATT through the procedure laid down by Article XXXIII GATT 1947. Upon the establishment of the WTO, membership could be obtained by GATT Contracting Parties and the European Communities, under what was called 'original membership'.[1] Non-GATT Contracting Parties have the possibility of seeking accession to the WTO through Article XII of the WTO Agreement, which provides for non-original membership. Chapter 3 highlighted that the outcome of the accession negotiations is contained in an 'accession package' which serves as the 'entry fee' to the multilateral trading system.[2] The legal status of the package, which consists of a protocol of accession, schedules of commitments and the working party report, is not clearly defined in the WTO Agreement. As a result of this, questions have arisen as to the enforceability of commitments that are contained in the accession package. In the absence of arguments to the contrary, WTO dispute settlement panels and the Appellate Body have consistently held that the commitments made by acceding states and customs territories in the course of accession negotiations can be enforced in WTO dispute settlement proceedings.[3] In the previous

[1] Article XI.1 of the WTO Agreement.

[2] Qin, Julia Ya (2017), Mind the Gap: Navigating Between the WTO Agreement and Its Accession Protocols, in Elsig, Manfred, Hoekman, Bernard and Pauwelyn, Joost (2017), *Assessing the World Trade Organization: Fit for Purpose?*, Cambridge, Cambridge University Press, at 249. Qin criticizes the 'entry fee' theory.

[3] Kennedy, Matthew (2013), 'The Integration of Accession Protocols into the WTO Agreement', *Journal of World Trade* (47) (1), pp. 45–76, at 49.

chapter it has been established that there are little to no references to either the terms 'Protocol of Accession', 'Working Party Report on Accession' or 'Accession Package' in the WTO Agreement, including the General Agreement on Tariffs and Trade 1994 and the Understanding on the Rules and Procedures Governing the Settlement of Disputes (DSU). The purpose of the first part of this chapter therefore is to analyse the legal grounds on which protocols of accession have been enforced in WTO dispute settlement proceedings. To this end, the chapter will start with a historical analysis of relevant GATT panel reports that dealt with documents related to the accession of GATT Contracting Parties. In the subsequent section, the rules and procedures governing the settlement of disputes in the WTO will be examined in more detail. In addition to an analysis of the rules concerning applicable law and jurisdiction, a separate section will discuss the role the Vienna Convention on the Law of Treaties (1969) plays in the reports of WTO panels and the Appellate Body.[4] Subsequently, the accession-related disputes are examined in detail. It is observed that the Appellate Body has adopted a pragmatic approach and has eschewed making general statements on the enforceability of protocols of accession. In response to this, the subsequent section presents a legal theory of enforceability. The establishment of this theory involves a discussion of the academic criticism on the approach adopted by panels and the Appellate Body in respect of the issue of enforceability is presented and discussed. The question is raised whether this issue has been completely settled, or whether there remains a possibility that an acceded Member, facing a complaint in which a violation of one of its protocol of accession commitments is alleged, can successfully challenge the jurisdiction of the panel examining the case. Finally, in the concluding paragraph of the first part of this chapter the findings are summarized and presented with the objective of enabling a discussion on the relationship between individual protocol of accession commitments and the WTO Agreement in the second part of this chapter. A highly debated question is whether the finding of enforceability respects the balance between the rights and obligations of original and non-original Members of the WTO. This chapter examines the relationship between certain individual commitments made in protocols of accession and the WTO Agreement. First, the legal basis for the creation of these additional rules commitments will be established. Second, a

[4] Vienna Convention on the Law of Treaties (23 May 1969) 1155 UNTS 331; 8 ILM 679 (1969); 63 AJIL 875 (1969), entered into force 27 January 1980 (Vienna Convention).

number of issues arising from the relationship between protocols of accession and the WTO Agreement will be examined. The major share of this chapter will be devoted to the issue of the availability of the general exceptions contained in Article XX of the GATT 1994 for the justification of measures that prima facie appear to be inconsistent with a commitment made in a protocol of accession. This particular issue cannot be addressed without examining some of the institutional aspects of the WTO, including the relationship between the covered agreements. Are there examples in which an obligation or a right contained in one agreement affects the rights and obligations contained in another agreement? Are there examples of agreements that specifically allow for recourse to provisions of another covered agreement? How does the Appellate Body's characterization of protocols of accession as 'integral parts' of the WTO Agreement impact the institutional balance between original and non-original Members of the WTO? The general exceptions contained in Article XX of the GATT 1994 can serve as justification for measures that would otherwise be GATT-inconsistent. After a general discussion on the substance of Article XX of the GATT 1994, we turn to its scope of application. Thereto, the availability of the general exceptions in Article XX GATT 1994 for the justification of non-GATT violations is addressed. A number of covered agreements contain references to Article XX of the GATT 1994. The question is to what extent and on what conditions the article can be used to remedy violations of non-GATT 1994 provisions. This analysis is conducted by examining the text of the covered agreements and, thereafter, by reviewing the case law of the panels and the Appellate Body in cases such as *China – Publications and Audiovisual Products*, *China – Raw Materials* and *China – Rare Earths*. This chapter concludes by answering the question whether the approach adopted by panels and the Appellate Body respects the balance between rights and obligations of new WTO Members. Second, an examination of the commitments that provide for rights or derogations to WTO Members (other than the acceding Member) is provided. Some commitments allow the WTO membership to act in a way that, presumably, would be inconsistent with their WTO obligations in the absence of the commitment in the protocol of accession. Third, the commitments that entail the foregoing of rights on the part of the acceding Member are examined. Although relatively rare, they constitute an important example of how accession negotiations may alter the balance between rights and obligations of the WTO membership. Fourth, the impact of commitments contained in protocols of accession on WTO Members other than the acceding Member is examined.

4.2 THE ENFORCEABILITY OF GATT AND WTO PROTOCOLS OF ACCESSION

4.2.1 Tracing the Roots: GATT Protocols of Accession

GATT instruments of accession never attracted a lot of attention in scholarship. Chapter 2 discussed the evolution of GATT membership, but did not fully address the outcome of the GATT accession process.[5] This section presents ten GATT disputes in which instruments of accession played a role.[6] Considering that the primary focus of the GATT was on the elimination of tariff barriers to international trade, the scope of the accession instruments was also relatively limited. Consequently, the relationship between the instruments and the GATT 1947 itself was not particularly problematic. The main issue that many of the GATT panel reports dealt with was that of the 'grandfather clause' – or the existing legislation exception – which was included in most GATT protocols of accession. Nevertheless, the GATT panel reports in which GATT accession instruments were at issue provide useful historic background information about the relationship between old and new parties to the multilateral trading system. An analysis of these reports will help to better understand why protocols of accession became a contentious issue in WTO dispute settlement practice.

In the first GATT accession dispute Uruguay complained against measures adopted by 15 Contracting Parties.[7] In the case of the complaints against Germany and Switzerland, the respondents noted that the challenged measures were justified under, or did not conflict with, the

[5] Beslać, Petra and Osakwe, Chiedu (2015), The Evolution of the GATT/WTO Accession Protocol: Legal Tightening and Domestic Ratification, in Dadush, Uri and Osakwe, Chiedu (eds) (2015), *WTO Accessions and Trade Multilateralism: Case Studies and Lessons from the WTO at Twenty*, Cambridge, Cambridge University Press, 348–93. In their contribution of the evolution of the GATT/WTO accession protocol, Beslać and Osakwe discuss the general features of the GATT accession process and the GATT accession protocols that emanated from this process. They refer to the 'streamlined procedures' that characterized this process, as well as the fact that the 'four-part structure of the protocol text … has provided the basic architecture for almost all subsequent Accession Protocols, including those under the WTO'.

[6] For an overview of GATT dispute settlement practice, see, for example, Davey, William J. (1987), 'Dispute Settlement in GATT', *Fordham International Law Journal* (11) (1), pp. 51–109.

[7] GATT Panel Report, *Uruguay – Recourse to Article XXIII.*

provisions of the instruments governing the accession of both countries to the GATT 1947. With respect to the German measure the Panel noted that:

> in the view of the Government of the Federal Republic of Germany, the import permit requirements and quotas as applied to meat and refined edible oils were justifiable in terms of the Torquay Protocol, under which the Federal Republic of Germany provisionally applied the GATT, because they resulted from the administration of marketing laws in force prior to Germany's accession.[8]

With respect to the Swiss measure the Panel noted that:

> Switzerland's relations with contracting parties were governed by the Declaration on the Provisional Accession of the Swiss Confederation to the General Agreement. Under the terms of the Declaration, Switzerland is permitted to maintain restrictions pursuant to certain laws which are specified in paragraph 1(b) of the Declaration. The Panel further noted that, in the opinion of the Government of Switzerland, the measures maintained either did not conflict with the provisions of the GATT or were provided for under the Declaration of Provisional Accession of Switzerland.[9]

The second GATT Panel Report in which GATT accession instruments played an explicit role is *Jamaica – Margins of Preference*.[10] In this dispute the United States had raised the issue of an increase in the margins of preference by Jamaica, upon its independence from the United Kingdom on 6 August 1962. Jamaica was one of the former colonies that had joined the GATT under the procedure laid down by Article XXVI:5(c) GATT 1947. Essentially the US requested Jamaica to return to the margins of preferences as applicable on 10 April 1947. Ultimately the Panel suggested that the Contracting Parties would take a decision that would 'change with respect to Jamaica the base date referred to in paragraph 4 of Article I from 10 April 1947, to 1 August 1962', in accordance with Article XXV:5 GATT 1947.[11] Similar to the situation in *Uruguay – Recourse to Article XXIII*, in *Spain – Soybean Oil* the issue arose whether the 'grandfather clause' in the form of a provision in the Spanish Protocol of Application permitted Spain to maintain GATT-inconsistent legislation that was adopted prior to its accession to

---

8 GATT Panel Report, *Uruguay – Recourse to Article XXIII*, at 31.
9 GATT Panel Report, *Uruguay – Recourse to Article XXIII*, at 48.
10 GATT Panel Report, *Jamaica – Margins of Preference*.
11 GATT Panel Report, *Jamaica – Margins of Preference*, para. 15.

the GATT 1947.[12] The US argued that the restrictions on the sale of soybean oil were inconsistent with Spain's obligations under the GATT and that they were not exempt from Spain's GATT obligations by virtue of the 'grandfather clause' (or the 'existing legislation clause'). The grandfather clause, typically found in a Protocol of Provisional Application (PPA) stipulates that 'Part II of the General Agreement will be applied to the fullest extent not inconsistent with legislation which existed on [...] the date of the Protocol providing for such accession.' Although the Panel ultimately found that Spain's measures did not violate the GATT, it nevertheless inquired into the question as to whether the measure would have been exempt from Spain's GATT obligations.

> The Panel noted that such a formula was customary on accession to the General Agreement and that Spain had it inserted in its Protocol of Accession. The Panel further noted that the 'existing legislation' clause had in past GATT practice been agreed to mean that 'a measure is so permitted, provided that the legislation on which it is based is by its terms or expressed intent of a mandatory character – that is, it imposes on the executive authority requirements which cannot be modified by executive action.' It also noted that the legislation invoked by Spain in this matter was in existence on the date of Spain's accession to the GATT and at the date of the Panel's examination.[13]

Eventually the Panel found, in *obiter dictum*, that 'the legislation invoked could not be considered to be of the kind that was covered by the "existing legislation" exception'.[14] In *US – Manufacturing Clause* the European Communities alleged that the manufacturing clause, which was part of US copyright legislation, infringed upon the US's GATT obligations.[15] The GATT Panel noted that the:

> central point of difference between the two parties to the dispute related to whether the Manufacturing Clause, despite the postponement by legislation of July 1982 of the expiry date of 1 July 1982 inserted in the Clause in 1976, could still qualify as 'existing legislation' under the Protocol of Provisional Application.[16]

It found that 'the Protocol of Provisional Application did not authorize contracting parties to enact legislation increasing the degree of GATT

---

[12] GATT Panel Report, *Spain – Soyabean Oil*.
[13] GATT Panel Report, *Spain – Soyabean Oil*, para. 4.10.
[14] GATT Panel Report, *Spain – Soyabean Oil*, para. 4.11.
[15] GATT Panel Report, *US – Manufacturing Clause*.
[16] GATT Panel Report, *US – Manufacturing Clause*, para. 35.

inconsistency of "existing legislation.'"[17] In *Norway – Apples and Pears*, the GATT Panel was asked to assess whether Norway's system of restrictive import licensing was covered by the 'existing legislation' clause.[18] Norway did not contest that the system was inconsistent with Article XI GATT 1947, but solely argued that this violation could be justified under the clause contained in the PPA. After a series of disputes in which this issue had been raised, the GATT Panel now was asked to provide clearer guidance on the conditions that had to be fulfilled in order to successfully invoke the 'existing legislation' clause. Bearing this in mind, the Panel started by revisiting the origins of this type of clause. Considering the importance of its statement, it is provided here in its entirety:

> The Panel noted in the first place that paragraph 1(b) of the Protocol served a well determined purpose in a particular historical situation. It was to enable, in 1947, governments to accept the obligations of Part II of the General Agreement without having to adjust their domestic legislation. The drafters of the Protocol expected the General Agreement to be superseded soon by the ITO Charter and they felt that legislative changes should not be required at that time because such changes would have delayed the acceptance of the obligations under the General Agreement and could have prejudged the outcome of the negotiations on the Charter (see Summary Record of the Preparatory Committee of the United Nations Conference on Trade and Employment, E/PC/T/TAC/SR 1, 2 and 6). In the light of this purpose of the existing legislation clause, the Panel considered that it would not be justified to give this clause four decades after the entry into force of the Protocol an interpretation that would extend its functions beyond those it was originally designed to serve.[19]

The GATT Panel subsequently assessed the interpretation that had been given to the term 'existing legislation' by earlier GATT panels. It found that in order for legislation to qualify as 'existing legislation' in the sense of the PPA, such legislation must be i) legislation in a formal sense; ii) predate the Protocol; and iii) be mandatory in character by its terms or expressed intent.[20] Ultimately, the GATT Panel found that Norway's 1934 Act was not mandatory in character and that therefore the 'existing legislation' clause was not applicable in this particular dispute.[21] Less than a year after the GATT Panel in *Norway – Apples and Pears* had

17 GATT Panel Report, *US – Manufacturing Clause*, para. 39.
18 GATT Panel Report, *Norway – Apples and Pears*.
19 GATT Panel Report, *Norway – Apples and Pears*, para. 5.5
20 GATT Panel Report, *Norway – Apples and Pears*, para. 5.7.
21 GATT Panel Report, *Norway – Apples and Pears*, para. 6.1.

circulated its Report, the GATT Panel in *Thailand – Cigarettes* was asked to determine whether Thailand's Tobacco Act of 1966 fell within the scope of the existing legislation exception.[22] The US had complained that the restrictions on the imports of cigarettes that were based on this Act were inconsistent with Article XI of the GATT 1947. Thailand, in addition to its argument that the alleged violation of Article XI GATT 1947 could be justified by Article XX(b) of the GATT 1947, argued that the Act fell within the scope of the existing legislation clause as contained in its PPA.[23] In order to assess Thailand's claim with regard to the 'existing legislation' clause, the Panel applied the three-tier analysis as developed by the GATT Panel in *Norway – Apples and Pears*. It referenced a 1949 Working Party Report that stated that the existing legislation clause would only be applicable in respect of 'legislation which is of a mandatory character by its terms or expressed intent – that is, it imposes on the executive authority requirements which cannot be modified by executive action'.[24] The Panel, in referencing Section 27 of the Tobacco Act of 1966 dismissed Thailand's argument regarding the mandatory nature of the Act. It held that the Act 'did not, by its terms or expressed intent, impose on the Thai executive authorities a requirement to restrict imports that could not be modified by executive action. On the contrary, Section 27 of the Act explicitly gives the Thai executive authorities the power to grant import licences.'[25] Consequently, the fact that there was discretion on the side of the executive meant that the legislation in question was not mandatory in nature. Similarly to the previous disputes dealing with the 'existing legislation' clause, the GATT Panel in *EEC – Bananas II* was asked whether legislation that was inconsistent with Article XI GATT 1947 could be justified under this clause in the EEC's PPA.[26] Again, the GATT Panel extensively relied on the findings made by the Panel in *Norway – Apples and Pears* in order to find that the legislation in question could not be considered 'mandatory'.[27] Consequently, the respondents could not rely on the 'existing legislation' clause in order to justify their GATT-inconsistent legislation.

---

[22] GATT Panel Report, *Thailand – Cigarettes.*

[23] GATT Panel Report, *Thailand – Cigarettes*, para. 12.

[24] GATT Panel Report, *Thailand – Cigarettes*, para. 83; GATT Document, Working Party on 'Notifications of existing measures and procedural questions' (BISD III/49, para. 99 at 62; approved by the Contracting Parties on 10 August 1949).

[25] GATT Panel Report, *Thailand – Cigarettes*, para. 83.

[26] GATT Panel Report, *EEC – Bananas II.*

[27] GATT Panel Report, *EEC – Bananas II*, para. 356.

GATT dispute settlement practice in relation to new GATT Contracting Parties thus mostly dealt with the issue of whether, and under which conditions, legislation that had been enacted prior to the state or customs territory in question obtaining GATT membership could be considered as falling within the scope of the 'existing legislation' clause as incorporated in PPAs. The next section deals with the way in which WTO protocols of accession have been featured in WTO dispute settlement proceedings. It starts with an analysis of the WTO's dispute settlement system from an institutional and procedural perspective, examining, inter alia, jurisdiction, applicable law and the interpretative techniques that have been used.

4.2.2 WTO Dispute Settlement: The Enforceability of WTO Protocols of Accession

The WTO dispute settlement system is often heralded as the jewel in the crown of the WTO.[28] It is widely regarded as one of the most effective and well-functioning international dispute settlement systems.[29] In fact, it is sometimes argued that the success of the dispute settlement pillar of the WTO poses a threat to the negotiating arm of the organization, at least to the extent that in the absence of new rules agreed upon by Members, the adjudicative organs of the WTO are increasingly called upon to decide on issues that are beyond the scope of the WTO Agreement.[30] This in turn leads to concerns in respect of the express warnings against acts of 'judicial activism' as found in Articles 3.2 and

---

[28] See, for example, WTO (1997), The Future Path of the Multilateral Trading System, Speech by former D-G Renato Ruggiero, Seoul, 17 April. Available at https://www.wto.org/english/news_e/sprr_e/seoul_e.htm (last accessed at 1 June 2017).

[29] Van Damme, Isabelle (2010), 'Treaty Interpretation by the WTO Appellate Body', *European Journal of International Law* (21) (3), pp. 605–48, at 648.

[30] See, inter alia, Shaffer, Gregory, Elsig, Manfred and Puig, Sergio (2016), 'The Extensive (but Fragile) Authority of the WTO Appellate Body, Law and Contemporary Problems', *Law and Contemporary Problems* (79), pp. 237–73; Shlomo-Agon, Sivan (2015), 'Clearing the Smoke: The Legitimation of Judicial Power at the WTO', *Journal of World Trade* (49) (4), pp. 539–90, at 568. Shlomo-Agon references comments made by a staff member of the Appellate Body (AB) Secretariat who noted that 'the AB does not make policy', 'this is what the negotiators do', the AB 'interprets the law' and 'would never overlook the treaty provisions'.

19.2 of the DSU.[31] Additionally, the increased workload of the dispute settlement system leads to an increased burden on the legal staff of the WTO Secretariat.[32] In this section the WTO dispute settlement system is examined with a particular focus on disputes that have involved acceded Members and their protocols of accession. First, the legal basis for WTO dispute settlement, in the form of the Understanding on the Rules and Procedures Governing the Settlement of Disputes (Dispute Settlement Understanding, or DSU), is examined. What is the scope of the jurisdiction that has been conferred upon the institutions that feature in WTO dispute settlement proceedings? What is the applicable law in these proceedings? To what extent can WTO dispute settlement organs rely on sources of law that originate outside of the WTO in order to assist them in interpreting certain provisions? What role does the Vienna Convention play in the interpretative techniques used by panels and the Appellate Body?[33]

---

[31] Jackson, John H. (2011), Modern Approaches to Treaty Interpretation, in Govaere, Inge, Quick, Reinhard and Bronckers, Marco (eds) (2011), *Trade and Competition Law in the EU and Beyond*, Cheltenham, UK and Northampton, MA, USA, Edward Elgar, pp. 187–93. Jackson notes that the fear for judicial overreach should not be overstated and that 'too much rigidity' in terms of textualism also has its defects.

[32] WTO (2014), Azevêdo Says Success of WTO Dispute Settlement Brings Urgent Challenges, 26 September. Available at https://www.wto.org/english/news_e/spra_e/spra32_e.htm (last accessed at 1 June 2017). Noting, inter alia, that '[u]nder the current situation the 7 member AB can handle around 10–12 appeals at most per year. That's stretching the envelope. And this is with AB Members working almost full-time. This operational cap is thus simply not enough given the level of demand.' See also WTO (2015), Azevêdo Seeks WTO Members' Views on How to Meet Increasing Demand for Dispute Settlement, 28 October. Available at https://www.wto.org/english/news_e/spra_e/spra94_e.htm (last accessed at 1 June 2017).

[33] See, in general and in addition to the aforementioned contributions, International Law Commission, Third Report on Subsequent Agreements and Subsequent Practice in Relation to the Interpretation of Treaties, UN Doc. A/CN.4/683 (7 April 2015) (prepared by Special Rapporteur Georg Nolte); Aust, Anthony (2007), *Modern Treaty Law and Practice*, Second Edition, New York, Cambridge University Press; Brownlie, Ian (2003), *Principles of Public International Law*, Sixth Edition, Oxford, Oxford University Press; McNair, Lord (1961), *The Law of Treaties*, 2003 Reprint, Oxford, Oxford University Press; Nolte, Georg (ed.) (2013), *Treaties and Subsequent Practice*, Oxford, Oxford University Press; Villiger, Mark E. (2009), *Commentary on the 1969 Vienna Convention on the Law of Treaties*, Leiden, Martinus Nijhoff; Murphy, Sean (2013), The Relevance of Subsequent Agreement and Subsequent Practice for the Interpretation of Treaties, in Nolte, Georg (ed.) (2013), *Treaties and Subsequent*

4.2.2.1 The DSU

The establishment of the WTO in 1995 coincided with the conclusion of the Understanding on the Rules and Procedures Governing the Settlement of Disputes (or the DSU) as Annex 2 to the WTO Agreement.[34] The DSU provided the multilateral trading system with a much more enhanced and well-developed institutional framework for the settlement of disputes as compared to the system that prevailed under the WTO's predecessor, the GATT 1947. In this section the concepts of jurisdiction and applicable law as they apply in WTO dispute settlement are discussed.

4.2.2.1.1 Jurisdiction The scope of WTO dispute settlement is defined by Article 1 of the DSU which provides:

> The rules and procedures of this Understanding shall apply to disputes brought pursuant to the consultation and dispute settlement provisions of the agreements listed in Appendix 1 to this Understanding (referred to in this Understanding as the 'covered agreements'). The rules and procedures of this Understanding shall also apply to consultations and the settlement of disputes between Members concerning their rights and obligations under the provisions of the Agreement Establishing the World Trade Organization (referred to in this Understanding as the 'WTO Agreement') and of this Understanding taken in isolation or in combination with any other covered agreement.

Appendix 1 provides that the 'covered agreements' mentioned in Article 1 of the DSU are i) Agreement Establishing the World Trade Organization; ii) Multilateral Trade Agreements such as those included in

---

Practice, Oxford, Oxford University Press, 82–94; Murphy, Sean D. (2015), 'Identification of Customary International Law and Other Topics: The Sixty-Seventh Session of the International Law Commission', *The American Journal of International Law* (109) (4), pp. 822–44; Abi-Saab, Georges (2010), The Appellate Body and Treaty Interpretation, in Fitzmaurice, Malgosia, Elias, Olufemi and Merkouris, Panos (eds) (2010), *Treaty Interpretation and the Vienna Convention on the Law of Treaties: 30 Years On*, Leiden, Nijhoff; Stern, Brigitte (2010), Interpretation in International Trade Law, in Fitzmaurice, Malgosia, Elias, Olufemi and Merkouris, Panos (eds) (2010), *Treaty Interpretation and the Vienna Convention on the Law of Treaties: 30 Years On*, Leiden, Nijhoff, pp. 111–28; Van Damme, Isabelle (2009), *Treaty Interpretation by the WTO Appellate Body*, Oxford, Oxford University Press; Marceau, Gabrielle (2006), Balance and Coherence by the WTO Appellate Body: Who Could Do Better?, in Sacerdoti, Giorgio, Yanovich, Alan and Bohanes, Jan (eds) (2006), *The WTO at Ten: The Contribution of the Dispute Settlement System*, Cambridge, Cambridge University Press, at 326.

[34] Understanding on Rules and Procedures Governing the Settlement of Disputes, 1869 U.N.T.S. 401, entered into force 1 January 1995 (DSU).

Annex 1A: Multilateral Agreements on Trade in Goods, Annex 1B: General Agreement on Trade in Services, Annex 1C: Agreement on Trade-Related Aspects of Intellectual Property Rights and Annex 2: Understanding on Rules and Procedures Governing the Settlement of Disputes; and iii) Plurilateral Trade Agreements, such as those mentioned in Annex 4 to the WTO Agreement. Note that Annex 1A was amended by means of a Protocol of Amendment to insert the Agreement on Trade Facilitation into that Annex. Thereby the Agreement on Trade Facilitation has been made part of the 'covered agreements' and is henceforth enforceable under the DSU. Notably, this approach was, as will be established below, not adopted in respect of protocols of accession.

Article 2 of the DSU establishes the Dispute Settlement Body (DSB) and bestows upon it the authority to 'establish panels, adopt panel and Appellate Body reports, maintain surveillance of implementation of rulings and recommendations, and authorize suspension of concessions and other obligations under the covered agreements'. Article 3.2 of the DSU subsequently makes clear that the object and purpose of the WTO's dispute settlement system is twofold. It serves i) 'to preserve the rights and obligations of Members under the covered agreements', and ii) 'to clarify the existing provisions of those agreements in accordance with customary rules of interpretation of public international law'. Further, '[r]ecommendations and rulings of the DSB cannot add to or diminish the rights and obligations provided in the covered agreements'. The compulsory and exclusive nature of the jurisdiction of the WTO's dispute settlement is incorporated in Article 23.1 of the DSU which provides that in the event of a dispute WTO Members 'shall have recourse to, and abide by, the rules and procedures of this Understanding'. A final article that could be relevant in this regard is Article 11 of the DSU, which requires panels to 'make an objective assessment of the matter before it, including an objective assessment of the facts of the case and the applicability of and conformity with the relevant covered agreements'.

4.2.2.1.2 Applicable law Article 3.2 of the DSU does not mention the concept of 'applicable law':

> There is no single test to answer the question of how much other international law, apart from the WTO covered agreements, is part of the applicable law. It is a matter to be decided by WTO members and, in the absence of such a decision, it is a test to be designed by panels and the Appellate Body. The covered agreements are obviously part of the applicable law in WTO dispute

> settlement. But the WTO covered agreements are incomplete, and sometimes it becomes necessary to apply other international law.[35]

As mentioned in the previous section, the scope of the jurisdiction of the WTO's dispute settlement system is limited to the 'covered agreements' (the agreements listed in Appendix 1). In general terms this means that disputes arising under other – non-WTO – sources of international law cannot be brought before the DSB.[36] Protocols of accession and accession working party reports are not listed under Appendix 1. Consequently, they cannot be considered to be 'covered agreements' in the sense of the DSU. This raises the question as to what the legal basis is for the adjudication of disputes that arise from commitments contained in the accession package. This question will be addressed by examining how this issue has been dealt with in the relevant reports of panels and the Appellate Body.

4.2.2.1.3 The DSU and the Vienna Convention Article 3.2 of the DSU provides the WTO's Dispute Settlement Body and the organs involved in WTO settlement with the authority 'to clarify the existing provisions of those agreements in accordance with customary rules of interpretation of public international law'. In its first ever Report, the WTO's Appellate Body affirmed that some rules contained in the Vienna Convention form part of 'the customary rules of interpretation of public international law'.[37] More precisely, it held that the general rule of treaty interpretation as contained in Article 31 of the Vienna Convention forms part of this body of customary rules of interpretation.[38] Consequently, although the applicable law of the dispute settlement system of the WTO is confined to the 'covered agreements' listed in Appendix 1 of the DSU, the direction contained in Article 3.2 of the DSU reveals 'a measure of recognition that the General Agreement is not to be read in clinical isolation from public international law'.[39]

---

35 Van Damme (2010), Treaty Interpretation by the WTO Appellate Body, at 647.

36 Wouters, Jan, Coppens, D. and Geraets, D. (2012), The Influence of General Principles of Law, in Gaines, Sanford E., Olsen, Britte Egelund and Sørensen, Karsten Engsig (eds), *Liberalizing Trade – in the EU and the WTO – a Legal Comparison*, Cambridge, Cambridge University Press, pp. 43–74, at 46.

37 Appellate Body Report, *US – Gasoline*, at 17.

38 Article 31.1 Vienna Convention provides: 'A treaty shall be interpreted in good faith in accordance with the ordinary meaning to be given to the terms of the treaty in their context and in the light of its object and purpose.'

39 Appellate Body Report, *US – Gasoline*, at 17.

4.2.2.2 WTO dispute settlement practice involving protocols of accession

The first WTO Member to accede under the procedure laid down by Article XII of the WTO Agreement was Ecuador on 21 January 1996. However, it took until March 2006 for a complaint to be filed against an acceded Member based on an alleged violation of its accession protocol commitments. Up until October 2017, 33 requests for consultations cited the alleged violation of a commitment contained in a protocol of accession.[40] All but five of these disputes have featured China as either the complainant or respondent.[41] This section provides a brief discussion of all relevant disputes so as to allow for a detailed analysis of the way in which protocols of accession have been interpreted by panels and the Appellate Body in the next section. That final section of this chapter will provide an overview of the critique on the Appellate Body case law relating to protocols of accession and their status in the legal framework of the WTO.

To date, there have been 28 disputes involving China in which the measure at issue was allegedly inconsistent with one or more of the provisions of China's Protocol of Accession.[42] In seven of these disputes

---

[40] See WTO, Disputes by Agreement. Available at https://www.wto.org/english/tratop_e/dispu_e/dispu_agreements_index_e.htm?id=A30 (last accessed at 1 June 2017).

[41] In one dispute the alleged violation of an accession protocol commitment was only included in the request for the establishment of a panel, and was not yet part of the request for consultations. See Request for the Establishment of a Panel by Ukraine, Armenia – Measures Affecting the Importation and Internal Sale of Cigarettes and Alcoholic Beverages, WT/DS411/2/Rev.1, 8 October 2010. In the other disputes involving an accession protocol commitment, Viet Nam challenged a US anti-dumping investigation on shrimp. See United States – Anti-Dumping Measures on Certain Shrimp from Viet Nam, WT/DS404/1, 4 February 2010. The most recent request for consultations citing a provision of a protocol of accession is Ukraine – Measures relating to Trade in Goods and Services, WT/DS525/1, 1 June 2017.

[42] The relevant disputes are China – Measures Affecting Imports of Automobile Parts (Complainants: European Communities, United States and Canada) (DS339, DS340 and DS342), China – Certain Measures Granting Refunds, Reductions or Exemptions from Taxes and Other Payments (Complainants: United States and Mexico) (DS358, DS359), China – Measures Affecting Trading Rights and Distribution Services for Certain Publications and Audiovisual Entertainment Products (Complainant: United States) (DS363), China – Measures Affecting Financial Information Services and Foreign Financial Information Suppliers (Complainants: United States and Canada) (DS373, DS378), United States – Definitive Anti-Dumping and Countervailing Duties on Certain

a Report was issued by the Panel.[43] In four of these disputes China acted as the respondent. In the three remaining disputes, China challenged measures by the EU or the US that it alleged were inconsistent with one of the provisions incorporated in China's Protocol of Accession. It should be noted at the outset that the discussion of the disputes below focuses only on the discussion of the relationship between protocols of accession and the WTO Agreement by panels and the Appellate Body. It does not deal with the substantive issues of each particular dispute since those

---

Products from China (Complainant: China) (DS379), China – Grants, Loans and Other Incentives (Complainants: United States, Mexico and Guatemala) (DS387, DS388 and DS390), China – Measures Related to the Exportation of Various Raw Materials (Complainants: United States, European Communities and Mexico) (DS394, DS395 and DS398), European Communities – Definitive Anti-Dumping Measures on Certain Iron or Steel Fasteners from China (Complainant: China) (DS397), United States – Measures Affecting Imports of Certain Passenger Vehicle and Light Truck Tyres from China (Complainant: China) (DS399), European Union – Anti-Dumping Measures on Certain Footwear from China (Complainant: China) (DS405), China – Measures Concerning Wind Power Equipment (Complainant: United States) (DS419), China – Measures Related to the Exportation of Rare Earths, Tungsten and Molybdenum (Complainants: United States, European Union and Japan) (DS431, DS432, DS433), United States – Countervailing Duty Measures on Certain Products from China (Complainant: China) (DS437), China – Certain Measures Affecting the Automobile and Automobile-Parts Industries (Complainant: United States) (DS450), China – Measures Relating to the Production and Exportation of Apparel and Textile Products (Complainant: Mexico) (DS451); China – Tax Measures Concerning Certain Domestically Produced Aircraft (Complainant: United States) (DS501); China – Export Duties on Certain Raw Materials (Complainant: United States) (DS508); China – Duties and Other Measures Concerning the Exportation of Certain Raw Materials (Complainant: European Union) (DS509); and China – Tariff Rate Quotas for Certain Agricultural Products (DS517).

[43] In China – Certain Measures Granting Refunds, Reductions or Exemptions from Taxes and Other Payments (Complainants: United States and Mexico) (DS358, DS359) and China – Measures Affecting Financial Information Services and Foreign Financial Information Suppliers (Complainants: United States and Canada) (DS373, DS378) a mutually agreed solution was reached, and the dispute was withdrawn. China – Grants, Loans and Other Incentives (Complainants: United States, Mexico and Guatemala) (DS387, DS388 and DS390), China – Measures Concerning Wind Power Equipment (Complainant: United States) (DS419), China – Certain Measures Affecting the Automobile and Automobile-Parts Industries (Complainant: United States) (DS450), China – Measures Relating to the Production and Exportation of Apparel and Textile Products (Complainant: Mexico) (DS451) and China – Tax Measures Concerning Certain Domestically Produced Aircraft (Complainant: United States) (DS501) are still 'in consultations'.

issues relate to the commitments that have been made in protocols of accession, which are dealt with in the final chapters.

4.2.2.2.1 Absence of arguments on enforceability In *China – Auto Parts*, the European Communities, the United States and Canada complained against Chinese measures that, inter alia, determined whether imported automotive parts and components constituted complete vehicles.[44] In the view of the complainants, these measures were inconsistent with Article III of the GATT 1994, Article 2 of the Trade-Related Investment Measures (TRIMS) Agreement and Article 3 of the SCM Agreement. Moreover, the measures were alleged to be inconsistent with several paragraphs of China's Protocol of Accession and several paragraphs of the corresponding Working Party Report on the Accession of China.[45] The requests for consultations of the US and Canada both refer to China's Protocol of Accession as 'an integral part of the Marrakesh Agreement Establishing the World Trade Organization'. Interestingly, the EC's Request for Consultations does not explicitly state that the Protocol of Accession is an integral part of the Marrakesh Agreement, but rather states that 'China has acted inconsistently with its obligations under the Marrakesh Agreement Establishing the World Trade Organization, as set out in the Protocol on the Accession of the People's Republic of China to the WTO.' From this it may be inferred that the EC, at the time, inferred that the commitments contained in China's Protocol of Accession were part of the Marrakesh Agreement Establishing the World Trade Organization. In its Report, the Panel in *China – Auto Parts* noted that both parties 'agree that China's commitments under its Working Party Report are enforceable in WTO dispute settlement proceedings'.[46]

---

[44] WTO, Request for Consultations, China – Measures Affecting Imports of Automobile Parts (Complainant: European Communities), WT/DS339/1; WTO, Request for Consultations, China – Measures Affecting Imports of Automobile Parts (Complainant: United States), WT/DS340/1; and WTO, Request for Consultations, China – Measures Affecting Imports of Automobile Parts (Complainant: Canada), WT/DS432/1.

[45] The EC's Request for Consultations identifies Part I, para. 7.3 of the Protocol of Accession of China and para. 203 of the Working Party Report on the Accession of China in conjunction with Part I, para. 1.2 of the Protocol of Accession of China, and para. 342 of the Working Party Report. The Request for Consultations by the United States also refers to para. 90 of the Working Party Report, whereas Canada's Request for Consultations also refers to para. 93 of the Working Party Report.

[46] Panel Reports, *China – Auto Parts*, para. 7.740. Subsequently the Panel went on to find that: 'The Accession Protocol is an integral part of the WTO

On appeal the Appellate Body examined these findings by the Panel and noted that neither of the parties had disputed the Panel's findings on this particular point, and summarized the Panel's approach:

> The Panel proceeded, therefore, on the basis that the commitment made by China in paragraph 93 of its Accession Working Party Report is enforceable in WTO dispute settlement proceedings and should be interpreted in accordance with the customary rules of interpretation as codified in Articles 31 and 32 of the Vienna Convention. Neither of these propositions has been disputed at any point in these proceedings, including in this appeal.[47]

In the first dispute involving a protocol of accession, neither of the parties thus put forward any arguments relating to the status of these protocols in the legal framework of the WTO, nor to their enforceability in WTO dispute settlement proceedings. In *China – Publications and Audiovisual Products*, the US alleged, inter alia, that a number of Chinese measures were inconsistent with Paragraphs 5.1 and 5.2 of China's Protocol of Accession, and with Paragraph 1.2 of the Protocol of Accession in so far as it incorporates the commitments contained in Paragraphs 83 and 84 of the Working Party Report on the Accession of China.[48] According to the US '[t]he Accession Protocol forms part of the terms of accession agreed between China and the WTO and is an integral part of the Marrakesh Agreement Establishing the World Trade Organization'.[49] In the absence of any arguments to the contrary, the Panel in *China – Publications and Audiovisual Products* simply assumed that a protocol of accession was enforceable in WTO dispute settlement proceedings. It did, however, address the issue of the relationship between commitments made in China's Working Party Report and China's Protocol of Accession itself. The Panel Report contains the text of Paragraph 342 of the Working Party Report, which lists all the paragraphs of the Working Party Report containing commitments made by

Agreement pursuant to Part I, Article 1.2 of the Accession Protocol. In turn, paragraph 342 of China's Working Party Report incorporates China's commitments under its Working Party Report, including paragraph 93, into the Accession Protocol. Therefore, China's commitment in paragraph 93 of the Working Party Report is also an integral part of the WTO Agreement.'

47 Appellate Body Reports, *China – Auto Parts*, para. 214.

48 WTO, Request for Consultations, China – Measures Affecting Trading Rights and Distribution Services for Certain Publications and Audiovisual Entertainment Products (Complainant: United States), WT/DS363/1, at 2.

49 WTO, Request for Consultations, China – Measures Affecting Trading Rights and Distribution Services for Certain Publications and Audiovisual Entertainment Products (Complainant: United States), WT/DS363/1, at 3.

China. The Panel made reference to the concluding sentence of that paragraph to indicate that the commitment-containing paragraphs had become an integral part of the Protocol of Accession.[50] The crucial paragraph in the Appellate Body Report in *China – Publications and Audiovisual Products* is Paragraph 133, in which the Appellate Body reiterates the statement in the Protocol of Accession that it shall 'be an integral part of the WTO Agreement'.[51] The Appellate Body noted that neither of the parties appealed this finding, and therefore proceeded to examine the claim on the merits.[52] The Panel in *China – Raw Materials* set out – in quite some detail – what it considered to be the essential characteristics of the WTO accession process. It emphasized the fact that the outcome of accession negotiations reflects 'a delicate balance of rights and obligations' which constitutes the 'entry fee' to the WTO.[53] It then reiterated that protocols of accession are 'integral parts' of the WTO Agreement. Presumably since neither of the parties put forward any argument as to the enforceability of commitments contained in protocols of accession, the Panel proceeded to discuss the substantive issues before it.[54] Indeed, the Panel held:

> In this dispute, as with previous disputes concerned with China's Accession Protocol, all parties agree that China's Accession Protocol forms an integral part of the WTO Agreement. Moreover, all parties agree that WTO Members can initiate WTO dispute settlement proceedings on the basis of a claim of violation of China's Accession Protocol. Finally, all parties agree that commitments included in the related Working Party Report, and incorporated into the Accession Protocol by cross-reference, are binding and enforceable through WTO dispute settlement proceedings.[55]

---

[50] Panel Report, *China – Publications and Audiovisual Products*, para. 7.232.

[51] Appellate Body Report, *China – Publications and Audiovisual Products*, para. 133. Further, the Appellate Body noted that '[t]he Panel observed that paragraphs 83(d) and 84(a) and (b) of China's Accession Working Party Report are incorporated into China's Accession Protocol and, hence, the WTO Agreement'.

[52] Appellate Body Report, *China – Publications and Audiovisual Products*, para. 140.

[53] Panel Reports, *China – Raw Materials*, para. 7.112.

[54] Panel Reports, *China – Raw Materials*, paras. 7.114–7.116.

[55] Panel Reports, *China – Raw Materials*, para. 7.114 (footnote omitted). The Panel referenced the findings in *China – Auto Parts*, adopted on 15 December 2008 and in *China – Publications and Audiovisual Products*, adopted on 19 January 2010 when both panels and Appellate Body assessed claims based on China's Accession Protocol.

Ultimately the Panel decided that it would 'interpret the provisions of China's Accession Protocol – *like those of the WTO covered agreements* – in accordance with the customary rules of interpretation of public international law, including those codified in Articles 31, 32 and 33 of the Vienna Convention'.[56] The Appellate Body in *China – Rare Earths* began its analysis with the observation that the parties agreed on the fact that the provisions of China's Protocol of Accession should be interpreted in accordance with Articles 31 and 32 of the Vienna Convention. Referencing its findings in *China – Raw Materials*, the Appellate Body reiterated that these customary rules of treaty interpretation are, 'pursuant to Article 3.2 of the DSU, applicable [...] in clarifying the meaning of Paragraph 11.3 of the Protocol'. Interestingly, the Appellate Body then addressed China's novel line of argumentation and noted that:

> [a]lthough China has developed its own explanation as to why the DSU, including the interpretative rules set out in Article 3.2, is applicable to China's Accession Protocol, *it does not question the proposition itself.* We further note that *the mandatory nature of much of the language used* in China's Accession Protocol *supports the view that its drafters intended it to be enforceable under the DSU.* Indeed, it is uncontested that China's Accession Protocol is enforceable under the DSU.[57]

The footnote to these last sentences stipulates:

> We note that this proposition *has not been contested* either in the present disputes or in any prior dispute involving China's Accession Protocol. In addition, we take note of the Panel's statement that, in all prior cases involving China's Accession Protocol, panels and the Appellate Body 'have proceeded on the assumption' that Paragraph 1.2 serves, *inter alia*, the function of making the obligations in China's Accession Protocol *enforceable* under the DSU. According to the Panel, this is because the Marrakesh Agreement is a covered agreement listed in Appendix 1 to the DSU and, as such, the provisions of that Agreement, together with the provisions of China's Accession Protocol, which is 'an integral part' of that agreement, are subject to the WTO dispute settlement mechanism set out in the DSU. (Panel Reports, para. 7.85) We also take note of the fact that the DSU is one of the Multilateral Trade Agreements annexed to the Marrakesh Agreement. The Marrakesh Agreement is enforceable under the DSU pursuant to its Appendix 1.[58]

---

[56] Panel Reports, *China – Raw Materials*, para. 7.115.

[57] Appellate Body Reports, *China – Rare Earths*, para. 5.19 (emphasis added).

[58] Appellate Body Reports, *China – Rare Earths*, para. 5.19, footnote 422 (emphasis added).

Consequently, WTO dispute settlement practice has consistently treated the commitments contained in protocols of accession and working party reports as enforceable under the DSU.

4.2.2.2.2 The legal status of commitments in working party reports: treaty text In addition to the question of enforceability of protocols of accession and the commitments contained in working party reports, panels and the Appellate Body have addressed the question whether the entire accession package has become an integral part of the WTO Agreement, or whether merely some of the commitments contained in the working party report have. In the request for consultations in *EU – Footwear*, China put forward that it considered that Council Regulation (EC) No. 1472/2006 of 5 October 2006 imposing definitive anti-dumping duties and collecting definitively the provisional anti-dumping duties imposed on imports of certain footwear with uppers of leather from inter alia China, was inconsistent with, inter alia, Part I, Paragraph 15 (a) (ii) of China's Protocol of Accession and Paragraph 151(e) and (f) of the Report of the Working Party on the Accession of China.[59] The Panel had to deal with the issue of the relationship between paragraphs in the Working Party Report that had not been explicitly mentioned in Paragraph 342 of the Working Party Report, and which, therefore, had not become an integral part of the WTO Agreement. Given the importance of this finding, it is warranted to quote the relevant paragraph of the Panel Report in full:

> Section 1(2) of China's Accession Protocol provides, in relevant part, '[t]his Protocol, which shall include the commitments referred to in paragraph 342 of China's Accession Working Party Report, shall be an integral part of the WTO Agreement.' Section 1(2) of China's Accession Protocol, which is the only incorporation of commitments from China's Accession Working Party Report into the WTO Agreement, is clear on its face, and cannot be understood to incorporate commitments from paragraphs not listed in Paragraph 342. Paragraph 151 of China's Accession Working Party Report is not among the paragraphs listed in Paragraph 342 of China's Accession Working Party Report. It is thus clear Paragraph 151 of China's Accession Working Party Report is not a 'commitment [...] referred to in Paragraph 342', and consequently, is not part of the WTO Agreement. Paragraph 151 of China's Accession Working Party Report therefore cannot be understood to impose a

[59] WTO, Request for Consultations, European Union – Anti-Dumping Measures on Certain Footwear from China (Complainant: China), WT/DS405/1, at 2.

legally binding obligation on any WTO Member, and cannot be the basis of a claim in WTO dispute settlement.[60]

The Panel also disagreed with arguments raised by China that the use of the term 'comply' in Paragraph 151 signalled the existence of a legally binding commitment 'and that since Paragraph 342 only lists the commitments "given by China", a commitment given by other WTO Members would naturally not be included in Paragraph 342'.[61] The Panel stated that:

> Even if Paragraph 14 were understood to mean that Paragraphs 15 to 342 all refer to 'commitments', Paragraph 1(2) of China's Accession Protocol refers to Paragraph 342 specifically, and exclusively, in establishing which of the paragraphs of China's Accession Working Party Report contain commitments that are to be incorporated in the Protocol, and consequently become legally binding. Paragraph 14 of China's Accession Working Party Report, in itself, cannot make commitments expressed in China's Accession Working Party Report legally binding.[62]

Moreover, China argued that commitments given by other Members in respect of product-specific safeguards were also legally binding, despite not being listed in Paragraph 342.[63] The Panel responded by referring to the fact that the binding legal commitments in respect of the transitional product-specific safeguard mechanism arose out of Section 16 of China's Protocol of Accession, and not out of China's Working Party Report.[64]

In the second, and so far most recent, dispute involving a protocol of accession that did not involve China as either the complainant or the respondent, Viet Nam again challenged the WTO-consistency of a US anti-dumping investigation on shrimp.[65] The main findings by the Panel for the purpose of this chapter can be found in Paragraph 7.175 of its Report. There the Panel reaffirmed the findings made by previous panels

---

60 Panel Report, *EU – Footwear*, para. 7.181 (footnotes omitted).

61 Panel Report, *EU – Footwear*, para. 7.182.

62 Panel Report, *EU – Footwear*, para. 7.183.

63 Panel Report, *EU – Footwear*, para. 7.184.

64 Panel Report, *EU – Footwear*, para. 7.185. This section had become an integral part of the WTO Agreement. The Panel concluded that '[t]here is nothing in China's Accession Protocol that sets out "commitments" equivalent to the matters addressed in Paragraph 151(e) and (f) of China's Accession Working Party Report'.

65 WTO, Request for Consultations, United States – Anti-Dumping Measures on Certain Shrimp from Viet Nam (Complainant: Viet Nam), WT/DS429/1, at 2.

and the Appellate Body to the extent they had found that the commitments contained in working party reports are enforceable to the extent that they have been included in the list of paragraphs of the working party report that is incorporated by reference in the Protocol of Accession. The Panel stated:

> Provisions contained in Accession Protocols are binding upon the parties and are therefore treaty text to be interpreted pursuant to customary rules of interpretation, in particular Articles 31 and 32 of the Vienna Convention. By virtue of paragraph 2 of Viet Nam's Accession Protocol, the commitment contained in paragraph 255 of its Working Party Report is incorporated by reference into the Accession Protocol and is therefore treaty language. *In contrast, paragraph 254 is not referred to in Viet Nam's Accession Protocol and, therefore, is not treaty text.*[66]

None of the findings of the Panel relating to the commitment in Viet Nam's accession Working Party Report were appealed, and hence the Appellate Body did not discuss the matter further.[67]

4.2.2.2.3 Interim conclusion From the foregoing overview it becomes apparent that panels and the Appellate Body have consistently held that commitments contained in protocols of accession are enforceable in WTO dispute settlement. Equally, commitments contained in paragraphs of accession working party reports that have been included in the concluding paragraph of the report that is 'incorporated by reference' into the protocol of accession are enforceable under the DSU.[68] It is safe to say that the interpretative approach adopted by panels and the Appellate Body has been influenced to a large extent by the fact that it appears to have been the wish of the WTO, and, indeed, the states and customs territories that have acceded to it post-1995, that the commitments entered into would be subject to WTO dispute settlement proceedings. At no point during any of the disputes that have involved protocols of accession have Members questioned the enforceability of these commitments. Although only one acceded Member (China) has found itself on the respondent-side in all protocol of accession-related disputes, it has chosen not to question the enforceability of the commitments contained in its Protocol of Accession before the DSU. One of the grounds on

[66] Panel Report, *US – Shrimp II (Vietnam)*, para. 7.175 (footnote omitted) (emphasis added).

[67] Appellate Body Report, *US – Shrimp II (Vietnam)*.

[68] See Panel Report, *US – Shrimp II (Vietnam)*, para. 7.175 (footnote omitted) (emphasis added).

which it could have done so can be found in Article 11 of the DSU, which requires panels to 'make an objective assessment of the matter before it, including an objective assessment of the facts of the case *and the applicability of and conformity with the relevant covered agreements*'. Such an argument would have forced the panel, and indeed the Appellate Body, to assess and pronounce whether a protocol of accession is a covered agreement – which it is not – and to determine on what basis the commitments contained therein can be enforced.[69] However, for now it appears therefore that panels and the Appellate Body have adopted a rather pragmatic approach that is aimed at satisfying the wishes of the membership of the WTO. This particular approach by the panels and the Appellate Body has, however, attracted criticism in legal scholarship. Several academics have expressed concern about the systemic implications of the approach that has been adopted.[70] These concerns will be discussed in detail in the next section of this chapter.

4.2.2.3 Beyond practice: a legal theory of enforceability

For quite some time the idea that commitments contained in protocols of accession could be enforced in WTO dispute settlement proceedings was not controversial.[71] However, some have considered the development of a coherent interpretation on the legal basis for the enforceability of accession protocol commitments as a necessary step to be taken before one could start thinking about the interpretation of such commitments.[72]

---

[69] Kennedy (2013), The Integration of Accession Protocols into the WTO Agreement, at 49–50.

[70] See below, inter alia, Kennedy (2013), The Integration of Accession Protocols into the WTO Agreement, at 47.

[71] Qin, Julia Ya (2003), '"WTO-Plus" Obligations and Their Implications for the World Trade Organization Legal System: An Appraisal of the China Accession Protocol', *Journal of World Trade* (37)(3), pp. 483–522, at 509. Qin already foresaw that China's Protocol of Accession would likely be considered enforceable under WTO dispute settlement proceedings, since the Protocol of Accession 'constitutes an integral part of the WTO Agreement' and, as such, becomes part of a covered agreement for the purpose of the DSU and is, therefore, 'fully enforceable through the WTO dispute settlement procedure'; see also Qin, Julia Ya (2004), 'WTO Regulation of Subsidies to State-Owned Enterprises (SOEs): A Critical Appraisal of the China Accession Protocol', *Journal of International Economic Law* (7) (4), pp. 863–919, at 883.

[72] Charnovitz, Steve (2008), 'Mapping the Law of WTO Accession', in Janow, Merit E., Donaldson, Victoria and Yanovich, Alan (eds), *The WTO: Governance, Dispute Settlement and Developing Countries*, Huntington, NY, Juris Publishing, pp. 855–920, at 856. In a footnote to that statement, Charnovitz

It could indeed be argued that the mere fact that protocols of accession declare *themselves* to be 'an integral part' of the WTO Agreement is insufficient as 'the justification for enforceability has to be extrinsic to any language included in the accession protocol itself'.[73] The issue attracted more attention from the moment that the Panel Report in *China – Auto Parts* was issued. Some started exploring the implications of the accession process for the single undertaking approach and questioned the grounds on which the Panel and the Appellate Body had found that the commitments contained in a protocol of accession were indeed enforceable.[74] The conclusion that this issue was, in the absence of arguments of the parties, not addressed, corresponds with the finding in the previous section that panels and the Appellate Body adopt a pragmatic approach when certain issues are not disputed.[75] This interpretative approach has also been defined as an 'all-purpose response', noting that 'the basis on which WTO accession protocols take legal effect has not

---

recognized that although the development of such an interpretation would be most welcome, it would depend on the line of argumentation adopted by the respondent in a particular dispute: 'By "enforceable," I mean that a WTO Member is legally entitled to lodge a complaint about a lack of implementation of an accession commitment. If China does not contest that its commitments are enforceable, then the question of why an accession commitment is enforceable may not be directly addressed by this panel.'

73 Charnovitz (2008), Mapping the Law of WTO Accession, at 883. Charnovitz suggests that holding otherwise 'would carry the implication that the WTO General Council has a general power to make agreements with governments, or with international organizations, that create (or diminish) enforceable obligations in the WTO'.

74 Kennedy, Matthew (2011), 'Two Single-Undertakings: Can the WTO Implement the Results of a Round?', *Journal of International Economic Law* (14) (1), pp. 77–120, at 98. Kennedy notes that '[a]n accession protocol is annexed to the WTO Agreement by means not expressly set out in the WTO Agreement, although Article XII offers at least a fig leaf for the procedure'.

75 Kennedy (2011), Two Single-Undertakings: Can the WTO Implement the Results of a Round?, at 99. Noting that '[t]he Panel and Appellate Body in *China – Audiovisual Services* […] refrained from elucidating the basis of their jurisdiction to enforce them'. According to Kennedy the jurisprudence 'shows that [panels and the Appellate Body] do not take a strict legal approach when the parties do not raise potential defects'. He further discusses the finding in *China – Auto Parts* that the enforceability of such commitments had not been disputed and the lack of explanation provided by the Panel and the Appellate Body in *China – Publications and Audiovisual Products* on the statement that these commitments could be enforced.

been elucidated in dispute settlement practice'.[76] Some have referred to the issue of individual non-original Members taking up different rules commitments to express concern about the 'legitimacy, authority and enforceability of the AP [accession protocol] as an instrument'.[77] WTO Members do not seem overly concerned with this particular issue, to the surprise of some scholars.[78] However, it should be noted that, to this date, no Members other than China and Viet Nam have been involved in WTO dispute settlement proceedings involving protocols of accession that have reached the panel stage. It is safe to say that in future disputes involving these two Members any argument relating to the enforceability of their WTO protocol of accession would most likely be easily dismissed given the earlier acceptance of the jurisdiction of the DSB in relation to their accession protocol commitments by these Members. Five potential legal bases for the enforcement of the commitments contained in protocols of accession have been suggested so far: i) the 'Integral Part' reasoning, ii) amendment or modification of the WTO Agreement, iii) Article XII of the WTO Agreement as the cause of action, iv) the protocol of accession as a 'subsequent agreement' in the sense of Article 31(3)(a) of the Vienna Convention, and v) protocols of accession as 'subsequent practice' modifying the WTO agreements in the sense of Article 31(3)(b) of the Vienna Convention.[79] There is thus ample debate on the question as to what the legal basis for such enforcement should be. Ultimately, however,

---

[76] Kennedy (2013), The Integration of Accession Protocols into the WTO Agreement, at 47.

[77] Tyagi, Mitali (2012), 'Flesh on a Legal Fiction: Early Practice in the WTO on Accession Protocols', *Journal of International Economic Law* (15) (2), pp. 391–441, at 397.

[78] Tyagi (2012), Flesh on a Legal Fiction: Early Practice in the WTO on Accession Protocols, at 441. Tyagi concludes with some very critical remarks on the extent to which the WTO is willing to adhere to principles commonly associated with the rule of law: 'the arguments in this article demand that the WTO examine its practice with respect to APs and establish a position on the impact they can have on the single undertaking. Is the Ministerial Conference capable of extending the jurisdiction of the DSB? Do accessions exist as exceptions to the MFN obligation and the prohibition on reservations? Are members aware of the political powers of the Ministerial Council capable of being exercised without consensus? Thus far it appears that, despite the questionable legality of APs and the abundance of legal tools to examine APs, neither the Members nor the DSBs have sought guidance outside the political strength of an agreement reached within the secretive walls of the WTO working groups on accession.'

[79] Charnovitz (2008), Mapping the Law of WTO Accession, at 883–905; and Qin, Julia Ya (2015), 'The Conundrum of WTO Accession Protocols: In

there is broad agreement that commitments included in protocols of accession are enforceable. Nevertheless, although the likelihood of panels and the Appellate Body ever having to address the issue is small, the potential legal bases for enforceability are examined in the following subsections.

4.2.2.3.1 Protocols of accession as an integral part In the sections discussed above it has become clear that panels and the Appellate Body have consistently ruled that the commitments contained in protocols of accession are enforceable in WTO dispute settlement proceedings. As the Appellate Body referred to the findings of the Panel in *China – Rare Earths*:

> this is because the Marrakesh Agreement is a covered agreement listed in Appendix 1 to the DSU and, as such, the provisions of that Agreement, together with the provisions of China's Accession Protocol, which is '*an integral part*' of that agreement, are subject to the WTO dispute settlement mechanism set out in the DSU.[80]

The fundamental question that has to be asked in order to determine whether this particular line of reasoning – although not contested by either of the parties – is correct, is whether a protocol of accession can declare itself to be 'an integral part' of another agreement, in this case the Marrakesh Agreement Establishing the World Trade Organization. It has been argued that this interpretation suffers from the '*petitio principii*' fallacy as 'neither the WTO Ministerial Conference nor the General Council has a general competence to conclude an agreement with another subject of international law and then to incorporate the agreement into the WTO using an integral clause'.[81] This critique is aptly summarized by the following quote:

> Regardless of the impressive lineage of 'integral part,' there is a big difference between a provision of a treaty stating that its own annexes will be an integral part of the treaty, and a negotiation held long after the treaty goes into force

Search of Legality and Legitimacy', *Virginia Journal of International Law* (55) (2), pp. 370–450, at 407–11.

[80] Appellate Body Reports, *China – Rare Earths*, para. 5.19, footnote 422 (emphasis added), referring to Panel Reports, *China – Rare Earths*, para. 7.85.

[81] Charnovitz (2008), Mapping the Law of WTO Accession, at 886. Charnovitz submits that drafters of the new WTO-era protocols of accession may have considered the inclusion of the phrase 'an integral part' as a convenient way to ensure enforceability.

> that purports to make the results an integral part of a pre-existing treaty. An analogy to Article II of the GATT 1994 would be relevant only if Article XII of the WTO Agreement stated that any accession terms will be an 'integral part' of the WTO. But Article XII does not state this. So it seems clear that simply by importing the language 'integral part' from the other WTO contexts does not itself justify using the integral clause to transform the contents of an accession protocol into a discipline enforceable in the WTO dispute settlement system.[82]

However, there should be no doubt that the parties that have been involved in dispute settlement proceedings dealing with protocol of accession commitments intended these commitments to be enforceable. The approach adopted by panels and the Appellate Body is another example of the large degree of deference granted to the Members of the WTO with respect to their intentions as taken from the text of the agreements that they have concluded. Whether this approach is correct from a normative perspective will be discussed in more detail below. For now it suffices to note that, indeed, the Appellate Body seems to award great value to the actual language used in the agreements and treaty texts it interprets.

4.2.2.3.2 Protocols of accession as an amendment or modification of the WTO Agreement As an alternative to the 'integral part' reasoning developed by the parties and the Appellate Body, it has been suggested that protocols of accession should be seen as an amendment or modification of the WTO Agreement.[83] Article X of the WTO Agreement lays

---

[82] Charnovitz (2008), Mapping the Law of WTO Accession, at 888–9. See also Qin (2015), The Conundrum of WTO Accession Protocols: In Search of Legality and Legitimacy, at 413–14. Qin notes that 'The legal effect of this integration clause, however, is questionable. As a matter of treaty law, it is unclear how an accession protocol, which is a bilateral treaty between an acceding country and the WTO, can transform itself into a multilateral one among the members of the WTO. As a matter of legal logic, one treaty cannot make itself part of another treaty without express authorization of the latter. Indeed, it is common to find within the WTO treaty framework that one instrument designates another as its integral part, but each of such designations is made through explicit provision in the primary instrument, not the other way around.'

[83] Ehlermann, Claus-Dieter and Ehring, Lothar (2005), 'Decision-Making in the World Trade Organization: Is the Consensus Practice of the World Trade Organization Adequate for Making, Revising and Implementing Rules on International Trade?', *Journal of International Economic Law* (8) (1), pp. 51–75, at 57. Ehlermann and Ehring submit that 'the Accession Protocol is an agreement

down the criteria that have to be fulfilled for a successful amendment. However, the article is completely silent on any issues relating to the protocol of accession. Moreover, Article XII of the WTO Agreement does not discuss the option of protocols of accession constituting an amendment. This particular interpretation would entail that Article XII WTO Agreement could serve as a means of evading the criteria put forth in Article X WTO Agreement.[84] Nevertheless:

> [a]lthough regular amendments are regulated in Article X, not XII of the WTO Agreement, one can speak of an amendment also in the case of an accession because, first, of the addition of a new Member (the WTO Agreement is modified so as to cover an additional subject of international law) and, second, of potential alteration of the WTO Agreement for the purposes of the new Member (plus and minus).[85]

Such an interpretation would indeed imply that the Ministerial Conference, based on Article XII of the WTO Agreement, has the authority to amend the WTO Agreement – in addition to the formal procedures laid

---

between the new Member and the WTO (Article XII:1 of the WTO Agreement), not an (amendment) agreement between the new and the old Members'.

[84] Parenti, Antonio (2000), 'Accession to the World Trade Organization: A Legal Analysis', *Legal Issues of Economic Integration* (27) (2), pp. 141–57, at 156. Parenti argues that this would amount to a violation of WTO rules in itself: '[a]ny alteration to the obligations of a WTO Member is possible only in the cases and according to the conditions specifically foreseen in the Agreement. These are of two kinds, specific and general. Specific ones include the possibility for a Member to increase the level of the customs duties beyond the consolidated one in case of balance of payment problems, as foreseen in Articles XII and XVIII GATT. Those of a general nature would have to be considered tantamount to an amendment of the WTO Agreement, and as such, governed by the provisions and procedures foreseen in Article X WTO. An alteration occurring in case of an accession would therefore not be consistent with the WTO rules. This could not be rectified by even the eventual unanimous voting on the terms of accession, because such an alteration would have occurred without the respect of the rules of the WTO.'

[85] Ehring, Lothar (2013), Nature and Status of WTO Accession Commitments: 'WTO-Plus' Obligations and Their Relationship to Other Parts of the WTO Agreement, in Cremona, Marise, Hilpold, Peter, Lavranos, Nikos, Staiger, Stefan Schneider and Ziegler, Andreas R. (eds), *Reflections on the Constitutionalisation of International Economic Law: Liber Amicorum for Ernst-Ulrich Petersmann*, Leiden, Martinus Nijhoff Publishers, pp. 337–61, at 345. Ehring notes that this particular interpretation is contrary to what Parenti has argued.

down in Article X WTO Agreement.[86] Some argue that the WTO has acted 'without the respect of' its own rules.[87] The Appellate Body has not used the recent cases to express itself unequivocally on the issue of enforceability and Members seem to have accepted the situation as it is. In fact, the accessions that have been concluded after the most recent accession-related disputes also involve the conclusion of rules commitments and the corresponding protocols of accession equally pronounce themselves to constitute an integral part of the WTO Agreement. Moreover, even if a potential ultra vires argument has merit, it is extremely unlikely that the Appellate Body would be willing to entertain an argument in which it is asked to rule on the competence of the Ministerial Conference.[88] Although questionable from an institutional law perspective – and perhaps even from a rule of law perspective – it is clear that, although the possibility has not been explicitly provided for by the drafters of the WTO Agreement, the Members of the WTO intended protocols of accession to have the effect of prescribing the relationship between the acceded Member and the WTO, by rectifying, amending or modifying the WTO Agreement with the entry into force of a protocol of accession. Twenty years of accession practice shows that applicants, members of accession working parties, and indeed the WTO have negotiated rules commitments that are contained in protocols of accession.

---

[86] Beslać and Osakwe (2015), The Evolution of the GATT/WTO Accession Protocol: Legal Tightening and Domestic Ratification, at 357. Noting that '[w]hile the scope of specific accession obligations has varied, reflecting the particular dynamics of individual accession negotiations and the specificities of foreign trade regimes, it has nevertheless been accepted that the WTO Agreement is *rectified, amended and modified* with the entry into force of Accession Protocols of each new Article XII Member' (emphasis added).

[87] Qin (2015), The Conundrum of WTO Accession Protocols: In Search of Legality and Legitimacy, at 412. Indeed, Qin has stated that 'a strong argument can be made that the Ministerial Conference has acted *ultra vires* in approving accession terms that de facto amend the provisions of the WTO agreements'. Referencing Charnovitz (2008), Mapping the Law of WTO Accession, at 900–901 (concluding that '[g]iven the lack of any legal standard in Article XII regarding the content of accession agreements, there may not be any accession terms that are *ultra vires*' (footnotes omitted)); and Tyagi (2012), Flesh on a Legal Fiction: Early Practice in the WTO on Accession Protocols, at 412–14 (claiming that the Ministerial Conference has exceeded its authority in approving the rule-modifying provisions of the accession protocols).

[88] Qin (2015), The Conundrum of WTO Accession Protocols: In Search of Legality and Legitimacy, at 412–13.

4.2.2.3.3 Article XII of the WTO Agreement as the legal basis Another argument for the enforceability of commitments in protocols of accession is based on the text of Article XII of the WTO Agreement which governs accession.[89] This argument supposedly finds support in the text of Article 1.1 of the DSU, which provides:

> The rules and procedures of this Understanding shall apply to disputes brought pursuant to the consultation and dispute settlement provisions of the agreements listed in Appendix 1 to this Understanding (referred to in this Understanding as the 'covered agreements'). The rules and procedures of this Understanding shall also apply to consultations and the settlement of disputes between Members concerning their *rights and obligations* under the provisions of the Agreement Establishing the World Trade Organization (referred to in this Understanding as the 'WTO Agreement') and of this Understanding taken in isolation or in combination with any other covered agreement. [emphasis added]

It has been submitted that the rights and obligations referred to in this article extend to the rights and obligations contained in protocols of accession that are concluded pursuant to Article XII of the WTO Agreement.[90] However, a more convincing argument is that Article XII of the WTO Agreement does not confer any rights to WTO Members, but rather prescribes the authority and decision-making process of the Ministerial Conference regarding accession and the scope of accession.[91] Indeed, the argument that Article XII WTO Agreement confers rights would 'arbitrarily extend the scope of Article XII' and would 'grant limitless legislative powers to the political organs of the WTO under the guise of accession'.[92] Nevertheless, the question is whether this is indeed what such an interpretation would result in. The legislative powers arguably granted by Article XII of the WTO Agreement are confined to the accession negotiations between an applicant state and the WTO. It is difficult to imagine how this could equate to 'limitless legislative

---

[89] Charnovitz (2008), Mapping the Law of WTO Accession, at 894–5. Charnovitz has argued that the basis for enforceability can be found in this provision, and more specifically in the use of the word 'terms' therein. He provides seven arguments for the interpretation that 'a term agreed to in an Article XII treaty is enforceable through the DSU', finding further support in the text of Article 1.1 DSU.

[90] Charnovitz (2008), Mapping the Law of WTO Accession, at 895.

[91] Qin (2015), The Conundrum of WTO Accession Protocols: In Search of Legality and Legitimacy, at 416.

[92] Tyagi (2012), Flesh on a Legal Fiction: Early Practice in the WTO on Accession Protocols, at 402.

powers', as the procedures for, for example, amendments, waivers and interpretations would still remain in place. Although the term 'terms' indeed results in a wide degree of discretion granted to the WTO and the applicant state to determine the conditions under which the latter may become a Member of the WTO, this is hardly the same as 'limitless legislative powers' being conferred upon the political organs of the WTO. It appears unlikely that Article XII of the WTO can validly be considered as the basis for jurisdiction over protocols of accession.[93]

4.2.2.3.4 Protocols of accession as a successive treaty relating to the same subject matter Article 30 of the Vienna Convention prescribes how to deal with situations in which a treaty is concluded that deals with the same subject matter as a treaty that is already in place.[94] Paragraph 2 stipulates that '[w]hen a treaty specifies that it is subject to, or that it is not to be considered as incompatible with, an earlier or later treaty, the provisions of that other treaty prevail'. Paragraph 3 contains a conflict clause that stipulates that '[w]hen all the parties to the earlier treaty are parties also to the later treaty but the earlier treaty is not terminated or suspended in operation under article 59, the earlier treaty applies only to the extent that its provisions are compatible with those of the later treaty'. In *China – Rare Earths*, China submitted that '[i]rrespective of the interpretation of Article XII:1 [of the Marrakesh Agreement] and Paragraph 1.2 of China's Accession Protocol', its Accession Protocol is properly characterized as a 'subsequent agreement' relating to the same subject matter in the sense of Article 30 of the Vienna Convention.[95] It thus put forward an argument in which protocols of accession are

---

93 Ehring (2013), Nature and Status of WTO Accession Commitments: 'WTO-Plus' Obligations and Their Relationship to Other Parts of the WTO Agreement, at 346. Ehring notes that '[t]he required legal basis for the decisive incorporation of Accession into the WTO Agreement arguably resides also in Article XII:I and the "terms to be agreed", but one must admit that this falls short of an evident or compelling reasoning. In the past, a (small) number of observers had doubts as to the enforceability of WTO accession obligations, but WTO Members probably considered these obligations fully enforceable under the dispute settlement system.' He also mentions the fact that China has used its Protocol of Accession as an 'offensive' instrument as well, for example in *US – Anti-Dumping and Countervailing Duties (China).*

94 Villiger (2009), *Commentary on the 1969 Vienna Convention on the Law of Treaties*, at 405–6. See also Aust (2007), *Modern Treaty Law and Practice*, at 217.

95 Appellate Body Reports, *China – Rare Earths*, para. 2.26. See also footnote 113 to that paragraph, in which the Appellate Body noted that 'Article

considered as a 'subsequent agreement that modifies the WTO agreements with respect to their application to the acceded member'.[96] The use of the term 'subsequent agreement' in this context was not quite appropriate, as Article 30 of the Vienna Convention does not contain that exact term. Rather, Article 30 refers to 'successive treaties relating to the same subject matter'. The term 'subsequent agreement' is, however, used in Article 31(3) of the Vienna Convention. In the proceedings, the European Union argued that Article 30(3) of the Vienna Convention 'is inapposite because there is no question of "incompatibility" between the provision at issue – that is, Paragraph 11.3 of China's Accession Protocol – and the GATT 1994'.[97] Arguably a protocol of accession constitutes a treaty in its own right as it comports with the description of a treaty provided in Article 2 of the Vienna Convention.[98] A protocol of accession is concluded between the acceding state or customs territory in question and the WTO. All WTO Members are party to the WTO Agreement, as the constitutive document of the WTO. Yet the question is whether all WTO Members are also, individually, party to an accession protocol. A protocol of accession is concluded between the acceding Member and the WTO. As such, the parties to the treaty, the protocol of accession, are different from those to the WTO Agreement.[99] Nevertheless, as stated, the fact remains that all parties to the WTO Agreement are also Members of the WTO. Consequently, the organization, in its capacity as party to the protocol of accession, has the authority to declare that this protocol

30 of the Vienna Convention concerns the "[a]pplication of successive treaties relating to the same subject-matter"'.

96 Qin (2015), The Conundrum of WTO Accession Protocols: In Search of Legality and Legitimacy, at 404.

97 Appellate Body Reports, *China – Rare Earths*, para. 2.133.

98 Article 2 of the Vienna Convention provides in para. (a) that a '"treaty" means an international agreement concluded between States in written form and governed by international law, whether embodied in a single instrument or in two or more related instruments and whatever its particular designation'. It should be noted that the Appellate Body has so far refrained from characterizing protocols of accession as treaties. Rather, the term 'legal instrument' has been used to describe them. For example, in *China – Rare Earths* it stated that '[t]he word "apply" in the second sentence [of Article XII:1 WTO Agreement] "is not referring to the ... application of a legal instrument or document", *such as the terms of accession*'. Appellate Body Reports, *China – Rare Earths*, para. 5.29 (emphasis added).

99 Qin (2017), Mind the Gap: Navigating Between the WTO Agreement and Its Accession Protocols, at 237.

shall be 'an integral part of the WTO Agreement'.[100] Thereby, the protocol of accession as the legal instrument containing the terms of accession becomes part of the 'same treaty', namely the WTO Agreement.[101] China's argument was presented for the first time during the oral hearing of the dispute. However, the Appellate Body rejected the argument completely:

> These arguments [...] do not, in our view, comport well with the analysis that we have set out above. [...] In the same vein, we do not consider Article 30(3) of the Vienna Convention to be apposite for understanding the relationship between the different components of this single package of rights and obligations, all of which form part of 'the same treaty' to which China acceded in 2001.[102]

There has been fierce criticism in respect of the 'summary dismissal' of this argument by the Appellate Body.[103] It has been argued that 'the Appellate Body completely overlooked the need to resolve conflict between *the provisions of the accession protocols* and *the provisions of the WTO agreements on the same subject matter*'.[104] There are two arguments that can be raised against this interpretation and criticism of the Appellate Body's decision. First, a protocol of accession is concluded between the applicant state and the WTO. As such, it is not governed by the Vienna Convention as that treaty only applies to treaties concluded

---

[100] It is acknowledged that the legal basis for this approach is questionable, as mentioned in section 4.2.2.3.1. However, so far no party to a dispute involving a protocol of accession has questioned the enforceability of these legal instruments.

[101] Appellate Body Reports, *China – Rare Earths*, para. 5.70, referring to Appellate Body Report, *Argentina – Footwear (EC)*, para. 81.

[102] Appellate Body Reports, *China – Rare Earths*, para. 5.70.

[103] Qin (2015), The Conundrum of WTO Accession Protocols: In Search of Legality and Legitimacy, at 428. In Qin's view 'VCLT Article 30(3) is not only "apposite", but indispensable' 'for understanding the relationship between specific provisions of accession protocols and the provisions of the WTO agreements'.

[104] Qin (2015), The Conundrum of WTO Accession Protocols: In Search of Legality and Legitimacy, at 429 (emphasis added). According to Qin, without first identifying and resolving such conflict, however, 'it is impossible to interpret the accession protocols and other components of the WTO Agreement as the "single package of rights and obligations" in a truly consistent and coherent manner'. Her criticism seems to originate from the finding by the Appellate Body that protocols of accession become part of 'the same treaty' (a single package of rights and obligations) consisting of different components.

between states.[105] Nevertheless, to the extent that Articles 30, 31 and 32 of the Vienna Convention reflect customary rules of interpretation of public international law, they could be considered as applicable, even between an international organization and a state. Second, this interpretation appears to rest on a rather broad interpretation of the notion of conflict in international law. Under international law there are three criteria that have to be fulfilled before we can speak of conflict:

> First, two States must be bound by two different treaties, or two different obligations. Second, the treaties (or the obligations) must cover the same substantive subject-matter. Third, the provisions must conflict, in the sense that the provisions must impose mutually exclusive obligations.[106]

Even assuming that an applicant's protocol of accession and the WTO Agreement are two different treaties – which arguably the Appellate Body does not think to be the case – and that (a commitment in) a protocol of accession and (a provision of) the WTO Agreement cover the same subject matter, it would take some creativity to consider these commitments and provisions as imposing 'mutually exclusive obligations'.[107] The Appellate Body has so far adopted a rather narrow notion of the concept of conflict in its reports. For example, in *Guatemala – Cement I* it held that:

> A special or additional provision should only be found to prevail over a provision of the DSU in a situation where adherence to the one provision will lead to a violation of the other provision, that is, in the case of a conflict between them.[108]

This notion of conflict, which corresponds to a large extent to that proposed by, among others, Wilfried Jenks, has attracted strong criticism.[109] In the context of protocols of accession it entails that there is only a situation of conflict when the adherence to a commitment in a

---

[105] Qin (2015), The Conundrum of WTO Accession Protocols: In Search of Legality and Legitimacy, at 429. Qin acknowledges that the Vienna Convention does not apply to the WTO as it is an international organization.

[106] Marceau, Gabrielle (2001), 'Conflicts of Norms and Conflicts of Jurisdictions: The Relationship Between the WTO Agreement and MEAs and Other Treaties', *Journal of World Trade* (35) (6), pp. 1081–131, at 1084.

[107] See, in particular, the interpretation provided by the Appellate Body in *China – Rare Earths*.

[108] Appellate Body Report, *Guatemala – Cement I*, para. 65.

[109] Pauwelyn, Joost (2003), *Conflict of Norms in Public International Law: How WTO Law Relates to Other Rules of International Law*, Cambridge,

protocol of accession or a provision in a covered agreement leads to the violation of a provision of a covered agreement or an accession protocol commitment respectively. In any event, it is clear that to determine whether a conflict exists, a case-by-case analysis is required.[110] The threshold for finding a conflict between a provision of the WTO Agreement (including all of its annexes) and a commitment in a protocol of accession should, nevertheless, be relatively high.[111] After all, by negotiating its accession and by signing the protocol, the applicant state expresses its intention to be bound by the obligations laid down by the WTO Agreement. The rights and obligations assumed at the moment of accession must therefore, as a matter of logic, be considered as – at a minimum – compatible with each other. It would make little sense for an applicant member, or indeed for the WTO, to insist on the inclusion of a commitment in a protocol of accession that would *require* the applicant to act inconsistently with one of the obligations contained in the WTO Agreement. Indeed, 'since the main objective of interpretation rules is to identify the intention of the parties, it is suggested that "conflicts" should be interpreted narrowly, in order to keep as much as possible of the agreement of the parties'.[112] Indeed, it can be concluded that there is

---

Cambridge University Press, at 161–200; Bartels, Lorand (2008), Treaty Conflicts in WTO Law: A Comment on William J. Davey's Paper 'The Quest for Consistency', in Griller, Stefan (ed.) (2008), *At the Crossroads: The World Trading System and the Doha Round*, Vienna, Springer, at 134–37.

[110] A more elaborate analysis of the relationship between commitments in protocols of accession and the provisions of the WTO Agreement is carried out in the context of the mapping exercise in Chapters 5 and 6.

[111] Chase, Claude (2012), 'Norm Conflict Between WTO Covered Agreements: Real, Apparent or Avoided?', *The International and Comparative Law Quarterly* (61) (4), 791–821. Chase notes that, in respect of intra norm conflict between norms arising in the covered agreements, 'the single-undertaking nature of WTO rights and obligations presumes that WTO norms constitute an integrated and coherent system of multilateral rules; creates *a heavy presumption against conflict*; demands cumulative and simultaneous compliance with all WTO norms; disengages the application of conflict rules under international law such as the *lex posterior* rule codified in Article 30 of the VCLT; and appears to privilege an application of the principle of *lex specialis* that, to some degree, diverges from the understanding of that principle under general international law' (emphasis added).

[112] Marceau (2001), Conflicts of Norms and Conflicts of Jurisdictions: The Relationship Between the WTO Agreement and MEAs and Other Treaties, at 1086. A broader definition 'would lead to providing a third party (an adjudication body or an interpreter) with the power to set aside a provision that has been voluntarily negotiated by States'.

conflict 'where adherence to the one provision will necessarily lead to a violation of the other provision and the provisions cannot, therefore, be read as complementing each other'.[113] There is, therefore, a strong argument against considering the relationship between commitments contained in protocols of accession and the provisions of the WTO Agreement in terms of 'conflict', and an approach based on Article 30 of the Vienna Convention does not appear to be sound.

4.2.2.3.5 Protocols of accession as subsequent practice or subsequent agreement The rules on treaty interpretation contained in the Vienna Convention reflect the idea that parties to a treaty may, through subsequent practice or through the conclusion of a subsequent agreement, have provided new indications as to the correct interpretation of a particular term in an older agreement. Article 31 of the Vienna Convention provides:

> 1. A treaty shall be interpreted in good faith in accordance with the ordinary meaning to be given to the terms of the treaty in their context and in the light of its object and purpose.
> 2. The context for the purpose of the interpretation of a treaty shall comprise, in addition to the text, including its preamble and annexes:
>   (a) any agreement relating to the treaty which was made between all the parties in connection with the conclusion of the treaty;
>   (b) any instrument which was made by one or more parties in connection with the conclusion of the treaty and accepted by the other parties as an instrument related to the treaty.
> 3. There shall be taken into account, together with the context:
>   (a) any subsequent agreement between the parties regarding the interpretation of the treaty or the application of its provisions;
>   (b) any subsequent practice in the application of the treaty which establishes the agreement of the parties regarding its interpretation;
>   (c) any relevant rules of international law applicable in the relations between the parties.
> 4. A special meaning shall be given to a term if it is established that the parties so intended.

Article 31(1) stipulates that, in interpreting a treaty, a treaty interpreter shall do so in good faith and in accordance with the ordinary meaning

---

[113] Van den Bossche, Peter and Zdouc, Werner (2013), *The Law and Policy of the World Trade Organization*, Third Edition, Cambridge, Cambridge University Press, at 45. In a footnote it is explained that in international law 'there is a strong presumption against conflict as it can be assumed that countries will not undertake conflicting obligations'.

given to the terms of the treaty in light of their context and object and purpose. Article 31(2) subsequently provides what that context shall comprise of. Article 31(3) further stipulates in subparagraphs (a) and (b) that, together with the context, any subsequent agreement between the parties regarding the interpretation of the treaty or the application of its provisions and any subsequent practice in the application of the treaty which establishes the agreement of the parties regarding its interpretation shall be taken into account. The International Law Commission (ILC) has prepared a number of reports on the correct interpretation of the terms subsequent agreement and subsequent practice in the interpretation of constituent instruments of international organizations. The reports notes that the subsequent practice of the parties to constituent instruments of international organizations, the practice of organs of an international organization, and a combination of the two may constitute relevant practice for the purpose of the interpretation of a constituent instrument of an international organization.[114] In respect of subsequent agreements regarding the interpretation of constituent instruments of international organizations, the report identifies two forms: self-standing agreements between the parties and agreements between the parties in the form of a decision of a plenary organ of an international organization.[115] The foregoing serves as illustration for the consideration of a final argument that has been put forward as a basis for the enforceability of protocols of accession: considering them as 'subsequent practice of the WTO that modifies the WTO Agreements'.[116] It has been argued that:

> The 'subsequent practice' explanation is more consistent with the constitutionalist approach, as opposed to the traditional functionalist approach, towards international organizations. Although the WTO remains largely a member-driven institution, it is undeniable that the Organization has acquired independent power and authority over its members through its highly effective dispute settlement mechanism. The trend of expanding global governance, of

---

[114] International Law Commission, Third Report on Subsequent Agreements and Subsequent Practice in Relation to the Interpretation of Treaties, UN Doc. A/CN.4/683 (7 April 2015) (prepared by Special Rapporteur Georg Nolte), para. 31.

[115] International Law Commission, Third Report on Subsequent Agreements and Subsequent Practice in Relation to the Interpretation of Treaties, UN Doc. A/CN.4/683 (7 April 2015) (prepared by Special Rapporteur Georg Nolte), para. 58.

[116] Qin (2015), The Conundrum of WTO Accession Protocols: In Search of Legality and Legitimacy, at 407–11.

> which the WTO plays an important part, comports more with a constitutionalist perspective on the Organization. For these reasons, it is submitted here that 'subsequent practice' of the WTO offers a better explanation for the phenomenon of modifications of WTO agreements through accession protocols.[117]

It is of note that it is not defined which exact term in the WTO Agreement is being interpreted when referring to the concepts of subsequent practice and subsequent agreement. Is it Appendix 1 of the DSU, which contains the covered agreements? Is that appendix 'modified' by the practice of WTO Members to advocate the enforcement of protocols of accession? Or is it, rather, the term 'terms' in Article XII of the WTO Agreement, which Qin contends was only meant to refer to the content of goods and services schedules of commitments?[118] Or is it perhaps any particular term in any provision of the WTO Agreement that is invoked in conjunction with the relevant commitment in a protocol of accession? It is submitted that using these concepts is ultimately not helpful in determining the relationship between commitments contained in protocols of accession and the WTO Agreement. The Appellate Body has set out a clear test in respect of the concept of subsequent agreement in *US – Clove Cigarettes*, which essentially boils down to the question whether the agreement is an agreement 'bearing specifically upon the interpretation of the treaty'.[119] It is clear that, contrary to the factual

---

[117] Qin (2015), The Conundrum of WTO Accession Protocols: In Search of Legality and Legitimacy, at 411 (footnotes omitted). To illustrate this point, Qin argues that in fact it is the 'integration clause' – the sentence in protocols of accession declaring themselves to be an integral part of the WTO Agreement – that constitutes subsequent practice effectively amending the WTO Agreement. Notably, at 418 Qin states that '[u]ltimately, treating accession protocols as "covered agreements" is yet another example of "subsequent practice" of the WTO that effectively amends *the DSU*' (emphasis added).

[118] Qin (2015), The Conundrum of WTO Accession Protocols: In Search of Legality and Legitimacy, at 417. Qin notes that '[s]ince the practice of routinely demanding additional rule commitments (i.e., commitments not incorporated into the GATT and GATS schedules) did not develop until years after the conclusion of the WTO Agreement, it is difficult to conclude that enforceability of such rule commitments was the original intention behind Article XII'. It is submitted that the practice of 'demanding additional rule commitments' can be witnessed as early as Ecuador's accession. Further evidence is provided by Bulgaria's and Mongolia's protocols of accession, which are the first to contain commitments on the elimination of export duties.

[119] Appellate Body Report, *US – Clove Cigarettes*, paras. 262–8. See also International Law Commission, Third Report on Subsequent Agreements and

circumstances in that particular case, none of the protocols of accession bears specifically upon the interpretation of a particular treaty term. Protocols of accession do not have that purpose. They contain the terms on which a state or customs territory may become a Member of the WTO. This is something fundamentally different than the situation in which WTO Members gather to clarify the meaning of a particular treaty term, as they did in the case of the Doha Ministerial Decision on Implementation-Related Issues and Concerns which referred explicitly to a particular term in the TBT Agreement.[120] Moreover, it appears that when referring to the concept of subsequent agreement and subsequent practice on the one hand and successive treaties on the other, the different approaches referred to in Article 30 and Article 31 of the Vienna Convention have been conflated.[121] Article 31 is relevant to the extent that these agreements or practices might assist in determining the meaning of a particular treaty term. Article 30 of the Vienna Convention provides the priority or conflict rules between the provisions of successive treaties relating to the same subject matter. It is then noted that '[i]n accordance with Article 30, in relation between the acceded member and other members of the WTO, the provisions of the accession protocol shall prevail over the prior WTO agreements to the extent they are inconsistent or incompatible or in conflict with each other'.[122] The interpretation provided by the Appellate Body in *China – Rare Earths*, indicates that this approach has been rejected.[123] The Appellate Body's line of reasoning seems to suggest that the terms contained in these protocols are merely criteria for a state to become a Member of the WTO. As such, these 'terms', and the accession package they are contained in, become

---

Subsequent Practice in Relation to the Interpretation of Treaties, UN Doc. A/CN.4/683 (7 April 2015) (prepared by Special Rapporteur Georg Nolte), paras. 63–7.

[120] The term clarified was 'reasonable interval'.

[121] The difficulty in pointing out exactly how protocols of accession should be used becomes apparent when Qin notes that: '[t]he characterization of a WTO accession protocol either as a subsequent agreement modifying the WTO agreements, or as a subsequent practice of the WTO modifying its underlying treaties, provides a conceptual foundation for defining such a relationship properly'. If they constitute subsequent practice, they can only be considered to be of help in interpreting a particular treaty term in the constitutive treaty by virtue of Article 31(3)(b) of the Vienna Convention. Qin, however, proceeds with the argument that Article 30 Vienna Convention provides the principle and that protocols of accession should be seen as successive treaties.

[122] For a rejection of this 'conflict' approach, see section 4.2.2.3.4.

[123] Appellate Body Reports, *China – Rare Earths*, paras. 2.133 and 5.70.

part of 'the same treaty'. It is submitted that, rather than modifying the WTO agreements, the commitments in protocols of accession provide for additional criteria that new Members have to adhere to as part of their WTO membership. Some of these criteria, or rules, might be additional, depending on the extent to which they are already dealt with in the WTO Agreement, others may merely prescribe a particular method of how to implement the obligations contained in that agreement.[124] In any event, the intention of the members of the working party on the accession of a particular state or customs territory and the state or customs territory in question appears to be to negotiate a coherent framework of rights and obligations that governs its WTO membership. Consequently, there is very little reason to assume that commitments contained in a protocol of accession and the rights and obligations arising under the WTO Agreement should be considered to be in conflict with each other. In fact, Article XII of the WTO Agreement provides the main argument in support of this approach. It refers to the fact that accession is possible to 'this Agreement [the WTO Agreement] and the Multilateral Trade Agreements annexed thereto'. It would appear somewhat illogical to assume that a state or customs territory would want to accede to the WTO Agreement and the Multilateral Trade Agreements, subject to 'the terms to be agreed' between it and the membership, only then to argue that the terms it had negotiated are in conflict with the rights and obligations contained in those agreements. Consequently, an approach based on Article 30 Vienna Convention does not appear to be appropriate either.

4.2.2.3.6 Interim conclusion on enforceability: acquiescence? The foregoing suggests that there is no generally accepted theory on the issue of enforceability of protocols of accession in WTO dispute settlement proceedings. Considering that there are 35 other WTO Members who have acceded through the procedure stipulated by Article XII of the WTO Agreement, the question to what extent these Members would be in a position to successfully challenge a panel's jurisdiction over claims arising under their protocol of accession can validly be raised. One could, for instance, imagine the Russian Federation or any other acceded Member challenging the jurisdiction of the DSB in such a situation. This would force the panel in question to develop a more elaborate legal reasoning on the grounds for enforceability of protocol of accession commitments. However, Members appear to have given their tacit

---

124 For a detailed typology of accession commitments, see Chapter 5.

acceptance that the commitments contained in these protocols can indeed be enforced, regardless of the precise legal basis for such enforcement. In general international law a tacit and unilateral consent conveyed by a state 'through silence or inaction, in circumstances such that a response expressing disagreement or objection in relation to the conduct of another state would be called for', is known as the doctrine of acquiescence.[125] Considering the multilateral nature of WTO dispute settlement proceedings where reports of panels and the Appellate Body are adopted by the DSB, Members that were not party to a dispute involving a protocol of accession, but which would have had objections against the enforceability of the commitments contained therein, could have expressed this disagreement or objection during the DSB meetings in which the adoption of such reports was on the agenda. However, in none of the instances where this was the case has a WTO Member objected to enforceability. Certain Members have expressed their disagreement with substantive aspects of the reports that were up for adoption; however, none of them, including the Russian Federation, has objected to the enforceability of accession protocols as such.[126] It may therefore be assumed that future challenges to the enforceability of accession protocols would easily be rejected, even though in this case the doctrine of acquiescence would not relate to the non-objection to a substantive obligation, but rather to the non-objection against the enforceability of protocols of accession containing such commitments and obligations. The subsequent section deals with the relationship between these commitments and the provisions of the WTO agreements in order to determine whether, as some have

---

[125] Marques, Antunes and Nuno, Sérgio (2006), Acquiescence, in Wolfrum, Rüdiger (ed.), *Max Planck Encyclopedia of Public International Law* [MPEPIL], Oxford University Press, para. 2. Available at http://opil.ouplaw.com/view/10.1093/law:epil/9780199231690/law-9780199231690-e1373#law-9780199231690-e1373 (last accessed at 1 June 2017), as cited by Ziegler, Andreas R. and Baumgartner, Jorun (2015), Good Faith as a Principle of (International) Law, in Mitchell, Andrew D., Sornajah, M. and Voon, Tania (eds) (2015), *Good Faith and International Economic Law*, Oxford, Oxford University Press, pp. 9–36, at 23.

[126] WTO, Dispute Settlement Body, Minutes of the Meeting of 29 August 2014, WT/DSB/M/349, 23 October 2014, para. 8.9. '[T]he Russian Federation regretted the Appellate Body's rulings in relation to an issue of systemic importance raised by Russia as a third party to this dispute. Russia believed that this issue remained unresolved and that this may create room for concern from a legal perspective.' This remark related to the applicability of the general exceptions in Article XX of the GATT 1994 to commitments contained in protocols of accession and not the enforceability of these commitments as such.

suggested, the lack of a clearly established jurisdictional basis for the enforcement is problematic.

4.3 THE RELATIONSHIP BETWEEN COMMITMENTS IN PROTOCOLS OF ACCESSION AND THE WTO AGREEMENT

Absent any clear indication as to the exact legal status of protocols of accession and the commitments contained in their related working party reports, panels and the Appellate Body have resolved issues dealing with the relationship between these instruments and the WTO Agreement on an ad hoc and case-by-case basis.[127] In section 3.2.4.3 it was explained that the negotiation of rules commitments forms part of the WTO accession process. This section examines the legal basis for the conclusion of these commitments. Moreover, it examines four of the most prominent issues arising from the relationship between such commitments and the WTO Agreement. First, it assesses the issue of the applicability of the exceptions clauses contained in the GATT 1994 to the commitments contained in protocols of accession and working party reports. This has been far the most controversial issue in accession-related disputes. Second, it analyses the commitments in these instruments that create additional 'rights' for WTO Members other than the acceding Member. Third, this section examines whether there have been instances in which applicants have explicitly foregone rights that would normally accrue to them under the WTO Agreement. Fourth, this section examines the way in which the commitments contained in the protocol of accession and working party report of one Member might potentially impact the interpretation of provisions of the WTO Agreement and the protocols of accession of other Members.

4.3.1 Legal Basis for Rules Commitments

In Chapter 3 it was noted that in some accession negotiations additional rules commitments have been agreed upon that exceed the scope of the WTO Agreement. Consequently, the results of some of the negotiations

[127] Qin (2017), Mind the Gap: Navigating Between the WTO Agreement and Its Accession Protocols, at 226–7.

on rules commitments have been controversial.[128] The fact that some applicants have had to accept more 'stringent' terms than others in order to be allowed access to the organization has led some to argue that the WTO has a two-tiered membership. It cannot be denied that, indeed, the commitments entered into by various applicants sometimes differ. Some acceded Members have accepted rules commitments that are not applicable to original WTO Members, or even to other acceded Members. Ultimately, this fact is the logical outcome of an accession process that grants the freedom to the organization and the applicant to determine 'the terms on which' the latter may accede to the organization.[129] It has been suggested that treating Article XII and the subsequent practice of WTO as the legal basis for country-specific rule-making has grave implications for the legal system of the WTO and would lead to 'a dismantling of the uniformity of WTO rules'.[130] Considering the gravity of such an argument, several observations are in order. Although the WTO has a uniform set of rules applicable to all Members, in certain areas there are multiple speeds of liberalization and different sets of rules apply to different types of Members.[131] In most instances these different rules have been designed for the benefit of developing and least-developed country Members. Although the situation in respect of protocols of accession is arguably different, this in any event points at the fact that the uniformity of trade rules is debatable. Moreover, the existence of multiple speeds of trade liberalization and the corresponding difference in rules does not necessarily constitute a problem. Indeed, as will be explored below, it is highly questionable whether, as has been suggested, 'this has created a new exception to the non-discrimination principle of the WTO' through which 'an acceded member may be treated less favourably than the original members under the WTO Agreement'.[132] The next section

[128] Qin (2017), Mind the Gap: Navigating Between the WTO Agreement and Its Accession Protocols.

[129] Qin (2017), Mind the Gap: Navigating Between the WTO Agreement and Its Accession Protocols. Qin has been critical of the way in which WTO Members have used this 'freedom' and has suggested that the 'terms to be agreed' should be understood as merely referring to market access commitments. See below, Chapter 5.

[130] Qin (2017), Mind the Gap: Navigating Between the WTO Agreement and Its Accession Protocols, at 238.

[131] Consider, for example, the rules on Special and Differential Treatment and the existence of plurilateral agreements such as the Information Technology Agreement and the Agreement on Government Procurement.

[132] Qin (2017), Mind the Gap: Navigating Between the WTO Agreement and Its Accession Protocols, at 239. Qin transposes the concept of non-discrimination

examines some of the issues in the relationship between the commitments resulting from the accession negotiations and the WTO Agreement.

4.3.2 Issues in the Relationship between Commitments in Protocols of Accession and the WTO Agreement

4.3.2.1 Article XX of the GATT 1994

Article XX of the GATT 1994 contains the general exceptions and provides for a list of potential grounds for justifications that a Member can invoke in order to 'remedy' an otherwise GATT-inconsistent measure. Consequently, the article will only be invoked once a measure taken by a Member has been found to be in violation of one of the obligations contained in the GATT 1994. For example, Members have invoked Article XX(g) of the GATT 1994 to justify an import restriction – inconsistent with Article XI of the GATT 1994 – on grounds of the preservation of 'clean air'.[133] Similarly, Members have had recourse to Article XX of the GATT 1994 in order to justify measures that had been found to be inconsistent with the national treatment obligation contained in Article III GATT 1994 and the MFN treatment obligation contained in Article I GATT 1994.[134]

4.3.2.1.1 The substance of Article XX of the GATT 1994 Article XX GATT 1994 consists of 11 paragraphs and a chapeau. The paragraphs contain a number of societal objectives that Members may pursue in violation of their obligations under the GATT 1994, provided that they fulfil the criteria stipulated. The chapeau serves as an anti-abuse provision that seeks to ensure that the pursuit of such a societal objective does not serve as a guise for protectionist intentions. The requirements of the paragraphs and the chapeau apply in conjunction, as the Appellate Body explained in *US – Gasoline*:

> In order that the justifying protection of Article XX may be extended to it, the measure at issue must not only come under one or another of the particular exceptions – paragraphs (a) to (j) – listed under Article XX; it must also satisfy the requirements imposed by the opening clauses of Article XX. The analysis is, in other words, two-tiered: first, provisional justification by reason

---

as applied to trade in goods and services under the GATT 1994 and GATS to the treatment of WTO Members. Language such as 'treated less favourably' borrows from the national treatment provisions in these agreements.

133 Appellate Body Report, *US – Gasoline*, at 13–15.

134 See, for example, Panel Report, *EC – Asbestos*; Appellate Body Reports, *EC – Seal Products*.

of characterization of the measure under XX(g); second, further appraisal of the same measure under the introductory clauses of Article XX.[135]

This subsection briefly discusses the paragraphs of Article XX GATT 1994 that have been invoked most often in WTO dispute settlement practice, as well as the operation of the chapeau.[136]

Article XX(a) of the GATT 1994 concerns measures necessary for the protection of public morals. The case law on this particular paragraph is limited. The article was referred to in a limited number of GATT panel reports and was invoked in WTO dispute settlement proceedings in, inter alia, *China – Publications and Audiovisual Products*.[137] This paragraph was also invoked by the European Union in *EC – Seal Products*.[138] In that dispute the Appellate Body upheld the Panel's finding that 'the EU Seal Regime is provisionally deemed necessary within the meaning of Article XX(a) of the GATT 1994'. The finding attracted a lot of attention from scholars wondering whether the interpretation does not result in the scope of the exception becoming too broad.[139] In *Colombia – Textiles* the Panel heard the argument that Colombia's policies aimed at combating money laundering were necessary to protect public morals.[140] Although the Panel accepted that in theory such policies could fall within the scope of the public morals exception, Colombia in this dispute had not shown that the compound tariff that formed part of the policy was 'designed to' protect public morals.[141] Theoretically, the Panel could have stopped its

135 Appellate Body Report, *US – Gasoline*, at 22.

136 For a more elaborate discussion on the operation of the general exceptions in Article XX of the GATT 1994 see, inter alia, Van den Bossche and Zdouc (2013), *The Law and Policy of the World Trade Organization*, at 545–82; Lester, Simon, Mercurio, Bryan and Davies, Arwel (2012), *World Trade Law: Text, Materials and Commentary*, Oxford, Hart Publishing, at 363–418.

137 Appellate Body Report, *China – Publications and Audiovisual Products*, paras. 205–33. Delimatsis, Panagiotis (2011), 'Protecting Public Morals in a Digital Age: Revisiting the WTO Rulings on US – Gambling and China – Audiovisual Products', *Journal of International Economic Law* (14) (2), pp. 257–93.

138 Appellate Body Reports, *EC – Seal Products*, para. 5.290.

139 See, inter alia, Cooreman, Barbara (2016), 'Extraterritorial Environmental Concerns and Public Morals: Testing the Limits of Article XX(a) GATT after Seals', *Journal of International Trade and Arbitration Law* (5) (2), pp. 519–57; Howse, Robert, Langille, Joanna and Sykes, Katie (2015), 'Pluralism in Practice: Moral Legislation and the Law of the WTO after Seal Products', *George Washington International Law Review* (48), pp. 81–150.

140 Panel Report, *Colombia – Textiles*, circulated 27 November 2015.

141 Panel Report, *Colombia – Textiles*, para. 7.401.

analysis at this stage. However, presumably to enable the Appellate Body to have a better record of facts and arguments, the Panel proceeded by analysing the necessity of the measure. The conclusion of this second step of the analysis, determining whether the measure is 'necessary' to fulfil the policy objective, was that this was not the case.[142] Inter alia, the Panel found that Colombia had 'not demonstrated the contribution of the compound tariff to the alleged objective of combating money laundering'.[143]

The second paragraph of Article XX concerns measures that are 'necessary to protect human, animal or plant life or health'. Similarly to Article XX(a) the paragraph contains a two-tier test. Provisional justification under Article XX(b) GATT 1994 is present if: i) the policy objective of the measure is the protection of the life or health of humans, animals or plants; and ii) the measure is necessary to fulfil that policy objective.[144] In respect of the first part of this two-tier test, panels and the Appellate Body have shown 'a significant degree of deference in accepting that the policy objective of a measure was to protect life or health of humans, animals or plants'.[145] According to the Appellate Body the second step of determining necessity involves 'weighing and balancing' which is 'a holistic operation that involves putting all the variables of the equation together and evaluating them in relation to each other after having examined them individually, in order to reach an overall judgement'.[146]

Article XX(g) deals with measures that are aimed at addressing the exhaustion of natural resources and the corresponding environmental concerns.[147] More specifically, the article deals with measures taken as part of policies that relate to the conservation of exhaustible natural resources.[148] The test of paragraph (g) of Article XX GATT is three-tiered. It requires that a measure i) relates to the 'conservation of

---

142 Panel Report, *Colombia – Textiles*, para. 7.470.

143 Panel Report, *Colombia – Textiles*, para. 7.445.

144 Van den Bossche and Zdouc (2013), *The Law and Policy of the World Trade Organization*, at 554.

145 Van den Bossche and Zdouc (2013), *The Law and Policy of the World Trade Organization*, at 555.

146 Appellate Body Report, *Brazil – Retreaded Tyres*, para. 182.

147 Van den Bossche and Zdouc (2013), *The Law and Policy of the World Trade Organization*, at 565.

148 Chi, Manjiao (2014), 'Exhaustible Natural Resource in WTO Law: GATT Article XX (g) Disputes and Their Implications', *Journal of World Trade* (48) (5), pp. 939–66; Franke, Martina (2011), 'WTO, China – Raw Materials: Ein Beitrag zum fairen Rohstoffhandel?', Beiträge zum Transnationalen

exhaustible natural resources', ii) 'relates to' the conservation of exhaustible natural resources and iii) be 'made effective in conjunction with' restrictions on domestic production or consumption. As part of the first step in the three-tier test, in *US – Shrimp* the Appellate Body adopted a broad, 'evolutionary' interpretation of the concept of 'exhaustible natural resources', holding that:

> The words of Article XX(g), 'exhaustible natural resources', were actually crafted more than 50 years ago. They must be read by a treaty interpreter in the light of contemporary concerns of the community of nations about the protection and conservation of the environment. While Article XX was not modified in the Uruguay Round, the preamble attached to the WTO Agreement shows that the signatories to that Agreement were, in 1994, fully aware of the importance and legitimacy of environmental protection as a goal of national and international policy. The preamble of the WTO Agreement – which informs not only the GATT 1994, but also the other covered agreements – explicitly acknowledges 'the objective of sustainable development'.
>
> [...]
>
> From the perspective embodied in the preamble of the WTO Agreement, we note that the generic term 'natural resources' in Article XX(g) is not 'static' in its content or reference but is rather 'by definition, evolutionary'. It is, therefore, pertinent to note that modern international conventions and declarations make frequent references to natural resources as embracing both living and non-living resources.[149]

The Appellate Body, referencing its earlier Report in *US – Shrimp*, summarized the second step of the three-tier test as follows in *China – Raw Materials*:

> In order to fall within the ambit of subparagraph (g) of Article XX, a measure must 'relat[e] to the conservation of exhaustible natural resources'. The term 'relat[e] to' is defined as 'hav[ing] some connection with, be[ing] connected to'. The Appellate Body has found that, for a measure to relate to conservation in the sense of Article XX(g), there must be 'a close and genuine relationship of ends and means'. The word 'conservation', in turn, means 'the preservation of the environment, especially of natural resources'.[150]

Wirtschaftsrecht, Heft 114, Institut für Wirtschaftsrecht, Martin-Luther Universität Halle-Wittenberg.

149 Appellate Body Report, *US – Shrimp*, paras. 129–30 (in relevant part, footnotes omitted).

150 Appellate Body Reports, *China – Raw Materials*, para. 355 (footnotes omitted); Liu, Han-Wei and Maughan, John (2012), 'China's Rare Earths Export

Finally, the third step in the three-tier test – that the measure be 'made effective in conjunction with' restrictions on domestic production or consumption – is a requirement of 'evenhandedness'.[151] In *China – Raw Materials* the Appellate Body interpreted the term 'in conjunction' to mean that 'the trade restriction must operate jointly with the restrictions on domestic production or consumption'.[152] It held that 'Article XX(g) permits trade measures relating to the conservation of exhaustible natural resources if such trade measures work together with restrictions on domestic production or consumption, which operate so as to conserve an exhaustible natural resource'.[153] Consequently it reversed the Panel's finding on this point, as the Panel had interpreted the phrase 'made effective in conjunction with' in Article XX(g) of the GATT 1994 as requiring a separate showing that the purpose of the challenged measure must be to make effective restrictions on domestic production or consumption.[154]

Notably, the Panel agreed with China's argument that the principle of sovereignty over natural resources should be taken into account in the interpretation of Article XX(g) of the GATT 1994. China had argued that 'nothing should interfere with their sovereignty over such natural resources'.[155] The Panel ultimately held that, in light of Article 31(3)(c) of the Vienna Convention, the interpretation of Article XX(g) GATT 1994:

> should 'take into account' the principle of sovereignty over natural resources. The principle of sovereignty over natural resources affords Members the opportunity to use their natural resources to promote their own development while regulating the use of these resources to ensure sustainable development. Conservation and economic development are not necessarily mutually exclusive policy goals; they can operate in harmony. So too can such policy goals operate in harmony with WTO obligations, for Members must exercise their sovereignty over natural resources consistently with their WTO obligations. In

---

Quotas: Out of the China – Raw Materials Gate, but Past the WTO's Finish Line?', *Journal of International Economic Law* (15) (4), pp. 971–1005.

151 Van den Bossche and Zdouc (2013), *The Law and Policy of the World Trade Organization*, at 567.

152 Appellate Body Reports, *China – Raw Materials*, para. 356.

153 Appellate Body Reports, *China – Raw Materials*, para. 360.

154 Panel Reports, *China – Raw Materials*, paras. 7.465–7.467; Appellate Body Reports, *China – Raw Materials*, para. 361.

155 Panel Reports, *China – Raw Materials*, para. 7.356. See, inter alia, Gu, Bin (2011), 'Mineral Export Restraints and Sustainable Development: Are Rare Earths Testing the WTO's Loopholes?', *Journal of International Economic Law* (14) (4), pp. 765–805.

> the Panel's view, Article XX(g) has been interpreted and applied in a manner that respects WTO Members' sovereign rights over their own natural resources.[156]

The second part of the two-tier test laid down by Article XX GATT 1994 involves an assessment of whether the measure meets the requirements of the chapeau of that article. The chapeau reads (in relevant part):

> Subject to the requirement that such measures are not applied in a manner which would constitute a means of arbitrary or unjustifiable discrimination between countries where the same conditions prevail, or a disguised restriction on international trade, nothing in this Agreement shall be construed to prevent the adoption or enforcement by any contracting party of measures.

Consequently, once a measure has been provisionally justified under one of the paragraphs of Article XX GATT 1994 discussed above, it is necessary to determine whether the measure is applied in a way that would constitute 'a misuse or abuse of the exceptions of Article XX GATT 1994'.[157]

The Appellate Body has held that the discrimination test included in the chapeau of Article XX GATT 1994 does not prohibit discrimination per se, but rather arbitrary and unjustifiable discrimination.[158] Referencing its earlier Reports in *US – Shrimp* and *Brazil – Retreaded Tyres*, the Appellate Body in *EC – Seal Products* declared that:

> [o]ne of the most important factors in the assessment of arbitrary or unjustifiable discrimination is the question of whether the discrimination can be reconciled with, or is rationally related to, the policy objective with respect to which the measure has been provisionally justified under one of the subparagraphs of Article XX.

The finding by the Appellate Body in *US – Shrimp* has been summarized as follows: 'when a measure is applied in a rigid and inflexible manner, the application of the measure may constitute "arbitrary discrimination" within the meaning of the chapeau of Article XX'.[159] With respect to the term 'unjustifiable discrimination' the Appellate Body noted in *US –*

---

[156] Panel Reports, *China – Raw Materials*, para. 7.381.

[157] Van den Bossche and Zdouc (2013), *The Law and Policy of the World Trade Organization*, at 573.

[158] Appellate Body Report, *US – Gasoline*, at 23. See also Van den Bossche and Zdouc (2013), *The Law and Policy of the World Trade Organization*, at 574.

[159] Van den Bossche and Zdouc (2013), *The Law and Policy of the World Trade Organization*, at 575.

Gasoline that 'the resulting discrimination [from the application of the measure] must have been foreseen' and should not merely be 'inadvertent or unavoidable'.[160] Therefore, the deliberate nature of the discrimination is crucial. The term 'disguised restriction on international trade' has not been interpreted in WTO dispute settlement proceedings since *US – Gasoline*. There the Appellate Body stated that the term 'whatever else it covers, may properly be read as embracing restrictions amounting to arbitrary or unjustifiable discrimination in international trade under the guise of a measure formally within the terms of an exception listed in Article XX'.[161] Since the terms 'arbitrary or unjustifiable discrimination' and 'disguised restriction on trade' encompass an analysis of the same considerations, panels and the Appellate Body have been able to limit themselves to examining the first term.[162]

4.3.2.1.2 The scope of application of Article XX of the GATT 1994

The 'chapeau' of Article XX of the GATT 1994 ends with the phrase that '*nothing* in *this* Agreement shall be construed to prevent the adoption or enforcement by any contracting party of measures', followed by several paragraphs.[163] The term 'nothing' implies that Article XX GATT 1994 is capable of justifying inconsistencies with *any* of the GATT obligations.[164] The language of Article XX GATT 1994 dates back to the GATT 1947, which already contained this provision. In the GATT era the term 'this' simply referred to the provisions of the GATT 1947. At the time when the provision was drafted, there was no other agreement that could contain a provision that could 'be construed to prevent the adoption or enforcement' of measures taken by a GATT Contracting Party. With the establishment of the WTO at the end of the Uruguay Round of Multilateral Trade Negotiations the scope of the multilateral trading system expanded significantly. The WTO Agreement operates as an umbrella agreement to which many agreements are annexed. The text of the GATT

---

160 Appellate Body Report, *US – Gasoline*, at 28–9.

161 Appellate Body Report, *US – Gasoline*, at 25.

162 Smith, Fiona (2015), 'Natural Resources and Global Value Chains: What Role for the WTO?', *International Journal of Law in Context* (11) (2), pp. 135–52; Switzer, Stephanie, Gerber, Leonardus and Sindico, Francesco (2015), 'Access to Minerals: WTO Export Restrictions and Climate Change Considerations', *Laws*, (4), pp. 617–37.

163 Emphasis added.

164 Van den Bossche and Zdouc (2013), *The Law and Policy of the World Trade Organization*, at 548.

1947 is incorporated into the WTO framework through a reference in the GATT 1994, Article 1 of which provides (in relevant part):

> The General Agreement on Tariffs and Trade 1994 ('GATT 1994') shall consist of:
>
> the provisions in the General Agreement on Tariffs and Trade, dated 30 October 1947, annexed to the Final Act Adopted at the Conclusion of the Second Session of the Preparatory Committee of the United Nations Conference on Trade and Employment (excluding the Protocol of Provisional Application), as rectified, amended or modified by the terms of legal instruments which have entered into force before the date of entry into force of the WTO Agreement.

The GATT 1994 thus consists of inter alia, the GATT 1947. Considering that the GATT 1994 is not the only multilateral trade agreement on trade in goods annexed to the WTO Agreement, the question has arisen whether provisions contained in the GATT 1994 are also applicable to these other non-GATT instruments. This section examines under what conditions this might be the case, with a particular focus on the disputes involving protocols of accession that have dealt with this issue. Note that this chapter does not include any argument as to the supposed applicability of Article XX GATT 1994 exceptions to agreements such as the Agreement on Subsidies and Countervailing Measures (SCM Agreement) or the Agreement on the Application of Sanitary and Phytosanitary Measures (SPS Agreement).[165]

---

[165] In the context of *Canada – Renewable Energy/Feed-in Tariff* (DS412 and DS426), the International Institute for Sustainable Development (IISD), the Canadian Environmental Law Association (CELA) and Ecojustice Canada jointly filed an Amicus Curiae submission in which it was argued that Article XX of the GATT 1994 should be applicable to measures that had been found inconsistent with the SCM Agreement. The submission put forward inter alia, that '[t]he term "this Agreement" in the chapeau of Article XX of the GATT 1994 has no clear "ordinary" meaning of its own. This term was contained in the GATT 1947, prior to the Uruguay Round, when the GATT 1947 itself constituted the primary multilateral trade agreement. The GATT 1947 was carried over into the WTO Agreement essentially as it is, without being rewritten to take into account its new place as one of many related "goods" agreements, bound together in an annex. The reference to "this Agreement" must, therefore, necessarily be interpreted in the light of today's placement of this provision and the link of the GATT 1994 to other Annex 1A agreements, as discussed above.' See also, inter alia, Andemariam, Senai (2006), 'Can (Should) Article XX(b) GATT be a Defense to Inconsistencies with the SPS/TBT Agreements?', *The Journal of World Investment & Trade* (7) (4), pp. 519–44; and Shadikhodjaev, Sherzod

4.3.2.1.2.1 REFERENCES TO ARTICLE XX OF THE GATT IN WTO AGREEMENTS A number of agreements annexed to the WTO Agreement include explicit references to Article XX of the GATT 1994, whereas others, such as the General Agreement on Trade in Services, include their own article containing general exceptions. Article 3 to the Agreement on Trade-Related Investment Measures (TRIMS Agreement) stipulates that '[a]ll exceptions under GATT 1994 shall apply, as appropriate, to the provisions of this Agreement'. Article 2.6 of the Agreement on Preshipment Inspection refers to Article XX of the GATT 1994 in respect of additional transparency procedures. It provides (in relevant part): 'in emergency situations of the types addressed by Articles XX and XXI of GATT 1994, such additional requirements or changes may be applied to a shipment before the exporter has been informed'. This is, however, something entirely different from declaring that the general exceptions contained in Article XX of the GATT 1994 are available to justify inconsistencies with the obligations of the Agreement on Preshipment Inspection. The SPS Agreement contains two references to Article XX(b) of the GATT 1994. First, the preamble provides that the drafters desired to 'elaborate rules for the application of the provisions of GATT 1994 which relate to the use of sanitary or phytosanitary measures, in particular the provisions of Article XX(b)'.[166] Second, Article 2.4 of the SPS Agreement provides:

> Sanitary or phytosanitary measures which conform to the relevant provisions of this Agreement shall be presumed to be in accordance with the obligations of the Members under the provisions of GATT 1994 which relate to the use of sanitary or phytosanitary measures, in particular the provisions of Article XX(b).

The SPS Agreement thus serves as an elaboration of the test contained in Article XX(b) of the GATT. It does not incorporate any of the other paragraphs of that article into the text of the agreement. On a side note, the Agreement on Import Licensing Procedures does not contain a reference to the general exceptions of Article XX of the GATT 1994, but does refer to the national security exceptions contained in Article XXI of the GATT 1994.[167] Given the wide variety in the ways in which Article XX of the GATT 1994 has been referenced in other WTO agreements, it can be assumed that the drafters of these agreements were aware of the

---

(2015), 'Renewable Energy and Government Support: Time to "Green" the SCM Agreement?', *World Trade Review* (14) (3), pp. 479–506.

[166] Footnote 1 to the SPS Agreement provides that '[i]n this Agreement, reference to Article XX(b) includes also the chapeau of that Article'.

[167] Article 1.10 of the Agreement on Import Licensing Procedures.

implications of these different approaches. Where they explicitly intended to make the general exceptions applicable to a non-GATT agreement, they specifically incorporated the article by reference. Where they chose to only make available another exception included in the GATT 1994, such as the national security exception, only a reference to Article XXI of the GATT 1994 is present. This is telling as it shows that Members were aware of the importance to reference certain provisions. Consequently, the absence of an explicit reference should also be attributed weight. This is confirmed by the Agreement on Trade Facilitation (TFA), which was adopted in 2014 and entered into force in February 2017.[168] Article 24.7 of the TFA provides that '[a]ll exceptions and exemptions under the GATT 1994 shall apply to the provisions of this Agreement'.

In addition to explicit references to Article XX of the GATT 1994 or the 'exceptions' under the GATT 1994, there is language in certain non-GATT agreements that led some authors to conclude that Article XX GATT 1994 would be available to justify measures that would otherwise be inconsistent with non-GATT agreements. These conclusions have mostly been drawn after the interpretation developed by the Appellate Body in the context of *China – Publications and Audiovisual Products* which is discussed in detail below. At this stage it suffices to mention that the Appellate Body's finding that the phrase 'in a manner consistent with the WTO Agreement' – contained in the relevant paragraph of China's Protocol of Accession – allowed for recourse to Article XX 1994 has been interpreted by some as allowing for the possibility to rely on Article XX of the GATT 1994 to justify violations of non-GATT provisions.[169]

[168] Agreement on Trade Facilitation, Annex to the Protocol Amending the Marrakesh Agreement Establishing the World Trade Organization. Protocol Amending the Marrakesh Agreement Establishing the World Trade Organization, WTO, General Council, 27 November 2014, WT/L/940.

[169] Lester, Mercurio and Davies (2012), *World Trade Law*, at 367. They note that '[t]he question of whether Article XX applies outside the context of the GATT is an important one with systemic implications. Perhaps wisely, the Appellate Body has resisted putting forward an overall solution to the issue, instead waiting to see if defendants invoke Article XX and then addressing the issue on a case-by-case basis. As a result, however, it is difficult to draw any broad conclusions on how the issue will be dealt with under specific provisions.' This statement is important in light of the subsequent section. Although this contains an overview of explicit and (potential) implicit references to Article XX of the GATT 1994, it should always be recalled that, although the text of the commitment is very important, an interpretation in the context of a specific dispute would always take into account the context of the relevant provision as

4.3.2.1.2.2 References to Article XX of the GATT 1994 in protocols of accession In addition to the references in agreements that are annexed to the WTO Agreement, such as the TRIMS Agreement and the SPS Agreement discussed above, Article XX of the GATT 1994 has been referenced in a number of protocols of accession. The references are typically included in respect of certain commitments that have been made by the acceding state or customs territory. Only references that are included in a commitment paragraph are shown in this overview, as only these paragraphs constitute treaty text.[170] Although these 'non-treaty text' paragraphs might constitute 'legal context', the analysis of whether that is so under a particular set of circumstances would have to rest on a case-by-case analysis.

Table 4.1 shows that there are a variety of ways in which Article XX of the GATT 1994 has been referenced in the context of WTO protocols of accession. The reference is most commonly included in the working party report which contains the commitments on specific matters entered into by the applicant state. In some instances the reference is explicit. This is so where the commitment, for example, reads 'from the date of accession, Tonga's applied laws and regulations regarding export restrictions would be in conformity with the relevant provisions of the WTO, including Articles XI, XVII, *XX* and XXI of the GATT 1994'.[171]

---

well. As a result it is important to bear in mind that a case-by-case analysis will always be required.

170 Panel Report, *US – Shrimp II (Vietnam)*, para. 7.175. For an earlier finding on this particular issue, see Panel Reports, *China – Raw Materials*, para. 7.145. Para. 7.145 reads: 'Paragraph 155 of China's Working Party Report has the same content as Paragraph 11.3 of China's Accession Protocol, providing that "taxes and charges should be eliminated unless applied in conformity with GATT Article VIII or listed in Annex 6 to the Draft Protocol". Paragraph 156 provides: "China noted that the majority of products were free of export duty, although 84 items, including tungsten ore, ferrosilicon and some aluminium products, were subject to export duties". There is no reference, explicit or implicit, to the availability of Article XX defences for such commitments. Although they do not form part of the explicit commitments covered by China's Accession Protocol, the provisions of Paragraphs 155 and 156 of China's Working Party Report are part of the legal context of Paragraph 11.3 of China's Accession Protocol and articulate clearly the concerns of WTO Members at the time with respect to China's use of export duties.'

171 WTO, Report of the Working Party on the Accession of Tonga to the World Trade Organization, WTO/ACC/TON/17, WT/MIN(05)/4, 2 December 2005, para. 84 (emphasis added).

Table 4.1 References to Article XX of the GATT 1994

Member and Commitment Paragraph in Working Party Report (in order of Accession)[172]	Reference (in relevant part)	Type
Ecuador (38)	The representative of Ecuador said that any prior authorizations or license requirements incompatible with the provisions of the General Agreement 1994 or the Multilateral Trade Agreements, in particular the WTO Agreement on Import Licensing Procedures, would be eliminated at the time of accession. From the date of accession additional measures would only be applied as provided for in the Articles of the General Agreement 1994, for instance Articles III and XX, and the WTO Agreements. If justified under relevant provisions, restrictions would be implemented in accordance with the Agreement on Import Licensing Procedures	Applicability of Article XX to prior authorizations and license requirements. Article XX is not referenced in the Agreement on Import Licensing Procedures
Bulgaria (49)	In conclusion the representative of Bulgaria confirmed that, in the context of its accession to the Agreement Establishing the WTO, the Bulgarian Government would use its authority to suspend or prohibit imports and exports or otherwise restrict their quantities in conformity with the provisions of the GATT 1994 in particular Articles XI, XII, XIII, XIX, XX and XXI	Confirmation of GATT provisions

[172] In many instances other paragraphs of the Working Party Report (also) contain references to Article XX of the GATT 1994. However, as they do not constitute treaty text, they are not listed here.

Table 4.1 (continued)

Member and Commitment Paragraph in Working Party Report (in order of Accession)	Reference (in relevant part)	Type
Mongolia (20)	The representative of Mongolia said that Mongolia commits that, from the date of accession, the authority of its Government to suspend imports and exports or to apply licensing requirements that can be used to suspend trade in the products under license would be applied in conformity with the requirements of the WTO, in particular GATT 1994 Articles VI, XI, XVIII, XIX, XX, and XXI, and the Multilateral Trade Agreements on Agriculture, Sanitary and Phytosanitary Measures, Import Licensing Procedures, and Technical Barriers to Trade and that his Government would not maintain from the date of accession non-tariff import measures, including bans, quotas, permits and licences, that cannot be justified specifically under WTO provisions	Confirmation of GATT provisions
Panama (42)	The representative of Panama confirmed that, from the date of accession, the authority of his Government to suspend imports and exports or to apply licensing requirements that could be used to suspend, ban, or otherwise restrict the quantity of trade would be applied in conformity with the requirements of the WTO, in particular Articles XI, XIII, XVIII, XIX, XX, and XXI of the GATT 1994, and the Multilateral Trade Agreements on Agriculture, Sanitary and Phytosanitary Measures, Import Licensing Procedures, Safeguards and Technical Barriers to Trade, and that his Government would eliminate from the date of its accession, non-tariff import measures, including bans, quotas, permits, prior authorization requirements and licences that could not be justified specifically under WTO provisions	Confirmation of GATT provisions

Member and Commitment Paragraph in Working Party Report (in order of Accession)	Reference (in relevant part)	Type
Kyrgyz Republic (60)	The representative of the Kyrgyz Republic confirmed that the Kyrgyz Republic would, from the date of accession, eliminate and shall not introduce, re-introduce or apply quantitative restrictions on imports or other non-tariff measures such as licensing, quotas, bans, permits, prior authorization requirements, licensing requirements and other restrictions having equivalent effect that cannot be justified under the provisions of the WTO Agreements	Indirect reference to 'justified under the provisions of the WTO Agreements'
Latvia (59)	[The representative of Latvia] further confirmed that the legal authority of the Government of Latvia to suspend imports and exports or to apply licensing requirements that could be used to suspend, ban, or otherwise restrict the quantity of trade will be applied from the date of accession in conformity with the requirements of the WTO, in particular Articles XI, XII, XIII, XVIII, XIX, XX and XXI of the GATT 1994, and the Multilateral Trade Agreements on Agriculture, Sanitary and Phytosanitary Measures, Import Licensing Procedures, Safeguards and Technical Barriers to Trade	Confirmation of GATT provisions
Estonia (83)	The representative of Estonia confirmed that any remaining export control requirements were fully consistent with WTO provisions, including those contained in Articles XI, XVII, XX and XXI of the GATT 1994[173]	Confirmation of GATT provisions

[173] This will be referred to as the Standard Commitment.

Table 4.1 (continued)

Member and Commitment Paragraph in Working Party Report (in order of Accession)	Reference (in relevant part)	Type
Jordan (88)	The representative of Jordan confirmed that Jordan would, from the date of accession, eliminate and shall not introduce, re-introduce or apply quantitative restrictions on imports, or other non-tariff measures such as licensing, quotas, bans, permits, prior authorization requirements, licensing requirements and other restrictions having equivalent effect that cannot be justified under the provisions of the WTO Agreement. Any further amendments to the import licensing regime after accession would be fully in accordance with all relevant provisions of the WTO, including the Agreement on Import Licensing Procedures. Jordan would replace non-automatic import licensing with automatic import licensing for 'milk for industrial use' within 3 years from the date of accession. He further confirmed that the legal authority of the Government of Jordan to suspend imports and exports or to apply licensing requirements that could be used to suspend, ban, or otherwise restrict the quantity of trade will be applied from the date of accession in conformity with the requirements of the WTO, in particular Articles XI, XII, XIII, XVIII, XIX, XX and XXI of the GATT 1994	Confirmation of GATT provisions
Georgia (86)	Standard Commitment, see above	Confirmation of GATT provisions
Albania (90)	Standard Commitment, see above	Confirmation of GATT provisions
Oman (77)	Standard Commitment, see above	Confirmation of GATT provisions

Member and Commitment Paragraph in Working Party Report (in order of Accession)	Reference (in relevant part)	Type
Croatia (73)	The representative of Croatia confirmed that Croatia would, from the date of accession, eliminate and shall not introduce, re-introduce or apply quantitative restrictions on imports, or other non-tariff measures such as licensing, quotas, bans, permits, prior authorization requirements, licensing requirements and other restrictions having equivalent effect that cannot be justified under the provisions of the WTO Agreement. He further confirmed that the legal authority of the Government of Croatia to suspend imports and exports or to apply licensing requirements that could be used to suspend, ban, or otherwise restrict the quantity of trade will be applied from the date of accession in conformity with the requirements of the WTO, in particular Articles XI, XII, XIII, XVIII, XIX, XX and XXI of the GATT 1994	Confirmation of GATT provisions
Lithuania (29)	Standard Commitment, see above	Confirmation of GATT provisions
Moldova (83)	Standard Commitment, see above	Confirmation of GATT provisions

Table 4.1 (continued)

Member and Commitment Paragraph in Working Party Report (in order of Accession)	Reference (in relevant part)	Type
China (Paragraph 5.1 Protocol of Accession)	Without prejudice to China's right to regulate trade in a manner consistent with the WTO Agreement, China shall progressively liberalize the availability and scope of the right to trade, so that, within three years after accession, all enterprises in China shall have the right to trade in all goods throughout the customs territory of China, except for those goods listed in Annex 2A which continue to be subject to state trading in accordance with this Protocol	'in a manner consistent with the WTO Agreement', interpreted by the Appellate Body as allowing recourse to Article XX of the GATT 1994 in China – Publications and Audiovisual Products[174]
Paragraph 7.2 Protocol of Accession	In implementing the provisions of Articles III and XI of the GATT 1994 and the Agreement on Agriculture, China shall eliminate and shall not introduce, re-introduce or apply non-tariff measures that cannot be justified under the provisions of the WTO Agreement	Confirmation of GATT provisions
122	The representative of China confirmed that China would not introduce, re-introduce or apply non-tariff measures other than listed in Annex 3 of the Draft Protocol unless justified under the WTO Agreement	Confirmation of GATT provisions
162	Moreover, export restrictions and licensing would only be applied, after the date of accession, in those cases where this was justified by GATT provisions	Confirmation of GATT provisions

[174] Appellate Body Report, *China – Publications and Audiovisual Products*, paras. 205–33.

Member and Commitment Paragraph in Working Party Report (in order of Accession)	Reference (in relevant part)	Type
165	The representative of China confirmed that upon accession, remaining non-automatic restrictions on exports would be notified to the WTO annually and would be eliminated unless they could be justified under the WTO Agreement or the Draft Protocol	Confirmation of GATT provisions
217	The representative of China stated that China would ensure that no price increase in respect to imports, in particular by state trading enterprises, would result in protection beyond that allowed in its Schedule of Concessions and Commitments on Goods or that was not otherwise justified under WTO rules	Confirmation of GATT provisions
Chinese Taipei (73)	The representative of Chinese Taipei said that Chinese Taipei also undertook to eliminate and not reintroduce or apply import bans, quantitative restrictions, licensing restrictions, or other non-tariff measures having similar effect which were not justified under specific provisions of the WTO Agreement	Confirmation of GATT provisions
Armenia (87)	Standard Commitment, see above	Confirmation of GATT provisions
FYR Macedonia (107)	Standard Commitment, see above	Confirmation of GATT provisions
Nepal (50)	Standard Commitment, see above	Confirmation of GATT provisions
84	The representative of Nepal confirmed that from the date of accession, Nepal would apply its export licensing requirements and other export control requirements in conformity with WTO provisions, including those contained in Articles XI, XVII, XX and XXI of the GATT 1994	Confirmation of GATT provisions
Cambodia (82)	Standard Commitment, see above	Confirmation of GATT provisions

Table 4.1 (continued)

Member and Commitment Paragraph in Working Party Report (in order of Accession)	Reference (in relevant part)	Type
116	The representative of Cambodia stated that, from the date of accession, Cambodia would ensure that it applied its laws and regulations governing export measures and would act in conformity with the relevant provisions of the WTO, including Articles I and XI of the GATT 1994 and the Agreement on Subsidies and Countervailing Measures	Confirmation of GATT provisions
Saudi Arabia (132)	With respect to Satellite Internet Receivers, HS [Harmonized System] 85291000, the representative of Saudi Arabia noted that these products were currently listed in Annex F as banned imports. He confirmed that Saudi Arabia would permit imports of these products, subject to a non-automatic licence, within three years of the date of Saudi Arabia's accession to the WTO. In his government's view, non-automatic licensing was necessary to protect public morals. He further stated that internet service providers transmitting to such satellite internet receivers would be required to use a Saudi internet filtering facility	Confirmation of GATT provisions
155	Standard Commitment, see above	Confirmation of GATT provisions
158	Standard Commitment, see above	Confirmation of GATT provisions

Table 4.1 (continued)

Member and Commitment Paragraph in Working Party Report (in order of Accession)	Reference (in relevant part)	Type
179	Some members of the Working Party enquired whether the Kingdom of Saudi Arabia maintained any export controls. In response, the representative of Saudi Arabia stated that Saudi Arabia maintained no export bans, except on some items such as date seedlings, breeding horses and subsidized wheat and wheat flour. He informed the Working Party that the legal basis of the bans was the authority of the Council of Ministers and that the bases for the individual bans were as set out in Annex I (List of Banned Exports), i.e., GATT 1994 Article XX(a), (b), (d), (f) and (j). Some members of the Working Party asked whether Saudi Arabia intended to remove those bans prior to its accession to the WTO. In response, the representative of Saudi Arabia stated that there was no ban on the export of wheat and wheat flour; an export licence would be approved unless the wheat and wheat flour had been subsidized and the subsidy had not been repaid (i.e., if the subsidy had been returned to the government, the product could be exported). He further added that Saudi Arabia banned the export of date seedlings and breeding horses because the local breeds and varieties of these two items were pure and rare. The representative indicated that a list of banned exports was attached to the Working Party Report at Annex I; a list of exports subject to authorization/licensing was attached at Annex J. In reply to questions from a member of the Working Party, the representative stated that any trader or manufacturer could apply for an export licence, for which no fees were charged.	Confirmation of GATT provisions. Prejudging an analysis of panels and the Appellate Body on the consistency of certain measures with the requirements of certain paragraphs of Article XX of the GATT 1994

Table 4.1 (continued)

Member and Commitment Paragraph in Working Party Report (in order of Accession)	Reference (in relevant part)	Type
	He further said that there were no activity licensing requirements and that the application for the licence had to be submitted to the concerned ministry, i.e., the Ministries of Commerce and Industry, Agriculture, Health, Interior or Petroleum and Mineral Resources. He reported that the licenses were either automatic or non-automatic as indicated in Annex J and that the time period for obtaining the licence depended upon the nature of the exported product. At a later stage, the representative of Saudi Arabia added that Annexes I and J identified all products subject to export bans or export licensing, some of which were discussed below in response to questions from members of the Working Party. In response to a question from a member of the Working Party, the representative of Saudi Arabia stated that export traders needing licenses were required to have commercial registration. He added that information on export licensing procedures was available on the website of the Ministry of Commerce and Industry. He further added that the list of products subject to export licensing was presently not published but that, prior to accession, it would be published in the official gazette. He added that updates on export restrictions will also be published	
183	Standard Commitment, see above	Confirmation of GATT provisions
Viet Nam (215)	Standard Commitment, see above	Confirmation of GATT provisions
227	Standard Commitment, see above	Confirmation of GATT provisions

Member and Commitment Paragraph in Working Party Report (in order of Accession)	Reference (in relevant part)	Type
Tonga (84)	Standard Commitment, see above	Confirmation of GATT provisions
106	The representative of Tonga stated that from the date of accession, Tonga's applied laws and regulations regarding export restrictions would be in conformity with the relevant provisions of the WTO, including Articles XI, XVII, XX and XXI of the GATT 1994	Confirmation of GATT provisions
Ukraine (173)	The representative of Ukraine confirmed that from the date of accession Ukraine would maintain transparent and science based standards for trade in ground beef. He further confirmed that Ukraine would not introduce a ban on this product that could not be justified under the provisions of the WTO Agreement	Confirmation of GATT provisions
192	Standard Commitment, see above	Confirmation of GATT provisions
240	The representative of Ukraine confirmed that at present export duties were applied only to the goods listed in Table 20(a). He further confirmed that Ukraine would reduce export duties in accordance with the binding schedule contained in Table 20(b). He also confirmed that as regards these products, Ukraine would not increase export duties, nor apply other measures having an equivalent effect, unless justified under the exceptions of the GATT 1994. He further confirmed that the current duties and any changes in their application would be published in the Official Gazette. The representative of Ukraine also confirmed that from the date of accession, Ukraine will not apply any obligatory minimum export prices. The Working Party took note of these commitments. The Working Party agreed that these commitments do not constitute a reinterpretation of GATT 1994, nor affect the rights and obligations of other members in respect of provisions on the application of export duties, that are measures in accordance with GATT 1994	Explicit reference to the 'exceptions of the GATT 1994'

Table 4.1 (continued)

Member and Commitment Paragraph in Working Party Report (in order of Accession)	Reference (in relevant part)	Type
255	The representative of Ukraine confirmed that from the date of accession the export licensing requirements and other export restrictions and control requirements listed in Table 22(b) and paragraphs 242, 243 and 250 of this Report or any introduced in the future would be applied in conformity with WTO provisions, including those contained in Articles XI, XVII, XX and XXI of the GATT 1994	Confirmation of GATT provisions
Cape Verde (123)	Standard Commitment, see above	Confirmation of GATT provisions
Montenegro (114)	Standard Commitment, see above	Confirmation of GATT provisions
135	The representative of Montenegro confirmed that from the date of accession, any export licensing requirements and other export restrictions and control requirements with similar effect applied by Montenegro would either be eliminated or applied in conformity with WTO provisions, including those contained in Articles XI, XVII, XX and XXI of the GATT 1994	Confirmation of GATT provisions
Samoa (109)	Standard Commitment, see above	Confirmation of GATT provisions
134	The representative of Samoa confirmed that any quantitative export restrictions, including prohibitions, quotas and licensing systems would be applied in conformity with WTO provisions	Confirmation of GATT provisions
Russian Federation (487)	Standard Commitment, see above	Confirmation of GATT provisions

Member and Commitment Paragraph in Working Party Report (in order of Accession)	Reference (in relevant part)	Type
668	The representative of the Russian Federation confirmed, that, from the date of accession, quantitative restrictions on exports or restrictions on the sale for export of goods, such as quotas, bans, permits, prior authorization requirements, licensing requirements (including the requirements listed in Table 33), domestic market supply requirements or measures having equivalent effect that could not be justified under the provisions of the WTO Agreement, would be eliminated and not introduced, re-introduced or applied, whether by the Russian Federation or the competent bodies of the CU [Customs Union]. He further confirmed that discretionary authority to temporarily ban exports or otherwise restrict exports, including under provisions of the Agreement on Licensing, the Precious Stones and Metals Regulations, or Federal Law No. 164-FZ of 8 December 2003 'On the Fundamentals of State Regulation of Foreign Trade Activity' whether exercised by the Russian Federation or the competent bodies of the CU, would be applied from the date of accession in conformity with the provisions of the WTO Agreement. He also confirmed that, if the Russian Federation took recourse to Article XX(i) of the GATT 1994, with respect to any measures, whether applied by the Russian Federation or the competent bodies of the CU, restricting exports of domestic materials necessary to ensure essential quantities of such materials to a domestic or CU processing industry, such measures would not operate to increase the exports of or the protection of such industry	Confirmation of GATT provisions
Vanuatu (63)	Standard Commitment, see above	Confirmation of GATT provisions

Table 4.1 (continued)

Member and Commitment Paragraph in Working Party Report (in order of Accession)	Reference (in relevant part)	Type
Lao PDR (82)	Standard Commitment, see above	Confirmation of GATT provisions
Tajikistan (137)	Standard Commitment, see above	Confirmation of GATT provisions
181	The representative of Tajikistan confirmed that from the date of accession, Tajikistan would apply its export licensing requirements, quantitative restrictions and other export control requirements in conformity with WTO provisions, including those contained in Articles XI, XVII, XX and XXI of the GATT 1994	Confirmation of GATT provisions
Yemen (93)	The representative of Yemen said that imports were prohibited or restricted for environmental, health, national security and religious reasons, i.e. if considered contrary to Shari'a Law. Products subject to import prohibitions are listed in Table 12. In his view, these import prohibitions were consistent with Articles XX and XXI of the GATT 1994. Yemen also prohibited the importation of coffee and mango, and maintained seasonal restrictions on potatoes (other than seed potatoes), tomatoes, lettuce and chicory, oranges, mandarins, lemons, grapes, melons and papayas [...] The seasonal restrictions consisted of periods when importation was prohibited, and 'allowed' periods when the goods were subject to an additional duty of 35 per cent over and above the ordinary tariff of 25 per cent. Information on the production seasons, and the domestic production and consumption of these goods was provided in document WT/ACC/YEM/32 (pages 6–7). He confirmed that the import ban on coffee and mango and the seasonal import restrictions on agricultural products [...] would be removed from the date of accession	Confirmation of GATT provisions

Member and Commitment Paragraph in Working Party Report (in order of Accession)	Reference (in relevant part)	Type
107	The representative of Yemen confirmed that, from the date of accession, Yemen would eliminate and would not introduce, re-introduce or apply quantitative restrictions on imports or other non-tariff measures such as licensing, quotas, bans, permits, prior authorization requirements, licensing requirements, and other restrictions having equivalent effect, that cannot be justified under the provisions of the WTO Agreement. He also confirmed that, if balance-of-payments measures were necessary, Yemen would impose them in a manner consistent with the relevant WTO provisions, including Articles XII and XVIII of the GATT 1994 and the Understanding on Balance-of-Payments Provisions of the GATT 1994. He further confirmed that from the date of accession, Yemen would use its legal authority to suspend imports and exports, or to apply licensing requirements that could otherwise restrict the quantity of trade, only in conformity with the requirements of the WTO Agreement	Confirmation of GATT provisions
Seychelles (191)	Standard Commitment, see above	Confirmation of GATT provisions
240	The representative of Seychelles confirmed that, from the date of accession, Seychelles would apply its laws and regulations governing export measures, including prohibitions, export licensing requirements and other export control requirements, in conformity with WTO provisions including those contained in Articles XI, XVII, XX and XXI of the GATT 1994	Confirmation of GATT provisions

Table 4.1 (continued)

Member and Commitment Paragraph in Working Party Report (in order of Accession)	Reference (in relevant part)	Type
Kazakhstan (559)	The representative of Kazakhstan confirmed that, from the date of accession, quantitative restrictions on exports or restrictions on the sale for export of goods, such as quotas, bans, permits, prior authorization requirements, licensing requirements (including the requirements listed in Annex 6 of this Report), domestic market supply requirements or measures having equivalent effect that could not be justified under the provisions of the WTO Agreement, would be eliminated and not introduced, re-introduced or applied, whether by Kazakhstan or the competent bodies of the EAEU [Eurasian Economic Union]. She further confirmed that discretionary authority to temporarily ban exports or otherwise restrict exports, whether exercised by Kazakhstan or the competent bodies of the EAEU, would be applied from the date of accession in conformity with the provisions of the WTO Agreement. She also confirmed that, if Kazakhstan took recourse to Article XX(i) of the WTO General Agreement on Tariffs and Trade 1994, with respect to any measures, whether applied by Kazakhstan or the competent bodies of the EAEU, restricting exports of domestic materials necessary to ensure essential quantities of such materials to a domestic or EAEU processing industry, such measures would not operate to increase the exports of or the protection of such industry. The Working Party took note of these commitments	Additional commitment to ensure that 'such measures would not operate to increase the exports of or the protection of such industry'

Member and Commitment Paragraph in Working Party Report (in order of Accession)	Reference (in relevant part)	Type
Afghanistan	None[175]	
Liberia	None	

In two working party reports reference is made to Article XX in the context of measures that the acceding state appears to want to 'pre-emptively justify' by stating that they fall within the scope of the article. For example, Paragraph 179 of the Report on the Accession of Saudi Arabia lists certain measures, including bans, that Saudi Arabia considered that 'the bases for the individual bans were as set out in Annex I (List of Banned Exports), i.e., GATT 1994 Article XX(a), (b), (d), (f) and (j)'. Similarly, the Working Party Report on the Accession of Yemen contains the following statement:

> The representative of Yemen said that imports were prohibited or restricted for environmental, health, national security and religious reasons, i.e. if considered contrary to Shari'a Law. Products subject to import prohibitions are listed in Table 12. In his view, these import prohibitions were consistent with Articles XX and XXI of the GATT 1994.[176]

In other instances the reference is explicit, but even more general. For example, the Working Party Report on the Accession of Ukraine contains a commitment on the reduction of certain export duties. In this respect the Report provides that 'Ukraine would not increase export duties, nor apply other measures having an equivalent effect, unless justified under the exceptions of the GATT 1994.'[177] However, the paragraph then concludes by stating that 'these commitments do not constitute a reinterpretation of GATT 1994, nor affect the rights and obligations of other members in respect of provisions on the application of export

[175] No reference to Article XX of the GATT 1994 in one of the commitment paragraphs. However, Annex 10 contains measures that are currently in place, along with their justification under Article XX GATT 1994. Annex 10 is, however, not referenced in any of the commitment paragraphs.

[176] WTO, Report of the Working Party on the Accession of Yemen to the World Trade Organization, WT/ACC/YEM/42, 4 October 2013, para. 93.

[177] WTO, Report of the Working Party on the Accession of Ukraine to the World Trade Organization, WT/ACC/UKR/152, 25 January 2008, para. 240.

duties, that are measures in accordance with GATT 1994'. This statement raises at least two questions: i) could the commitments entered into by an acceding Member upon its accession to the WTO ever constitute a 'reinterpretation' of GATT 1994, and if so, how? and, ii) why did the members of the Working Party – and indeed the WTO itself – deem it necessary to include this type of language? Interestingly, similar types of statements were not included in other accession working party reports until the Accession of Kazakhstan.[178] The relevant paragraph in its Working Party Report does, as such, not deal with the relationship between a commitment and the applicability of Article XX of the GATT 1994. Rather, the statement was made in the context of several paragraphs that deal with a commitment by Kazakhstan to eliminate export duties on certain products. In that context some Members 'stated that this was without prejudice to their views in respect of the status and legality of export duties in the framework of the WTO Agreement'. Although this statement is different from the one included in the Working Party Report on the Accession of Ukraine, it reflects the same concern that the commitments included in protocols of accession may lead to a 're-interpretation' of GATT 1994 and of the rights and obligations of other Members.

4.3.2.1.2.3 ARTICLE XX GATT 1994, PROTOCOLS OF ACCESSION AND WTO DISPUTE SETTLEMENT As mentioned above, *China – Publications and Audiovisual Products* was the first dispute in which the Panel and the Appellate Body had to rule on the relationship between commitments in protocols of accession and Article XX of the GATT 1994. The Panel recognized the existence of 'complex legal issues' in this particular dispute, as a result of the – yet to be established – relationship between protocols of accession and certain GATT 1994 provisions.[179] It proceeded with the substantive analysis of Article XX of the GATT 1994 and ultimately reached the conclusion that the measure could not be provisionally justified under

---

178 These statements are a reflection of the idea that, potentially, the commitments contained in protocols of accession may, even though they would appear to be specifically catered for the acceding Member, have an impact on the interpretation of other provisions of the covered agreements. Indeed, if a particular interpretative approach is adopted in respect of certain commitments contained in these protocols, this may have a bearing on the interpretation of similar provisions in the WTO Agreement.

179 Panel Report, *China – Publications and Audiovisual Products*, paras. 7.742–7.745.

paragraph (a) of that provision.[180] On appeal China requested the Appellate Body to reverse the Panel's findings under paragraph (a), to complete the analysis under the chapeau of Article XX of the GATT 1994 and to find that China could rely on Article XX(a) of the GATT 1994 to justify its measure in the event of an inconsistency with the commitments in its Protocol of Accession.[181] The Appellate Body rejected the *arguendo* approach adopted by the Panel, stating that 'assuming arguendo that China can invoke Article XX(a) could be at odds with the objective of promoting security and predictability through dispute settlement'.[182] Subsequently it examined the text of Paragraph 5.1 in order to determine whether a link with Article XX GATT 1994 was present.

Paragraph 5.1 of China's Protocol of Accession provides (in relevant part):

> Without prejudice to China's right to regulate trade in a manner consistent with the WTO Agreement, China shall progressively liberalize the availability and scope of the right to trade, so that, within three years after accession, all enterprises in China shall have the right to trade in all goods throughout the customs territory of China, except for those goods listed in Annex 2A which continue to be subject to state trading in accordance with this Protocol. Such right to trade shall be the right to import and export goods.

The Appellate Body noted that:

> We read the phrase 'in a manner consistent with the WTO Agreement' as referring to the WTO Agreement as a whole, including its Annexes. We note, in this respect, that we see the 'right to regulate', in the abstract, as an inherent power enjoyed by a Member's government, rather than a right bestowed by international treaties such as the WTO Agreement. [...] When what is being regulated is trade, then the reference in the introductory clause to 'consistent with the WTO Agreement' constrains the exercise of that

---

180 Panel Report, *China – Publications and Audiovisual Products*, paras. 7.910–7.914. As a result the Panel decided it was not necessary i) to decide on whether the Chinese measure fulfilled the requirements of the chapeau, and ii) to resolve the fundamental issue of whether the text of China's Protocol of Accession allowed it to have recourse to Article XX of the GATT in the first place.

181 Appellate Body Report, *China – Publications and Audiovisual Products*, para. 211.

182 Appellate Body Report, *China – Publications and Audiovisual Products*, paras. 213–15.

> regulatory power such that China's regulatory measures must be shown to conform to WTO disciplines.[183]

And:

> [W]TO Members' regulatory requirements may be WTO consistent in one of two ways. First, they may simply not contravene any WTO obligation. Secondly, even if they contravene a WTO obligation, they may be justified under *an applicable exception*. The reference to 'a manner consistent with the WTO Agreement' seems to us to encompass both types of WTO-consistency. Thus, we read the phrase 'right to regulate trade in a manner consistent with the WTO Agreement' as a reference to: (i) rights that the covered agreements affirmatively recognize as accruing to WTO Members, namely, the power of Members to take specific types of regulatory measures in respect of trade in goods when those measures satisfy prescribed WTO disciplines and meet specified criteria; and (ii) certain rights to take regulatory action that derogates from obligations under the *WTO Agreement* – that is, to relevant exceptions.[184]

In light of these observations the Appellate Body then continued its analysis to determine whether, in this particular case, Article XX of the GATT 1994 was available to China to justify measures inconsistent with its Protocol of Accession. It held:

> Any exercise of China's right to regulate trade will be protected under the introductory clause of paragraph 5.1 only if it is consistent with the WTO Agreement. This will be the case when China's measures regulating trade are of a type that the WTO Agreement recognizes that Members may take when they satisfy prescribed disciplines and meet specified conditions. Yet, these are not the only types of WTO-consistent measures that may be protected under the introductory clause of paragraph 5.1. Whether a measure regulating those who may engage in the import and export of goods falls within the scope of China's right to regulate trade may also depend on whether the measure has a clearly discernible, objective link to the regulation of trade in the goods at issue.[185]

In this particular case the Appellate Body found that there was, indeed, a 'clearly discernible, objective link' between the measure and the regulation of trade in the goods at issue, and that, therefore, China could rely

[183] Appellate Body Report, *China – Publications and Audiovisual Products*, para. 222.

[184] Appellate Body Report, *China – Publications and Audiovisual Products*, para. 223.

[185] Appellate Body Report, *China – Publications and Audiovisual Products*, para. 230.

on the general exceptions contained in Article XX of the GATT 1994.[186] Ultimately the Appellate Body concluded that China had not demonstrated that the measure at issue was 'necessary' in the context of Article XX(a) of the GATT 1994 and that, therefore, the measure could not be justified.[187] One of the most important elements of the Appellate Body's analysis was indeed that the answer to the question whether a violation of a commitment contained in a protocol of accession can be remedied by having access to the general exceptions contained in Article XX of the GATT 1994 is dependent on the text of the commitment in question. The need for a textual reference to 'connect' the relevant commitment to the relevant article in the GATT became present in this dispute. The Appellate Body refrained from making any general statements on the applicability of Article XX GATT 1994 to commitments contained in protocols of accession. The initial response to the Appellate Body's findings in *China – Publications and Audiovisual Products* was mixed.[188] It has been argued that the Appellate Body limits 'its legal reasoning to textual analysis, rather than discussing the treaty terms in their broader systemic context and in the light of their "object and purpose", which would entail inquiries into the underlying policy considerations'.[189] This

---

[186] Appellate Body Report, *China – Publications and Audiovisual Products*, para. 233.

[187] Appellate Body Report, *China – Publications and Audiovisual Products*, para. 337.

[188] Qin, Julia Ya (2011), 'Pushing the Limits of Global Governance: Trading Rights, Censorship and WTO Jurisprudence – A Commentary on the China-Publications Case', *Chinese Journal of International* Law (10), pp. 271–322, at 293–5. Qin stated, inter alia, that 'the AB's ruling on the availability of GATT Article XX to the Accession Protocol is a welcome development in WTO jurisprudence' and that 'it should not be difficult to establish the availability of GATT general exceptions to other WTO agreements regulating trade in goods, such as the Antidumping Agreement and the SCM [Agreement]'.

[189] Qin (2011), Pushing the Limits of Global Governance: Trading Rights, Censorship and WTO Jurisprudence – A Commentary on the China-Publications Case, at 316. Referencing remarks made by Irwin and Weiler who described the Appellate Body's approach as one of 'textual fetishism and policy phobia'. See, Irwin, Douglas A. and Weiler, Joseph (2008), 'Measures Affecting the Cross-Border Supply of Gambling and Betting Services (DS285)', *World Trade Review* (7) (1), pp. 71–113, at 89–95. One of the criticisms put forward by Irwin and Weiler is best summarized by their statement that '[e]xaggerated textualism is as undermining as is exaggerated teleology since, among many other concerns, at a profound level it severs the legitimating nexus between the law as the handmaiden of its social, political, and economic goals'. See also, Diamond, Richard (2008), 'Privatization and the Definition of Subsidy: A Critical Study of

argument for taking into account the object and purpose has, however, rightfully been challenged, since ascertaining the object and purpose of a particular WTO provision is inherently difficult.[190] Moreover, it is questionable whether, from a normative perspective, it is desirable for the judicial organs of the WTO to 'speculate on the object and purpose of the WTO system when WTO Members themselves are unable to articulate it in the first place'.[191] In any event, the Appellate Body's reasoning meant that in future cases there would always have to be an examination into the relationship between the relevant non-GATT agreement, such as a protocol of accession or indeed agreements such as the SPS Agreement or the SCM Agreement, and the allegedly 'closely intertwined' or 'closely related' GATT obligation.[192] The potential systemic implications of the findings by the Appellate Body have also been discussed at length.[193] These potential implications and the related concern emanating therefrom were evidently recognized by the Appellate Body. Subsequent cases show that the Appellate Body has adopted an approach which is aimed at harnessing the obligations that Members of the WTO have

---

Appellate Body Texturalism', *Journal of International Economic Law* (11) (3), pp. 649–78; Junqueira, Carla (2011), 'The Interpretive Technique of the WTO Appellate Body', *Global Trade and Customs Journal* (6) (1), pp. 29–34.

190 Du, Michael Ming (2012), 'Letter to the Editors: Has the WTO Appellate Body Pushed the Limits of Global Governance in the China-Publications Case? A Reply to Julia Qin', *Chinese Journal of International Law* (11), pp. 227–34, at 231.

191 Du (2012), Letter to the Editors: Has the WTO Appellate Body Pushed the Limits of Global Governance in the China-Publications Case? A Reply to Julia Qin, at 231.

192 Piérola, Fernando (2010), 'The Availability of a GATT Article XX Defence with Respect to a Non-GATT Claim: Changing the Rules of the Game? Comments on the Appellate Body Report in China – Measures Affecting Trading Rights and Distribution Services for Certain Publications and Audiovisual Entertainment Products', *Global Trade and Customs Journal* (5) (4), pp. 172–5, at 174. See also Voon, Tania (2010), 'China and Cultural Products at the WTO', *Legal Issues of Economic Integration* (37) (3), pp. 253–9, at 257. See also Ngangjoh-Hodu, Yenkong (2011), 'Relationship of GATT Article XX Exceptions to Other WTO Agreements', *Nordic Journal of International Law* (80), pp. 219–34, at 230.

193 Pauwelyn, Joost (2010), 'Case Note: Squaring Free Trade in Culture with Chinese Censorship – The WTO Appellate Body Report on China – Audiovisuals', *Melbourne Journal of International Law* (11) (1), pp. 119–40, at 136. On this issue, see also Conconi, Paola and Pauwelyn, Joost (2011), 'Trading Cultures: Appellate Body Report on China – Audiovisuals (WT/DS363/AB/R, adopted 19 January 2010)', *World Trade Review* (10) (1), pp. 95–118, at 103–6.

subscribed to, even though, in some instances, this may result in a finding that would appear to restrict their regulatory autonomy in a way that may have been unexpected.

The approach adopted in *China – Publications and Audiovisual Products* was maintained in subsequent cases that dealt with the same issue. In *China – Raw Materials*, China sought to justify an inconsistency with its commitment to eliminate certain export duties contained in Paragraph 11.3 of its Protocol of Accession.[194]

In its Report, the Panel observed that:

> the phrase 'in conformity with the GATT 1994' does not appear in Paragraph 11.3. Nor do the words '[w]ithout prejudice to China's right to regulate trade in a manner consistent with the WTO Agreement' appear in that paragraph. However, it does appear in Paragraphs 11.1 and 11.2, quoted above. In the Panel's view, this difference in wording between the three sequential sub-paragraphs is evidence of a *deliberate choice* made by China and the WTO Members in setting out China's rights and obligations and it must be given effect and respected. In addition, the fact that Paragraph 11.3 does not include the language 'in conformity with WTO obligations' (which appears in Paragraphs 11.1 and 11.2) can only be understood to reflect *agreement at the time of China's accession* that since China's export duties commitments arose exclusively from China's Accession Protocol, Article XX would not apply to such commitments.[195]

Moreover, it stated that:

> If China and WTO Members wanted the defences of GATT Article XX to be available to violations of China's export duty commitments, they could have said so in Paragraph 11.3 or elsewhere in China's Accession Protocol. In addition, China and the WTO Members could have agreed that China's export duty commitments were an integral part of China's commitments under the GATT 1994. For instance, WTO Members could have done this by incorporating China's export duties commitments into China's GATT 1994 Schedule. If China's export duties commitments were part of China's GATT 1994 Schedule, the general defences of Article XX of the GATT 1994 would be available to justify potential violations. However, this is not what China and WTO Members chose to do.[196]

---

[194] Para. 11.3 stipulates: 'China shall eliminate all taxes and charges applied to exports unless specifically provided for in Annex 6 of this Protocol or applied in conformity with the provisions of Article VIII of the GATT 1994.'

[195] Panel Reports, *China – Raw Materials*, para. 7.138 (emphasis added).

[196] Panel Reports, *China – Raw Materials*, para. 7.140 (footnote omitted).

Focusing further on the intentions of China and the members of the Working Party which negotiated its accession, the Panel found that 'China could have made reference to the defences of GATT Article XX – the way they did, for instance, concerning the use of quantitative restrictions in Paragraphs 164 and 165 of China's Working Party Report – but the WTO Members and China evidently decided not to do so'.[197] On appeal China raised three arguments against the interpretation developed by the Panel. China i) argued that the Panel erred in finding that there is 'no textual basis' in the Protocol of Accession of China for it to invoke Article XX of the GATT 1994; ii) argued that the Panel's finding that the absence of express language granting the right to regulate trade was a reflection of the intention of China and the other Members to deprive China of the right to have recourse to Article XX GATT 1994; and iii) argued that WTO Members have an 'inherent right' to regulate trade.[198] The Appellate Body upheld the findings made by the Panel by stating, inter alia, that:

> as China's obligation to eliminate export duties arises exclusively from China's Accession Protocol, and not from the GATT 1994, we consider it reasonable to assume that, had there been a common intention to provide access to Article XX of the GATT 1994 in this respect, language to that effect would have been included in Paragraph 11.3 or elsewhere in China's Accession Protocol.[199]

Interestingly, the Appellate Body, like the Panel, made use of the opportunity to mention the explicit references to Article XX of the GATT 1994 in other non-GATT WTO agreements to illustrate its point.[200]

The response to the Appellate Body Report in *China – Raw Materials* was one of severe criticism. Although it was acknowledged that the outcome of the dispute could have been predicted in light of the Appellate Body's interpretative approach in *China – Publications and Audiovisual Products*, there was still outrage at the fact that China, which had agreed to WTO-Plus commitments in its Protocol of Accession, was prevented from having recourse to the general exceptions contained in Article XX of the GATT 1994 because of the absence of a textual link to that provision. At the Meeting of the DSB during which the Panel and Appellate Body Reports in *China – Raw Materials* were adopted, China itself stated:

---

197 Panel Reports, *China – Raw Materials*, para. 7.129.

198 Appellate Body Reports, *China – Raw Materials*, para. 274.

199 Appellate Body Reports, *China – Raw Materials*, para. 293.

200 Appellate Body Reports, *China – Raw Materials*, paras. 303–6.

> Given the fundamental importance of Article XX to the rules governing the trade in goods, it could not be lightly concluded that a Member had abandoned its inherent right to pursue 'fundamental societal interests' other than trade, unless the Member concerned had given up such right through explicit and specific language.[201]

It has been considered that the Appellate Body's decision is strongly objectionable.[202] Some have argued that it should have paid more attention to concepts such as object and purpose.[203] On a more fundamental level it has been considered wrong for the judicial organs of the WTO to consider the text of protocols of accession as equivalent to treaty text.[204] Indeed, as has been noted, 'the unavailability of Articles XX, XXI etc. purely based on the formal location of a substantively identical export duty commitment may appear particularly surprising and to many

---

[201] WTO, Dispute Settlement Body, Minutes of the Meeting of 22 February 2012, WT/DSB/M/312, 22 May 2012, at 112.

[202] Bronckers, Marco and Maskus, Keith A. (2014), 'China – Raw Materials: A Controversial Step Towards Evenhanded Exploitation of Natural Resources', *World Trade Review* (13) (2), pp. 393–408, at 399. They note that 'admitting public policy exceptions in respect of a commitment on export duties does not necessarily open the door to admitting an appeal to Article XX in respect of other commitments on goods, such as for example the obligations set forth in the WTO Agreement on Subsidies and Countervailing Measures (SCM)'. Moreover, 'the Appellate Body could have given more weight, for instance, to language in other parts of China's accession documents'.

[203] Bronckers and Maskus (2014), China – Raw Materials: A Controversial Step Towards Evenhanded Exploitation of Natural Resources, at 401. See also Baroncini, Elisa (2012), 'The China – Rare Earths WTO Dispute: A Precious Chance to Revise the China – Raw Materials Conclusions on the Applicability of GATT Article XX to China's WTO Accession Protocol', *Cuadernos de Derecho Transnacional* (4) (2), pp. 49–69, at 64; and Baroncini, Elisa (2013), 'The Applicability of GATT Article XX to China's WTO Accession Protocol in the Appellate Body Report of the China – Raw Materials Case: Suggestions for a Different Interpretative Approach', *China-EU Law Journal* (1) (3–4), pp. 1–34.

[204] Bronckers and Maskus (2014), China – Raw Materials: A Controversial Step Towards Evenhanded Exploitation of Natural Resources, at 400. Stating that '[h]olding China to a drafting error is a deplorable outcome. We are not looking at a private contract, where parties can more easily choose to contract out of certain rights or be held to their negotiating mistakes. Here, we are looking at the rights and duties of sovereign states to regulate the public good. Notions of "contracting out", or "negotiating mistakes", are entirely misplaced here.' Moreover, they argued that it appears as if the Appellate Body considered that China made a drafting error in failing to explicitly reference Article XX of the GATT 1994 in its commitment on the elimination of export duties.

also doubtful'.[205] Nevertheless, it has also been observed that a public policy problem does not really seem to exist because China would have other means available to it to achieve the same objective.[206] It is submitted that this observation holds merit. Nothing prevents China, or any other acceded Member that undertook a similar commitment without an explicit link with Article XX of the GATT 1994, to adopt measures that restrict the quantity of exports and to seek and justify them under Article XX of the GATT 1994.

Only six weeks after the Appellate Body circulated its Report in *China – Raw Materials*, and only three weeks after the adoption of the Report by the DSB, the US, the EU and Japan filed a request for consultations against China, alleging, inter alia, that certain export duties on rare earth elements were inconsistent with its obligations under Paragraph 11.3 of the Protocol of Accession.[207] The Panel, applying the same reasoning as was used in *China – Raw Materials*, found that – since the export duties at issue had not been included in Annex 6 to China's Protocol of Accession – China had acted inconsistently with Paragraph 11.3 of the Protocol.[208] Subsequently, China argued – as it had done in *China – Raw Materials* – that the violation could be justified under Article XX(b) of the GATT 1994.[209] It presented three arguments that the Panel summarized as follows:

> (i) 'Paragraph 11.3 of China's *Accession Protocol* has to be treated as an integral part of the GATT 1994'; (ii) 'The terms "nothing in this Agreement" in the chapeau of Article XX of the GATT 1994 do not exclude the availability of Article XX to defend a violation of Paragraph 11.3 of China's *Accession Protocol*'; and (iii) 'An appropriate holistic interpretation, taking

---

[205] Ehring (2013), Nature and Status of WTO Accession Commitments: 'WTO-Plus' Obligations and Their Relationship to Other Parts of the WTO Agreement, at 360. He continues, stating that 'not just China, but possibly also the other WTO Members had no intention of creating Chinese export duty commitments that are unqualified by exceptions'.

[206] Ehring (2013), Nature and Status of WTO Accession Commitments: 'WTO-Plus' Obligations and Their Relationship to Other Parts of the WTO Agreement, at 361. Noting that '[t]here has yet to be an example of a policy based on Article XX the pursuit of which requires the imposition of an export duty and is impossible through a non-tariff export restriction'.

[207] WTO, China – Measures Related to the Exportation of Rare Earths, Tungsten and Molybdenum, Requests for Consultations by the United States, the European Union and Japan, WT/DS431/1, WT/DS432/1 and WT/DS433/1, 15 March 2012.

[208] Panel Reports, *China – Rare Earths*, para. 7.48.

[209] Panel Reports, *China – Rare Earths*, para. 7.49.

> due account of the object and purpose of the *WTO Agreement*, confirms that China may justify export duties through recourse to Article XX of the GATT 1994'.[210]

First, China argued that the absence of a specific textual reference to Article XX of the GATT 1994 in its Protocol of Accession is not in and of itself dispositive in answering the question whether the exceptions are available. It argued that there were 'cogent reasons' for the Panel to depart from the Reports in *China – Raw Materials* in which this interpretation had been put forward. The Panel, however, disagreed, holding that:

> China's reliance on *US – Carbon Steel* is misplaced and its argument that 'textual silence in a treaty provision is not, in and of itself, dispositive' cannot be regarded as a 'cogent reason' for departing from the Appellate Body's finding that the obligation in Paragraph 11.3 of China's Accession Protocol is not subject to the general exceptions in Article XX of the GATT 1994.[211]

Second, China put forward that, in the words of the Panel:

> i) the legal effect of Paragraph 1.2 of China's Accession Protocol and Article XII:1 of the Marrakesh Agreement is to make China's Accession Protocol an 'integral part' of the Marrakesh Agreement, and also to make each of the Accession Protocol-specific provisions an integral part of one of the Multilateral Trade Agreements (e.g. GATT 1994) annexed to the Marrakesh Agreement; and that ii) [t]he determination of which Multilateral Trade Agreement(s) (e.g. GATT 1994) a particular provision of the Accession Protocol is an 'integral part' must be based on an evaluation of which Multilateral Trade Agreement(s) the provision at issue is 'intrinsically' related to.[212]

The Panel, again, dismissed both arguments and found that there were no 'cogent reasons' to depart from the *China – Raw Materials* jurisprudence.[213] Third, China argued that '[t]he terms "nothing in this Agreement" in the chapeau of Article XX of the GATT 1994 do not exclude the availability of Article XX to defend a violation of Paragraph 11.3 of China's *Accession Protocol*'.[214] Focusing on the fact that China, as a

---

210 Panel Reports, *China – Rare Earths*, para. 7.62 (footnotes omitted) (emphasis in the original).

211 Panel Reports, *China – Rare Earths*, para. 7.72.

212 Panel Reports, *China – Rare Earths*, para. 7.76.

213 Panel Reports, *China – Rare Earths*, para. 7.99.

214 Panel Reports, *China – Rare Earths*, para. 7.100. According to China, 'the exceptions under Article XX of the GATT 1994 are also available to excuse

result of the commitment in its Protocol of Accession, was only prevented from using *one type* of measure – export duties – to achieve environmental objectives, the Panel concluded that there was no reason to assume that the interpretation developed by the Appellate Body in *China – Raw Materials* was inconsistent with the object and purpose of the WTO Agreement.[215] However, the Panel disagreed with China that this is the result of the Appellate Body's finding that 'the obligation in Paragraph 11.3 of China's Accession Protocol is not subject to the general exceptions in Article XX of the GATT 1994.'[216] Conscious of the controversy surrounding this particular issue the Panel emphasized the limited scope of its finding and, moreover, that the only implications of this ruling are that China cannot use export duties to attain its environmental objectives.[217] One panellist was unable to agree with the findings of the Panel and, rather exceptionally, issued a separate opinion.[218] The concluding paragraph of this opinion reads as follows:

> Paragraph 11.3 of China's Accession Protocol is an integral part of China's obligations on trade in goods in the sense that it adds to the basic obligations of the GATT 1994 relating to border tariffs. A proper interpretation on the availability of Article XX of the GATT 1994 to Paragraph 11.3 of China's Accession Protocol should take into account the fact that Paragraph 11.3 must be read cumulatively and simultaneously with related GATT Articles II and XI and as an integral part of the GATT system of rights and obligations. Therefore, in my view, unless China explicitly gave up its right to invoke Article XX of GATT 1994, which it did not, the general exception provisions of the GATT 1994 are available to China to justify a violation of Paragraph 11.3 of its Accession Protocol. I see nothing in China's Accession Protocol that clearly indicates such a waiver. In my view, finding that the obligation in Paragraph 11.3 is subject to the general exceptions in Article XX of the GATT 1994 allows China to exercise its rights and obligations with a view to favouring its sustainable development. This concludes my separate opinion.[219]

---

violations of [...] intrinsically GATT-related "WTO-plus" provisions contained in post-1994 accession protocols'.

[215] Panel Reports, *China – Rare Earths*, paras. 7.113–7.114.

[216] Panel Reports, *China – Rare Earths*, para. 7.114.

[217] Panel Reports, *China – Rare Earths*, paras. 7.116–7.117. The Panel further stressed that it made no statement on the general question as to the applicability of Article XX of the GATT 1994 to China's – or indeed other Member's – Protocol of Accession.

[218] Panel Reports, *China – Rare Earths*, paras. 7.118–7.138.

[219] Panel Reports, *China – Rare Earths*, para. 7.138.

Although the majority of the Panel found that recourse to Article XX of the GATT 1994 was not available to China, it still proceeded – on an *arguendo* basis – with the substantive analysis under that provision.[220] Although it acknowledged that 'the mining and production of rare earths, tungsten, and molybdenum have caused grave harm to the environment and to the life and health of humans, animals, and plants in China', it held that China had not demonstrated that 'its export duties are designed and structured to protect human, animal or plant life or health'.[221] The Panel also found that the measures at issue were not apt to making a contribution to the achievement of the stated objective.[222] Finally, it found that China had failed to establish that the proposed alternatives to the measure were not reasonably available to it, or that they would not be able to make the same contribution as the measure at issue.[223] Since the measure at issue also did not meet the requirements of the chapeau of Article XX of the GATT 1994, the Panel found that, even if Article XX of the GATT 1994 would be available to justify inconsistencies with commitments in China's Protocol of Accession, China had, in the context of this dispute, not established that its measure would justify the requirements of that article.[224]

On appeal China challenged the Panel's findings in relation to the relationship between Article XX of the GATT and commitments contained in its Protocol of Accession.[225]

> In China's view, the Panel's interpretation of Paragraph 1.2 would 'jeopardize the internal coherence' of the WTO legal framework, which consists of an 'overarching institution agreement' (i.e. the Marrakesh Agreement) and several Multilateral Trade Agreements. For China, the Panel's interpretation means that a 'WTO-plus' commitment regarding trade in goods would have to be read as an integral part of the overarching institutional provisions of the WTO – i.e. the Marrakesh Agreement – rather than as an integral part of a substantive agreement, such as the GATT 1994. China maintains that it is the Multilateral Trade Agreements, rather than the 'overarching institutional agreement', that stipulate each Member's substantive obligations, as well as the applicable exceptions. Thus, China emphasizes that a treaty interpreter assessing a provision in China's Accession Protocol must undertake the additional analytical step of determining with which Multilateral Trade Agreement that provision has an 'intrinsic relationship'. This additional

220 Panel Reports, *China – Rare Earths*, paras. 7.139–7.196.
221 Panel Reports, *China – Rare Earths*, paras. 7.156–7.171.
222 Panel Reports, *China – Rare Earths*, para. 7.179.
223 Panel Reports, *China – Rare Earths*, para. 7.187.
224 Panel Reports, *China – Rare Earths*, para. 7.196.
225 Appellate Body Reports, *China – Rare Earths*, paras. 2.10–2.27.

> analytical step is required as it allows the interpreter to determine the precise Multilateral Trade Agreement of which a particular provision of the Protocol is an integral part, thereby giving effective meaning to Paragraph 1.2, second sentence, of China's Accession Protocol.[226]

In doing so, China argued, 'the treaty interpreter's initial task is to analyse to which of the covered agreements listed in Appendix 1 to the DSU that Protocol provision *intrinsically relates*'.[227] After this preliminary step, the commitment contained in a protocol of accession would have to be treated as 'an integral part' of the relevant covered agreement. China's argument essentially revolved around the characterization of protocols of accession as 'successive treaties relating to the same subject matter' (somewhat unfortunately referred to as subsequent agreements) in the sense of Article 30(3) of the Vienna Convention. In this light, according to China, when 'a given accession commitment stands in conflict with one or more provisions in the Marrakesh Agreement or the Multilateral Trade Agreements annexed thereto, such conflict is resolved according to the rule under Article 30(3) of the Vienna Convention'.[228] Notably, China did not ask the Appellate Body to reverse the Panel's finding that Article XX of the GATT 1994 was not available to justify a breach of Paragraph 11.3 of China's Protocol of Accession.[229] The US, EU and Japan did not support the interpretation proposed by China.

---

226 Appellate Body Reports, *China – Rare Earths*, para. 2.13.

227 Appellate Body Reports, *China – Rare Earths*, para. 2.22. In para. 2.25 of the Appellate Body Report China's argument is presented in the following manner: 'China uses the analogy of a house to illustrate the nature of the WTO single undertaking, whereby the Marrakesh Agreement provides the foundation, outer walls, and the roof of the "WTO House", and the Multilateral Trade Agreements annexed thereto are rooms in this house. According to China, a treaty interpreter analysing a provision of China's Accession Protocol must identify the appropriate "room" or "rooms" in the "WTO House" where each accession protocol provision will take up residence. Thus, China argues, the proper way to consider post-1994 accession protocols is to think of provisions contained therein as "new coats of paint or furniture items in the individual agreement rooms of the WTO House". A Member's "terms" of accession may therefore rewrite, or add new substantive provisions to, specific provisions of the Marrakesh Agreement and its annexed agreements' (footnotes omitted) (emphasis added).

228 Appellate Body Reports, *China – Rare Earths*, para. 2.26. China argued that 'Article XI:1 of the GATT 1994 has been modified by Paragraph 11.3 of China's Accession Protocol and, as a result, China may not impose export duties'.

229 Appellate Body Reports, *China – Rare Earths*, para. 2.27.

However, several of the third parties to the dispute expressed the wish that the Appellate Body would provide more clarity on the relationship between commitments in protocols of accession and the provisions of covered agreements, including Article XX of the GATT 1994.[230] The Russian Federation and Saudi Arabia, two Members who, like China, acceded through the procedure laid down by Article XII of the WTO Agreement, also expressed their opinion on the issue. The Russian Federation's concern is fundamental and therefore provided here in full:

> Russia submits that the Panel's finding that an explicit textual link between the GATT 1994 and Paragraph 11.3 of China's Accession Protocol is required for Article XX of the GATT to be available to justify a breach of the Protocol is of serious concern. Russia claims that, during its accession negotiations, upon assurance by the incumbent WTO Members that defences under the WTO agreements are equally available to all WTO Members, Russia agreed to delete the following statement from its Accession Protocol: 'nothing in these commitments shall be understood to derogate from the rights of the Russian Federation under the WTO Agreement as applied between the Members of the WTO by the date of accession of the Russian Federation to the WTO.' In Russia's view, the Panel's above finding means that the statement Russia agreed to delete should have been included in the accession protocols of all newly acceded WTO Members. Russia further maintains that the Panel's finding would apply to all other defences, including the security exceptions in Article XXI of the GATT 1994. For Russia, an acceding Member's intention to waive its right to protect important values such as life and health must be clearly and unambiguously explained. In this regard, Russia stresses its agreement with the views of the dissenting member of the Panel.[231]

Finally, Saudi Arabia put forward a more nuanced argument that can be seen as more in line with the findings of the Panel and the arguments of the complainants. In its view 'the fact that a Member's accession commitments must be read together with the covered agreements does not necessarily mean that all of the defences provided in the relevant covered agreements are automatically available to justify also the violation of the accession commitment'.[232] The Appellate Body began its

---

[230] Appellate Body Reports, *China – Rare Earths*, paras. 2.218–2.244. Other third parties, such as Canada and Norway agreed with the position taken by the complainants in this dispute.

[231] Appellate Body Reports, *China – Rare Earths*, para. 2.240.

[232] Appellate Body Reports, *China – Rare Earths*, para. 2.241. Moreover, it stated that 'absent direct or indirect references to the availability of such exceptions, the Member has agreed to abide by its accession commitment, without exception'.

analysis by examining the language used in Article XII of the WTO Agreement. Finding support in Japan's argumentation on the relationship between that article and Article II:2 of the WTO Agreement, it held that '[t]hese two provisions thus serve closely related, albeit distinct, functions; they are not merely duplicative of each other. Read together, they ensure that the fundamental principle of the single undertaking applies to both existing and acceded Members of the WTO.'[233] The Appellate Body's key findings on Article XII are summarized at the end of Paragraph 5.34:

> [b]eyond the general rule governing accession set out in its two sentences, Article XII:1 itself does not speak to the question of the specific relationship between individual provisions of an accession protocol and individual provisions of the Marrakesh Agreement and the Multilateral Trade Agreements. In particular, Article XII:1, alone, does not create a substantive relationship, 'intrinsic' or otherwise, between provisions of China's Accession Protocol (such as Paragraph 11.3) and provisions of the covered agreements (such as Article II or XI of the GATT 1994). In this regard, we note that the Marrakesh Agreement is the overarching institutional agreement of the WTO, and Article XII thereof does not directly address the question of the substantive relationship between individual provisions of a protocol of accession, on the one hand, and the provisions of the Marrakesh Agreement and the Multilateral Trade Agreements, on the other hand.[234]

In the second step of its analysis relating to the status of protocols of accession in the legal framework of the WTO, the Appellate Body examined the wording of Paragraph 1.2 of China's Protocol of Accession.[235] This paragraph contains language that can be found in all protocols of accession that have been drafted since 1994. Therefore the findings of the Appellate Body are of relevance for all other Members

---

233 Appellate Body Reports, *China – Rare Earths*, para. 5.30.

234 Appellate Body Reports, *China – Rare Earths*, para. 5.34.

235 'Part I – General Provisions 1. General: 1. Upon accession, China accedes to the WTO Agreement pursuant to Article XII of that Agreement and thereby becomes a Member of the WTO. 2. The WTO Agreement to which China accedes shall be the WTO Agreement as rectified, amended or otherwise modified by such legal instruments as may have entered into force before the date of accession. This Protocol, which shall include the commitments referred to in paragraph 342 of the Working Party Report, shall be an integral part of the WTO Agreement. 3. Except as otherwise provided for in this Protocol, those obligations in the Multilateral Trade Agreements annexed to the WTO Agreement that are to be implemented over a period of time starting with entry into force of that Agreement shall be implemented by China as if it had accepted that Agreement on the date of its entry into force.'

that acceded under the procedure of Article XII of the WTO Agreement. Point of dispute was whether the term 'the WTO Agreement' refers to the Marrakesh Agreement Establishing the World Trade Organization, that is, the founding treaty of the WTO or, as China argued, to that agreement *and* the Multilateral Trade Agreements that have been annexed to it.[236] On this point the Appellate Body noted that:

> it appears that the term 'the WTO Agreement' in the second sentence of Paragraph 1.2 may refer to the Marrakesh Agreement, that is, to 'the WTO Agreement' excluding the Multilateral Trade Agreements. At the same time, an examination of the term 'the WTO Agreement', as used throughout China's Accession Protocol, indicates that the definition of 'the WTO Agreement' contained in the preamble does not necessarily preclude the annexed Multilateral Trade Agreements from also falling within the scope of the term 'the WTO Agreement' in some instances. This term may, depending on the specific context, include a reference to the annexed Multilateral Trade Agreements, or it may refer to the Marrakesh Agreement alone.[237]

The Appellate Body further held that it did not consider that 'determining the scope of the term "the WTO Agreement" in Paragraph 1.2 was dispositive of the key legal question before the Panel'.[238] Rather, it stated:

> Paragraph 1.2 of China's Accession Protocol, and in particular its stipulation that the Protocol is to be an 'integral part' of 'the WTO Agreement', essentially serves to build a bridge between the package of protocol provisions and the existing package of WTO rights and obligations under the Marrakesh Agreement and the Multilateral Trade Agreements.[239]

However, '[t]he fact that such a bridge exists does not in itself answer the question as to *how individual provisions* in China's Accession Protocol are related or linked to individual provisions of the other WTO agreements'.[240] Indeed, a case-by-case analysis is always needed to ascertain the relationship between a specific commitment in a protocol of accession and the provisions of the Marrakesh Agreement and the Multilateral Trade Agreements.[241] The Appellate Body then continued to determine the relationship between Paragraph 11.3 of China's Protocol of Accession

---

[236] Appellate Body Reports, *China – Rare Earths*, para. 5.37.
[237] Appellate Body Reports, *China – Rare Earths*, para. 5.46.
[238] Appellate Body Reports, *China – Rare Earths*, para. 5.49.
[239] Appellate Body Reports, *China – Rare Earths*, para. 5.50.
[240] Appellate Body Reports, *China – Rare Earths*, para. 5.50 (emphasis in the original).
[241] Appellate Body Reports, *China – Rare Earths*, para. 5.50.

and the relevant provisions of the Marrakesh Agreement and the Multilateral Trade Agreements. Recalling that several commitments containing a potential reference to Article XX of the GATT 1994 have been identified in various Members' protocols of accession, the following finding of the Appellate Body is of note:

> In many instances, no express language identifying the relationship between specific terms and provisions of a Multilateral Trade Agreement with those of another Multilateral Trade Agreement or the Marrakesh Agreement is found in the agreements at issue. Where this is so, recourse to other interpretative elements will be necessary to determine the specific relationship among individual terms and provisions of the Multilateral Trade Agreements, and between such provisions and the Marrakesh Agreement.
>
> [...]
>
> Just as the Multilateral Trade Agreements are an integral part of the Marrakesh Agreement, and, thereby, of the single package of WTO rights and obligations, so too is China's Accession Protocol an integral part of the same package. Thus, like the approach to ascertaining the relationship among provisions of the Multilateral Trade Agreements, the specific relationship between the provisions of China's Accession Protocol, on the one hand, and the provisions of the Marrakesh Agreement and the Multilateral Trade Agreements, on the other hand, must also be determined on a case-by-case basis through a proper interpretation of all relevant provisions. Neither obligations nor rights may be automatically transposed from one part of the legal framework into another.[242]

The Appellate Body then discussed its findings in *China – Publications and Audiovisual Products* and explained that in some situations the case-by-case analysis yields a conclusion of applicability of the general exceptions in Article XX of the GATT 1994. However, in other situations, where a different provision of the relevant Protocol of Accession is at issue, the conclusion may very well be different. In *China – Rare Earths* the Appellate Body found that 'the existence of an express reference to a GATT provision (Article VIII of the GATT 1994) in a protocol provision does not compel the conclusion that Article XX of the GATT 1994 is available to justify a breach of the protocol provision'.[243] As was noted earlier, China argued that it was necessary to establish with which provision of the Marrakesh Agreement and the Multilateral Trade

[242] Appellate Body Reports, *China – Rare Earths*, paras. 5.56–5.57.
[243] Appellate Body Reports, *China – Rare Earths*, para. 5.63.

Agreements the commitment in the Protocol of Accession was 'intrinsically related'.[244] The Appellate Body, however, found no basis for this particular legal test – which China had failed to illustrate in sufficient detail. It held that China's test 'sits uncomfortably with our interpretation set out above that rights and obligations cannot be automatically transposed from one part of the WTO legal framework to another'.[245] Finally, the Appellate Body also dismissed several arguments that China made in the course of the appellate proceedings. For instance, China had attempted to argue that 'where a given accession provision "stands in conflict" with one or more provisions in the Marrakesh Agreement or the Multilateral Trade Agreements annexed thereto, such conflict is resolved according to the "later-in-time" rule under Article 30(3) of the Vienna Convention'.[246] However, the Appellate Body dismissed this argument as it did not 'consider Article 30(3) of the Vienna Convention to be apposite for understanding the relationship between the different components of this single package of rights and obligations, all of which form part of "the same treaty" to which China acceded in 2001'.[247]

This section discussed the way in which the panels and the Appellate Body have approached the issue of the applicability of Article XX of the GATT 1994 to commitments contained in protocols of accession and working party reports in *China – Publications and Audiovisual Products*, *China – Raw Materials* and *China – Rare Earths*. The next section provides a normative assessment of this approach and establishes whether it accurately reflects the balance between the rights and obligations of all WTO Members. At the outset it should be noted that the (non)-applicability of the general exceptions contained in Article XX of the GATT 1994 has been the source of severe criticism. It has been argued that the approach adopted by the Appellate Body results in a situation in which Members that acceded under the procedure laid down by Article XII of the WTO Agreement are severely restricted in their right to regulate. The next section addresses whether these concerns are warranted and whether, indeed, the 'policy space' or 'regulatory autonomy' of new Members is lessened in comparison to that available to original Members of the WTO.

---

244 Appellate Body Reports, *China – Rare Earths*, para. 5.66.
245 Appellate Body Reports, *China – Rare Earths*, para. 5.68.
246 Appellate Body Reports, *China – Rare Earths*, para. 5.69.
247 Appellate Body Reports, *China – Rare Earths*, para. 5.70 (footnote omitted).

4.3.2.1.3 Assessment: balancing rights and obligations arising from protocols of accession with the covered agreements The reasoning developed by panels and the Appellate Body in *China – Publications and Audiovisual Products*, *China – Raw Materials* and *China – Rare Earths* has led to fierce criticism.[248] Nevertheless, another part of the response

[248] See, for example, Qin, Julia Ya (2012), 'Reforming WTO Discipline on Export Duties: Sovereignty over Natural Resources, Economic Development and Environmental Protection', *Journal of World Trade* (46) (5), pp. 1147–90; Qin, Julia Ya (2012), 'The Predicament of China's "WTO-Plus" Obligation to Eliminate Export Duties: A Commentary on the China – Raw Materials Case', *Chinese Journal of International Law* (11) (2), pp. 237–46; Qin, Julia Ya (2014), 'Judicial Authority in WTO Law: A Commentary on the Appellate Body's Decision in China – Rare Earths', *Chinese Journal of International Law* (13) (4), pp. 639–51; DeMedeiros, Jose F. (2012), 'Global Trade Law: China's Export Restraints Found to be Inconsistent with Its Obligations as a Member of the World Trade Organization – China – Measures Related to the Exportation of Various Raw Materials, WT/DS394/R, WT/DS395/R and WT/DS398/R', *Suffolk Transnational Law Review* (35) (1), pp. 203–19; Espa, Ilaria (2012), 'The Appellate Body Approach to the Applicability of Article XX GATT In the Light of China – Raw Materials: A Missed Opportunity?', *Journal of World Trade* (46) (6), pp. 1399–424; Gu, Bin (2012), 'Applicability of GATT Article XX in China – Raw Materials: A Clash Within the WTO Agreement', *Journal of International Economic Law* (15) (4), pp. 1007–31; Van Calster, Geert (2013), 'Case Note: China, Minerals Export, Raw and Rare Earth Materials – A Perfect Storm for World Trade Organization Dispute Settlement', *Review of European Community and International Environmental Law* (22) (1), pp. 117–22; Bronckers and Maskus (2014), China – Raw Materials: A Controversial Step Towards Even-handed Exploitation of Natural Resources; Lim, C.L. and Senduk, J.H. (2014), 'The Wages of Belonging: Rare Earths from China and the Return of GATT À La Carte', *Global Trade and Customs Journal* (9) (9), pp. 380–96; Guan, Wenwei (2014), 'How General Should the GATT General Exceptions Be? A Critique of the "Common Intention" Approach of Treaty Interpretation', *Journal of World Trade* (48) (2), pp. 219–58; Au, Thomas H. (2013), 'Reconciling WTO General Exceptions with China's Accession Protocol', *Tsinghua China Law Review* (5) (2), pp. 95–125; Baroncini (2013), The Applicability of GATT Article XX to China's WTO Accession Protocol in the Appellate Body Report of the China – Raw Materials Case: Suggestions for a Different Interpretative Approach; Han, Xiuli and Gao, Bo (2013), 'Export Taxes under the WTO System: China's Way out of the Dilemma', *Manchester Journal of International Law* (10) (3), pp. 336–61; Liu, Ying (2014), 'The Applicability of Environmental Protection Exceptions to WTO-Plus Obligations: In View of the China – Raw Materials and China – Rare Earths Cases', *Leiden Journal of International Law* (27) (1), pp. 113–39; Bond, Eric W. and Trachtman, Joel (2015), '*China – Rare Earths*: Export Restrictions and the Limits of Textual Interpretation', *World Trade Review* (15) (2), pp. 189–209.

has been more appreciative of the interpretation developed by the Appellate Body.[249] During the DSB meeting at which the Appellate Body Reports in *China – Rare Earths* were adopted, China further elaborated upon its opinion that the 'terms of accession' enshrined in protocols of accession constitute 'subsequent agreements' in the sense of Article 30(3) of the Vienna Convention.[250] After *China – Rare Earths*, the following constitutes an adequate description of the state of play in accession-related case law:

> To the extent that the nature of the obligation assumed in a Protocol of Accession is the same as the obligation assumed by original WTO Members under the covered agreements (as was the case in Publications and Audio-visual Products) a recently acceded Member could have recourse to the general exceptions as other WTO Members could have. If, however, the obligation involves a WTO-plus provision that, by definition is not contained in any of the Multilateral Trade Agreements annexed to the Marrakesh Agreement (as was the case in Raw Materials/Rare Earths), then a recently acceded Member's ability to have recourse to the general exceptions must be specifically included in its Accession Protocol. However, a mere textual reference to a particular provision of the GATT 1994, or even to Article XX of the GATT 1994 specifically, is not dispositive. One still has to examine the nature of the obligation assumed by the acceding Member in the light of the

---

[249] For a more positive critique on the reasoning developed by the Appellate Body, see, for example, Valles, Cherise (2015), 'Appellate Body Report in China: Rare Earths – Addressing Violations of WTO-Plus Obligations', *Global Trade and Customs Journal* (10) (4), pp. 130–35; Matsushita, Mitsuo (2011), 'Export Control of Natural Resources: WTO Panel Ruling on the Chinese Export Restrictions of Natural Resources', *Trade, Law and Development* (3) (2), pp. 267–95; Matsushita, Mitsuo (2011), 'Export Controls of Natural Resources and the WTO/GATT Disciplines', *Asian Journal of WTO and International Health Law and Policy* (6) (2), pp. 281–312; Matsushita, Mitsuo (2012), 'A Note on the Appellate Body Report in the Chinese Minerals Export Restrictions Case', *Trade, Law and Development* (4) (2), pp. 400–420; Feld, Danielle Spiegel and Switzer, Stephanie (2014), 'Whither Article XX? Regulatory Autonomy under Non-GATT Agreements after China – Raw Materials', *Yale Journal of International Law Online* (38), pp. 16–30.

[250] WTO, Dispute Settlement Body, Minutes of the Meeting of 29 August 2014, WT/DSB/M/349, 23 October 2014, at 8.8. According to China '[terms of accession] thus served to stipulate, including by the means of "WTO-plus" provisions, how an acceding Member could take up the rights and obligations under the WTO's "single undertaking". In practical terms, this required an interpreter to find a home for each accession commitment under either the Marrakesh Agreement or one of the multilateral trade agreements annexed thereto.'

> commitments made in the Working Party Report and in the covered agreements in the light of the overall architecture of the WTO legal framework. This appears to be shorthand to suggest that if a WTO-plus obligation is at issue, it will likely be very difficult to find that a Member can have recourse to the general exceptions for breaches of those obligations.[251]

The crucial question is therefore which acceded Members have accepted such WTO-Plus obligations upon their accession to the WTO and what is the precise scope of these obligations?[252] This book contributes to existing scholarship by analysing the protocols of accession of all acceded Members in mapping the prevalence and scope of these WTO-Plus obligations. As was described in section 4.3.2.1.2.2, it can already be noted that in the field of export duties the Members that have accepted the most stringent commitments appear not to have access to Article XX of the GATT 1994 to justify a violation of these commitments. In the cases of China and Tajikistan this is for the reasons put forward by the Appellate Body in the disputes discussed in this chapter. In the case of Montenegro this is because there is no reference to the GATT in the paragraph containing the commitment.[253] Therefore, an assessment of whether the allegedly strict 'textualist' interpretative approach adopted by the Appellate Body does justice to the carefully drafted balance between the rights and obligations of acceded Members will ultimately need to take into account the nature of the commitments that these Members have agreed upon as a condition for their accession to the WTO. One has to take into account that criticism of the decision to require a link between a commitment contained in a protocol of accession and the general exceptions contained in Article XX of the GATT 1994 has implications that reach further than the context of protocols of accession.[254] Indeed, some authors have welcomed the decision of the Appellate Body in *China – Publications and Audiovisual Products* not to per se exclude the applicability of Article XX of the GATT 1994 to commitments contained in protocols of accession as it may serve as a precedent for the

---

[251] Valles (2015), Appellate Body Report in China: Rare Earths – Addressing Violations of WTO-Plus Obligations, at 135.

[252] See Chapter 6.

[253] WTO, Protocol on the Accession of the People's Republic of China, WT/L/432, 23 November 2001, para. 11.3; WTO, Report of the Working Party on the Accession of the Republic of Tajikistan, WT/ACC/TJK/30, 6 November 2012, para. 169; and WTO, Report of the Working Party on the Accession of Montenegro to the World Trade Organization, WT/ACC/CGR/38, 5 December 2011, para. 132.

[254] See section 4.3.2.

applicability of Article XX of the GATT 1994 to other non-GATT provisions.[255] Given the mandate that has been conferred upon these organs by the Members of the WTO, it is understandable that caution is exercised in determining the relationship between commitments contained in protocols of accession and the WTO Agreement.[256] In some instances this may have led to outcomes that, at least superficially, may appear to be at odds with ideas of the common structure of the WTO where there is a careful balance between rights and obligations. However, the case-by-case approach adopted by the Appellate Body, where in each situation a new assessment has to be made as to the relationship between commitments in protocols of accession and the relevant provision(s) of the Multilateral Trade Agreements, appears to be the one most capable of doing justice to the wording of the text of the relevant protocols and agreements. If the Appellate Body were to have adopted a more active and progressive approach, this may have resulted in upsetting the delicate balance between rights and obligations as reflected in the single undertaking which is, in the end, the outcome of the Uruguay Round. Although some commentators have suggested that, in some cases, this might actually be a desirable development, it is highly questionable whether, from the perspective of the separation of powers, this would have been more 'legitimate' than the current approach.[257] Declaring that, in the absence of a textual reference, provisions contained in a covered agreement could be applicable in respect of commitments contained in a protocol of accession, might ultimately have led to situations in which valid arguments could be made for the applicability of these provisions to other covered agreements. This seems completely contrary to the idea that takes the outcome of long and painful negotiations seriously. Cautious of such an outcome, it appears that the Appellate Body has

---

[255] Bronckers and Maskus (2014), China – Raw Materials: A Controversial Step Towards Evenhanded Exploitation of Natural Resources, at 399, footnote 23. 'We might add that we see no strong objection either to admitting these public policy exceptions in respect of other WTO commitments regarding trade in goods – though admitting an appeal to Article XX in respect of commitments in the SCM Agreement could effectively re-create a category of non-actionable subsidies.'

[256] Taking into account, in particular, Articles 3.2 and 19.2 of the DSU. Article 19.2 DSU provides: 'In accordance with paragraph 2 of Article 3, in their findings and recommendations, the panel and Appellate Body cannot add to or diminish the rights and obligations provided in the covered agreements.'

[257] See for an opposing view, for example, Irwin and Weiler (2008), Measures Affecting the Cross-Border Supply of Gambling and Betting Services (DS285), at 89–95.

opted for an approach that, in the short term at least, might attract severe criticism, but one which, ultimately, lays the responsibility for advancing WTO law in a certain direction with the organization's 'legislative' organ, that is, the Members of the WTO. Arguments that the Appellate Body's interpretative approach is too textualist and fails to take into account the object and purpose of provisions and their context have been around since the institution's very inception.[258] The WTO's dispute settlement is currently under severe pressure. Not because of the fact that Members do not consider the decisions rendered by it as illegitimate, but rather because they appear to have confidence in the system. Such confidence that in 20 years over 500 requests for consultations have been filed, more than 200 panel reports and more than 120 Appellate Body reports have been issued.[259] Although the outcome of certain cases might – from the outside at least – appear to be unwelcome, or sometimes even illogical or unjust, these numbers are testament to the fact that the Members, including the ones at the losing end of certain controversial decisions, consider that their disputes will be adjudicated in a fair and adequate manner, based on the text of the agreements that have been drafted by them. In the end, any discussion on the interpretative approach adopted by the Appellate Body in respect of the relationship between commitments contained in protocols of accession and the general exceptions of Article XX of the GATT 1994 amounts to a discussion on the proper role

---

[258] See, for example, Horn, Henrik and Weiler, Joseph H.H. (2005), 'European Communities – Trade Description of Sardines: Textualism and Its Discontent', *World Trade Review* (4) (Supplement S1), pp. 248–75; McRae, Donald (2006), Treaty Interpretation and the Development of International Trade Law by the WTO Appellate Body, in Sacerdoti, Giorgio, Yanovich, Alan and Bohanes, Jan (eds) (2006), *The WTO at Ten: The Contribution of the Dispute Settlement System*, Cambridge, Cambridge University Press; Ortino, Federico (2006), 'Treaty Interpretation and the WTO Appellate Body Report in US – Gambling: A Critique', *Journal of International Economic Law* (9) (1), pp. 117–48; Magnuson, William (2010), 'WTO Jurisprudence & Its Critiques: The Appellate Body's Anti-Constitutional Resistance', *Harvard International Law Journal Online* (51), pp. 121–54. Magnuson describes the Appellate Body's approach as 'textualism run amok'. Oesch, Matthias (2003), *Standards of Review in WTO Dispute Resolution*, Oxford, Oxford University Press, at 44. Oesch notes that the 'essentially inflexible and functionalist approach to interpretation corresponds to the fact that the authority and legitimacy of the WTO dispute settlement system is still relatively weak'. See also Stern (2010), Interpretation in International Trade Law.

[259] See WTO, Chronological List of Disputes Cases. Available at https://www.wto.org/english/tratop_e/dispu_e/dispu_status_e.htm (last accessed at 16 October 2017).

of the judiciary. Is it really upon the judiciary to venture substantially beyond the text of the agreements that have been negotiated by the legislature, in the context of the WTO, by its Members? What authority does it have to determine the object and purpose of certain provisions when even the Members themselves are unable to articulate it?[260] The confidence expressed by the Members of the WTO in its dispute settlement mechanism is telling. They have not voted with their feet. Although they may seek refuge in bilateral and plurilateral initiatives to negotiate new rules for international trade, they still travel to Geneva to submit their trade disputes to the WTO.

4.3.2.2 Rights for other WTO Members in protocols of accession

Some provisions in protocols of accession and commitments in working party reports provide for derogations from the existing rights and obligations of WTO Members towards the applicant in question. In essence these provisions and commitments create 'a right for', or 'permit', WTO Members to adopt measures that would, presumably, be inconsistent with their WTO obligations in the absence of these provisions. The provisions can be placed in two categories: provisions that establish separate regimes for safeguards, and provisions that allow for the use of special methodologies in the context of anti-dumping investigations.[261] Both categories are discussed in this section.

4.3.2.2.1 Transitional safeguards In *US – Tyres*, China complained about a US safeguard measure on tyres it alleged to be inconsistent with Articles I, II and XIX of the GATT 1994. Moreover, China argued, the measure could not be justified under the China-specific safeguard mechanism contained in its Protocol of Accession.[262] The Panel began its analysis by noting that the case was the first to deal with the transitional product-specific safeguard mechanism as contained in China's Protocol of Accession. According to the Panel this called for some general

---

[260] Du (2012), Letter to the Editors: Has the WTO Appellate Body Pushed the Limits of Global Governance in the China-Publications Case? A Reply to Julia Qin, at 231.

[261] See sections 6.4.1 and 6.4.2 for the scope and prevalence of these provisions and commitments in the examined protocols of accession and working party reports.

[262] WTO, Request for Consultations, United States – Measures Affecting Imports of Certain Passenger Vehicle and Light Truck Tyres from China (Complainant: China), WT/DS399/1, at 1. See Part III for a more detailed description of the Transitional Product-Specific Safeguard Mechanism.

observations.[263] The following observation by the Panel provides an insight into the way in which the outcome of accession negotiations between an applicant state or customs territory and the WTO has been treated in the context of WTO dispute settlement proceedings. Because of its significance, it is quoted in full:

> Having stated this important contextual background, the Panel was also aware that the issues before it involved the interpretation of the provisions of the transitional product-specific safeguard mechanism and that it was the task of the Panel to do that. It was not for the Panel to seek to recalibrate what the WTO Members had agreed to in the negotiations that led to the accession of China to the WTO in the light of what the Panel might perceive as changing economic circumstances that perhaps had not been considered when the Protocol was negotiated. That remains the prerogative of the WTO Members themselves.[264]

In the remainder of the Panel Report the relationship between China's Protocol of Accession and the WTO Agreement is not discussed in more detail. On appeal China challenged several findings made by the Panel. The Appellate Body began its analysis, contrary to the Panel, with a discussion on the status of China's Protocol of Accession. It held that:

> Paragraph 1.2 of China's Accession Protocol provides that the Protocol 'shall be an integral part' of the *WTO Agreement*. As such, the customary rules of interpretation of public international law, as codified in Articles 31 and 32 of the *Vienna Convention on the Law of Treaties* (the '*Vienna Convention*'), are, pursuant to Article 3.2 of the DSU, applicable in this dispute in clarifying the meaning of Paragraphs 16.1 and 16.4 of the Protocol.[265]

Here the Appellate Body for the first time explicitly acknowledged that the rules of treaty interpretation were applicable to a protocol of accession as a result of it becoming 'an integral part' of the WTO Agreement. After quoting the text of these two paragraphs, the Appellate Body noted that:

> The text of Section 16 of the Protocol resembles to some extent the language found in provisions of other WTO agreements, such as the *Agreement on Safeguards*. Yet, there are important textual and contextual differences between Section 16 of the Protocol and the relevant provisions of other WTO agreements that will inform our interpretative analysis. In the light of these

---

263 Panel Report, *US – Tyres (China)*, para. 7.2.

264 Panel Report, *US – Tyres (China)*, para. 7.10.

265 Appellate Body Report, *US – Tyres (China)*, para. 118.

> differences, and as we explain further below, we view Paragraphs 16.1 and 16.4 of the Protocol as establishing a distinct standard for the imposition of safeguard measures as compared to the standards set out in other WTO agreements.[266]

For a further analysis of this case and Section 16 of the Protocol, see section 6.4.1 below. Since the mechanism created a separate safeguard regime from that applicable under the Agreement on Safeguards, the case is of little assistance in providing insight on the relationship between the provisions contained in that Agreement and the commitment in the Protocol of Accession.

4.3.2.2.2 Non-market economy methodologies In terms of the non-market economy (NME) methodologies that are contained in the protocols of accession and working party reports of China, Viet Nam and Tajikistan, it should be noted that the commitments that permit the use of these methodologies by WTO Members are in essence a derogation of the existing obligations of these Members. The interpretation of these commitments and the relation between these commitments and the provisions of the Anti-Dumping Agreement and Article VI:2 of the GATT 1994 is discussed extensively in section 6.4.2.

4.3.2.3 Waivers in protocols of accession

In one instance, a Member that acceded under Article XII of the WTO Agreement has explicitly waived its right to make use of a certain provision in one of the WTO agreements. The commitment in question has been made by Kazakhstan and reads:

> To reflect the results of these negotiations, the CET [common external tariff] and the Accession Schedule will be modified. For goods subject to negotiation according to paragraph 309 Kazakhstan confirmed that it would not have recourse to Articles XXIV:6 or XXVIII of the GATT 1994 and will continue to apply the commitments contained in the Accession Schedule from the date of its accession until such time as the adjusted tariff rates are negotiated and agreed by consensus with the affected Members have been bound in the modified schedule of Kazakhstan and been implemented by the EAEU. In case the EAEU does not implement the adjusted rates, the commitments contained in the Accession Schedule would prevail. The Working Party took note of these commitments.[267]

---

[266] Appellate Body Report, *US – Tyres (China)*, para. 120.

[267] WTO, Report of the Working Party on the Accession of the Republic of Kazakhstan, WT/ACC/KAZ/93, 23 June 2015, para. 313.

Because of Kazakhstan's trade negotiations in the context of the EAEU, the members of the Working Party deemed it necessary to prevent Kazakhstan from having recourse to the provisions that govern the renegotiation of tariff concessions.[268] This commitment is the first in which a new Member explicitly agrees to forego a right to make use of a provision contained in a covered agreement. The Appellate Body dealt with the question of the relinquishment of rights under the DSU in *Peru – Agricultural Products*.[269] In reaching its conclusion, it recalled its earlier finding in *EC – Bananas III (Article 21.5 – Ecuador II/Article 21.5 – US)* that 'the relinquishment of rights granted by the DSU cannot be lightly assumed', and that 'the language in the Understandings must clearly reveal that the parties intended to relinquish their rights'.[270] Although this accession commitment does not deal with rights granted by the DSU, but rather by the GATT 1994, the finding of the Appellate Body in *Peru – Agricultural Products* is not without relevance. Considering the clear wording of the commitment – 'Kazakhstan confirmed that it would not have recourse to Articles XXIV:6 or XXVIII of the GATT 1994' – it appears that this commitment constitutes a 'modification' of the WTO Agreement as between Kazakhstan and the other Members to that agreement in the sense of Article 41 of the Vienna Convention.[271] In any event, the inclusion of this commitment in the Working Party

---

[268] Tariff renegotiations are normally available under Article XXVIII of the GATT 1994. For a more detailed overview, see Hoda, Anwarul (2001), *Tariff Negotiations and Renegotiations under the GATT and the WTO: Procedures and Practices*, Cambridge, Cambridge University Press.

[269] Appellate Body Report, *Peru – Agricultural Products*, paras. 5.20–5.28.

[270] Appellate Body Reports, *EC – Bananas III (Article 21.5 – Ecuador II)/EC – Bananas III (Article 21.5 – US)*, para. 217.

[271] Article 41 provides: '1. Two or more of the parties to a multilateral treaty may conclude an agreement to modify the treaty as between themselves alone if: (a) the possibility of such a modification is provided for by the treaty; or (b) the modification in question is not prohibited by the treaty and: (i) does not affect the enjoyment by the other parties of their rights under the treaty or the performance of their obligations; (ii) does not relate to a provision, derogation from which is incompatible with the effective execution of the object and purpose of the treaty as a whole. 2. Unless in a case falling under paragraph 1(a) the treaty otherwise provides, the parties in question shall notify the other parties of their intention to conclude the agreement and of the modification to the treaty for which it provides.'

Report on the Accession of Kazakhstan constitutes further evidence of the ad hoc rule-making process that forms part of the WTO accession negotiations.

4.3.2.4 Relevance of protocols of accession for the interpretation of other instruments

The question whether secondary sources of WTO law can impact the rights and obligations of Members under the covered agreements is very much relevant. It has been suggested that the commitments contained in protocols of accession and working party reports 'may shed' light on the meaning of WTO provisions when applied to the acceded Member. Additionally, it has been argued that 'for those protocol provisions that fall in the category of elaborating existing provisions of WTO agreements', they could also clarify 'the meaning of the existing WTO provisions when applied to other members generally'.[272] Most of the arguments raised against the way in which panels and the Appellate Body have interpreted the terms of China's Protocol of Accession relate to the lack of regard for the context of those terms. It has been suggested that '[i]f the WTO judges had examined other members' accession documents on the same issue, they might have looked into the reasons behind the different language on the export duty commitments'.[273] The question is therefore whether the terms in protocols of accession constitute context in the sense of Article 31(2) of the Vienna Convention. Article 31(2) stipulates that the context shall comprise, in addition to the text (including preamble and annexes): i) any agreement relating to the treaty which was made between all the parties in connection with *the conclusion of* the treaty; and ii) any instrument which was made by one or more parties in connection with *the conclusion of* the treaty and accepted by the other parties as an instrument related to the treaty.[274] The Appellate Body has held that the Harmonized System constitutes context in the sense of Article 31(2)(a) Vienna Convention since 'prior to, during, as well as after the Uruguay Round negotiations, there was broad consensus among the GATT Contracting Parties to *use* the Harmonized System as the basis

---

[272] Qin (2017), Mind the Gap: Navigating Between the WTO Agreement and Its Accession Protocols, at 258.

[273] Qin (2017), Mind the Gap: Navigating Between the WTO Agreement and Its Accession Protocols, at 270.

[274] Emphasis added.

for their WTO Schedules, notably with respect to agricultural products'.[275] In the Appellate Body's view, 'this consensus constitutes an "agreement" between WTO Members "relating to" the *WTO Agreement* that was "made in connection with the conclusion of" that Agreement, within the meaning of Article 31(2)(a) of the Vienna Convention'.[276] The question is whether a protocol of accession qualifies as 'any agreement' or 'any instrument' that has been made 'in connection with the conclusion of the treaty'. Presumably, the treaty in question would be the WTO Agreement. However, contrary to the Harmonized System – which was already in place upon conclusion of the Uruguay Round and the signing of the WTO Agreement – protocols of accession were drafted only after the conclusion of the WTO Agreement. Note that Article 31(2)(a) and Article 31(2)(b) do not speak of 'any agreement [...] made between all the parties in connection with the treaty' or 'any instrument which was made by one or more parties in connection with the treaty [...]'. The addition of the term 'the conclusion of' must be given meaning. Consequently, it could be argued that, although protocols of accession arguably constitute agreement and/or instruments, and although they relate to the WTO Agreement, they were not made in connection with 'the conclusion' of that treaty.[277] It is acknowledged that this interpretation might be contrary to the rather broad notion of context that was subsequently used by the Appellate Body in *China – Auto Parts*.[278] In that case, the Appellate Body focused its analysis on the relevance of the context, rather than on whether an agreement or instrument conformed to the formal criteria stipulated by Article 31(2). Nevertheless, it is submitted that a convincing argument could be made that protocols of accession should not be considered as context in the sense of Article 31(2) of the Vienna Convention since they were not concluded in connection with

---

[275] Appellate Body Report, *EC – Chicken Cuts*, para. 199 (emphasis in the original).

[276] Appellate Body Report, *EC – Chicken Cuts*, para. 199 (emphasis in the original).

[277] See on this point, in particular, Van Damme (2009), *Treaty Interpretation by the WTO Appellate Body*, at 255.

[278] Appellate Body Reports, *China – Auto Parts*, para. 151. The Appellate Body noted that '[t]he realm of context as defined in Article 31(2) is broad. "Context" includes all of the text of the treaty – in this case, the *WTO Agreement* – and may also extend to "any agreement relating to the treaty which was made between all the parties in connection with the conclusion of the treaty" and "any instrument which was made by one or more parties in connection with the conclusion of the treaty and accepted by the other parties as an instrument related to the treaty"'.

'the conclusion' of the WTO Agreement, but were rather concluded subsequent to the conclusion of that agreement. However, even assuming that protocols of accession of other Members could constitute 'context' in the sense of Article 31 Vienna Convention, it is doubtful whether the Member-specific commitments contained in these protocols could be of assistance in interpreting the commitments of another Member. In the context of the commitments on the reduction and elimination of export duties, it has been argued that had this been done 'the reasons behind the different language on the export duty commitments' might have been looked into.[279] Accordingly, 'the relevant contexts provided by other members' accession documents could have shed much light on how the silence in China's Accession Protocol regarding the availability of GATT exceptions to the export duty obligations should be interpreted'.[280] This raises the question of whether the absence of specific terms that could lead to the applicability of the general exceptions in one Protocol of Accession could be interpreted by using other protocols of accession – in which such recourse is provided for – as relevant context. Considering the differences in which the commitments on the elimination of export duties have been drafted (see section 6.4.3), the reliance on context might as well suggest that there is not one generally applicable outcome in terms of the applicability of Article XX of the GATT 1994 to those commitments.

4.4 CONCLUSION

In the first part of this chapter the status of WTO protocols of accession in the WTO legal system was examined with the main purpose of determining the legal basis for the enforceability of commitments contained in these protocols and their associated working party reports. In the first section the differences between GATT and WTO accession were briefly revisited in order to be able to analyse the differences between the role of GATT accession protocols in GATT dispute settlement proceedings and WTO protocols of accession in WTO dispute settlement. Section 4.2 highlighted the rather straightforward nature of the GATT accession process by examining GATT panel reports that had involved GATT instruments of accession. It was concluded that most of these disputes

---

[279] Qin (2017), Mind the Gap: Navigating Between the WTO Agreement and Its Accession Protocols, at 270.

[280] Qin (2017), Mind the Gap: Navigating Between the WTO Agreement and Its Accession Protocols, at 271.

focused on the 'grandfather clause'/'existing legislation exception'. Moreover, the role of WTO protocols of accession in WTO dispute settlement proceedings was examined in detail by scrutinizing the available panel and Appellate Body reports that deal with commitments contained in protocols of accession. It was found that the Members involved in these disputes have, until the time of writing, not challenged the jurisdiction of panels or the Appellate Body to hear these disputes. Considering that there is no clear basis in the DSU for the enforcement of protocols of accession, some had expected such a challenge. In the absence of any arguments to that effect, panels and the Appellate Body have so far been able to suffice by referring to the statement contained in protocols of accession that these protocols 'shall be an integral part' of the WTO Agreement. This has led to fierce criticism in scholarship, in particular because of the fact that this would signal that both the WTO Members and the judicial organs of the WTO would not pay sufficient attention to the rule of law. By accepting that protocols of accession can declare themselves to be 'an integral part' of the WTO Agreement, panels and the Appellate Body have implicitly accepted that the General Council has the power to amend the WTO Agreement. Although it is uncertain whether any acceded Member that so far has not been involved in WTO dispute settlement proceedings involving its protocol of accession could successfully challenge the enforceability of such a protocol, it is possible that at some stage panels and the Appellate Body may be required to develop a more elaborate reasoning on this issue. For now, however, the enforceability of WTO protocols of accession appears to be fully accepted by the membership, regardless of the exact legal basis for such enforceability. Having assessed enforceability, the subsequent main section of this chapter contains an in-depth analysis of the relationship between the commitments contained in acceded Members' protocols of accession, including the working party reports, and the provisions contained in the Marrakesh Agreement and the Multilateral Trade Agreements. This relationship is of crucial importance, in particular in light of the fact that certain commitments entered into by acceded Members may extend beyond the obligations that original WTO Members are under by virtue of their WTO membership. In particular, the question whether the general exceptions contained in Article XX of the GATT 1994 are available to justify violations of such 'more far-reaching' commitments is of relevance in assessing whether there is an appropriate balance between the rights and the obligations of acceded Members. In the first substantive section of this chapter an overview was presented of the functioning of this general exceptions clause. Taking into account the two-tier structure of the article, and using examples from case law, the grounds for justifying a measure that would otherwise be WTO-inconsistent were examined. Having reviewed the substance of Article XX of the GATT 1994, the attention turned towards its scope of application. Starting from the language of the treaties, an overview was presented of the way in which non-GATT agreements refer to the general exceptions clause. Moreover, an overview of commitments in protocols of accession that potentially contain a reference to Article XX GATT 1994 was presented. This exercise was conducted in light of the discussion of Protocol of Accession-related case law that was the subject of section 4.3.2.1.2.3. In three disputes involving China's Protocol of Accession, panels and the Appellate Body have developed an interpretative approach that determines whether or not the violation of a certain commitment in a protocol of accession can potentially be justified under the general exceptions of the GATT 1994. It has been observed that this interpretative approach has been heavily criticized in scholarship for being (too) textualist and for failing to take into account relevant policy considerations. Moreover, it has been argued that the approach is not consistent with the standard laid down by the Vienna Convention. Inter alia, it has been suggested that the approach does not accurately take into account the object and purpose of the relevant provisions of the WTO Agreement and the commitments contained in WTO protocols of accession. Additionally, it has been argued that the Appellate Body has failed to take into account relevant context. In doing so, the Appellate Body has – in the view of certain authors – adopted an approach that might eventually undermine the legitimacy and credibility of the WTO in general and the organization's dispute settlement mechanism in particular. In the final section of this chapter it has been observed that such criticism, however well-argued, fails to acknowledge the member-specific nature of protocols of accession. Moreover, it fails to acknowledge that if Members consider that this situation is undesirable, they always have the option of asking the WTO Ministerial Conference or the General Council to address it.[281] In the next part the scope and prevalence of WTO-Plus commitments contained in protocols of accession will be examined. The results of a mapping exercise of 36 protocols of accession are presented, allowing for an assessment of the implications of the interpretative approach discussed in this chapter.

---

[281] Liu, Jingdong (2014), 'Accession Protocols: Legal Status in the WTO Legal System', *Journal of World Trade* (48) (4), pp. 751–71.

PART III

Mapping exercise: the content of protocols of accession

5. Mapping exercise: methodology and typology – commitments on specific matters

5.1 INTRODUCTION

In the first two parts of this monograph the origins and workings of the WTO accession process and the legal status of commitments contained in protocols of accession were examined in detail.[1] It was shown that, pursuant to the interpretative approach developed by panels and the Appellate Body, the relationship between commitments contained in these protocols of accession and the rights and obligations contained in the WTO Agreement has to be assessed on a case-by-case basis.[2] General findings about the applicability of certain provisions contained in, for example the GATT 1994, have been carefully avoided by the adjudicative organs of the WTO.[3] Consequently, in order to understand the relationship between an accession protocol commitment and one of the provisions of the WTO Agreement, one has to establish in each and every case what the relationship is between these provisions. This requires a close examination of the individual commitments that have been made by WTO Members upon their accession to the organization post-1995. In Chapters 5 and 6 such an analysis is conducted in order to allow for a more normative analysis at a later stage, since, after all, one has to be cognizant of the intricacies in the relationships between these *individual* commitments and the obligations that *all* Members of the WTO are under.

In light of the foregoing the next chapter of this monograph presents the results of a mapping exercise of the commitments contained in the protocols of accession of all 36 WTO Members that have joined the organization under the procedure laid down by Article XII of the WTO

[1] See Chapters 1–4.
[2] See Chapter 4.
[3] Appellate Body Report, *China – Rare Earths*, paras. 5.71–5.72.

Agreement. The analysis of all these commitments allows for a comparison between the commitments entered into by different Members. As a result, the analysis will enable us to answer one of the fundamental questions underlying this research project: have the demands that have been placed upon states and customs territories wishing to accede to the WTO increased over time and has it become, as a result thereof, more difficult for states to establish themselves as an actor within the multilateral trading system? This question can be distinguished from a second assumption that could, potentially, serve as a contrasting hypothesis. Under this hypothesis one would assume that the demands placed upon acceding states are per definition country-specific, as each state has to negotiate its own 'entrance fee' to the organization.[4]

In this chapter a typology of accession protocol commitments is developed and presented. Several methodologies have been presented that enable us to better understand the content of these commitments, especially in relation to the rights and obligations contained in the WTO Agreement. The chapter starts with an assessment of these methodologies and typologies and explains the differences between them. Additionally, after having made these observations based on literature, a new, further refined typology is presented that will serve as the basis for the in-depth analysis of accession protocol commitments that will be presented in Chapter 6. Before doing so, however, it is necessary to establish what is considered as the 'baseline' obligations that all WTO Members – original or non-original – have to adhere to.[5] This step is a prerequisite for a

---

[4] This appears to be one of the conclusions reached by Osakwe in Osakwe, Chiedu (2015), Contributions and Lessons from WTO Accessions: The Present and Future of the Rules-Based Multilateral Trading System, in Dadush, Uri and Osakwe, Chiedu (eds) (2015), *WTO Accessions and Trade Multilateralism: Case Studies and Lessons from the WTO at Twenty*, Cambridge, Cambridge University Press, 219–308, at 249. Noting that 'there can never be a "one-size-fits-all" approach to WTO accession and that there "should never be"'. See Qin, Julia Ya (2017), Mind the Gap: Navigating Between the WTO Agreement and Its Accession Protocols, in Elsig, Manfred, Hoekman, Bernard and Pauwelyn, Joost (2017), *Assessing the World Trade Organization: Fit for Purpose?*, Cambridge, Cambridge University Press, pp. 223–75, at 223 for a critique on the 'entry fee' theory.

[5] Charnovitz, Steve (2008), 'Mapping the Law of WTO Accession', in Janow, Merit E., Donaldson, Victoria and Yanovich, Alan (eds), *The WTO: Governance, Dispute Settlement and Developing Countries*, Huntington, NY, Juris Publishing, pp. 855–920, at 868.

further research question that will be answered in this part: whether the amount of 'WTO-Plus' commitments that are sought from states and customs territories wishing to accede to the WTO has increased over time. Therefore, in tandem with the presentation of the typology of accession protocol commitments, an overview is presented of which types of commitments constitute WTO-Plus obligations.

5.2 EFFORTS TO CATEGORIZE COMMITMENTS IN PROTOCOLS OF ACCESSION

The issue of rules commitments being negotiated in the context of the WTO accession process has attracted the attention of international organizations and scholars for quite some time.[6] In 2001, in the context of a publication by the United Nations Conference on Trade and Development (UNCTAD), the first catalogue of the (more) stringent commitments that the 15 countries that had acceded until then had agreed to was compiled.[7] It was found, in particular, that the incumbent membership requests significant rules commitments as part of the accession negotiations.[8] Initially, most of the attention was bestowed upon China's Protocol of Accession and the 'WTO-Plus' obligations it contains.[9] Although many scholars followed this approach in respect of other protocols of accession, it was only in 2008 an elaborate analytical framework for assessing commitments in protocols of accession was presented.[10] In the same year, the WTO published its *Handbook on*

---

[6] See above, section 3.2.4.3.

[7] Butkeviciene, Jolita, Hayashi, Michiko, Ognivtsev, Victor and Yamaoka, Tokio (2001), 'Terms of WTO Accession' in United Nations Conference on Trade and Development (2001), *WTO Accessions and Development Policies*, Geneva, United Nations, UNCTAD/DITC/TNCD/11, pp. 155–76, at 155.

[8] Butkeviciene, Hayashi, Ognivtsev, and Yamaoka (2001), Terms of WTO Accession, at 155. It was found that applicants were denied the use of special and differential treatment (S&D) provisions, for example by declining the application of transition periods.

[9] Qin, Julia Ya (2003), '"WTO-Plus" Obligations and Their Implications for the World Trade Organization Legal System: An Appraisal of the China Accession Protocol', *Journal of World Trade* (37) (3), pp. 483–522.

[10] Charnovitz (2008), Mapping the Law of WTO Accession. His analysis is complete up until 2006. See also Watson, Keith William (2012), Interpreting WTO Accession Commitments According to Their Functional Relationship with Provisions of the WTO Agreements, Thesis submitted in partial satisfaction of

Accession.[11] Although the handbook systematically assesses the commitments contained in protocols of accession, it refrains from categorizing these commitments as 'more stringent', 'less stringent', 'WTO-Plus' or 'WTO-Minus'.[12] More recent contributions have aimed at further refining the typology of commitments contained in protocols of accession.[13] Rather than using terms such as 'WTO-Plus' and 'WTO-Minus', the following terminology has been suggested: i) more stringent obligations to an applicant as compared to the WTO Agreement; ii) less stringent obligations to an applicant compared to the WTO Agreement; iii) more stringent obligations to incumbent Members compared to the WTO Agreement; and iv) less stringent obligations to incumbent Members compared to the WTO Agreement.[14] The WTO itself has also stepped up its efforts in making the accession process more transparent by launching the Accession Commitments Database (ACDB).[15] This useful tool enables users to catalogue commitments contained in protocols of accession by Section, Keyword and Member. It does not, however, indicate the

---

the requirements for the degree of Master of Laws, Faculty of the George Washington University Law School, 20 May.

[11] Williams, Peter John (2008), *A Handbook on Accession to the WTO*, Cambridge, Cambridge University Press.

[12] Williams (2008), *A Handbook on Accession to the WTO*, at 50. Williams notes that 'Some Members have argued in the General Council/Ministerial Conference that new entrants should not be required to undertake Protocol commitments that are more stringent than those of original WTO Members at similar levels of economic development (sometimes referred to as WTO-plus commitments)'.

[13] Tyagi, Mitali (2012), 'Flesh on a Legal Fiction: Early Practice in the WTO on Accession Protocols', *Journal of International Economic Law* (15) (2), pp. 391–441, at 432. Tyagi also lists a sample of commitments that he considers beyond the scope of the WTO Agreement, finding that 'the modification and exclusion of WTO legal texts is rife in APs [accession protocols]'. See also Yamaoka, Tokio (2013), 'Analysis of China's Accession Commitments in the WTO: New Taxonomy of More and Less Stringent Commitments, and the Struggle for Mitigation by China', *Journal of World Trade* (47) (1), pp. 105–58. Yamaoka contributed to this field of scholarship by suggesting a 'new taxonomy of more and less stringent commitments'.

[14] Yamaoka (2013), Analysis of China's Accession Commitments in the WTO: New Taxonomy of More and Less Stringent Commitments, and the Struggle for Mitigation by China, at 118.

[15] WTO, Accession Commitments Database (ACDB). Available at http://acdb.wto.org/index.aspx (last accessed at 1 June 2017).

relationship of the commitment with the relevant (or corresponding) provision (if any) in the WTO Agreement. In addition to the ACDB, the WTO has also published a comprehensive study of 20 years of accession practice in the multilateral trading system.[16] The contribution contains many insightful case studies as well as a first comprehensive attempt by the WTO to present the content of commitments contained in protocols of accession in a systematic manner.[17] In the first comprehensive contribution of its kind, an 'accession results grid' is presented, outlining in great detail the different types of commitments that have been entered into by acceding Members.[18] Moreover, this is the first contribution to provide basic statistics on the amount of 'specific commitment paragraphs' that are contained in the relevant working party reports and protocols of accession.[19]

5.3 SCOPE OF THE MAPPING EXERCISE

The mapping exercise includes protocols of accession of Members that joined the WTO after its inception in 1995 until the accessions of Kazakhstan, Afghanistan and Liberia in December 2015. These 20 years of WTO accession practice provide a relevant time-frame for a comprehensive analysis. This section thereto first presents some accession-related statistics, in terms of the amount of Members that have acceded; the economic status of those Members and the amount of commitments contained in their respective protocols of accession and associated working party reports.

5.3.1 Numbers

Since 1995, 36 states or separate customs territories have acceded to the WTO.

---

[16] Dadush, Uri and Osakwe, Chiedu (eds) (2015), *WTO Accessions and Trade Multilateralism: Case Studies and Lessons from the WTO at Twenty*, Cambridge, Cambridge University Press.

[17] Osakwe (2015), Contributions and Lessons from WTO Accessions, at 252.

[18] Osakwe (2015), Contributions and Lessons from WTO Accessions, at 252.

[19] Osakwe (2015), Contributions and Lessons from WTO Accessions, at 300.

Table 5.1 Number of commitment paragraphs in working party reports on accessions

	WTO Member	Accession Date	Status	Paragraphs with Commitments
01	Ecuador	21 January 1996	DC	21
02	Bulgaria	1 December 1996	Developed	35
03	Mongolia	29 January 1997	DC	17
04	Panama	6 September 1997	DC	24
05	Kyrgyz Republic	20 December 1998	DC	29
06	Latvia	10 February 1999	Developed	22
07	Estonia	13 November 1999	Developed	24
08	Jordan	11 April 2000	DC	29
09	Georgia	14 June 2000	DC	30
10	Albania	8 September 2000	DC	29
11	Oman	9 November 2000	DC	26
12	Croatia	30 November 2000	Developed	27
13	Lithuania	31 May 2001	Developed	28
14	Moldova	26 July 2001	DC	28
15	China	11 December 2001	DC	Protocol of Accession + 139
16	Chinese Taipei	1 January 2002	DC	63
17	Armenia	5 February 2003	DC	39
18	FYR Macedonia	4 April 2003	DC	24
19	Nepal	23 April 2004	LDC	25
20	Cambodia	13 October 2004	LDC	29
21	Saudi Arabia	11 December 2005	DC	59
22	Viet Nam	11 January 2007	DC	70
23	Tonga	27 July 2007	DC	29
24	Ukraine	16 May 2008	DC	63
25	Cape Verde	23 July 2008	DC	26
26	Montenegro	29 April 2012	DC	35
27	Samoa	10 May 2012	LDC	37
28	Russian Federation	22 August 2012	DC	163
29	Vanuatu	24 August 2012	LDC	30
30	Lao PDR	2 February 2013	LDC	26
31	Tajikistan	2 March 2013	DC	40

	WTO Member	Accession Date	Status	Paragraphs with Commitments
32	Yemen	26 June 2014	LDC	28
33	Seychelles	26 April 2015	DC	40
34	Kazakhstan	30 November 2015	DC	118
35	Liberia	14 July 2016	LDC	31
36	Afghanistan	29 July 2016	LDC	37
				Total: 1520 paragraphs

At the time of their accession all of these countries were either developing countries or LDCs. Out of the 36 acceded Members, eight are classified as LDCs.[20] Five of the acceded Members have, since their accession, graduated to 'developed country' status. In all five cases this was because the Members in question acceded to the European Union.[21] Of equal importance as the distinction between LDCs and developing countries is the marked difference between the protocols of accession of 'non-market economies' (or states whose economies, at the time of their accession, were characterized by a substantial degree of governmental involvement) and the protocols of applicants that were considered market economies at the time of their accession. The difference between these two groups of countries is reflected in the number of paragraphs containing commitments on specific matters in their working party reports (see Table 5.1).

Although numbers in and of themselves do not tell the whole story – paragraphs may contain more than one commitment – they nevertheless provide a relevant starting point for this analytical exercise.[22] In total, the protocols of accession of the 36 countries that have acceded to the WTO since 1995 contain 1520 paragraphs with commitments on specific matters. On average that is 42.2 paragraphs per protocol (see Table 5.2). However, the protocols of accession of China (2001) and the Russian

[20] Nepal, Cambodia, Samoa, Vanuatu, Lao PDR, Yemen, Liberia and Afghanistan.

[21] EU5: Bulgaria, Latvia, Estonia, Croatia, Lithuania.

[22] See in this regard also Jones, Kent (2010), *The Doha Blues: Institutional Crisis and Reform in the WTO*, Oxford, Oxford University Press, at 67. Jones notes that 'the number of such commitments may be taken as a rough measure of the degree to which applicants have had to agree to special obligations of interest to incumbent WTO members'.

Federation (2012) contain far more – 139 and 163, respectively – paragraphs containing commitments on specific matters than the average. If these two Members are excluded from the analysis, there are 1218 paragraphs and 34 Members, an average of 35.8 paragraphs per acceded Member.

Table 5.2 Groups and categories of non-original Members

Group	Paragraphs	Average
All	1520	42.2
All – Excluding China and Russian Federation	1218	35.8
All – Excluding NMEs (China, Armenia, Viet Nam and Tajikistan) and Chinese Taipei, Saudi Arabia, Ukraine, Russian Federation and Kazakhstan	766	28.4
LDCs	243	30.4
NMEs (China, Chinese Taipei, Armenia, Saudi Arabia, Viet Nam, Ukraine, Russian Federation, Tajikistan and Kazakhstan)	754	83.8
All – Pre-2005 (including China, Chinese Taipei, Armenia and Saudi Arabia)	688	34.4
All – Post-2005 (including Viet Nam, Ukraine, Russian Federation, Tajikistan and Kazakhstan)	773	51.5
All – Pre-2005 (excluding China, Chinese Taipei, Armenia and Saudi Arabia)	447	26.3
All – Post-2005 (excluding Viet Nam, Ukraine, Russian Federation, Tajikistan and Kazakhstan)	319	31.9

From early on it has been established that applicants with an economy that is characterized by a significant degree of influence of the state have been asked to accept more stringent commitments.[23] What is evident from the numbers is that applicants in this category have accepted more commitments.[24] This group consisting of nine applicants accounts for almost 50 per cent of all paragraphs containing commitments, with an

[23] Williams (2008), *A Handbook on Accession to the WTO*, at 50.

[24] Although the categorization is open to discussion, based on the language used in the working party reports, this group includes China, Chinese Taipei, Armenia, Saudi Arabia, Viet Nam, Ukraine, the Russian Federation, Tajikistan and Kazakhstan.

average of 83.7 paragraphs per applicant.[25] If a comparison is made between accessions of states with a large degree of governmental involvement in their economies and accessions of states in which this is not the case, it can be observed that the average number of paragraphs containing commitments has increased with 5.1 (or nearly 20 per cent) in 20 years of accession practice.[26] NMEs that have acceded post-2005 have had to accept far more commitment-containing paragraphs than their market economy country parts.[27]

5.3.2 Substance

Since these numbers merely provide an indication with respect to the amount of commitments being agreed to, the actual substance of those commitments is evidently of greater importance. Many academic contributions on this issue have focused on the question whether acceding states have been required to agree to 'more stringent' commitments. In their respective analyses, most authors have focused on a comparison between the protocol commitment and the baseline obligation contained in the WTO Agreement. However, few contributions have assessed the wording of these commitments in detail. A five-category typology of accession protocol commitments has been suggested: descriptions, referential confirmations, express confirmations, extra-schedule bindings, and modifications.[28] Others have suggested cataloguing commitments in the following five categories: i) commercial commitments; ii) affirmation of

---

[25] Regarding commitment-containing paragraphs, 49.6% can be found in the working party reports and protocols of accession of these nine Members.

[26] This finding corresponds with earlier observations by Jones in this field. Jones found that 'The accessions coefficient was positive and highly significant in most regression variants, indicating an increase in the number of rule commitments by 0.6 to 1.1 for each additional accession completed prior to an applicant country's Working Party Report'. Among the applicant status and trade policy profile variables, the results were weaker, with some unusual results. An increase by 1 in the AD [anti-dumping] index resulted in three to five additional rule commitments, with 10% or better statistical significance in four out of five variants. LDC status resulted in 10 to 14 fewer rule commitments, with 10% or better significance in the four variants tested. This result is consistent with the official WTO proclamation to facilitate LDC accession. Jones (2010), *The Doha Blues*, at 71.

[27] This difference can be explained at least partially because of the fact that many of the other applicants have been LDCs.

[28] Watson (2012), Interpreting WTO Accession Commitments According to Their Functional Relationship with Provisions of the WTO Agreements, at 60.

obligations; iii) elaboration of existing provisions; iv) expansion of existing obligations; and v) derogation from existing obligations.[29] As discussed in Chapter 4, and in light of the Appellate Body's findings in *China – Raw Materials* and *China – Rare Earths*, it is submitted that the wording of the commitments, including the way in which the baseline obligations contained in the WTO Agreement are referenced, is of crucial importance in assessing the question to what extent any particular commitment is 'more stringent' than the baseline obligation.[30] Ultimately the question whether the commitments applicants have agreed to have become more stringent over time can only be answered by analysing these commitments in detail.[31]

5.4 TYPOLOGY

This section presents a new typology of considering commitments contained in WTO protocols of accession. More specifically, five categories of commitments are identified below. Each category contains a brief description of the type of commitment and the way in which it relates to the rights and obligations contained in the WTO Agreement. These rights and obligations in the WTO Agreement, including all of its annexes, constitute the baseline that all WTO Members have to adhere to. Therefore, to the extent that a particular commitment by an acceded Member deviates from this baseline commitment, we can theoretically speak of a WTO-Plus – in the case of a more stringent commitment – or a WTO-Minus – in the case of a less stringent commitment – obligation. However, many commitments contained in protocols of accession simply confirm the acceding state's intention to adhere to the obligations provided for in the WTO Agreement. Such confirmations make up a large part of the totality of commitments that has been investigated. In the subsequent subsections, five categories of accession protocol commitments are identified. The first category consists of commitments that relate to transitional periods and special and differential treatment for developing countries and, in particular, LDCs. The second category contains the commitments that serve as a confirmation of the acceding state's intention to adhere to the baseline obligation that is contained in

[29] Qin (2017), Mind the Gap: Navigating Between the WTO Agreement and Its Accession Protocols, at 4–5.

[30] See above, Chapter 4, for an analysis of the reports of panels and the Appellate Body that forms the basis for this particular conclusion.

[31] See Chapter 6.

the WTO Agreement. These 'confirmation commitments' can best be described as a commitment to signal an intent to 'ensure conformity' with these baseline obligations. A third category of commitments consists of commitments that are aimed at implementing WTO obligations and ensuring the conformity of the domestic trade policy with the obligations prescribed by the WTO. This is a major category of commitments, which includes commitments in the areas of, for example, transparency, state-owned enterprises (SOEs) and internal taxes. Often, these commitments already pre-judge the WTO-consistency of the acceding state's trade policy, prior to it being subject to WTO dispute settlement proceedings.[32] Some authors have questioned the legitimacy of this particular practice.[33] The fourth category of commitments is of a particular type in the sense that they provide other WTO Members with the authority to adopt certain measures or practices that, in the absence of the commitment, they would not be allowed to adopt under the baseline obligations contained in the WTO Agreement. This type of commitment can mainly be found in the sphere of anti-dumping and countervailing measures.[34] The fifth, and final, category of accession protocol commitments consists of the commitments that do not have a direct counterpart in the WTO Agreement. These commitments often prohibit an acceded Member from doing something which is not prohibited for original Members. So far it appears that it is this fifth and final type of commitment that has caused the most controversies in respect of WTO accessions.[35]

5.4.1 Category 1: Transitional Periods and Special and Differential Treatment

Many WTO agreements contain provisions that provide for the possibility for developing countries to make use of transitional periods. The Agreement on Trade-Related Investment Measures, the Agreement on Customs Valuation, the Agreement on the Trade-Related Aspects of Intellectual

---

[32] WTO, Report of the Working Party on the Accession of the Islamic Republic of Afghanistan to the World Trade Organization, WT/ACC/AFG/36, 13 November 2015, paras. 90 and 146, referring to Annex 10. Annex 10 contains four export measures maintained by Afghanistan at the time of accession and their apparent justification grounds under Article XX of the GATT 1994.

[33] Grynberg, Roman and Joy, Roy Mickey (2000), 'The Accession of Vanuatu to the WTO: Lessons for the Multilateral Trading System', *Journal of World Trade* (34) (6), pp. 159–73, at 159. See section 5.4.3.

[34] Countervailing measures seek to off-set the negative effects caused by subsidized imports.

[35] Section 5.3, above.

Property Rights and the Agreement on Subsidies and Countervailing Measures all provide that all, or certain, of its provisions will only be applied to developing countries after a certain period of time. In nearly all protocols of accession, the applicant Member has committed itself to apply the provisions of the relevant agreements from the date of accession, 'without recourse to a transition period'.[36] Only in certain cases, most notably in the case of LDC accessions, have transition periods been agreed. Such commitments have been qualified as more stringent obligations than contained in the WTO Agreement.[37]

5.4.2 Category 2: Ensuring Conformity

By far the largest category of commitments on specific matters consists of commitments that reflect the applicant's intention to ensure the WTO-consistency of its trade policy. The discussions in accession working parties appear to be focused on ensuring that the acceding state's domestic laws and regulations are consistent with the WTO obligations it is about to undertake. As such, they are aimed at identifying measures that the incumbent membership considers to be (potentially) WTO-inconsistent and ensuring that the applicant alters them prior to accession. In this context, the most straightforward are commitments that stipulate that it would apply its domestic laws and regulations in conformity with the requirements laid down by one of the provisions of the WTO Agreement including the Multilateral Trade Agreements. Commitments on the application of internal taxes are a good example:

> The representative of Oman stated that, from the date of accession, Oman would apply its domestic taxes on products in compliance with Articles I and III of the GATT 1994.[38]

---

[36] See, for example, WTO, Report of the Working Party on the Accession of Albania to the World Trade Organization, WT/ACC/ALB/51, 13 July 2000, paras. 104 and 108, stipulating that Albania would apply the TBT and SPS Agreements, respectively, from the date of accession, without recourse to any transition period.

[37] Yamaoka (2013), Analysis of China's Accession Commitments in the WTO: New Taxonomy of More and Less Stringent Commitments, and the Struggle for Mitigation by China, at 122.

[38] WTO, Report of the Working Party on the Accession of Oman to the World Trade Organization, WT/ACC/OMN/26, 28 September 2000, para. 51.

This commitment by Oman is nothing more than a commitment to ensure conformity with the obligations contained in Articles I and III of the GATT 1994.

Another example of a commitment to apply domestic measures into conformity with the applicant's WTO obligations relates to the field of 'trade remedies'. Commitments on matters relating to anti-dumping measures, countervailing measures and safeguard measures are similar across most protocols of accession. All but two protocols contain commitments on the way in which the acceding state will apply the Anti-Dumping Agreement, the SCM Agreement and the Agreement on Safeguards. In 20 years of accession practice a standard commitment seems to have evolved:

> The representative of [Applicant] confirmed that, from the date of accession, [Applicant] would not apply any anti-dumping, countervailing or safeguard measure until it had notified and enacted appropriate laws and implementing regulations in conformity with the provisions of the WTO Agreements on the Implementation of Article VI, on Subsidies and Countervailing Measures, and on Safeguards. He further confirmed that [Applicant] would ensure the full conformity of such laws and regulations with the WTO Agreement, including Articles VI and XIX of the GATT 1994 and the Agreements on the Implementation of Article VI, Subsidies and Countervailing Measures, and Safeguards. He also confirmed that, after such laws and implementing regulations were enacted, [Applicant] would apply any anti-dumping duties, countervailing duties and safeguard measures only in full conformity with WTO provisions.

5.4.3 Category 3: Implementing WTO Obligations and Bringing Measures into Conformity with WTO Obligations

Applicants have been asked to change laws and legislation prior to their accession. In these cases the incumbent membership has analysed the trading regime of the applicant and considered that a particular measure is inconsistent with the applicant's future WTO obligations. This practice has been criticized and described as 'akin to having a complainant at a panel act as the sole panellist'.[39] Nevertheless, it might be argued that this aspect of the accession process prevents the applicant from being subject to dispute settlement proceedings at a later stage. Most of the commitments that belong within this category can be summarized as 'doing X as a way to ensure conformity with a particular WTO

---

[39] Grynberg and Joy (2000), The Accession of Vanuatu to the WTO: Lessons for the Multilateral Trading System, at 159.

obligation'. Some commitments contain a detailed description of *the way in which* applicants are expected to conform to their WTO obligations. These commitments usually specify a particular line of action the acceding state will undertake in order to implement its obligations.

5.4.3.1 Internal taxes

In some protocols of accession, the incumbent membership has used the reports of panels and the Appellate Body. Consider the commitments on internal taxes in the protocols of accession of Georgia, Armenia, Nepal, Viet Nam and Vanuatu, for example:

> The representative of Georgia confirmed that [...] the excise tax on vodka would be increased to conform to Article III requirements as interpreted in recent dispute resolution cases.[40]

> [T]he representative of Armenia stated that legislation had been enacted by Armenia's Parliament in Law No. HO-415-N on 21 October 2002 and would be implemented before the date of accession to equalise the level of excise duties applied to all distilled beverages, vodka, cognac, liquor, etc. (HS 2208) and to equalise the level of excise duties applied to champagne, sparkling wines, wines, etc. (HS 2204).[41]

> The representative of Nepal confirmed that, from the date of accession, Nepal would apply its domestic taxes, including value-added and excise taxes, in a non-discriminatory manner consistent with Articles I and III of the GATT 1994. For beverages classified as 'chhyang', a fermented beverage similar to beer, Nepal would maintain an equal rate of excise duty for chhyang and beer from the date of accession. The Working Party took note of these commitments.[42]

> The representative of Viet Nam further confirmed that, within three years after the date of accession, Viet Nam would apply excise taxes and other internal taxes on distilled spirits and beer in accordance with the WTO Agreement, including Articles I and III of the GATT 1994. To this end, he further confirmed that, within three years after the date of accession, all distilled

[40] WTO, Report of the Working Party on the Accession of Georgia to the World Trade Organization, WT/ACC/GEO/31, 31 August 1999, para. 57.

[41] WTO, Report of the Working Party on the Accession of the Republic of Armenia to the World Trade Organization, WT/ACC/ARM/23, 26 November 2002, para. 70.

[42] WTO, Report of the Working Party on the Accession of the Kingdom of Nepal to the World Trade Organization, WT/ACC/NPL/16, 28 August 2003, para. 64.

spirits with an alcohol content of 20 per cent or higher would be subject to either a single specific rate per litre of pure alcohol or a single ad valorem rate.[43]

In reply to Members, the representative of Vanuatu stated that the schedule of excise taxes would be amended to remove, upon accession, the discrimination between like or similar alcoholic beverages, including for the excise tax applied to: Whiskies (HS2208.3010, HS2208.3020); Rum and other spirits obtained by distilling fermented sugarcane products (HS2208.4010, HS2208.4020); Gin and Geneva (HS2208.5010, HS2208.5020); Vodka (HS2208.6010, HS2208.6020); Liqueurs and cordials (HS2208.7010, HS2208.7020); and, other spirituous beverages (HS2208.9010, HS2208.9020).[44]

In these accessions, the incumbent membership appears to have used the finding by the Panel and the Appellate Body in *Japan – Alcoholic Beverages II* that shochu and vodka were like products.[45] However, likeness, according to the Working Party Report on Border Tax Adjustments (1970) and subsequent cases, is to be determined 'on a case-by-case basis' and 'in a given market'.[46] The Members who have made these commitments appear therefore to have given up their freedom to tax certain products differently, by accepting that they are 'like' in the sense of Article III:2 of the GATT 1994. This would appear to pre-judge the outcome of a potential WTO dispute on this issue and would seem to limit the regulatory freedom of these Members in a way that does not apply to other Members.

5.4.3.2 Transparency

Commitments on transparency are a good example of commitments that stipulate in a detailed manner *how* the applicant will implement the general obligation contained in the GATT 1994, in this case Article X of that agreement. This article requires WTO Members to promptly publish laws, regulations and judicial decisions to enable governments and traders to become acquainted with them. However, the article is silent on the way *in which* this should be done. Moreover, several other WTO agreements contain transparency obligations that Members have to

---

43 WTO, Report of the Working Party on the Accession of Viet Nam, WT/ACC/VNM/48, 27 October 2006, para. 198.

44 WTO, Report of the Working Party on the Accession of Vanuatu to the World Trade Organization, WT/ACC/VUT/18, 11 May 2011, para. 55.

45 Appellate Body Report, *Japan – Alcoholic Beverages II*, at 23.

46 GATT, Working Party Report, Border Tax Adjustments (1970), BISD 18S/97, para. 18.

adhere to. Examples include Article 12 of the Customs Valuation Agreement, Article 3 of the GATS and Article 63 of the TRIPS Agreement.[47] Working party reports contain a wide variety of commitments on this issue. The Seychelles Working Party Report contains a commitment stipulating that Seychelles would 'establish a website updated on a regular basis and readily available to WTO Members, individuals and enterprises, dedicated to the publication of all regulations and other measures pertaining to or affecting trade in goods, services, and TRIPS'.[48] Tajikistan took up a similar, but not identical, commitment that entails that it would 'post the contents of current and past editions of the Official Journal on the Government website and keep them current'.[49] Whether these commitments can be characterized as WTO-Plus obligations is doubtful. Although they prescribe a particular method of implementing the baseline obligation contained in Article X of the GATT 1994, they do not further restrict the new Member's ability to create policy. It could be argued that the new Member's policy space is restricted since it no longer has the option of choosing *the method* with which it desires to fulfil the obligation laid down in Article X, but this argument can be countered by the argument that, in accepting the accession protocol commitment, the Member in question has exercised its sovereignty and right to regulate by opting for a particular method in negotiating its terms of accession.[50] A far-reaching commitment in this category was made by China, stating that it 'would make available to

---

[47] For a detailed overview of all transparency requirements in the WTO agreements, see Marceau, Gabrielle and Pedersen, Peter N. (1999), 'Is the WTO Open and Transparent? A Discussion of the Relationship of the WTO with Non-Governmental Organizations and Civil Society's Claims for More Transparency and Public Participation', *Journal of World Trade* (33) (1), pp. 5–49, at 21–5. See also Ala'i, Padideh and D'Orsi, Matthew (2011), Transparency in International Economic Relations and the Role of the WTO, in Ala'i, Padideh and Vaughn, Robert G. (eds) (2011), *Research Handbook on Transparency*, Cheltenham, UK and Northampton, MA, USA, Edward Elgar, pp. 368–99.

[48] WTO, Report of the Working Party on the Accession of the Republic of Seychelles, WT/ACC/SYC/64, 5 November 2014, para. 407.

[49] WTO, Report of the Working Party on the Accession of the Republic of Tajikistan, WT/ACC/TJK/30, 6 November, 2012 para. 343.

[50] This was the argument used by the Panel in *China – Raw Materials*. See Panel Reports, *China – Raw Materials*, para. 7.156. The Panel noted that 'WTO Members have an inherent and sovereign right to regulate trade. WTO Members and China have exercised this right, *inter alia*, in negotiating and ratifying the WTO Agreement. China has exercised its inherent and sovereign right to regulate trade in negotiating, among other actions, *the terms of its accession into the WTO*' (footnote omitted) (emphasis added).

WTO Members translations into one or more of the official languages of the WTO all laws, regulations and other measures pertaining to or affecting trade in goods, services, TRIPS or the control of forex'.[51]

5.4.3.3 Accession to international agreements

Protocols of accession also contain commitments that entail that the applicant will accede to a particular international agreement. In most accessions, the applicant has confirmed that it will seek accession to two plurilateral trade agreements contained in Annex 4 of the WTO Agreement: the Agreement on Trade in Civil Aircraft and the Agreement on Government Procurement. Article XII:3 of the WTO Agreement explicitly stipulates that the accession to these agreements will be governed by the provisions of these agreements themselves. Since accession to either of these agreements is not mandatory for WTO Members, the commitment can be considered as 'more stringent' for the applicant. The language of these commitments differs slightly, ranging from 'an intention to accede' and a commitment to accede 'if the results of the negotiations are satisfactory to the interests of [Applicant]' to 'the representative of [Applicant] confirmed that [Applicant] would accede to the Agreement on Government Procurement (GPA) within one year of its accession to the WTO'.[52] Tyagi has argued that the failure to live up to the commitment to accede could potentially be challenged before – and enforced by – a panel.[53] In the case of commitments relating to accession to the Agreement on Government Procurement, it should be noted, however, that only Chinese Taipei and Montenegro stipulated a deadline for accession.[54] These two Members have indeed acceded to the Agreement on Government Procurement. With respect to the Agreement on Trade in Civil Aircraft the picture is different. Applicants who have made

---

[51] WTO, Report of the Working Party on the Accession of China, WT/ACC/CHN/49 and Corr. 1, 1 October 2001, para. 334. See also Qin (2003), 'WTO-Plus' Obligations and Their Implications for the World Trade Organization Legal System: An Appraisal of the China Accession Protocol, at 494; Ala'i and D'Orsi (2011), Transparency in International Economic Relations and the Role of the WTO, at 368.

[52] From the group of applicants to make a commitment on this issue, so far only Chinese Taipei, Armenia and Montenegro have acceded to the Agreement on Government Procurement.

[53] Tyagi (2012), Flesh on a Legal Fiction: Early Practice in the WTO on Accession Protocols, at 416.

[54] Cambodia, Cape Verde, Ecuador, Lao PDR, Nepal, Samoa, Tonga, Viet Nam and Yemen did not undertake commitments with respect to either of the plurilateral agreements.

a commitment on this particular issue have nearly all agreed to join the agreement from the date of accession. However, applicants such as Armenia, FYR Macedonia, Oman, Tajikistan and Ukraine have so far not acceded to the Agreement on Trade in Civil Aircraft, thereby failing to act in conformity with their commitment.[55] Tyagi's argument that this type of commitment could equally be enforced in WTO dispute settlement proceedings raises the question of how such a 'commitment violation' could be addressed. Is the failure to sign and ratify, and thereby accede, to the Agreement on Trade in Civil Aircraft a measure that can be challenged before a panel? If this is the case, does a panel have the authority to recommend that a non-conforming Member address this inconsistency by ratifying the Agreement on Trade in Civil Aircraft? What if the Member, in spite of the panel's ruling, still does not comply? Would this allow for the suspension of concessions by the complaining Member? These are all questions that illustrate the potential problems that this type of 'commitment' might pose in WTO dispute settlement proceedings. However, it is important to note that it is extremely unlikely that a fellow WTO Member will file a complaint against the failure to sign up to an international agreement. First, such a claim is unlikely to be supported by a particular industry. In the large majority of WTO disputes there is an affected industry that seeks the removal of a particular measure. It is unlikely that there is an industry that would be negatively affected by the failure of a WTO Member to sign up to an international agreement. Second, this 'best-efforts' type of obligation is more diplomatic and political in nature than some of the other commitments. It is likely that the commitment was merely introduced into the working party report to highlight the importance of that particular agreement.

In the case of Seychelles, a commitment was made to accede to the International Union for the Protection of New Varieties of Plants (UPOV). The representative of Seychelles 'confirmed that his Government would notify, no later than the end of 2015, the accession to the Convention of International Union for the Protection of New Varieties of Plants'.[56] This commitment contains 'the way in which' Seychelles would implement the obligation contained in Article 27.3(b) of the

[55] There were 32 signatories to the Agreement on Trade in Civil Aircraft at the time of writing. See WTO, Agreement on Trade in Civil Aircraft. Available at https://www.wto.org/english/tratop_e/civair_e/civair_e.htm (last accessed at 1 June 2017).

[56] WTO, Report of the Working Party on the Accession of the Republic of Seychelles, WT/ACC/SYC/64, 5 November 2014, para. 372.

TRIPS Agreement, which requires Members to 'provide for the protection of plant varieties either by patents or by an effective *sui generis* system or by any combination thereof'. Interestingly, the government of Nepal explicitly 'rejected the kind of "WTO-plus" commitment the adoption of UPOV 91 would entail'.[57] The commitment by Seychelles is the first in which an applicant made a commitment to accede to a 'non-WTO' international agreement.

5.4.3.4 State-owned enterprises

Accession working party reports also contain sections on the issue of SOEs. It has been observed that many of the states that have acceded through the procedure laid down by Article XII of the WTO Agreement feature state trading practices.[58] This term is not explicitly used in the context of the GATT 1994, which – dating back to 1947 – still uses the term 'State Trading Enterprises' in the context of Article XVII GATT 1994. This article stipulates (in relevant part):

> 1. (*a*) Each contracting party undertakes that if it establishes or maintains a State enterprise, wherever located, or grants to any enterprise, formally or in effect, exclusive or special privileges, such enterprise shall, in its purchases or sales involving either imports or exports, act in a manner consistent with the general principles of non-discriminatory treatment prescribed in this Agreement for governmental measures affecting imports or exports by private traders.
>
> (*b*) The provisions of sub-paragraph (*a*) of this paragraph shall be understood to require that such enterprises shall, having due regard to the other provisions of this Agreement, make any such purchases or sales solely in accordance with commercial considerations, including price, quality, availability, marketability, transportation and other conditions of purchase or sale, and shall afford the enterprises of the other contracting parties adequate opportunity, in accordance with customary business practice, to compete for participation in such purchases or sales.

---

[57] ICTSD (International Centre for Trade and Sustainable Development), Nepal Ready to Enter WTO Without UPOV Membership, 5 September 2003. Available at http://www.ictsd.org/bridges-news/biores/news/nepal-ready-to-enter-wto-without-upov-membership (last accessed at 1 June 2017).

[58] Bratanov, Dimitar (2015), Disciplining State Trading Practices: Lessons from WTO Accession Negotiations, in Dadush, Uri and Osakwe, Chiedu (eds) (2015), *WTO Accessions and Trade Multilateralism: Case Studies and Lessons from the WTO at Twenty*, Cambridge, Cambridge University Press, pp. 764–94, at 774.

In the context of trade in services, Article VIII of the GATS also refrains from using the term 'state-owned', referring to 'monopoly supplier' and 'exclusive service supplier' instead.

In the first four accessions to the WTO, commitments relating to Article XVII GATT 1994 and Article VIII GATS were made under the heading 'State-Trading', followed by either 'enterprises' or 'entities'. Nevertheless, in the context of Bulgaria's accession, the term 'state-owned' was used in the context of its commitment to fulfil the notification requirements contained in the WTO agreements. In the Working Party Report on the accession of the Kyrgyz Republic, the heading 'State ownership and privatization' was used for the first time. The commitment on state trading entities in Jordan's Working Party Report is the first to refer to 'state-owned enterprises' in the context of a commitment to observe Article XVII GATT 1994 and Article VIII GATS. Additionally, the commitment is the first to explicitly refer to the language used in Article XVII:1(b) GATT 1994 by stipulating that Jordan would observe these provisions 'in particular abiding by the provisions for notification, non-discrimination, and *the application of commercial considerations* for trade transactions'. A similar commitment is found in Oman's WPR. China's commitments on the issue of SOEs are detailed as they elaborate on the term 'commercial considerations' using the language found in Article XVII GATT 1994. Paragraph 46 of its WPR stipulates:

> The representative of China further confirmed that China would ensure that all state-owned and state-invested enterprises would make purchases and sales based solely on commercial considerations, e.g., price, quality, marketability and availability, and that the enterprises of other WTO Members would have an adequate opportunity to compete for sales to and purchases from these enterprises on non-discriminatory terms and conditions.

This type of commitment is quite common. It can be found in 16 other accession WPRs. The second part of the paragraph continues by stipulating that:

> In addition, the Government of China would not influence, directly or indirectly, commercial decisions on the part of state-owned or state-invested enterprises, including on the quantity, value or country of origin of any goods purchased or sold, except in a manner consistent with the WTO Agreement. The Working Party took note of these commitments.

It has been argued that this provision 'apparently extends the discipline of GATT Article XVII on state trading enterprises to *all* state-owned and state-invested enterprises in China'.[59] Similar commitments have been made by Viet Nam, Cape Verde, Vanuatu, Lao PDR and Yemen. The Russian Federation has also undertaken commitments in this area, but they are phrased in a slightly different manner. The commitment only refers to enterprises that operate within the scope of 'the services commitments of the Russian Federation' and requires the Russian Federation to 'ensure that such enterprises would act in accordance with the provisions set-out in this paragraph'.[60]

Moreover, Paragraph 10.2 of China's Protocol of Accession stipulates that 'for purposes of applying Articles 1.2 and 2 of the SCM Agreement, subsidies provided to state-owned enterprises will be viewed as specific if, *inter alia*, state-owned enterprises are the predominant recipients of such subsidies or state-owned enterprises receive disproportionately large amounts of such subsidies'. A similar commitment is contained in Paragraph 190 of the WPR on the accession of Tajikistan.

Interestingly, 'accession negotiations could be seen as a barometer of the direction in which multilateral disciplines in [the area of state owned enterprises] may yet evolve'.[61] This is important as SOEs and state-trading enterprises are a field in which new disciplines are still needed, something which is also reflected by the attention given to this topic in the context of pluri- and bilateral negotiations in the context of, for example, the Trans-Pacific Partnership (TPP) and the Transatlantic Trade and Investment Partnership (TTIP).[62]

---

[59] Qin, Julia Ya (2004), 'WTO Regulation of Subsidies to State-Owned Enterprises (SOEs): A Critical Appraisal of the China Accession Protocol', *Journal of International Economic Law* (7) (4), pp. 863–919, at 884. See also Du, Michael Ming (2014), 'When China's National Champions Go Global: Nothing to Fear but Fear Itself?', *Journal of World Trade* (48) (6), pp. 1127–66.

[60] Bratanov observed that there have been four substantive 'shifts' in the evolution of the language of commitments relating to state owned enterprises. Bratanov (2015), Disciplining State Trading Practices: Lessons from WTO Accession Negotiations, at 774.

[61] Bratanov (2015), Disciplining State Trading Practices: Lessons from WTO Accession Negotiations, at 793. Noting that '[t]he experience that WTO Members that have gone through the process of accession have with reporting on SOEs is very valuable', and, accordingly, 'they are well placed to influence further work in the development of more comprehensive disciplines pertaining to the operations of STEs [state-trading enterprises]'.

[62] Willemyns, Ines (2016), 'Disciplines on State-Owned Enterprises in International Economic Law: Are We Moving in the Right Direction?', *Journal of International Economic Law* (19) (3), pp. 657–80; Du, Ming (2015), 'Explaining

5.4.4 Category 4: 'Allowing Other Members to Do Something they Would Otherwise Not Be Allowed to Do'

In addition to the standard commitment on anti-dumping, countervailing duties and safeguard measures, three applicants have accepted a commitment that enables other WTO Members to use a different methodology in the context of anti-dumping investigations.[63] In the context of the WTO, dumping is regulated by the Agreement on Implementation of Article VI of the General Agreement on Tariffs and Trade 1994 (Anti-Dumping Agreement).[64] The Anti-Dumping Agreement lays down a set of rules that WTO Members have to adhere to in the context of anti-dumping investigations. However, it does not contain any provisions concerning NMEs. Rather, it stipulates how anti-dumping investigations should be conducted by investigating authorities and which principles should guide such investigations. Article 2.1 Anti-Dumping Agreement stipulates (in relevant part):

> a product is to be considered as being dumped, i.e. introduced into the commerce of another country at less than its normal value, if the export price of the product exported from one country to another is less than the comparable price, in the ordinary course of trade, for the like product when destined for consumption in the exporting country.

China's Tripartite Strategy Towards the Trans-Pacific Partnership (TPP) Agreement', *Journal of International Economic Law* (18) (2), pp. 407–32, at 417.

[63] An example of the standard commitment can be found in the Working Party Report on the Accession of Croatia: 'The representative of Croatia said that Croatia would not apply any anti-dumping, countervailing or safeguard measure until it had notified and implemented appropriate laws in conformity with the provisions of the WTO Agreements on the Implementation of Article VI, on Subsidies and Countervailing Measures, and on Safeguards. In the elaboration of any legislation concerning anti-dumping duties, countervailing duties and safeguards, Croatia would ensure their full conformity with the relevant WTO provisions, including Article VI and XIX of the GATT 1994 and the Agreement on the Implementation of Article VI, the Agreement on Subsidies and Countervailing Measures and the Agreement on Safeguards. After such legislation was implemented, Croatia would only apply any anti-dumping duties, countervailing duties and safeguard measures in full conformity with the relevant WTO provisions. The Working Party took note of these commitments'. See WTO, Report of the Working Party on the Accession of Croatia to the World Trade Organization, WT/ACC/HRV/59, 29 June 2000, para. 99.

[64] Agreement on Implementation of Article VI of the General Agreement on Tariffs and Trade 1994, 1868 U.N.T.S. 201, entered into force 1 January 1995 (the 'Anti-Dumping Agreement').

Article 9 of the Anti-Dumping Agreement stipulates how anti-dumping duties should be imposed and collected. Article 6 of the Anti-Dumping Agreement determines the role of evidence in anti-dumping investigations and further indicates that investigating authorities shall determine 'individual margins of dumping' for each known exporter or producer.[65]

Although (or because) the Anti-Dumping Agreement is silent on the treatment of imports from NMEs, the incumbent membership of the WTO has made this particular issue part of the accession negotiations of NMEs. Commitments on specific matters relating to anti-dumping can be found in the protocols of accession of China (2001), Viet Nam (2007) and Tajikistan (2013).[66] For example, Paragraph 15 of China's Protocol of Accession stipulates (in relevant part):

> **15. Price Comparability in Determining Subsidies and Dumping**
>
> Article VI of the GATT 1994, the Agreement on Implementation of Article VI of the General Agreement on Tariffs and Trade 1994 ('Anti-Dumping Agreement') and the SCM Agreement shall apply in proceedings involving imports of Chinese origin into a WTO Member consistent with the following:
>
> (a) In determining price comparability under Article VI of the GATT 1994 and the Anti-Dumping Agreement, the importing WTO Member shall use either Chinese prices or costs for the industry under investigation or a methodology that is not based on a strict comparison with domestic prices or costs in China based on the following rules:
>
> (i) If the producers under investigation can clearly show that market economy conditions prevail in the industry producing the like product with regard to the manufacture, production and sale of that product, the importing WTO Member shall use Chinese prices or costs for the industry under investigation in determining price comparability;
>
> (ii) The importing WTO Member may use a methodology that is not based on a strict comparison with domestic prices or costs in China if the producers under investigation cannot clearly show that market economy conditions prevail in the industry producing the like product with regard to manufacture, production and sale of that product.
>
> (b) [...]
>
> (c) [...]

---

[65] See in particular Article 6.10 Anti-Dumping Agreement.

[66] The year of accession is indicated. None of the 33 other protocols of accession contain similar provisions as the ones discussed below.

> (d) Once China has established, under the national law of the importing WTO Member, that it is a market economy, the provisions of subparagraph (a) shall be terminated provided that the importing Member's national law contains market economy criteria as of the date of accession. In any event, the provisions of subparagraph (a)(ii) shall expire *15 years after the date of accession*. In addition, should China establish, pursuant to the national law of the importing WTO Member, that market economy conditions prevail in a particular industry or sector, the non-market economy provisions of subparagraph (a) shall no longer apply to that industry or sector.[67]

Obligations similar to those contained in Paragraph 15 of China's Protocol of Accession can be found in the working party reports on the accessions of Viet Nam and Tajikistan. Contrary to China's Protocol of Accession, Viet Nam's Protocol stipulates an exact expiry date concerning the provisions laid down in subparagraph (a)(ii).[68] These provisions shall expire on 31 December 2018 (almost 12 years after WTO accession), whereas China's Protocol stipulates that similar provisions contained in that protocol would expire 15 years after accession. In the case of Tajikistan, the negotiators have not opted for an exact date of expiration of the provisions in subparagraph (a)(ii) (as in the case of Viet Nam), but have (as in the case of China) opted for an expiration time of 15 years after accession.[69] Tajikistan acceded on 2 March 2013, hence subparagraph (a)(ii) will remain applicable until March 2028, unless Tajikistan can establish, under the laws of the importing Member, that it is a market economy.

The commitments accepted by China, Viet Nam and Tajikistan allow WTO Members to use a methodology 'that is not based on a strict comparison with domestic prices or costs in China'. The commitment thus does not require any of the three acceding states to *do* something, but rather it enables the incumbent membership to do something (may use a methodology) that it otherwise would not be allowed to do.[70] It should be noted that in light of the expiration of China's protocol commitment in this regard there is a fierce and ongoing debate as to

---

[67] WTO, Protocol of Accession of the People's Republic of China, WT/L/432, 23 November 2001 (emphasis added).

[68] WTO, Report of the Working Party on the Accession of Viet Nam, WT/ACC/VNM/48, 27 October 2006, para. 225.

[69] WTO, Report of the Working Party on the Accession of the Republic of Tajikistan, WT/ACC/TJK/30, 6 November 2012, para. 164.

[70] It appears that the Members of the Working Parties assumed that in the absence of protocol commitments to this effect, the application of NME methodologies is inconsistent with the provisions of the Anti-Dumping Agreement.

whether WTO law requires its Members to abstain from the use of this type of methodology (see section 6.4.2). Notably, on the day after the expiration of Paragraph 15(a)(ii) of China's Protocol of Accession, China filed Requests for Consultations against the United States and the European Union.[71]

5.4.5 Category 5: 'Prohibitions'

The final category of commitment consists of commitments that limit the regulatory freedom of the applicant, by creating an obligation that prohibits the applicant from adopting particular measures. This type of commitment is quite rare.[72] The most prominent example of such a commitment is the commitment to reduce or eliminate export duties. These commitments are perhaps the single most discussed of all protocol of accession commitments.[73] The WTO Agreement itself is silent on the issue of export duties and does, as such, not prohibit them. Article XI of the GATT 1994 only applies to quantitative export restrictions and does

---

[71] See DS515, United States – Measures Related to Price Comparison Methodologies, WT/DS515/1, 15 December 2016 and DS516, European Union – Measures Related to Price Comparison Methodologies, WT/DS516/1, 15 December 2016.

[72] Qin (2003), 'WTO-Plus' Obligations and Their Implications for the World Trade Organization Legal System: An Appraisal of the China Accession Protocol, at 488. Qin, referencing the note compiled by the WTO's Secretariat, notes that 'Except in the case of China, these commitment paragraphs are generally of the following types: (a) Obligations to abide by existing WTO rules, e.g., a commitment to bring specific national measures into conformity with WTO provisions on the subject in question; (b) Obligations relating to transitional periods permitted under the various WTO agreements, e.g., a commitment not to have recourse to specific WTO provisions providing for transitional periods for developing country Members; (c) Authorization to depart temporarily from specific WTO rules or from market access commitments contained in the goods schedules; and (d) Obligations to abide by rules created by the commitment paragraph and not contained in the Multilateral Trade Agreements. These relate to a commitment to comply with "WTO obligations and other international obligations" of the acceding country, privatization, sub-central governments, government procurement, trade in civil aircraft and publication.'

[73] Primo Braga, Carlos and Cattaneo, Olivier (2011), Global Trade Governance and Development: The WTO Accession Conundrum, in Deere-Birkbeck, Carolyn (ed.) (2011), *Making Global Trade Governance Work for Development: Perspectives and Priorities from Developing Countries*, Cambridge, Cambridge University Press, at 364–6.

not regulate export duties.[74] Commitments on export duties (or export taxes) have, however, been made in 15 accessions.[75] In a number of cases, applicants have accepted a commitment relating to export duties as part of their protocol of accession. The ways in which this commitment has been phrased differ substantially, as will be explained in more detail in Chapter 6.

5.5 CONCLUSION

This chapter presents a typology that will enable an assessment of the type of commitments included in WTO protocols of accession. The phenomenon of specific commitments contained in these protocols has been examined by a number of scholars. These efforts have been examined in an introductory section. Building upon these assessments, the remainder of this chapter has provided a slightly modified typology that is used in answering four further research questions in the remainder of this monograph. First, to what extent do the specific commitments contained in WTO protocols of accession deviate from the WTO baseline obligations and to what extent can we therefore truly speak of 'WTO-Plus' and 'WTO-Minus' obligations? Second, is there evidence of a discernible trend in WTO accession practice that points at increased demands on states and customs territories that have tried to accede to the WTO in the past 20 years? Has accession indeed become more burdensome on applicants? Third, what relationship is there between the type of economic structure that prevails in a given applicant and the amount and type of specific commitments that are requested from it by the WTO? In other words, does it matter – in terms of the amount and scope of the commitments entered into – whether an applicant is a market or a 'non-market' economy country? Fourth, is it true that applicant states that

---

[74] Article XI:1 of the GATT 1994 stipulates: 'No prohibitions or restrictions other than duties, taxes or other charges, whether made effective through quotas, import or export licences or other measures, shall be instituted or maintained by any contracting party on the importation of any product of the territory of any other contracting party or on the exportation or sale for export of any product destined for the territory of any other contracting party.' Qin argues that Article XI:1 GATT 1994 thereby 'explicitly permits the use of export duties on any products'. See Qin (2017), Mind the Gap: Navigating Between the WTO Agreement and Its Accession Protocols, at 243.

[75] Export duty commitments were made by Bulgaria, Mongolia, Latvia, Estonia, Georgia, Croatia, China, Saudi Arabia, Viet Nam, Ukraine, Montenegro, Russian Federation, Tajikistan, Kazakhstan and Afghanistan.

have entered into the most stringent commitments also have had to forego the rights that could have mitigated the negative effects these commitments might have on their regulatory autonomy? In order to answer these questions, this book proceeds in two further chapters. In Chapter 6 the detailed results of the mapping exercise will be presented. Whereas this chapter contains an analysis of some commitments in protocols of accession by means of example, the next chapter provides a more complete overview of the commitments entered into, specifically by cataloguing them in line with the typology developed in this chapter. Finally, Chapter 7 contains a normative analysis of 20 years of WTO accession practice. In addition to highlighting the specific challenges that have been posed by the rather 'political' nature of the accession process, the chapter also contains a number of recommendations that could assist countries that are still in the process of acceding to the WTO.

6. Mapping exercise: the results

6.1 INTRODUCTION: RULES COMMITMENTS IN PROTOCOLS OF ACCESSION

This penultimate chapter presents the findings of the mapping exercise carried out in respect of the results of all 36 WTO accessions completed so far. Using the typology developed in Chapter 5, the commitments are analysed and examined in order to obtain a more precise picture of the scope and prevalence of the rules commitments that arguably exceed the WTO baseline. The commitments discussed in this chapter will mainly be those that amount to more than a simple confirmation of the baseline obligation. Hence, commitments that fall into the second category ('Ensuring Conformity') identified in Chapter 5 will not be extensively discussed. The main focus of this chapter will be on the commitments that fall within the fourth and fifth categories as these commitments most clearly and explicitly depart from the WTO baseline commitments. The structure of this chapter follows the structure of the working party reports and, as such, contains the same headings and subheadings. Where there are differences with the structure adopted in the working party reports, for example in respect of state-owned enterprises (SOEs), this is explicitly indicated in the text. In addition to highlighting the type of commitments that applicants have entered into, this chapter indicates to what extent certain commitments deviate from the baseline obligations in the WTO Agreement. Particular emphasis will be placed on those commitments that exemplify new trends in international trade lawmaking. In areas such as technical barriers to trade, sanitary and phytosanitary measures and transparency, commitments have been undertaken that fit well within the current trend of focusing on concepts such as 'regulatory cooperation' in bi- and plurilateral trade agreements such as the Transatlantic Trade and Investment Partnership (TTIP) and the Transpacific Partnership (TPP).

6.2 ECONOMIC POLICIES

The first substantive section of a working party report contains an overview of the economic policies in the applicant state in question. Typically there are six subheadings: 'monetary and fiscal policies', 'foreign exchange and payments', 'investment regime', 'state ownership, state-trading entities and privatization', 'pricing policies' and 'competition policy'. The amount of actual commitments made in this section is rather limited. Substantive commitments on the investment regime and state-owned or state-trading entities are more often made under their respective headings in the section 'policies affecting trade in goods' (see section 6.4 below). Non-market economies (NMEs) often make commitments under the subheading 'State Ownership and Privatization; State-Trading Entities' to confirm their intention to apply principles of transparency in the course of the privatization process. A typical commitment can be found in Kazakhstan's Working Party Report:

> The representative of Kazakhstan confirmed the readiness of Kazakhstan to ensure the transparency of its privatization process. Kazakhstan would provide annual reports to WTO Members (along the lines of the information provided to the Working Party) on developments in its privatization process for as long as the process continued. The Working Party took note of this commitment.[1]

Kazakhstan also undertook a novel and interesting commitment under the heading 'Investment Regime':

> In response to questions from some Members, the representative of Kazakhstan stated that Kazakhstan would provide foreign invested juridical persons of Kazakhstan, producing crude oil and gas in accordance with the national legislation of Kazakhstan, *non-discriminatory access to pipelines* which were partly or fully owned and regulated by the Government in accordance with the national legislation within the available remaining capacities of such pipelines, based on existing rights of access. The access would be allocated in a fair and equitable manner, and proportional to the production capacity of companies producing crude oil and gas in Kazakhstan. When applying measures relating to such pipeline transportation, including access to pipelines for foreign invested juridical persons of Kazakhstan producing crude oil and

---

[1] WTO, Report of the Working Party on the Accession of the Republic of Kazakhstan, WT/ACC/KAZ/93, 23 June 2015, para. 101. Similar commitments can be found in the working party reports on the accessions of Seychelles, Tajikistan, Russian Federation, Samoa, Montenegro, Cape Verde, Ukraine, Viet Nam, Saudi Arabia, Cambodia, FYR Macedonia, Armenia, Moldova, Lithuania, Croatia, Albania, Georgia, Estonia, Latvia, Kyrgyz Republic and Bulgaria.

> gas in Kazakhstan, the Government of Kazakhstan would ensure that the following principles were respected: (i) fully transparent legal and regulatory measures on access and pipeline transportation tariffs; (ii) non-discrimination with respect to the origin of crude oil and gas production within the territory of Kazakhstan and the destination; and (iii) application of non-discriminatory transportation tariffs with respect to foreign and domestic investors.[2]

Extending principles of non-discrimination to the energy (oil and gas sector) is a relatively novel development in WTO accession practice. Previous accessions have included commitments on the issue of freedom of transit. Ukraine's commitment reads:

> The representative of Ukraine confirmed that Ukraine would apply all its laws, regulations and other measures governing transit of goods (*including energy*), such as those governing charges for transportation of goods in transit, in conformity with the provisions of Article V of the GATT 1994 and other relevant provisions of the WTO Agreement.[3]

Whereas Montenegro's commitment stipulates:

> The representative of Montenegro confirmed that, from the date of accession, Montenegro would apply all its laws, regulations and other measures governing transit of goods (*including energy*), such as those governing charges for transportation of goods in transit, in conformity with the WTO Agreement, including Article V of the GATT 1994.[4]

These commitments already provided an indication of the WTO's increased attention for energy-related issues.[5] By including these commitments it has been made clear that, at least in the context of the

---

[2] WTO, Report of the Working Party on the Accession of the Republic of Kazakhstan, WT/ACC/KAZ/93, 23 June 2015, para. 87 (footnote omitted).

[3] WTO, Report of the Working Party on the Accession of Ukraine to the World Trade Organization, WT/ACC/UKR/152, 25 January 2008, para. 367 (emphasis added).

[4] WTO, Report of the Working Party on the Accession of Montenegro to the World Trade Organization, WT/ACC/CGR/38, WT/MIN(11)/7, 5 December 2011, para. 185 (emphasis added).

[5] See, inter alia, Marceau, Gabrielle (2010), 'The WTO in the Emerging Energy Governance Debate', *Global Trade and Customs Journal* (5) (3), pp. 83–3; Milthorp, Peter and Christy, David (2011), Energy Issues in Selected WTO Accessions, in Selivanova, Yulia (ed.), *Regulation of Energy in International Trade Law, WTO, NAFTA and Energy Charter*, Alphen aan den Rijn, Kluwer Law International, 259–302; Cossy, Mireille (2012), Energy Trade and

commitments made by these Members, the concept of goods should be understood as including energy.[6] As noted by Cossy, '[t]he specific reference to energy arguably aims at ensuring that Article V disciplines will apply to transport of gas irrespective of the means of transport, i.e. including transport through fixed infrastructure'.[7] The commitment made by Kazakhstan does, however, go considerably further than any of the other earlier commitments made on this particular issue. By seeking to ensure that Kazakhstan will adhere to the principles mentioned in Paragraph 87 of its Working Party Report, the members of the Working Party have attempted to guarantee that Kazakhstan would give access to its energy infrastructure on a non-discriminatory basis. As explained by Milthorp and Christy, Russia had attempted to 'monopolize supplies of Kazakhstan gas to cement Russia's position as a dominant supplier position in the region'.[8] This commitment can be seen as an attempt to break this monopoly.[9] It is likely that commitments such as the ones agreed to by acceding countries such as Ukraine, Montenegro, the Russian Federation and Kazakhstan will form the starting point for new negotiations on trade in energy. These countries will seek to ensure that they do not end up in a less advantageous position as a result of agreeing

WTO Rules: Reflexions on Sovereignty over Natural Resources, Export Restrictions and Freedom of Transit, in Herrmann, Christoph and Terhechte, Jörg Philipp (eds) (2012), *European Yearbook of International Economic Law*, vol. 3, Heidelberg, Springer, pp. 281–306; and Pogoretskyy, Vitaliy (2013), 'Freedom of Transit and the Principles of Effective Right and Economic Cooperation: Can Systemic Interpretation of GATT Article V Promote Energy Security and the Development of an International Gas Market?', *Journal of International Economic Law* (16) (2), pp. 313–52.

[6] As noted by Pogoretskyy, it is questionable whether Article V of the GATT 1994 in itself is sufficiently precise to warrant the conclusion that energy is covered by the GATT 1994. Consequently, he concludes his contribution by stating that 'if WTO Members decide to extend or elaborate the disciplines of GATT Article V to explicitly cover issues essential to energy trade, such as the third-party access and capacity establishment rights (inter alia, in the course of the Doha negotiations on trade facilitation or in a separate energy-related agreement), such a progressive development of WTO law must necessarily take into account the existing relevant principles, crystallized in a broader environment of public international law'. Pogoretskyy (2013), Freedom of Transit and the Principles of Effective Right and Economic Cooperation, at 352.

[7] Cossy (2012), Energy Trade and WTO Rules, at 300.

[8] Milthorp and Christy (2011), Energy Issues in Selected WTO Accessions, at 290.

[9] Milthorp and Christy (2011), Energy Issues in Selected WTO Accessions, at 291.

to commitments that contain disciplines that are not applicable to other states.[10] That new negotiations are needed is widely recognized, however, it remains uncertain to what extent these negotiations could reasonably be expected to lead to the conclusion of an 'Agreement on Trade in Energy'.[11] In any event, the foregoing illustrates how the WTO accession process can serve – even if only to a rather limited extent – as a forum for discussions on novel issues relating to international trade. Members of the accession working parties have attempted to address their concerns in respect of certain issues arising from the policy framework of the applicant in question by developing commitments laying down disciplines that are otherwise not covered by the WTO Agreement. Undoubtedly, these commitments constitute 'WTO-Plus' rules.

6.3 FRAMEWORK FOR MAKING AND ENFORCING POLICIES

Having access to and being able to rely on an independent judiciary is of great importance for firms contemplating to invest in a particular state. Similarly, traders have to be able to have recourse in a court of law against decisions taken by executive organs such as tax and customs authorities. It has been noted that '[o]verall, the WTO constrains the role of legislatures to provide protectionism, *catalyses the creation and professionalization of bureaucratic agencies, and promotes the strengthening of judiciaries*'.[12] As explained, several provisions of the covered

---

[10] Milthorp and Christy (2011), Energy Issues in Selected WTO Accessions, at 301.

[11] Cossy (2012), Energy Trade and WTO Rules, at 306; and Pogoretskyy (2013), Freedom of Transit and the Principles of Effective Right and Economic Cooperation.

[12] Shaffer, Gregory (2015), 'How the World Trade Organization Shapes Regulatory Governance', *Regulation and Governance* (9) (1), pp. 1–15, at 8. Shaffer moreover finds that the 'WTO affects the relative role of courts and tribunals in national legal systems. Formalist legal scholarship has addressed the lack of direct effect of WTO law before domestic courts in the US and Europe, so that private parties do not have standing to enforce it. WTO rules, nonetheless, have significant effects in multiple ways on the authority and scope of activity of national courts. Multiple WTO agreements require mechanisms of judicial review, in particular for customs, import relief, and intellectual property law. This form of administrative governance can be viewed as a US export, facilitated through the WTO.' This contribution of the WTO to the development of the rule of law in developing countries should not be underestimated, especially in light

agreements contain transparency-related obligations that are aimed at ensuring that traders can become acquainted with the relevant laws and regulations of the WTO Member they are seeking to export to.[13] Such obligations can, inter alia, be found in Article X of the GATT 1994, Article 12 of the Customs Valuation Agreement, Article 3 of the GATS and Article 63 of the TRIPS Agreement.[14] The importance of these obligations was illustrated, inter alia, by the Appellate Body Report in *US – Countervailing and Anti-Dumping Measures on Certain Products from China*.[15] Further, it has been observed that 'the Appellate Body has emphasized the importance of GATT Article X:2 as a tool of the system to ensure transparency and protect traders' expectations regarding the publication and implementation of certain measures'.[16] Trying to improve transparency and the functioning of the rule of law in the applicant state is, therefore, also one of the main objectives of the often lengthy accession process. As part of this process applicants 'need to provide a description of the structure and powers of the government, describing the constitution and its relation to the main branches of government, the executive, legislative, and judiciary and the powers of each'.[17] Article XVI:4 of the WTO Agreement provides that WTO Members shall 'ensure the conformity of its laws, regulations and administrative procedures with its obligations as provided in the annexed Agreements' and several provisions of the covered agreements, such as the GATT 1994 and the GATS, contain provisions that provide for a right to appeal administrative

---

of the additional focus that is placed on issues such as transparency and judicial review in the context of WTO accession proceedings.

[13] Marceau, Gabrielle and Pedersen, Peter N. (1999), 'Is the WTO Open and Transparent? A Discussion of the Relationship of the WTO with Non-Governmental Organizations and Civil Society's Claims for More Transparency and Public Participation', *Journal of World Trade* (33) (1), pp. 5–49, at 21–5.

[14] Ala'i, Padideh and D'Orsi, Matthew (2011), Transparency in International Economic Relations and the Role of the WTO, in Ala'i, Padideh and Vaughn, Robert G. (eds) (2011), *Research Handbook on Transparency*, Cheltenham UK and Northampton, MA, USA, Edward Elgar, pp. 368–99, at 371–3.

[15] Appellate Body Report, *US – Countervailing and Anti-Dumping Measures (China)*.

[16] Romero, Johel and Piérola, Fernando (2014), 'Traders Beware: The Obligation to Publish Trade Measures before Enforcement and Its Treatment in the Dispute "United States – Countervailing and Anti-Dumping Measures on Certain Products from China"', *Global Trade and Customs Journal* (9) (11–12), pp. 517–20, at 520.

[17] Williams, Peter John (2008), *A Handbook on Accession to the WTO*, Cambridge, Cambridge University Press, at 66.

decisions.[18] Tonga's accession protocol commitment was one of the first to specifically give effect to the obligations laid down in Article X of the GATT and Article VI:2 of the GATS as it stipulates (in relevant part) that:

> Tonga would establish or designate tribunals or procedures for the prompt review of all administrative actions relating to the implementation of laws, regulations, judicial decisions and administrative rulings of general application referred to in *Article X:I of the GATT 1994* and *Article VI of the GATS*. The tribunals or procedures would also include actions relating to the implementation of national treatment, conformity assessment, the regulation, control, supply or promotion of a service, including the grant or denial of a licence to provide a service and other matters. The tribunals or procedures responsible for such reviews would be impartial and independent of the agency entrusted with administrative enforcement and shall not have any substantial interest in the outcome of the matter. The review procedure would include the opportunity for appeal, without penalty, by individuals and enterprises affected by any administrative action subject to review. If the initial right of appeal was to an administrative body, there should be the opportunity to choose to appeal the decision to a judicial body. Notice of the decision on appeal should be given to the appellant and the reasons for such a decision provided in writing.[19]

Of particular interest are the commitments entered into by Viet Nam, Ukraine, the Russian Federation and Kazakhstan. Their commitments establish a system of notice-and-comment on draft legislation that relates to trade in goods, trade in services or the trade-related aspects of intellectual property. Viet Nam, which acceded in 2006, and Ukraine, which acceded in 2008, made commitments under the heading 'Transparency'. Viet Nam's commitment reads (in relevant part):

> The representative of Viet Nam confirmed that [...] all laws, regulations, decrees, judicial decisions and administrative rulings of general application pertaining to or affecting customs issues, trade in goods, services, intellectual property and the control of foreign exchange *would be published promptly* in a manner that fulfils the WTO requirements, and no such laws, regulations, decrees, judicial decisions and administrative rulings of general application would become effective or be enforced prior to such publication, except for those regulations, judicial decisions and administrative rulings of general application, and other measures involving national emergency or security, or

---

[18] See Article X of the GATT and Article VI:2 of the GATS; Marceau and Pedersen (1999), Is the WTO Open and Transparent?, at 37–40.

[19] WTO, Report of the Working Party on the Accession of Tonga to the World Trade Organization, WTO/ACC/TON/17, WT/MIN(05)/4, 2 December 2005, para. 43 (emphasis added).

> for which publication would impede law enforcement. To this end, he further confirmed that Viet Nam would, as of the date of accession, establish or designate an official journal or website for each of the topics (or an aspect of a topic) identified above, dedicated to the publication, prior to their entry into force, of all regulations, decisions, orders, and administrative rulings of general application, pertaining to or affecting that topic. Such journals or websites would be updated on a regular basis, notified to the WTO, and readily available to WTO Members, individuals, associations and enterprises. The websites or journals where these measures would be published are listed in Table 23. The publication of such regulations and other measures would include, as appropriate, the following: (i) the names of the authorities (including contact points) responsible for implementing a particular measure; and (ii) the effective date of the measure. The representative of Viet Nam confirmed that with respect to proposed laws, ordinances, decrees and other regulations and measures issued by the National Assembly and the Government pertaining to or affecting trade in goods, services, and intellectual property, Viet Nam *would provide a reasonable period*, i.e., no less than *60 days*, for Members, individuals, associations and enterprises *to provide comments* to the appropriate authorities before such measures are adopted. The Government *would take into account* any comments received during the period for commenting. The only exceptions to this opportunity for comment would be for those regulations and other measures involving national emergency or security, or for which publication would impede law enforcement.[20]

The Working Party Report on the accession of Ukraine contains a similar commitment but specifies a reasonable period for comments of only 30 days, instead of the 60 days provided for in the case of Viet Nam.[21] In the case of the Russian Federation and Kazakhstan the commitment is found under the heading 'Framework for Making and Enforcing Policies' and it relates to acts that are adopted in the context of the Eurasian Economic Union (EAEU).[22] Kazakhstan's commitment reads:

> The representative of Kazakhstan confirmed that Commission Decision No. 308 'Decision-Making at the Commission of the Customs Union' of 18 June 2010 had been amended to establish and put into effect a mechanism for

---

[20] WTO, Report of the Working Party on the Accession of Viet Nam, WT/ACC/VNM/48, 27 October 2006, para. 518 (emphasis added).

[21] WTO, Report of the Working Party on the Accession of Ukraine to the World Trade Organization, WT/ACC/UKR/152, 25 January 2008, para. 499.

[22] WTO, Report of the Working Party on the Accession of the Russian Federation to the World Trade Organization, WT/ACC/RUS/70, WT/MIN(11)/2, 17 November 2011, para. 183; WTO, Report of the Working Party on the Accession of the Republic of Kazakhstan, WT/ACC/KAZ/93, 23 June 2015, para. 250. Both commitments, however, refer to the Transparency sections of the respective working party reports.

> publication of proposed EAEU legal acts covered under paragraph 1141 of Section 'Transparency' of this Report before their adoption and to provide a *reasonable period of time* for Members and interested persons *to provide comments* to the competent EAEU body, which was authorized to take these comments into account in its consideration of the proposed legal act. Moreover, from the date of Kazakhstan's accession to the WTO, pursuant to this mechanism, no EAEU legal act covered under paragraph 1146 of Section 'Transparency' of this Report would become effective prior to publication as provided for in the applicable provisions of the WTO Agreement.[23]

The increasing importance of the involvement of all types of stakeholders in the legislative process has been discussed in detail.[24] It has been noted that the question is not 'whether business participation is needed, but how businesses shall participate'.[25] Considering the wide diversity in protocol commitments in this field, this call for more uniformity in respect of the notice-and-comment procedures is warranted.[26] It is of interest to note at this stage that certain commitments made under other headings of the working party report also include notice-and-comment obligations.[27] It

---

[23] WTO, Report of the Working Party on the Accession of the Republic of Kazakhstan, WT/ACC/KAZ/93, 23 June 2015, para. 250.

[24] Wang, Heng (2010), Enhancing Business Participation in Trade Policy-Making: Lessons from China, in Steger, Debra P. (ed.) (2010), *Redesigning the World Trade Organization for the Twenty-First Century*, Ottawa, Centre for International Governance Innovation, pp. 257–84.

[25] Wang (2010), Enhancing Business Participation in Trade Policy-Making, at 277.

[26] Wang (2010), Enhancing Business Participation in Trade Policy-Making, at 278. As Wang notes, 'extending a more generalized notice-and-comment requirement to all WTO Members is a logical progression in the movement for greater transparency'.

[27] See, for example, these two commitments made by Tajikistan under the heading Policies Affecting Trade in Services: '[T]he representative of Tajikistan confirmed that Tajikistan would publish all laws, regulations and other measures of general application pertaining to or affecting trade in services. Publication of such laws, regulations and other measures would include the effective date of these measures and the general scope of services or activities affected. He further confirmed that Tajikistan would publish a list of all organizations that were responsible for authorizing, approving or regulating service activities for each service sector. In addition, Tajikistan would publish in the official journal all of its licensing procedures and conditions upon accession' and 'The representative of Tajikistan also confirmed that Tajikistan would (a) *publish in advance* any regulations or other implementing measures of general application that it proposed to adopt and the purpose of the regulation or other implementing measure; (b) provide interested persons and other Members a reasonable opportunity *to comment* on such proposed regulation or other implementing

would be desirable to have broader agreement on this issue as notice-and-comment procedures appear to be one of the most fruitful ways of ensuring that new laws and regulations do not constitute unnecessary barriers to trade. Involvement of the business sector at early stages of the legislative process might result in more efficient regulation. Interestingly, these developments at the level of WTO accession are also present in other areas of international trade lawmaking. Particularly in the field of the SPS and TBT chapters of certain regional and plurilateral trade agreements, there is a tendency to include provisions that allow for enhanced transparency and notice-and-comment procedures.[28] For example, Mathis makes reference to a provision of the Australia-US Free Trade Agreement which provides for a TBT-Plus notice-and-comment procedure.[29] Through the inclusion of these provisions, trade negotiators seek to ensure that private actors such as corporations have the possibility to engage, at an early stage, in the lawmaking process at the domestic level. This is indicative of a wider appreciation for what has been called 'regulatory cooperation'.[30] With average MFN tariffs at an all-time low and growing awareness that trade liberalization will increasingly be realized through the reduction of non-tariff barriers (NTBs) attention has shifted towards the elimination, and preferably the prevention, of regulatory barriers. These trends are clearly visible in so-called 21st Century Trade Agreements such as the TTIP and the TPP.[31] Whether in hindsight

measure; and (c) allow *reasonable time* between publication of the final regulation or other implementing measure and its effective date.' See, WTO, Report of the Working Party on the Accession of Tajikistan, WT/ACC/TJK/30, 6 November 2012, paras. 336 and 337. Seychelles and Kazakhstan made similar commitments. See WTO, Report of the Working Party on the Accession of Seychelles, WT/ACC/SYC/64, 5 November 2014, paras. 395 and 396; and WTO, Report of the Working Party on the Accession of the Republic of Kazakhstan, WT/ACC/KAZ/93, 23 June 2015, paras. 1131 and 1133.

[28] Steger, Debra P. (2012), 'Institutions for Regulatory Cooperation in "New Generation" Economic and Trade Agreements', *Legal Issues of Economic Integration* (39) (1), pp. 109–26, at 123.

[29] Mathis, James (2012), 'Multilateral Aspects of Advanced Regulatory Cooperation: Considerations for a Canada-EU Comprehensive Trade Agreement (CETA)', *Legal Issues of Economic Integration* (39) (1), pp. 73–91, at 89.

[30] See, for example, Hufbauer, Gary Clyde and Cimino-Isaacs, Cathleen (2015), 'How Will TPP and TTIP Change the WTO System?', *Journal of International Economic Law* (18) (3), pp. 679–96.

[31] See, inter alia, Alemanno, Alberto (2015), 'The Regulatory Cooperation Chapter of the Transatlantic Trade and Investment Partnership: Institutional Structures and Democratic Consequences', *Journal of International Economic Law* (18) (3), pp. 625–40; Lester, Simon and Barbee, Ine (2013), 'The Challenge

it will be possible to consider that the commitments made in the context of WTO accession negotiations broke new ground in this respect remains to be seen. However, what is clear is that WTO Members at least have attempted to introduce new disciplines in this field by means of accession negotiations. This is further evidence of the fact that, although the outcome of the accession process may – in some instances – result in the applicant being under more stringent obligations than the other Members of the organization, the relative ad hoc nature of the accession process allows for the creation of new rules in fields where the WTO has not ventured before. The question whether these benefits outweigh the downsides that this approach may have from a normative perspective will be answered in the final chapter.[32]

6.4 POLICIES AFFECTING TRADE IN GOODS

6.4.1 Transitional Safeguards

Article XIX of the GATT 1994 and the Agreement on Safeguards contain rules that determine under which circumstances WTO Members may temporarily increase import tariffs to prevent injury to their domestic industry as a result of a sudden and unexpected increase in imports. In the context of the accession of China, a special, product-specific safeguard mechanism was negotiated that was incorporated into the text of China's Protocol of Accession. Paragraph 16 of the Protocol provides:

> **16. Transitional Product-Specific Safeguard Mechanism**
>
> 1. In cases where products of Chinese origin are being imported into the territory of any WTO Member in such increased quantities or under such conditions as to cause or threaten to cause market disruption to the

---

of Cooperation: Regulatory Barriers in the Transatlantic Trade and Investment Partnership', *Journal of International Economic Law* (16) (4), pp. 847–67; and Hufbauer and Cimino-Isaacs (2015), How Will TPP and TTIP Change the WTO System?, at 692. Noting that adopting '[a] so-called "horizontal approach" to cooperation [as opposed to adopting standards] would entail greater transparency, more stakeholder participation, and close communication across the Atlantic – with the end goal of ensuring that both sides are better informed about the costs and benefits of their domestic regulatory measures as they affect the other party'.

[32] Qin, for example, argues that the assumption that 'Article XII of the Marrakesh Agreement authorizes the making of all country-specific rules in accession agreements' is questionable. See, Qin (2017), Mind the Gap: Navigating Between the WTO Agreement and Its Accession Protocols, at 233.

domestic producers of like or directly competitive products, the WTO Member so affected may request consultations with China with a view to seeking a mutually satisfactory solution, including whether the affected WTO Member should pursue application of a measure under the Agreement on Safeguards. Any such request shall be notified immediately to the Committee on Safeguards.

2. If, in the course of these bilateral consultations, it is agreed that imports of Chinese origin are such a cause and that action is necessary, China shall take such action as to prevent or remedy the market disruption. Any such action shall be notified immediately to the Committee on Safeguards.
3. If consultations do not lead to an agreement between China and the WTO Member concerned within 60 days of the receipt of a request for consultations, the WTO Member affected shall be free, in respect of such products, to withdraw concessions or otherwise to limit imports only to the extent necessary to prevent or remedy such market disruption. Any such action shall be notified immediately to the Committee on Safeguards.
4. Market disruption shall exist whenever imports of an article, like or directly competitive with an article produced by the domestic industry, are increasing rapidly, either absolutely or relatively, so as to be a significant cause of material injury, or threat of material injury to the domestic industry. In determining if market disruption exists, the affected WTO Member shall consider objective factors, including the volume of imports, the effect of imports on prices for like or directly competitive articles, and the effect of such imports on the domestic industry producing like or directly competitive products.
5. Prior to application of a measure pursuant to paragraph 3, the WTO Member taking such action shall provide reasonable public notice to all interested parties and provide adequate opportunity for importers, exporters and other interested parties to submit their views and evidence on the appropriateness of the proposed measure and whether it would be in the public interest. The WTO Member shall provide written notice of the decision to apply a measure, including the reasons for such measure and its scope and duration.
6. A WTO Member shall apply a measure pursuant to this Section only for such period of time as may be necessary to prevent or remedy the market disruption. If a measure is taken as a result of a relative increase in the level of imports, China has the right to suspend the application of substantially equivalent concessions or obligations under the GATT 1994 to the trade of the WTO Member applying the measure, if such measure remains in effect more than two years. However, if a measure is taken as a result of an absolute increase in imports, China has a right to suspend the application of substantially equivalent concessions or obligations under the GATT 1994 to the trade of the WTO Member applying the measure, if such measure remains in effect more than three years. Any such action by China shall be notified immediately to the Committee on Safeguards.

7. In critical circumstances, where delay would cause damage which it would be difficult to repair, the WTO Member so affected may take a provisional safeguard measure pursuant to a preliminary determination that imports have caused or threatened to cause market disruption. In this case, notification of the measures taken to the Committee on Safeguards and a request for bilateral consultations shall be effected immediately thereafter. The duration of the provisional measure shall not exceed 200 days during which the pertinent requirements of paragraphs 1, 2 and 5 shall be met. The duration of any provisional measure shall be counted toward the period provided for under paragraph 6.
8. If a WTO Member considers that an action taken under paragraphs 2, 3 or 7 causes or threatens to cause significant diversions of trade into its market, it may request consultations with China and/or the WTO Member concerned. Such consultations shall be held within 30 days after the request is notified to the Committee on Safeguards. If such consultations fail to lead to an agreement between China and the WTO Member or Members concerned within 60 days after the notification, the requesting WTO Member shall be free, in respect of such product, to withdraw concessions accorded to or otherwise limit imports from China, to the extent necessary to prevent or remedy such diversions. Such action shall be notified immediately to the Committee on Safeguards.
9. Application of this Section shall be terminated 12 years after the date of accession.

This Transitional Product-Specific Safeguard Mechanism (TPSSM) is a unique feature of China's Protocol of Accession.[33] None of the other protocols of accession contains a similar provision.[34] The introduction of the TPSSM is a reflection of the concern that certain Members of the WTO had in respect of China's WTO accession and the increase of cheap-imports that its accession would entail.[35] The application of the commitment has been considered 'a vivid illustration of an incumbent

---

[33] Ahn, Dukgeun (2005), Critical Review on the WTO Safeguard System: To Safeguard the Safeguard System, in Gao, Henry and Lewis, Donald (eds) (2005), *China's Participation in the WTO*, London, Cameron May. See also, Huang, Dongli (2006), 'Legal Interpretation of Paragraph 242 of the Report of the Working Party on the Accession of China under the World Trade Organization Legal Framework', *Journal of World Trade* (40) (1), pp. 137–52.

[34] Lingliang, Zeng (2005), The Legal Effectiveness and Appropriateness of Transitional Product-Specific Safeguard Mechanism Against China, in Gao, Henry and Lewis, Donald (eds) (2005), *China's Participation in the WTO*, London, Cameron May, at 98.

[35] Andersen, Scott and Lau, Christian (2002), 'Hedging Hopes with Fears in China's Accession to the World Trade Organization: The Transitional Special-Product Safeguard for Chinese Exports', *The Journal of World Intellectual Property* (5) (3), pp. 405–76, at 405.

WTO-Minus accession law in operation'.[36] The TPSSM was terminated in 2013, in accordance with Paragraph 16.9 of China's Protocol of Accession. Shortly after China's accession to the WTO several commentators expressed their concern as to the efficacy of the TPSSM and, indeed, the fact that the WTO had opted for a country-specific type of commitment in respect of China. At the time it was argued that the mechanism poses 'serious risks of market closing and market disruption for those Chinese imports that best reflect the comparative advantages of Chinese producers over other producers in the world' and that it 'could well punish Chinese national and foreign investors in China for efficiently producing low-cost, high-quality, non-dumped and non-subsidized products offering better value than domestically produced products'.[37] Moreover, it was noted that the application of the mechanism could erode support for the WTO in China.[38] Some expressed the expectation that the TPSSM may often be invoked, noting that although 'it could be argued that the transitional product-specific safeguard is such a politically aggressive instrument that it would never be used, this seems unlikely'.[39] Others have referenced the drafting history of the TPSSM in their analysis.[40] As will be explained in section 6.4, the fact that there was still a substantial degree of state influence in the Chinese economy, at the time of its accession negotiations, played an important role in the drafting of the mechanism.[41] Now that the application period of the TPSSM has lapsed stock can be taken of its use. One WTO dispute concerning the

---

36 Charnovitz, Steve and Hoekman, Bernard (2013), '*US – Tyres*: Upholding a WTO Accession Contract – Imposing Pain for Little Gain', *World Trade Review* (12) (2), pp. 273–96, at 294.

37 Andersen and Lau (2002), Hedging Hopes with Fears in China's Accession to the World Trade Organization, at 465. See in this respect also Bown, Chad P. and Crowley, Meredith A. (2010), 'China's Export Growth and the China Safeguard: Threats to the World Trading System?', *Canadian Journal of Economics* (43) (4), pp. 1353–88.

38 Andersen and Lau (2002), Hedging Hopes with Fears in China's Accession to the World Trade Organization, at 466. See also Messerlin, Patrick A. (2004), 'China in the World Trade Organization: Antidumping and Safeguards', *World Bank Economic Review* (18) (1), pp. 105–30, at 127–8.

39 Messerlin (2004), China in the World Trade Organization, at 128.

40 Spadi, Fabio (2002), 'Discriminatory Safeguards in the Light of the Admission of the People's Republic of China to the World Trade Organization', *Journal of International Economic Law* (5) (2), pp. 421–43.

41 Spadi (2002), Discriminatory Safeguards, at 426–30.

application of the TPSSM arose whilst the mechanism was in force.[42] In *US – Tyres*, China complained about the use of the mechanism by the US which had adopted safeguard measures against the importation of tyres from China.[43] Ultimately the Appellate Body found that the US had not acted inconsistently with any of its WTO obligations in applying the TPSSM to imports of tyres from China.[44] As was discussed in section 4.3.2.2, the case highlighted some important issues concerning the relationship between commitments contained in protocols of accession and the WTO Agreement. Furthermore, the dispute is an important illustration of the increasing importance of global value chains (GVCs) in international trade.[45] GVCs are an apt description of a world in which 'the concept of trade has changed from a final good crossing from one country to another to complex and sophisticated structures of trade in inputs across national borders before they become a final good'.[46] Reference has been made to the fact that the safeguard investigation was started upon request of US labour unions, rather than upon request of the domestic industry.[47] Indeed, the Panel had noted that:

---

[42] WTO, Request for Consultations, United States – Measures Affecting Imports of Certain Passenger Vehicle and Light Truck Tyres from China (Complainant: China), WT/DS399/1.

[43] Panel Report, *US – Tyres (China)*; Appellate Body Report, *US – Tyres (China)*. For a discussion see Charnovitz and Hoekman (2013), *US – Tyres*: Upholding a WTO Accession Contract – Imposing Pain for Little Gain; and Lee, Yong-Shik (2012), 'First WTO Case on Transitional Product-Safeguard Measure under Section 16 of the Protocol of China's Accession to the WTO: Affirming Discriminatory Safeguard Measure by the WTO?', *Journal of World Trade* (46) (4), pp. 913–36.

[44] Appellate Body Report, *US – Tyres (China)*, WT/DS399/AB/R, adopted 5 October 2011, para. 339.

[45] For a detailed analysis of global value chains as a new phenomenon in international trade and a proposal for a framework for analysis, see Sobel-Read, Kevin B. (2014), 'Global Value Chains: A Framework for Analysis', *Transnational Legal Theory* (5) (3), pp. 364–407, at 368–9. For an analysis of the challenges posed by GVCs to traditional concepts such as Rules of Origin, see Geraets, Dylan, Carroll, Colleen and Willems, Arnoud R. (2015), 'Reconciling Rules of Origin and Global Value Chains: The Case for Reform', *Journal of International Economic Law* (18) (2), pp. 287–305.

[46] Van der Marel, Erik (2015), 'Positioning on the Global Value Chain Map: Where Do You Want To Be?', *Journal of World Trade* (49) (6), pp. 915–50.

[47] Charnovitz and Hoekman (2013), *US – Tyres*: Upholding a WTO Accession Contract – Imposing Pain for Little Gain, at 291.

> [T]his case involved the invocation of a mechanism designed to protect a domestic industry that did not want that protection and by its own actions had precipitated the events that were now being invoked to justify the application of the transitional product-specific safeguard mechanism of China's Protocol of Accession. [...] [T]he investigation had been initiated by a labour union, a body that was concerned with job losses resulting from this transfer of manufacturing capacity to China, and not by the domestic producers themselves. Thus, the Panel was aware that this aspect of the case raised the question of the suitability or relevance of safeguard mechanisms in the context of 'outsourcing' and 'globalization', matters of considerable systemic interest to WTO Members.[48]

It appears that, leaving the *US – Tyres* controversy aside, the TPSSM has not caused problems of the kind that were expected by some authors.[49] Rather, the use of the non-market economy methodologies that will be discussed in the subsequent section appears to have caused far greater tensions between China and other Members of the WTO. Moreover, the fact that this type of commitment has not been included in any of the subsequent protocols of accession serves as further confirmation that WTO-Plus or WTO-Minus commitments are in most instances country-specific. The inclusion of the TPSSM in China's Protocol of Accession is a reflection of the fear among WTO Members that imports from an NME would threaten their domestic industries. With the accession of all major economies to the WTO it appears highly unlikely that another product-specific safeguard mechanism would be included in the accession protocol of any of the other states or customs territories that are currently in the process of accession.

6.4.2 Non-Market Economy Methodologies in Anti-Dumping Investigations

6.4.2.1 NMEs and the GATT 1947

The theory supporting the multilateral trading system is deeply rooted in the concept of comparative advantage and the idea of the liberalization of

---

[48] Panel Report, *US – Tyres (China)*, para. 7.9.

[49] See Huang, Thomas Weishing (2007), 'Taiwan's Protocol 16 Special Safeguard and Anti-Dumping Enforcement on Imports from China', *Journal of World Trade* (41) (2), 371–409, for a discussion of the application of the mechanism by Taiwan. Huang also discusses the tension between rule-based diplomacy and power diplomacy, noting that 'China's handling of this episode seems to bear out the prediction that China would not like any legal dispute with Taiwan to be paraded in any international forum like the WTO.'

international trade.[50] The preamble of the WTO Agreement, however, makes clear that the liberalization of trade is a means to and not an end in itself.[51] Consequentially, the ideological underpinnings of the multilateral trading system are not reflected in general membership criteria. Accession to the GATT 1947 was governed by the procedure laid down in Article XXXIII GATT 1947 which provides (in relevant part) that a 'government not party to this Agreement, or a government acting on behalf of a separate customs territory possessing full autonomy in the conduct of its external commercial relations and of the other matters provided for in this Agreement, may accede to this Agreement'. The language of this provision is mirrored in Article XII of the WTO Agreement. Article XII stipulates (in relevant part) 'any State or separate customs territory possessing full autonomy in the conduct of its external commercial relations and of the other matters provided for in this Agreement and the Multilateral Trade Agreements may accede to this Agreement'. Although the term 'government' has been changed to the term 'state', there is no substantial difference between the accession provisions in both agreements. Neither provision contains any requirements or characteristics that the government, state or customs territory seeking to accede has to possess in order to be accepted. There is, for example, no requirement that stipulates that governments or states seeking to accede have to conduct their internal economic affairs in a particular manner.

Although both agreements are based on the concepts of trade liberalization, reference to such explicit 'market economy' terminology is missing from the GATT 1947 and from the WTO Agreement. This is not to say that the GATT 1947 is completely silent on states that are characterized by a large degree of governmental involvement in the operation of their economy.[52] However, as has been noted, '[w]hile GATT takes into consideration the existence of state trading enterprises

---

[50] In the context of the Preamble of the GATT 1947, the term 'liberalization' has not been used as such. The term is, however, included in the Preamble to the WTO Agreement which stipulates (in relevant part) '[...] *Resolved*, therefore, to develop an integrated, more viable and durable multilateral trading system encompassing the General Agreement on Tariffs and Trade, the results of past trade liberalization efforts, and all of the results of the Uruguay Round of Multilateral Trade Negotiations [...]' (emphasis in the original).

[51] Rovnov, Yury (2015), 'The Relationship Between the MFN Principle and Anti-Dumping Norms of the WTO Revisited', *Journal of World Trade* (49) (1), pp. 173–98, at 194–5.

[52] See for a more elaborate discussion, section 2.2.3.2 above.

and other forms of State intervention in the economy, its entire theoretical and practical framework is suited for essentially market-oriented systems'.[53]

In sum, therefore, although the theoretical underpinnings of the multilateral trading system are rooted in the ideas of liberalization, comparative advantage and free markets, these underpinnings did not translate themselves into assumptions concerning the types of economies that would ultimately be able to join the system. Although the drafters of GATT were aware of the differences in economic systems between the non-market economy countries and the market economy countries, this did not result in a set of criteria a country would have to fulfil in order to be allowed to join the multilateral trading system. Rather, several ad hoc mechanisms were created that were aimed at mitigating the potential negative effects caused by imports from countries with a high degree of state influence in the economy.[54]

6.4.2.2 NMEs in the WTO

Non-market economies (NMEs) form a particular group of acceded Members. Because of their economic structure and the degree of state influence in the economy, NMEs are, on average, more often subject to more stringent commitments.[55] Arguably this follows from the fact that many of these NMEs 'have yet to fully implement the basic premises of the GATT – transparency, reciprocity, and the rule of law – notwithstanding on-going market reforms'.[56] Within the group of 36 acceded Members there are a number of countries that could arguably be characterized as NMEs at the time they were seeking to accede to the WTO.[57] This list includes Georgia (2000), China (2001), Armenia

---

[53] Spadi (2002), Discriminatory Safeguards, at 427.

[54] Spadi (2002), Discriminatory Safeguards, at 426; Blumental, David M. (1999), 'Applying GATT to Marketizing Economies: The Dilemma of WTO Accession and Reform of China's State-Owned Enterprises (SOEs)', *Journal of International Economic Law* (2) (1), pp. 113–53; Náray, Péter (2001), *Russia and the World Trade Organization*, Basingstoke, Palgrave.

[55] See section 5.3.1. It was noted that 'This group [...] accounts for nearly 50% of all paragraphs containing commitments, with an average of 79.5 paragraphs per applicant'.

[56] Blumental (1999), Applying GATT to Marketizing Economies, at 114.

[57] Thirty-six accessions had been completed at the time of completion of this book. On 12 October 2017 it was reported that the accession of Comoros was approaching the final stages. It is expected that it may become the 37th country to accede to the WTO. See WTO (2017), Members Commend Sustained Engagement by Comoros as It Approaches Final WTO Accession Stages.

(2003), Cambodia (2004), Viet Nam (2007), Tajikistan (2013) and Kazakhstan (2015).[58] It has been argued that whereas during the GATT era the Contracting Parties sought to find a way to incorporate different types of economic systems within the multilateral trading system, this approach has been abandoned in the WTO. Based on Jackson's 'interface principle' and Ruggie's theory on 'embedded liberalism', it has been described how the multilateral trading system has moved from a situation of acceptance to a situation where change (through marketization) is being sought.[59] Through the frame of 'coercive diplomacy', it has been argued that the WTO now 'promotes a specific kind of trade regime'.[60]

Of particular relevance are the commitments that NMEs have entered into in respect of their economic policies and the policies affecting trade in goods. Although the WTO Agreement purportedly does not impose a specific type of economic structure or organization, the incumbent membership has attempted on numerous occasions to direct applicant states into the direction of a market economy. These obligations are mostly, but not solely, related to the field of anti-dumping. They can also be found in the context of commitments on the abolishment of price controls and the use of special adjustments in subsidy calculations.[61] Moreover, the TPSSM that was included in China's Protocol of Accession, as discussed in section 6.4.1, provides a further example of the way in which the WTO has attempted to ensure that mechanisms were

Available at https://www.wto.org/english/news_e/news17_e/acc_com_12oct17_e.htm (last accessed at 18 October 2017).

[58] For an analysis of China's state capitalism and the WTO, see Du, Michael Ming (2014), 'China's State Capitalism and World Trade Law', *International and Comparative Law Quarterly* (63) (2), pp. 409–48.

[59] Huang, Chieh (2009), 'Non-Market Economies' Accessions to the WTO: Evolution of the Approach and Implications for the Organization', *The Hague Journal of Diplomacy* (4), at 69–72.

[60] Huang (2009), Non-Market Economies' Accessions to the WTO, at 79. Toohey, Lisa and Crowe, Jonathan (2014), 'The Illusory Reference of the Transitional State and Non-Market Economy Status', *The Chinese Journal of Comparative Law* (2) (2), pp. 314–36; Urdinez, Francisco and Masiero, Gilmar (2015), 'China and the WTO: Will the Market Economy Status Make Any Difference after 2016?', *The Chinese Economy* (48) (2), pp. 155–72.

[61] Yamaoka, Tokio (2013), 'Analysis of China's Accession Commitments in the WTO: New Taxonomy of More and Less Stringent Commitments, and the Struggle for Mitigation by China', *Journal of World Trade* (47) (1), pp. 105–58, at 122–5. Yamaoka has also suggested that, in the context of China's Protocol of Accession, allowing importing states to resort to different methodologies to determine the dumping margin is not, as such, a WTO-Plus (in his terminology: more stringent or less stringent) commitment.

available to mitigate the potential negative effects of NME exports on domestic industries. However, regardless of the terminology used, it cannot be denied that several provisions of China's Protocol of Accession allow other WTO Members to engage in conduct that would otherwise be prohibited under the rules contained in the covered agreements. These commitments are a continuation of the GATT practice discussed above that was directed at facilitating the accession of NMEs, whilst providing for an additional layer of protection for the domestic industries of market economy Contracting Parties.[62]

6.4.2.2.1 Accession protocol commitments on anti-dumping In the context of the WTO, dumping is regulated by the Agreement on Implementation of Article VI of the General Agreement on Tariffs and Trade 1994 (Anti-Dumping Agreement). The Anti-Dumping Agreement lays down a set of rules that WTO Members have to adhere to in the context of anti-dumping investigations. As was already indicated above, the Anti-Dumping Agreement does not contain any provisions concerning non-market economies.[63] Rather, it stipulates how anti-dumping investigations should be conducted by investigating authorities and which principles should guide such investigations. Article 2.1 Anti-Dumping Agreement stipulates (in relevant part):

> a product is to be considered as being dumped, i.e. introduced into the commerce of another country at less than its normal value, if the export price of the product exported from one country to another is less than the comparable price, in the ordinary course of trade, for the like product when destined for consumption in the exporting country.

Article 9 of the Anti-Dumping Agreement stipulates how anti-dumping duties should be imposed and collected. Article 6 of the Anti-Dumping

---

[62] Qin argues that '[t]he limited number of country-specific rules in GATT accession agreements [...] did not exceed the scope of the GATT provisions'. See, Qin (2017), Mind the Gap: Navigating Between the WTO Agreement and Its Accession Protocols, at 236. However, the Polish commitment to increase the value of imports from the Contracting Parties by 7% annually does not appear to have a counterpart in the GATT 1947. See Protocol for the Accession of Poland, BISD 15S/46. At the same time, however, Qin notes that 'the WTO practice of using accession protocols to modify the WTO Agreement is in keeping with GATT tradition'.

[63] Guan, Wenwei (2014), 'International Trade "From Status to Contract" and Back: A Critique of the NME Normal Value Determination and Beyond', *Journal of East Asia and International Law* (7) (1), pp. 77–104.

Agreement determines the role of evidence in anti-dumping investigations and further indicates that investigating authorities shall determine 'individual margins of dumping' for each known exporter or producer.[64]

Although (or because) the Anti-Dumping Agreement is silent on the treatment of imports from non-market economies, the incumbent membership of the WTO has made this particular issue part of the accession negotiations of NMEs. Commitments on specific matters relating to anti-dumping can be found in the protocols of accession of China (2001), Viet Nam (2007) and Tajikistan (2013).[65] For example, Section 15 of China's Protocol of Accession stipulates (in relevant part):

> **15. Price Comparability in Determining Subsidies and Dumping**
>
> Article VI of the GATT 1994, the Agreement on Implementation of Article VI of the General Agreement on Tariffs and Trade 1994 ('Anti-Dumping Agreement') and the SCM Agreement shall apply in proceedings involving imports of Chinese origin into a WTO Member consistent with the following:
>
> (a) In determining price comparability under Article VI of the GATT 1994 and the Anti-Dumping Agreement, the importing WTO Member shall use either Chinese prices or costs for the industry under investigation or a methodology that is not based on a strict comparison with domestic prices or costs in China based on the following rules:
> (i) If the producers under investigation can clearly show that market economy conditions prevail in the industry producing the like product with regard to the manufacture, production and sale of that product, the importing WTO Member shall use Chinese prices or costs for the industry under investigation in determining price comparability;
> (ii) The importing WTO Member may use a methodology that is not based on a strict comparison with domestic prices or costs in China if the producers under investigation cannot clearly show that market economy conditions prevail in the industry producing the like product with regard to manufacture, production and sale of that product.
>
> (b) […]
> (c) […]
> (d) Once China has established, under the national law of the importing WTO Member, that it is a market economy, the provisions of subparagraph (a) shall be terminated provided that the importing Member's national law contains market economy criteria as of the date of accession. In any event, the provisions of subparagraph (a)(ii) shall expire *15*

[64] See in particular Article 6.10 Anti-Dumping Agreement.

[65] The year of accession is indicated. None of the 33 other protocols of accession contain similar provisions as the ones discussed below.

> *years after the date of accession.* In addition, should China establish, pursuant to the national law of the importing WTO Member, that market economy conditions prevail in a particular industry or sector, the non-market economy provisions of subparagraph (a) shall no longer apply to that industry or sector.[66]

Obligations similar to those contained in Section 15 of China's Protocol of Accession can be found in the working party reports on the accessions of Viet Nam and Tajikistan.

Paragraph 255 of Viet Nam's Working Party Report stipulates (in relevant part):

> 255. The representative of Viet Nam confirmed that, upon accession, the following would apply – Article VI of the GATT 1994, the Agreement on Implementation of Article VI of the General Agreement on Tariffs and Trade 1994 ('Anti-Dumping Agreement') and the SCM Agreement shall apply in proceedings involving exports from Viet Nam into a WTO Member consistent with the following:
>
> (a) In determining price comparability under Article VI of the GATT 1994 and the Anti-Dumping Agreement, the importing WTO Member shall use either Vietnamese prices or costs for the industry under investigation or a methodology that is not based on a strict comparison with domestic prices or costs in Viet Nam based on the following rules:
> (i) If the producers under investigation can clearly show that market economy conditions prevail in the industry producing the like product with regard to the manufacture, production and sale of that product, the importing WTO Member shall use Vietnamese prices or costs for the industry under investigation in determining price comparability;
> (ii) The importing WTO Member may use a methodology that is not based on a strict comparison with domestic prices or costs in Viet Nam if the producers under investigation cannot clearly show that market economy conditions prevail in the industry producing the like product with regard to manufacture, production and sale of that product.
>
> (b) [...]
>
> (c) [...]
>
> (d) Once Viet Nam has established, under the national law of the importing WTO Member, that it is a market economy, the provisions of subparagraph (a) shall be terminated provided that the importing Member's national law contains market economy criteria as of the date of accession. In any event, the provisions of subparagraph (a)(ii) shall expire on

---

[66] Protocol of Accession of the People's Republic of China, WT/L/432, 23 November 2001 (emphasis added).

> *31 December 2018*. In addition, should Viet Nam establish, pursuant to the national law of the importing WTO Member, that market economy conditions prevail in a particular industry or sector, the non-market economy provisions of subparagraph (a) shall no longer apply to that industry or sector.
>
> The Working Party took note of these commitments.[67]

Note that contrary to China's Protocol of Accession, Viet Nam's Protocol stipulates an exact expiry date concerning the provisions laid down in subparagraph (a)(ii). These provisions shall expire on 31 December 2018 (almost 12 years after WTO accession), whereas China's Protocol stipulates that similar provisions contained in that protocol would expire 15 years after accession. Finally, the Protocol of Accession of Tajikistan stipulates (in relevant part):

> 164. The representative of Tajikistan confirmed that, upon accession, the following would apply – Article VI of the GATT 1994, the WTO Agreement on Implementation of Article VI of the General Agreement on Tariffs and Trade 1994 (Anti-Dumping Agreement) and the SCM Agreement shall apply in proceedings involving exports from Tajikistan into a WTO Member consistent with the following:
>
> (a) In determining price comparability under Article VI of the GATT 1994 and the Anti-Dumping Agreement, the importing WTO Member shall use either Tajikistan's prices or costs for the industry under investigation or a methodology that is not based on a strict comparison with domestic prices or costs in Tajikistan based on the following rules: (i) if the producers under investigation can clearly show that market economy conditions prevail in the industry producing the like product with regard to the manufacture, production and sale of that product, the importing WTO Member shall use Tajikistan's prices or costs for the industry under investigation in determining price comparability; (ii) the importing WTO Member may use a methodology that is not based on a strict comparison with domestic prices or costs in Tajikistan if the producers under investigation cannot clearly show that market economy conditions prevail in the industry producing the like product with regard to manufacture, production and sale of that product.
>
> Once Tajikistan has established, under the national law of the importing WTO Member, that it is a market economy, the provisions of sub-paragraph (a) shall be terminated provided that the importing Member's national law contains market economy criteria as of the date of accession. In any event, the provisions of sub-paragraph (a)(ii) shall expire *15 years after the date of accession*. In addition, should Tajikistan

[67] Report of the Working Party on the Accession of Viet Nam, WT/ACC/VNM/48, 27 October 2006 (emphasis added).

> establish, pursuant to the national law of the importing WTO Member, that market economy conditions prevail in a particular industry or sector, the non-market economy provisions of sub-paragraph (a) shall no longer apply to that industry or sector.

> The Working Party took note of these commitments.[68]

Notably, in the case of Tajikistan, the negotiators have not opted for an exact date of expiration of the provisions in subparagraph (a)(ii) (as in the case of Viet Nam), but have (as in the case of China) opted for an expiration time of 15 years after accession. Tajikistan acceded on 2 March 2013, hence subparagraph (a)(ii) will remain applicable until March 2028, unless Tajikistan can establish, under the laws of the importing Member, that it is a market economy. Given the largely self-judging nature of this last part of the commitment, WTO Members have given themselves a large degree of discretion to judge at what point prior to March 2028 Tajikistan could potentially become a market economy, thereby increasing their leverage over Tajikistan in other elements of future negotiations.

6.4.2.2.2 Challenges against the treatment of NMEs in anti-dumping investigations Anti-dumping investigations are carried out by domestic investigating authorities, often upon request of the domestic industry that is affected by the allegedly dumped imports. The investigation carried out by the domestic authorities has to comply with the requirements of the domestic laws and regulations setting out the conditions for conducting such an investigation. Moreover, the investigation also has to comply with the rules set out by the Anti-Dumping Agreement of the WTO. Consequently, the domestic rules governing anti-dumping investigations usually implement the WTO rules to a large extent. The EU's Basic Anti-Dumping Regulation (the Basic Regulation) lays down the procedures that the EU investigating authorities have to adhere to when conducting an anti-dumping investigation.[69] Article 2(7) of the Basic Regulation stipulates several ways of determining 'normal value' in the case of imports from NMEs.[70] Article 9(5) of the Basic Regulation

---

[68] Report of the Working Party on the Accession of the Republic of Tajikistan, WT/ACC/TJK/30, 6 November 2012 (emphasis added).

[69] Council Regulation (EC) No 1225/2009 on protection against dumped imports from countries not members of the European Community, 30 November 2009.

[70] Footnote 1 to Article 2.7 lists Azerbaijan, Belarus, North Korea, Tajikistan, Turkmenistan and Uzbekistan as examples of NMEs.

further provides for the possibility to impose country-wide rates of duties in the case of countries designated to fulfil the criteria as set out in Article 2(7)(a). It further provides that importers from such countries may apply for an individual rate of duty. In such a situation they have to fulfil the five criteria listed under Article 9(5) Basic Regulation.[71] Article 9(5) of the Basic Anti-Dumping Regulation thus establishes a presumption that producers or exporters that operate in NMEs are not entitled to individual treatment. Should NME exporters wish to qualify for such treatment, they bear the burden to demonstrate that they satisfy the criteria of the 'Individual Treatment' test.

Under US anti-dumping legislation a similar practice exists. The Antidumping Manual of the United States Department of Commerce (USDOC) implements Section VII of the US Tariff Act 1974. Chapter 10 of the Manual lays down a set of rules applicable to dumped imports from NMEs, including a set of factors that should be taken into account in order to determine whether a particular country is an NME.[72] The Manual further stipulates that:

> Individual dumping margins are automatically assigned to exporters in market-economy country cases. In NME cases, however, exporters must pass a separate rate test to receive a rate that is separate from the NME-wide rate.[73]

In the past five years the EU and US practices have been challenged in domestic courts and under the WTO's dispute settlement mechanism by exporters or producers in NMEs and by the states that have been assigned

---

[71] They would have to establish that: (i) exporters are free to repatriate capital and profits; (ii) export prices and quantities are freely determined; (iii) the company is independent from state interference; (iv) exchange rate conversions are carried out at market rates; and (v) 'State interference is not such as to permit circumvention of measures if individual exporters are given different rates of duty.'

[72] The Manual lists the following factors: the extent to which the currency of the foreign country is convertible into the currency of other countries; the extent to which wage rates in the foreign country are determined by free bargaining between labour and management; the extent to which joint ventures or other investments by firms of other foreign countries are permitted in the foreign country; the extent of government ownership or control of the means of production; the extent of government control over the allocation of resources and over the price and output decisions of enterprises; and such other factors as the administering authority considers appropriate. The Manual is available at http://ia.ita.doc.gov/admanual/index.html (last accessed at 18 October 2017).

[73] Section III 'Separate Rates'.

NME status under EU or US law.[74] The following sections discuss these challenges and the relevance of the commitments made in protocols of accession.

6.4.2.2.2.1 Challenges against the EU *EC – Fasteners* After a number of disputes in which commitments contained in China's Protocol of Accession had been used as a sword against China, in the sense that measures were allegedly inconsistent with one of these commitments, in *EC – Fasteners* the content of a working party report commitment was used *by* China for the first time to allege the inconsistency of a measure taken by the European Communities.[75] In the request for consultations, China noted that the EC's Basic Anti-Dumping Regulation and Council Regulation 91/2009 of 26 January 2009 are inconsistent with the EC's obligations under the GATT 1994 and the Anti-Dumping Agreement. Moreover, the request notes, the measures are inconsistent with the 'Protocol of Accession of the People's Republic of China ('China") which is an integral part of the Marrakech Agreement Establishing the World Trade Organization'.[76] This last statement could serve as confirmation that, indeed, China too considers that its Protocol of Accession is an integral part of the WTO Agreement. Allegedly, by not providing 'the opportunity to the interested parties to see all relevant information including, but not limited to, the identity of the applicants, non-confidential summaries of the questionnaire responses of EC producers, data concerning the normal value in the analogue country and information on the adjustments for differences affecting price comparability', the EC acted inconsistently with Article 6 of the Anti-Dumping Agreement and Paragraph 15 of China's Protocol of Accession.[77] In *EC – Fasteners* China challenged the EU's practice of using a country-wide

---

[74] See, inter alia, Zang, Michelle Q. (2009), 'The WTO Contingent Trade Instruments Against China: What Does Accession Bring?', *International and Comparative Law Quarterly* (58), pp. 321–51; Zang, Michelle Q. (2011), 'EC – Fasteners: Opening the Pandora's Box of Non-Market Economy Treatment', *Journal of International Economic Law* (14) (4), pp. 869–92.

[75] WTO, Request for Consultations, European Communities – Definitive Anti-Dumping Measures on Certain Iron or Steel Fasteners from China (Complainant: China), WT/DS397/1, at 1.

[76] WTO, Request for Consultations, European Communities – Definitive Anti-Dumping Measures on Certain Iron or Steel Fasteners from China (Complainant: China), WT/DS397/1, at 1.

[77] WTO, Request for Consultations, European Communities – Definitive Anti-Dumping Measures on Certain Iron or Steel Fasteners from China (Complainant: China), WT/DS397/1, at 3.

rate for producers and exporters in NME countries.[78] The Appellate Body began by discussing the relevance of Section 15 of China's Protocol of Accession. It noted, at the outset, that the contents of this Section are similar to that of the second *Ad* Note to Article VI:1 of the GATT 1994. The Appellate Body interpreted this provision as allowing 'investigating authorities to disregard domestic prices and costs of such an NME in the determination of normal value and to resort to prices and costs in a market economy third country'.[79] In a footnote the Appellate Body further clarified its interpretation of the second *Ad* Note to Article VI:1 GATT 1994:

> The recognition of special difficulties in determining price comparability in the second *Ad* Note to Article VI:1 **does not mean** that importing Members may depart from the provisions regarding the determination of export prices and the calculation of dumping margins and anti-dumping duties set forth in the *Anti-Dumping Agreement* and in the GATT 1994. While the second *Ad* Note to Article VI:1 refers to difficulties in determining price comparability in general, the text of this provision clarifies that these difficulties relate **exclusively to the normal value side** of the comparison. This is indicated by the operative part in the third sentence of this provision, which only allows importing Members to depart from a 'strict comparison with *domestic* prices'.[80]

The Appellate Body ultimately held that:

> Section 15 of China's Accession Protocol does not authorize WTO Members to treat China differently from other Members except for the determination of price comparability in respect of domestic prices and costs in China, which relates to the determination of normal value. We consider that, while Section 15 of China's Accession Protocol establishes special rules regarding the domestic price aspect of price comparability, it does not contain an **open-ended exception** that allows WTO Members to treat China differently for other purposes under the *Anti-Dumping Agreement* and the GATT 1994, such

---

78 Appellate Body Report, *EC – Fasteners (China)*, para. 282. China's claim was directed against Article 9(5) of the Basic Regulation, and not against the use of a different methodology by the EU. For a comprehensive analysis, see Bown, Chad P. and Mavroidis, Petros C. (2013), 'One (Firm) Is Not Enough: A Legal-Economic Analysis of EC – Fasteners', *World Trade Review* (12) (2), pp. 243–71.

79 Appellate Body Report, *EC – Fasteners (China)*, para. 285.

80 Appellate Body Report, *EC – Fasteners (China)*, para. 285, footnote 460 (italics original, bold emphasis added).

as the determination of export prices or individual versus country-wide margins and duties.[81]

The EU argued that the obligation contained in Article 6.10 of the Anti-Dumping Agreement to determine individual margins of dumping was merely 'a preference' and did not constitute an obligation as such. The Appellate Body squarely rejected this argument when it found that there is not 'any provision in the covered agreements that would allow importing Members to depart from the obligation to determine individual dumping margins only in respect of imports from NMEs'.[82] Section 15 of China's Protocol of Accession therefore did not provide a legal basis to form an exception to the requirement laid down in Article 6.10 of the Anti-Dumping Agreement.[83]

Similarly, the Appellate Body rejected the EU's argument under Article 9.2 of the Anti-Dumping Agreement. The EU had tried to argue that it could impose a country-wide rate on the basis of Article 9(5) Basic Regulation since naming individual suppliers would be 'impracticable'. Article 9.2 Anti-Dumping Agreement thus required the investigating authorities in the EU 'to specify an individual duty for each supplier, except where this is impracticable, when several suppliers are involved'.[84]

Finally, the Appellate Body found that China's Protocol of Accession did not contain the legal basis 'for a presumption that country-wide dumping margins be calculated and country-wide duties be imposed on all Chinese exporters of a product under investigation'.[85] *EC – Fasteners* therefore served as a first warning from the WTO that China's Protocol of Accession did not give other WTO Members unlimited discretion to apply NME methodologies.[86] In the subsequent compliance proceedings,

---

[81] Appellate Body Report, *EC – Fasteners (China)*, para. 290 (italics original, bold emphasis added).

[82] Appellate Body Report, *EC – Fasteners (China)*, para. 328.

[83] For a more elaborate analysis see Vermulst, Edwin (2013), Filling in the Blanks: The WTO Appellate Body's First Two Reports Concerning the NME-Related Aspects of TDI Against China, in Cremona, Marise, Hilpold, Peter, Lavranos, Nikos, Schneider, Stefan Staiger and Ziegler, Andreas R. (eds), *Reflections on the Constitutionalisation of International Economic Law: Liber Amicorum for Ernst-Ulrich Petersmann*, Leiden, Martinus Nijhoff Publishers, pp. 323–36, at 332.

[84] Appellate Body Report, *EC – Fasteners (China)*, para. 351.

[85] Appellate Body Report, *EC – Fasteners (China)*, para. 365.

[86] However, as Vermulst notes, 'although [...] the result to analogue country normal values for AD [anti-dumping] purposes, will expire in 2013 and 2016,

the European Union also lost on most counts, inter alia, because the Appellate Body found that the European Union had acted inconsistently with Article 2.4 of the Anti-Dumping Agreement.[87]

EU – Footwear

As already indicated, the EU's Basic Anti-Dumping Regulation allowed the EU, by virtue of Article 9(5), to impose a single country-wide duty on all dumping exports from China. China was one of the countries that had been assigned NME status by the EU. Article 9.2 of the Anti-Dumping Agreement, requires WTO Members to afford 'individual treatment' to exporters. The approach laid down in Article 9(5) of the Basic Anti-Dumping Regulation was challenged by China in *EU – Footwear*.[88] The Panel Report provided some guidance on the interpretative issues arising from the relationship between protocols of accession and the WTO Agreement. Ultimately the Panel decided that the EU had acted inconsistently with several provisions of the Anti-Dumping Agreement.[89] However, the Panel did not find that the EU had acted inconsistently with the commitment contained in Paragraph 15 of China's Protocol of Accession.[90]

Rusal Armenal ZAO v Council

Within the European Union itself, the treatment of exporters and producers in NMEs has also been challenged.[91] One of these challenges was lodged by Rusal Armenal ZAO, an Armenian manufacturer and exporter of aluminium products.[92] Armenia acceded to the WTO in February

---

respectively, WTO Members' investigating authorities can be expected to continue to conduct their TDI investigations in a way that curbs Chinese exports to the maximum extent permissible by WTO law, as interpreted by the AB at any given time. The limits on their discretion are likely to be tested in future cases.' Vermulst (2013), Filling in the Blanks, at 335–6.

87 Appellate Body Report, *EC – Fasteners (China) (21.5)*.

88 Panel Report, *EU – Footwear*.

89 Panel Report, *EU – Footwear*, paras. 8.1–8.2.

90 Panel Report, *EU – Footwear*, para. 8.3. For an analysis see, Dunoff, Jeffrey L. and Moore, Michael E. (2014), 'Footloose and Duty-Free? Reflections on European Union – Anti-Dumping Measures on Certain Footwear from China', *World Trade Review* (13) (2), pp. 149–78.

91 The WTO proceedings in *EC – Fasteners* and *EU – Footwear* had also been preceded by challenges before the European Court of Justice against the consistency of the EU anti-dumping investigations with the EU Basic Regulation.

92 Case T-512/09, Action brought on 21 December 2009 – *Rusal Armenal ZAO v Council of the European Union*, 2010/C 80/49.

2003, but, as has been established earlier, its Protocol of Accession does not contain a clause on anti-dumping matters such as the ones contained in the protocols of accession of China, Viet Nam and Tajikistan.[93]

Rusal Armenal ZAO alleged the Commission's decision to impose anti-dumping duties was in violation of Article 2(1) to (6) of the Basic Regulation and of Article 2.1 and 2.2 Anti-Dumping Agreement. It submitted that the only two exceptions to the obligation to determine normal value in accordance with Article 2.1 and 2.2 of the Anti-Dumping Agreement could arise from i) the second *Ad* Note to Article VI:1 GATT 1994 or ii) WTO protocols of accession.[94]

The General Court of the European Union (General Court) agreed with Rusal Armenal ZAO in finding that:

> Contrary to the institutions' claims, Article 2.1 and 2.2 of the Anti-dumping Agreement, on the one hand, and Article 2.7 and the second supplementary provision to paragraph 1 of Article VI of the GATT, on the other, are not two extremes (market economy as opposed to State monopoly of trade) between which there is a spectrum of situations where the Anti-dumping Agreement would allow WTO members the freedom to establish the rules that they regard as appropriate for calculating normal value, such as constructing normal value on the basis of data from undertakings in a third country if the producer concerned fails to show that market economy conditions prevail for the manufacture and sale by it of the like product.[95]

The General Court explicitly referred to the protocols of accession of China and Viet Nam to illustrate the possibility that other WTO Members may choose not to use Article 2 of the Anti-Dumping Agreement when exporters or producers cannot establish that they operate under market economy conditions. However, since such provision was not present in Armenia's Protocol of Accession, the only exception to the obligations in Articles 2.1 and 2.2 Anti-Dumping Agreement could arise from the second *Ad* Note to Article VI:1 GATT 1994. The *Ad* Note applies to 'countr[ies] which ha[ve] a complete or substantially complete monopoly of [their] trade and where all domestic prices are fixed by the State'.[96]

Ultimately it was found that:

---

93 See section 6.4.2.

94 Case T-512/09, *Rusal Armenal ZAO v Council*, para. 27.

95 Case T-512/09, *Rusal Armenal ZAO v Council*, para. 43.

96 Case T-512/09, *Rusal Armenal ZAO v Council*, para. 50.

> the argument that Armenia is an economy in transition between a market economy and the State monopoly described by the second supplementary provision to paragraph 1 of Article VI of the GATT is premised on the proposition that Armenia does not comply with the conditions for applying that provision.[97]

It has been argued that the second *Ad* Note to Article VI:1 GATT 1994 essentially revolves around the recognition that in determining the cost of production difficulties can arise and other methodologies than the ones prescribed by the Anti-Dumping Agreement may be used.[98] Investigating authorities therefore would enjoy a margin of discretion to determine the costs to be used.[99] Hence, 'the very existence, and the quality or openness, of the market of origin is, therefore, an essential and underlying element in all aspects of the construction of the normal value'.[100] Consequently, the second *Ad* Note to Article VI:1 GATT 1994 should be understood as laying down a need to 'compare the quality of markets for the purposes of fair comparison'.[101] However, it is submitted that such an interpretation would run counter to the terms 'in the case', 'in *such* cases' and 'in *such* a country' as found in the *Ad* Note.[102] These phrases appear to limit the scope of the *Ad* Note to countries which have 'a complete or substantially complete monopoly' of their trade and where 'all prices are fixed by the State'.

The judgment by the General Court was appealed by the institutions. The opinion by the Advocate-General was delivered on 23 April 2015. It

---

[97] Case T-512/09, *Rusal Armenal ZAO v Council*, para. 58.

[98] O'Connor, Bernard (2015), Constructing Normal Value in WTO Anti-Dumping Law: Giving Meaning to the Phrase Open, Market Oriented Policies in the Preamble to the Marrakesh Declaration, paper, Nctm Studio Legale, Italy, February. He arrives at this conclusion since he considers that normal value should be considered in light of the term 'ordinary course of trade', as used in Article 2.1 Anti-Dumping Agreement.

[99] O'Connor (2015), Constructing Normal Value in WTO Anti-Dumping Law, at 5. O'Connor articulates that 'given the WTO context, the concept of the ordinary course of trade must be an open market-oriented concept'.

[100] O'Connor (2015), Constructing Normal Value in WTO Anti-Dumping Law, at 7.

[101] O'Connor (2015), Constructing Normal Value in WTO Anti-Dumping Law, at 8. He argues that the phrase 'in the case of imports from a country which has a complete or substantially complete monopoly of its trade and where all domestic prices are fixed by the State' is exemplary, in that there may be other situations, which the drafters may not have foreseen, in which a distortion in the quality or openness of markets is present.

[102] Emphasis added.

was opined that the General Court erred in law by reviewing 'the lawfulness of the relevant provisions of the basic regulation [...] in the light of the Anti-Dumping Agreement itself'.[103] In the view of the Advocate-General, the EU legislature did not have the intention of implementing an international norm in the sense of the *Nakajima* case law. Although the EU Anti-Dumping Regulation is related to the WTO's Anti-Dumping Agreement, the decisive factor was that 'the EU legislature deliberately opted to take its own, very particular, approach to the regulation of nonmarket economies'.[104] In doing so, it 'did not intend to transpose any provisions from the Anti-Dumping Agreement'.[105] The Court of Justice of the European Union followed the Advocate-General's opinion.[106] It began by restating its earlier case law on the conditions that have to be fulfilled in order for it to be able to assess the validity of secondary EU legislation in light of the provisions of an international agreement, and more specifically the WTO Agreement.[107] Restating its findings in Nakajima, the Court of Justice of the European Union (CJEU) explained that such situations exist where, first, 'the European Union intends to implement a particular obligation assumed in the context of those WTO agreements' and second, 'where the EU act at issue refers explicitly to specific provisions of those agreements'.[108] In this particular case, the Court examined whether Article 2(7) of the Basic Anti-Dumping Regulation was an expression of the specific intention on behalf of the EU legislature to implement Article 2 of the Anti-Dumping Agreement.

> As regards Article 2(7) of the basic regulation, it must be pointed out at the outset that that provision, following on from recital 7 of that regulation, introduces a special regime laying down detailed rules for the calculation of normal value for imports from non-market economy countries, including Armenia. As regards those imports, Article 2(7)(a) provides that normal value

[103] Case C-21/14 P, Opinion of Advocate General Kokott, *European Commission v Rusal Armenal ZAO*, para. 52.

[104] Case C-21/14 P, Opinion of Advocate General Kokott, *European Commission v Rusal Armenal*, para. 51.

[105] Case C-21/14 P, Opinion of Advocate General Kokott, *European Commission v Rusal Armenal*, para. 50.

[106] Case C-21/14 P, Judgment of the Court, *European Commission v Rusal Armenal.*

[107] Case C-21/14 P, Judgment of the Court, *European Commission v Rusal Armenal*, paras. 37–9.

[108] Case C-21/14 P, Judgment of the Court, *European Commission v Rusal Armenal*, paras. 40–41.

> must be determined on the basis of the price or constructed value in a market economy third country, or the price from such a third country to other countries, including the European Union, or where those are not possible, on any other reasonable basis, including the price actually paid or payable in the European Union for the like product, duly adjusted if necessary to include a reasonable profit margin. In addition, Article 2(7)(b) stipulates that in anti-dumping investigations concerning imports from any non-market economy country which is a member of the WTO at the date of the initiation of the investigation, normal value is to be determined in accordance with Article 2(1) to (6), if it is shown that the market economy conditions, set out in Article 2(7)(c), prevail for this producer or producers in respect of the manufacture and sale of the like product concerned.[109]

According to the CJEU, this constitutes evidence that Article 2(7) of the Basic Regulation 'is the expression of the EU legislature's intention to adopt in that sphere an approach specific to the EU legal order'.[110] The Court further held that 'the rules laid down in Article 2(7) of the Basic Regulation and applicable to imports from nonmarket economy countries which are members of the WTO are based on the emergence, in those countries, following the economic reforms adopted, of firms for which market-economy conditions prevail'.[111] Notably the Court then considered the following:

> Since there are no specific rules relating to such a category of countries in the Anti-Dumping Agreement, a correlation cannot be established between, on the one hand, the rules in Article 2(7) of the basic regulation directed at the imports from non-market economy WTO member countries and, on the other, the rules set out in Article 2 of the Anti-Dumping Agreement. It follows that that provision of the basic regulation cannot be considered to be a measure intended to ensure the implementation in the EU legal order of a particular obligation assumed in the context of the WTO.[112]

Whereas the General Court had relied extensively on the text of the second *Ad* Note to Article VI:1 of the GATT 1994, the CJEU held that, although Article 2.7 of the Anti-Dumping Agreement refers to that provision, this in and of itself 'cannot call such a finding into question'.

---

[109] Case C-21/14 P, Judgment of the Court, *European Commission v Rusal Armenal*, para. 47.

[110] Case C-21/14 P, Judgment of the Court, *European Commission v Rusal Armenal*, para. 48.

[111] Case C-21/14 P, Judgment of the Court, *European Commission v Rusal Armenal*, para. 49.

[112] Case C-21/14 P, Judgment of the Court, *European Commission v Rusal Armenal*, para. 50.

According to the CJEU, 'in addition to the fact that that second supplementary provision does not lay down any specific rule governing the calculation of normal value, it is directed only at cases where a country has a complete or substantially complete monopoly of its trade and where all domestic prices are fixed by the State'.[113]

This particular finding warrants several observations. First, the finding that this provision 'does not lay down any specific rule governing the calculation of normal value' is rather obvious. The second *Ad* Note was negotiated in 1955, long before the conclusion of the WTO's Anti-Dumping Agreement. It was never intended to provide for detailed rules concerning the calculation of normal value as these rules were included in Article VI:1 of the GATT 1947, which defines normal value as 'the comparable price, in the ordinary course of trade, for the like product when destined for consumption in the exporting country'. WTO law thus leaves a certain amount of discretion to the domestic investigating authorities to determine the way in which normal value is calculated. Moreover, the text of the second *Ad* Note suggests that its scope is limited to countries which have 'a complete or substantially complete monopoly' of their trade and where 'all prices are fixed by the State'. Only in situations where this is the case does the *Ad* Note provide for the legal basis to deviate from the standard rule on the calculation of normal value. Therefore it seems warranted to conclude that Article 2(7) of the Basic Regulation is in fact correlated with Article 2 of the Anti-Dumping Agreement. However, from an EU perspective it is understandable that the CJEU would defer a decision of the consistency of the EU's anti-dumping investigation with WTO law to the WTO itself.[114] This discussion involves, inter alia, the question as to whether, and under what conditions, direct effect should be granted to provisions of WTO law

---

[113] Case C-21/14 P, Judgment of the Court, *European Commission v Rusal Armenal*, para. 51.

[114] Fabri, Hélène Ruiz (2014), 'Is There a Case – Legally and Politically – for Direct Effect of WTO Obligations?', *European Journal of International Law* (25) (1), pp. 151–73. See also, Bronckers, Marco (2008), 'From "Direct Effect" to "Muted Dialogue" – Recent Developments in the European Court's Case Law on the WTO and Beyond', *Journal of International Economic Law* (11) (4), pp. 885–98; and Bronckers, Marco (2011), The Domestic Law Effect of the WTO in the EU: A Dialogue with Jacques Bourgeois, in Govaere, Inge, Quick, Reinhard and Bronckers, Marco (eds) (2011), *Trade and Competition Law in the EU and Beyond*, Cheltenham, UK and Northampton, MA, USA, Edward Elgar, 240–56.

within the EU legal order.[115] In any event, the *Rusal Armenal* case cannot be seen in isolation from the upcoming expiration of Paragraph 16 of China's Protocol of Accession. In addition to the baseline rules contained in Article VI of the GATT 1994 and the Anti-Dumping Agreement, Paragraph 16 provides for a separate legal basis for the application of NME methodologies in respect of allegedly dumped imports from China. Had the CJEU held that the application of NME methodologies in the absence of such a special accession protocol commitment would be inconsistent with WTO law, this would have meant that the CJEU would have put the Commission in a precarious position. Considering that Paragraph 16 lapses at the end of 2016, it would have meant that the EU would be acting inconsistently with its own legislation if it decided to continue to apply NME methodologies in respect of allegedly dumped imports from China after that date.[116]

---

[115] Fabri aptly describes the CJEU's position as follows: 'The ECJ undoubtedly shares the view that the recognition of domestic effect to WTO rulings is not expected, and it therefore uses direct effect as a shield in the sharpest way, granting the European executive and legislative branches the margin of manoeuvre they want to keep in the implementation of international commitments while denying the invocability of those commitments by private parties or Member States, although they would obtain from it a right of which they are otherwise deprived.' See Fabri (2014), Is There a Case – Legally and Politically – for Direct Effect of WTO Obligations?, at 163. Fabri concludes that 'direct effect should, even in the name of fairness or justice, be handled with caution'. Ehlermann has expressed fierce opposition against granting of direct effect to norms of WTO law. See, Ehlermann, Claus-Dieter (2002), 'Tensions Between the Dispute Settlement Process and Treaty-Making Activities of the WTO', *World Trade Review* (1) (3), pp. 301–8, at 307.

[116] The issue of the end of the applicability of (parts of) Paragraph 16 of China's Protocol of Accession is not confined to the European Union. See for an analysis of this particular issue under Australian anti-dumping legislation, Zhou, Weihuan (2015), 'Australia's Anti-Dumping and Countervailing Law and Practice: An Analysis of Current Issues Incompatible with Free Trade with China', *Journal of World Trade* (49) (6), pp. 975–1010, at 991. For a take on the Brazilian situation, see Wei, Dan (2015), The Use of Trade Defense: Some Considerations for Brazil-China Bilateral Trade Relationship, in Wei, Dan (ed.) (2015), *Settlements of Trade Disputes Between China and Latin American Countries*, Berlin-Heidelberg, Springer-Verlag, at 32; and Kramer, Cynthia (2015), Brazilian Trade Remedies Practice Against China, in Wei, Dan (ed.) (2015), *Settlements of Trade Disputes Between China and Latin American Countries*, Berlin-Heidelberg, Springer-Verlag, at 49–51. An analysis of the Mexican approach can be found in Gómez-Altamirano, Daniela (2015), China-Mexico Trade Disputes: Fear of Competition? in Wei, Dan (ed.) (2015),

6.4.2.2.2.2 CHALLENGES AGAINST THE US The EU is not the only WTO Member to be challenged for its treatment of dumped imports from NMEs. In February 2012 Viet Nam requested consultations with the United States with respect to certain anti-dumping measures on certain frozen warm water shrimp. The Panel was established on 27 February 2013 and it circulated its Report on 17 November 2014.[117] Viet Nam raised three main claims in the dispute: i) the application of zeroing, ii) the application of an 'NME-wide entity' rate practice, and iii) claims concerning Section 129(c)(1) of the US Uruguay Round Agreements Act 1994. Only the second claim is of relevance to this particular contribution.

Viet Nam raised both 'as such' and 'as applied' claims in the dispute, but the main argument put forth was that the USDOC's NME-wide entity rate practice was inconsistent with Articles 6.10, 9.2, 9.4, 6.8 and Annex II of the Anti-Dumping Agreement.[118]

The Panel made extensive reference to the Appellate Body Report in *EC – Fasteners*, which it determined to be 'highly persuasive as to the correct interpretation' of Articles 6.10 and 9.2 of the Anti-Dumping Agreement.[119] It found that the USDOC's practice of presuming – in the context of anti-dumping investigations – that all companies belong to a single, NME-wide entity, and assigning a single rate to that entity is inconsistent with Articles 6.10 and 9.2 of the Anti-Dumping Agreement.[120]

The Panel then referred to Paragraph 255 of Viet Nam's Working Party Report and found that the exception provided in it is limited. The derogation in Paragraph 255(a) 'only concerns the determination of normal value, and does not extend to the determination of export price'. The Panel continued to find that:

> in anti-dumping proceedings involving imports from Viet Nam, paragraph 255 of Viet Nam's Working Party Report, as incorporated in Viet Nam's Accession Protocol, authorizes WTO Members to treat Viet Nam differently from other Members with respect to the determination of price comparability in respect of domestic prices and costs in Viet Nam, that is, the determination of normal value. However, this provision does not provide for a general exception permitting different treatment of Vietnamese exporters for other purposes,

---

Settlements of Trade Disputes Between China and Latin American Countries, Berlin-Heidelberg, Springer-Verlag, pp. 131–46.

117 Panel Report, *US – Shrimp II (Vietnam).*

118 Panel Report, *US – Shrimp II (Vietnam)*, para. 7.82.

119 Panel Report, *US – Shrimp II (Vietnam)*, para. 7.149.

120 Panel Report, *US – Shrimp II (Vietnam)*, para. 7.158.

> such as the application of a presumption that, in Viet Nam, all companies belong to a single, Viet Nam-wide entity, and should receive a single rate.[121]

Finally, the Panel, rejecting the US argument that paragraph 255 of Viet Nam's Protocol of Accession modifies Articles 6.10 and 9.2 of the Anti-Dumping Agreement, held that:

> paragraph 255 of Viet Nam's Working Party Report only allows importing Members to derogate from the disciplines of the Anti-Dumping Agreement with respect to the methodology used to calculate normal value. However, nothing in paragraph 255 indicates that this provision provides for a derogation from the obligations to assign an individual dumping margin pursuant to Article 6.10 and an individual anti-dumping duty rate pursuant to Article 9.2 of the Anti-Dumping Agreement.[122]

It is interesting to note that the Panel Report was appealed by Viet Nam with respect to the third claim on Section 129(c)(1) of the US Uruguay Round Agreements Act. The US did not file a notice of other appeal and thus seems to accept the findings of the Panel with respect to the NME-wide entity rate practice.

6.4.2.2.3 China's WTO challenge against EU and US anti-dumping practices in December 2016 As was already noted in Chapter 5, on the day after the expiration of Paragraph 15(a)(ii) of China's Protocol of Accession, China filed Requests for Consultations against the United States and the European Union. It alleged that the European Union acted inconsistently with its WTO obligations by continuing to calculate normal value based on a special calculation methodology, unless the producer meets certain criteria. The challenged measure is contained in Article 2(1) to (7) of the EU's Basic Anti-Dumping Regulation. The application of the special methodology is alleged to be inconsistent with Article I:1 of the GATT 1994, Article 2.1 and 2.2 of the Anti-Dumping Agreement and Article VI:1 of the GATT 1994, and the second paragraph of the *Ad* Note to Article VI:1 of the GATT 1994.[123] China alleged that 'the treatment afforded Chinese imports under Article 2(7) of the Basic Regulation ceased to be justifiable when paragraph 15(a)(ii) of China's

---

[121] Panel Report, *US – Shrimp II (Vietnam)*, para. 7.181.

[122] Panel Report, *US – Shrimp II (Vietnam)*, para. 7.192.

[123] WTO, Request for Consultations, European Union – Measures Related to Price Comparison Methodologies (Complainant: China), WT/DS516/1.

Accession Protocol expired on 11 December 2016 and is inconsistent with the WTO covered agreements'.[124]

Similarly, China alleged that the continued use of surrogate values to determine normal value and margins of dumping in anti-dumping investigations on Chinese products by the United States violated several provisions of the Anti-Dumping Agreement and the GATT 1994.[125] According to China 'the inconsistencies with the covered agreements [...] ceased to be justifiable when Section 15(a)(ii) of the Protocol expired on 11 December 2016 pursuant to Section 15(d) of the Protocol'. In China's view, '[a]fter that date, Section 15(a)(ii) of the Protocol does not provide a legal basis for Members to determine normal value using methodologies' that are 'not based on a strict comparison with domestic prices or costs in China'.[126]

In DS516 against the European Union, a Panel was established on 3 April 2017. At the time of submission of the manuscript, the Panel had, however, not yet been composed. In DS515 against the United States, China had not yet requested the establishment of a Panel at the time of the completion of this book in October 2017.

6.4.2.2.4 China's quest for market economy status in the EU and EU trade defence instruments reform There is an intense and ongoing debate on the meaning of Section 15 of China's Protocol of Accession.[127] In the European Union industry associations, parliamentarians and civil

---

[124] WTO, Request for Consultations, European Union – Measures Related to Price Comparison Methodologies (Complainant: China), WT/DS516/1, para. 9.

[125] WTO, Request for Consultations, United States – Measures Related to Price Comparison Methodologies (Complainant: China), WT/DS515/1.

[126] WTO, Request for Consultations, United States – Measures Related to Price Comparison Methodologies (Complainant: China), WT/DS515/1, at 3.

[127] Gatta, Brian (2014a), 'Between "Automatic Market Economy Status" and "Status Quo": A Commentary on "Interpreting Paragraph 15 of China's Protocol of Accession"', *Global Trade and Customs Journal* (9) (4), pp. 165–72; Gatta, Brian (2014b), 'Special Focus Issue: China's Market Economy Status after 2016', *Global Trade and Customs Journal* (9) (4), pp. 144–5; Graafsma, Folkert and Kumashova, Elena (2014), 'In re China's Protocol of Accession and the Anti-Dumping Agreement: Temporary Derogation or Permanent Modification?', *Global Trade and Customs Journal* (9) (4), pp. 154–9; Nastoll, Barbara (2013), 'EU Anti-Dumping Law, Imports from China and Treatment of Non-Market Economy Countries: Brosmann, Grünwald and Zhejiang Xinan', *Common Market Law Review* (50) (1), pp. 265–80; Nicely, Matthew R. (2014), 'Time to Eliminate Outdated Non-Market Economy Methodologies', *Global Trade and Customs Journal* (9) (4), pp. 160–64; O'Connor, Bernard (2015), 'Much Ado about "Nothing": 2016, China and Market Economy Status', *Global Trade and*

servants have all made their positions clear. In early January 2016, the European Commission decided that a full impact assessment on the effect of granting market economy status to China was needed. Reports have indicated that conducting a full impact assessment would mean that the EU would not grant market economy status to China before the deadline stipulated in Section 15 of the latter's Protocol of Accession. The legal service of the European Commission had earlier concluded that a change in China's status was obligatory, considering the language of the Protocol. This would have taken away the Commission's obligation to conduct a full impact assessment. Importantly, Members of the European Parliament (which has to approve the change in status), have also said that a full impact assessment would be required in order to enable them to take a decision on the matter.

Interestingly China's request for consultations in DS516, against the European Union, refers explicitly to subsequent amendments to the European Union's anti-dumping legislation, including not only the proposal to amend the methodology for determining dumping, but also the proposal to modernize the European Union's trade defence instruments (TDI).[128] Footnote 2 of its request for consultations stipulates that:

> China is aware of two legislative processes implicating potential changes to relevant provisions of the Basic Regulation: (i) the legislative process initiated by the European Commission's Proposal for a Regulation of the European Parliament and of the Council amending Regulation (EU) 2016/1036 on protection against dumped imports from countries not members of the European Union, dated 9 November 2016 (COM(2016) 721 final); and, (ii) the legislative process initiated by the European Commission's Proposal for a Regulation of the European Parliament and of the Council amending Council Regulation (EC) No 1225/2009 on protection against dumped imports

---

Customs Journal (10) (5), pp. 176–80; Pan, Rui (2015), 'China's WTO Membership and the Non-Market Economy Status: Discrimination and Impediment to China's Foreign Trade', *Journal of Contemporary China* (24) (94), pp. 742–57; Rao, Weijia (2013), 'China's Market Economy Status under WTO Antidumping Law after 2016', *Tsinghua China Law Review* (5), pp. 151–68; Ruessmann, Laurent and Beck, Jochen (2014), '2016 and the Application of an NME Methodology to Chinese Producers in Anti-Dumping Investigations', *Global Trade and Customs Journal* (9) (10), pp. 457–63; Rosenthal, Paul C. and Beckington, Jeffrey S. (2014), 'The People's Republic of China: A Market Economy or a Non-Market Economy in Anti-Dumping Proceedings Starting on December 12, 2016?', *Global Trade and Customs Journal* (9) (7–8), pp. 352–5.

[128] WTO, Request for Consultations, European Union – Measures Related to Price Comparison Methodologies (Complainant: China), WT/DS516/1, para. 11, footnote 2.

from countries not members of the European Community and Council Regulation (EC) No 597/2009 on protection against subsidised imports from countries not members of the European Community (COM(2013) 192 final).

Indeed, the European Commission has initiated the process of the reform of TDI. Earlier proposals date back to 2013, but the impending expiry of Section 15(a)(ii) placed renewed emphasis on the need to bring about reform. Leaving aside the question of whether it is possible to challenge 'legislative processes' as a measure at issue in WTO dispute settlement proceedings, China has expressed concern that the EU's TDI reform proposals will equally not withstand WTO scrutiny.

In part China's WTO challenge is aimed at the way in which the EU rejects Chinese market prices and costs when calculating normal value. In China's view the EU acts in a WTO-inconsistent manner by disregarding costs and prices in China in the absence of any legal basis to do so, in contradiction with Article 2.1 and 2.2 of the Anti-Dumping Agreement (ADA), Article VI:1 of the GATT 994 and the second paragraph of the *Ad* Note to Article VI:1 of the GATT 1994. In November 2016 the European Commission published its proposal for a Regulation amending the currently applicable trade defence instrument rules and in particular the methodology to be applied to determine dumping. This proposal departs from the application of the 'analogue country' methodology for NMEs, by replacing it with a horizontal methodology, not linked to the market economy status of a country. The horizontal methodology for the determination of normal value would be applicable in the same manner to all WTO Members. It would provide for the possibility to reconstruct normal value where it is demonstrated that domestic prices and costs in the exporting country are deemed inappropriate 'due to the existence of significant distortions'. Significant distortions would be deemed to exist inter alia 'when reported prices or costs, including the costs of raw materials, are not the result of free market forces as they are affected by government intervention'. Whether this is the case would be analysed on the basis of an illustrative list of factors relating to the degree of governmental control, through i) corporate state ownership, control or policy supervision or guidance; ii) the possibility to interfere with respect to prices or costs; iii) public policies or measures influencing free market forces; and iv) access to finance by institutions implementing public policy objectives.

As noted, Article VI:1 of the GATT 1994 provides that, in principle, normal value should be determined based on domestic prices of the like product or, in the absence of such prices, prices for export to a third country or prices constructed from the costs of production in the country of origin.

Article 2.2 of the ADA, however, provides for two exceptions to that principle:

1. Where there are no sales of the like product in the ordinary course of trade in the domestic market of the exporting country; or
2. Because of the particular market situation or the low volume of the sales in the domestic market.

In such cases, Article 2.2 of the ADA allows Members to determine the normal value 'by comparison with a comparable price of the like product when exported to an appropriate third country, provided that this price is representative, or with the cost of production in the country of origin plus a reasonable amount for administrative, selling and general costs and for profits'. If normal value is to be determined based on costs of production, Article 2.2.1.1 of the ADA, however, provides that:

> costs shall normally be calculated on the basis of records kept by the exporter or producer under investigation, provided that such records are in accordance with the generally accepted accounting principles of the exporting country and reasonably reflect the costs associated with the production and sale of the product under consideration.

In the Commission's proposal, it is suggested to disregard the domestic costs and prices of an exporter, where 'it is not appropriate to use domestic prices and costs in the exporting country due to the existence of significant distortions'. Significant distortions are defined to cover inter alia certain forms of state interventionism. In such instances:

> the normal value shall be constructed on the basis of costs of production and sale reflecting undistorted prices or benchmarks. For this purpose, the sources that may be used include undistorted international prices, costs, or benchmarks, or corresponding costs of production and sale in an appropriate representative country with a similar level of economic development as the exporting country, provided the relevant cost data are readily available. The constructed normal value shall include a reasonable amount for administrative, selling and general costs and for profits.[129]

In this respect the proposal closely resembles the position adopted by the EU when it used cost adjustment methodologies in an anti-dumping

[129] European Commission, Proposal for a Regulation of the European Parliament and of the Council amending Regulation (EU) 2016/1036 on protection against dumped imports from countries not members of the European Union, dated 9 November 2016 (COM(2016) 721 final), at 8.

investigation against biodiesel imports from Argentina and Indonesia, as it considered that a differential export tax (DET) led to a situation in which the true costs of production were not accurately reflected in the normal value. Yet, this practice was challenged before the WTO and the Panel and the Appellate Body in *EU – Biodiesel* partially upheld Argentina's challenge that the EU's method of calculating dumping margins was inconsistent with the provisions of the ADA.[130]

In *EU – Biodiesel*, the Panel and the Appellate Body inter alia found that the European Commission's costs adjustment methodology is not as such inconsistent with the ADA insofar as the European Commission is not required to establish the costs of production so as to reflect costs prevailing in other countries outside the country of origin, but retains a degree of discretion.[131] It was also found that Article 2.2 of the ADA requires the normal value to be constructed on the basis of inter alia the 'cost of production [...] in the country of origin'. Although this does not limit the source of information or evidence that may be used, out-of-country information must be adapted to correspond to a 'cost of production in the country of origin'. However, an investigating authority may not simply substitute the costs from outside the country of origin for the 'cost of production in the country of origin'.[132] Further, the Appellate Body held that Article 2.2.1.1 of the ADA does not allow costs to be disregarded solely because they are deemed 'artificially low', as this does not constitute, in itself, a sufficient basis for concluding that the producers' records did not reasonably reflect the costs of production. Thus, Article 2.2.1.1 does not involve an examination of the 'reasonableness' of the reported costs themselves, when the actual costs recorded in the records of the producer or exporter are otherwise found, within acceptable limits, to be accurate and faithful.[133] Such assessment must be made on an individual basis for each producer.[134]

---

[130] Appellate Body Report, *EU – Biodiesel*.

[131] Appellate Body Report, *EU – Biodiesel*, para. 6.225.

[132] Appellate Body Report, *EU – Biodiesel*, para. 6.58.

[133] Appellate Body Report, *EU – Biodiesel*, para. 6.3.

[134] See European Parliament's assessment of the impact of the ruling of the Panel in *EU – Biodiesel*: European Parliament (2016), Calculation of Dumping Margins: EU and US Rules and Practices in Light of the Debate on China's Market Economy Status, European Parliamentary Research Service (EPRS), 31 May. Available at http://www.europarl.europa.eu/thinktank/en/document.html?reference=EPRS_IDA(2016)583794 (last accessed at 18 October 2017).

In respect of the reform proposal it could be considered that under the 'non-standard methodology' costs are disregarded in a 'particular market situation', namely the existence of significant cost distortions caused by state interventionism. This could give rise to several new legal challenges. Indeed, a challenge could be brought on the basis of an *as such* violation of Article 2.2.1.1 of the ADA, insofar as the costs of all Chinese exporting producers would be disregarded as a result of alleged 'significant distortions' based on various forms of state interventionism, without assessing on an individual basis whether the costs recorded in the records of the individual producer or exporter are otherwise found, within acceptable limits, to be accurate and faithful. Similarly, one could envisage a challenge on the basis of an alleged *as applied* infringement of Article 2.2.1.1 of the ADA, to the extent that the European Commission would insufficiently substantiate the basis on which it considers that the individual Chinese exporting producers' records did not reasonably reflect the costs of production. It is therefore likely that the concrete application, if not the 'non-standard methodology' itself, would be liable to infringement, either *as such* or *as applied*, of certain provisions of the covered agreements.

Regardless of the way in which the EU will reform its trade defence instruments, and regardless of the way how other importing WTO Members will react to the expiry of Section 15(a)(ii), the heated debate on this particular issue evidences the fact that this type of commitment has served as the legal basis for treatment that, in the absence of that commitment, might very well be considered to be WTO-inconsistent.[135] Nevertheless, it should be noted that this type of commitment is relatively rare. Only China, Viet Nam and Tajikistan undertook such a commitment as a condition for their accession to the WTO. Moreover, China's commitment is bound to expire by the end of 2016, whereas Viet Nam's commitment will only be applicable until 2018. In sum, the commitments allowing for the use of a different type of methodology for the calculation of normal value in anti-dumping investigations are a good example

[135] In anticipation of the expiry of the relevant provision in China's Protocol of Accession, the EU has already started using alternative methodologies in the context of anti-dumping investigations. See, inter alia, Depayre, Gerard (2016), 'Why the EU Anti-Dumping Practice to Adjust Inputs Costs in Situations where Such Costs Are "Artificially Low" Is Legitimate and Justified', *Global Trade and Customs Journal* (11) (2), pp. 42–5; Müller, Sophia (2015), The Prospects of EU Trade Defence Against Chinese Imports after 2016: Taming the Dragon Through Countervailing Duties?, SSRN, SSRN-id2665960. Available at https://papers.ssrn.com/sol3/papers.cfm?abstract_id=2665960 (last accessed at 18 October 2017).

of the country-specific nature of more and less stringent commitments in protocols of accession. There is no evidence that these types of commitments are being imposed on a regular basis. Rather they reflect specific concerns in respect of the acceding country or customs territory, and thus constitute further evidence for the argument that Members have opted for a pragmatic and contract-like approach. This observation is shared by most authors. Some have, however, cautioned that '[w]hile rule-bargaining may have become a political reality in WTO accession practice, the adjudicators, as the judicial branch of the WTO, should at least be mindful of the detrimental impact of such practice on WTO rule of law.'[136]

6.4.3 Export Duties

Export restrictions have received attention in the context of the multilateral trading system since the beginning.[137] That attention has, however, been relatively limited in comparison to that awarded to restrictions on imports. In recent years, they have, however, become increasingly controversial, in particular when they are applied to raw materials.[138]

---

[136] Qin (2017), Mind the Gap: Navigating Between the WTO Agreement and Its Accession Protocols, at 260. In Qin's view 'the adjudicators [...] should be obliged to provide legal reasoning that would lessen the impact, rather than offering a legal cover for the practice'.

[137] See, inter alia, Roessler, Frieder (1975), 'GATT and Access to Supplies', *Journal of World Trade* (9) (1), pp. 25–40, at 27. Roessler notes that '[t]he attention of policy makers is no longer directed towards access to markets for primary products but rather towards access to supplies'; Rom, Michael (1984), 'Export Controls in GATT', *Journal of World Trade* (18) (2), pp. 125–54; Jackson, John H. (1984), 'The Changing International Law Framework for Exports: The General Agreement on Tariffs and Trade', *Georgia Journal of International and Comparative Law* (14) (3), pp. 505–20; Jones, Kent (1989), 'Voluntary Export Restraint: Political Economy, History and Role of the GATT', *Journal of World Trade* (23) (3), pp. 125–40; Karapinar, Baris (2011a), 'Export Restrictions and WTO Law: How to Reform Regulatory Deficiency', *Journal of World Trade* (45) (6), pp. 1139–55; Karapinar, Baris (2011b), 'China's Export Restriction Policies: Complying with "WTO Plus" or Undermining Multilateralism?', *World Trade Review* (10) (3), pp. 389–408; Karapinar, Baris (2012), 'Defining the Legal Boundaries of Export Restrictions: A Case Law Analysis', *Journal of International Economic Law* (15) (2), pp. 443–79.

[138] See for an excellent overview, Espa, Ilaria (2015), *Export Restrictions on Critical Minerals and Metals: Testing the Adequacy of WTO Disciplines*, Cambridge, Cambridge University Press; see also Ehring, Lothar and Selivanova, Yulia (2011), Export Restrictions in the Field of Energy, in Selivanova, Yulia

Export duties, or taxes on exports, typically lead to higher world prices and lower prices in the domestic market.[139] They therefore favour downstream domestic industries, especially if the taxes are applied in respect of raw materials.[140] Commitments on export duties (or export taxes) have been made in the context of 15 accessions.[141] In a number of cases, applicants have accepted a commitment relating to export duties as part of their protocol of accession.[142] The way in which this commitment has been phrased in working party reports differs substantially.[143] Bulgaria's Protocol of Accession contains a statement and a commitment on export duties. The Working Party had asked whether Bulgaria's export duties were 'necessary', to which the representative of Bulgaria responded that these taxes 'were specific taxes applied to prevent or relieve critical shortages of foodstuffs and other essential products, consistent with Article XI of the GATT 1994. This tax was temporary and would be dismantled when the domestic supply situation

---

(ed.), *Regulation of Energy in International Trade Law, WTO, NAFTA and Energy Charter*, Alphen aan den Rijn, Kluwer Law International; Malkawi, Bashar H. (2012), 'Trade in Oil and Export Restrictions: Taking the Organization of the Petroleum Exporting Countries to the WTO Court', *European Journal of Law Reform* (14) (1), 17–43; Smith, Michael P. (2015), 'Consistently Inconsistent: U.S. LNG Exportation Policy and the WTO', *Virginia Journal of International Law* (55) (1), pp. 257–89; Zhang, Weiwei (2016), 'Tracing GATT-Minus Provisions on Export Restrictions in Regional Trade Agreements', *Global Trade and Customs Journal* (11) (3), pp. 122–33.

[139] See, in respect of raw materials, Korinek, Jane and Kim, Jeonghoi (2011), 'Export Restrictions on Strategic Raw Materials and Their Impact on Trade and Global Supply', *Journal of World Trade* (45) (2), pp. 255–81.

[140] See for an assessment of China's export tax rebates, Chao, Chi-Chur, Chou, W.L. and Yu, Eden S.H. (2001), 'Export Duty Rebates and Export Performance: Theory and China's Experience', *Journal of Comparative Economics* (29), pp. 314–26; Chen, Chien-Hsun, Mai, Chao-Cheng and Yu, Hui-Chuan (2006), 'The Effect of Export Tax Rebates on Export Performance: Theory and Evidence from China', *China Economic Review* (17), 226–35.

[141] Export duty commitments were made by Bulgaria, Mongolia, Latvia, Estonia, Georgia, Croatia, China, Saudi Arabia, Viet Nam, Ukraine, Montenegro, Russian Federation, Tajikistan, Kazakhstan and Afghanistan.

[142] See, for example, China's commitment in this field. WTO, Protocol on the Accession of the People's Republic of China, WT/L/432, 23 November 2001, para. 11.3.

[143] See Espa (2015), *Export Restrictions on Critical Minerals and Metals: Testing the Adequacy of WTO Disciplines*, Chapter 4; and Qin, Julia Ya (2012), 'Reforming WTO Discipline on Export Duties: Sovereignty over Natural Resources, Economic Development and Environmental Protection', *Journal of World Trade* (46) (5), pp. 1147–90.

improved.'[144] Interestingly, although Article XI of the GATT 1994 does not apply to 'duties, taxes or charges', Bulgaria seemed to argue that its export taxes fell under the exception of Article XI:2(a) GATT 1994. Bulgaria confirmed that export taxes 'would be applied in accordance with the provisions of the WTO Agreement'.[145] Its representative noted that, at the current time, Bulgaria applied the export taxes only to the goods and services listed in Annex 2 to the Report. Bulgaria would, 'after accession, minimize its use of such taxes'. Mongolia made a commitment to transform the export prohibition on raw cashmere into an *ad valorem* export duty which would be phased out within ten years.[146] Again, no reference was made to Article XX of the GATT 1994. In Latvia's Protocol of Accession a commitment was made to 'abolish all export duties listed in Annex 3 by 1 January 2000 with the exception of the duty on antiques'. Its representative further confirmed that 'present export tariff rates related only to the goods listed in Annex 3 Export Duty Tariffs'.[147] An interesting question is whether the incumbent membership understood this paragraph as meaning that Latvia would also not introduce any new export duties on goods not listed in Annex 3 in the future. Similar to the protocols of Bulgaria and Mongolia, no reference was made to Article XX of the GATT 1994. Estonia's Protocol of Accession contains a commitment to 'minimize the use of export taxes'. 'Any such taxes applied would be in accordance with the provisions of the WTO Agreement.'[148] This commitment is vague in terms of its desired outcome. Estonia did not explicitly commit itself not to use export duties in the future, only to minimize such use. Interestingly, the phrase 'in accordance with the provisions of the WTO Agreement' has been added to the commitment. Recall that the WTO Agreement, and the GATT 1994, does not regulate the use of export duties. Presumably the drafters intended to confirm that in the event Estonia introduced an export duty, it would do so on a non-discriminatory basis, in accordance with Article I:1 of the GATT 1994. However, whether this phrase also indicates that in

[144] WTO, Report of the Working Party on the Accession of Bulgaria, WT/ACC/BGR/5, 20 September 1996, para. 38.

[145] WTO, Report of the Working Party on the Accession of Bulgaria, WT/ACC/BGR/5, 20 September 1996, para. 39.

[146] WTO, Report of the Working Party on the Accession of Mongolia, WT/ACC/MNG/9, 27 June 1996, para. 24.

[147] WTO, Report of the Working Party on the Accession of Latvia to the World Trade Organization, WT/ACC/LVA/32, 30 September 1998, para. 69.

[148] WTO, Report of the Working Party on the Accession of Estonia to the World Trade Organization, WT/ACC/EST/29, 9 April 1999, para. 80.

the event Estonia's export duty measures were to be found inconsistent with its accession protocol commitment or with one of the obligations of the WTO Agreement it could resort to the general exceptions contained in Article XX of the GATT 1994 is unclear.[149] Georgia's and Croatia's commitments are similar to that of Estonia, although Croatia only committed itself to applying export duties 'in accordance with the provisions of the WTO Agreement'. China's commitment is contained in the body of its protocol of accession and not, as in the case of all other acceded Members, in its Working Party Report.[150] The commitment reads: 'China shall eliminate all taxes and charges applied to exports unless specifically provided for in Annex 6 of this Protocol or applied in conformity with the provisions of Article VIII of the GATT 1994.' Its commitment was the most far-reaching at the time, indicating that it would eliminate all taxes and charges on exports, except for the ones levied on products explicitly mentioned. Contrary to other protocols of accession, there is no phrase that indicates that the export duties levied on the products listed in Annex 6 would be applied 'in accordance with the provisions of the WTO Agreement'. The lack of such reference prompted the Appellate Body to conclude that China could not rely on the general exceptions contained in Article XX of the GATT 1994. Interestingly, China, like other non-original Members, undertook a commitment with regard to export restrictions. This commitment is contained in Paragraph 162 of its Working Party Report and reads (in relevant part) 'export restrictions and licensing would only be applied, after the date of accession, in those cases where this was justified by GATT provisions'. This provision has been interpreted by the Panels and the Appellate Body in *China – Raw Materials* and *China – Rare Earths*. The conclusion after these two cases is that China, by agreeing to the commitment in Paragraph 11.3 of its Protocol of Accession, restricted its regulatory autonomy in the sense that it gave up the freedom to use export taxes, except with respect to the products listed in Annex 6. Saudi Arabia's commitment in its Working Party Report reveals a discussion between it and the incumbent Members. Members concerned with Saudi Arabia's practice of using export duties:

> noted that the export duties applied by Saudi Arabia appeared to be imposed only for revenue purposes and would have trade-distorting effects. In response, the representative of Saudi Arabia stated that Article XI of the

---

[149] See the extensive discussion on this issue in section 4.3.2.1.

[150] WTO, Protocol on the Accession of the People's Republic of China, WT/L/432, 23 November 2001, para. 11.3.

> GATT 1994 expressly permitted the imposition of export duties, and did not restrict the right to impose such duties.[151]

In spite of this statement, the representative of Saudi Arabia confirmed that Saudi Arabia 'would not impose export duties on iron and steel scrap'. This is a limited commitment, especially when compared to the commitment undertaken by China. Viet Nam's Protocol of Accession contains a commitment to apply export duties 'in conformity with the GATT 1994'.[152] Furthermore, Viet Nam would incrementally reduce export duties on seven products from 45 per cent to 22 per cent and on one product from 35 per cent to 17 per cent in the course of five years. Interestingly, Viet Nam's commitment refers to the GATT 1994 and not to the WTO Agreement, as in the protocols of Estonia, Georgia and Croatia.[153] Ukraine's commitment on export duties is rather detailed:

> The representative of Ukraine confirmed that at present export duties were applied only to the goods listed in Table 20(a). He further confirmed that Ukraine would reduce export duties in accordance with the binding schedule contained in Table 20(b). He also confirmed that as regards these products, Ukraine would not increase export duties, nor apply other measures having an equivalent effect, unless justified under the exceptions of the GATT 1994. The Working Party took note of these commitments.[154]

The Working Party Report further indicates that incumbent Members were concerned about this particular issue and their rights to impose export duties:

> The Working Party agreed that these commitments do not constitute a reinterpretation of GATT 1994, nor affect the rights and obligations of other members in respect of provisions on the application of export duties, that are measures in accordance with GATT 1994.[155]

---

[151] WTO, Report of the Working Party on the Accession of the Kingdom of Saudi Arabia to the World Trade Organization, WT/ACC/SAU/61, 1 November 2005, para. 184.

[152] WTO, Report of the Working Party on the Accession of Viet Nam, WT/ACC/VNM/48, 27 October 2006, para. 260.

[153] This would seem to suggest that the probability of a successful argument on the applicability of Article XX of the GATT 1994 to any violation of this particular commitment is higher.

[154] WTO, Report of the Working Party on the Accession of Ukraine to the World Trade Organization, WT/ACC/UKR/152, 25 January 2008, para. 240.

[155] WTO, Report of the Working Party on the Accession of Ukraine to the World Trade Organization, WT/ACC/UKR/152, 25 January 2008, para. 240.

The fact that the Working Party felt the need to explicitly include this statement reflects concerns among the incumbent membership that provisions in protocols of accession might at one point be used to impact their rights and obligations. Later protocols have not repeated this particular expression. Nevertheless, one could reasonably assume that if the WTO has, over the course of 20 years of accession practice, consistently used a particular expression, which may be different from the text of the WTO Agreement itself, that this would influence the subsequent interpretation of that particular term in the context of WTO dispute settlement proceedings.

In terms of commitments on the reduction or elimination of export duties, Montenegro's commitment is the most far-reaching. The paragraph containing the commitment is extremely brief and stipulates that Montenegro 'would not apply or reintroduce any export duty'.[156] There is no reference to the WTO Agreement or to GATT 1994, meaning that there does not appear to be a possibility of having recourse to Article XX of the GATT 1994 to justify any violations of that particular commitment. In the Protocol of Accession of the Russian Federation a new way was found to ensure the applicability of the general exceptions of Article XX of the GATT 1994 to its commitment on export duties. In a long and detailed paragraph, it is explained that Part V of the Schedule of Concessions and Commitments on Goods of the Russian Federation contains a list of more than 700 products on which export duties will not be increased, reduced or eliminated. To this end, Part V of the Schedule stipulates:

> The Russian Federation undertakes not to increase export duties, or to reduce or to eliminate them, in accordance with the following schedule, and not to reintroduce or increase them beyond the levels indicated in this schedule, except in accordance with the provisions with GATT 1994.[157]

Moreover, the Paragraph in the Working Party Report stipulates that 'the Russian Federation would apply export duties in conformity with the WTO Agreement, in particular with Article I of the GATT 1994'. In addition to the availability of the general exceptions of Article XX of the GATT 1994, this technique ensures that the applicant may resort to

---

[156] WTO, Report of the Working Party on the Accession of Montenegro to the World Trade Organization, WT/ACC/CGR/38, 5 December 2011, para. 132.

[157] WTO, Report of the Working Party on the Accession of the Russian Federation to the World Trade Organization, WT/ACC/RUS/70, 17 November 2011, para. 683.

the procedure in Article XXVIII:1 of the GATT 1994 to renegotiate the level of its export duty bindings.[158] In all other cases, where the protocol of accession or the working party report itself contains a table stipulating the export duty bindings, renegotiations are not possible since there is no provision that allows for the modification of protocols of accession.[159] According to Espa, 'newly acceded Members are practically unable to renegotiate any of the export duty commitments assumed under individual accession protocol provisions, inasmuch as the renegotiation procedure provided for in Article XXVIII GATT is only applicable to export duty concessions included in GATT schedules and, therefore, incorporated into the GATT framework'.[160] Tajikistan's Protocol of Accession reflects a return to the approach used in China's Protocol. Its commitment states that Tajikistan 'shall not introduce and shall eliminate all duties, taxes, fees and charges applied to exports, unless specifically provided for in Table 9 of this Protocol or applied in conformity with the provisions of Article VIII of the GATT 1994'.[161] The Working Party Report on the accession of Kazakhstan contains a rather elaborate commitment on the elimination of export duties. The structure of the commitment is the same as the one undertaken by the Russian Federation in the sense that the relevant export duty rates are included in a separate part of the Schedule of Specific Commitments.[162] Afghanistan's commitment on export duties is quite special and therefore deserves to be quoted in full:

---

[158] Qin (2012), Reforming WTO Disciplines on Export Duties, at 1160.

[159] There has been some debate on the question whether Article XXVIII bis of the GATT 1994 also allows for the renegotiation of export duty commitments. In Qin's view, 'from a systemic perspective, the principle and rationale underlying Article XXVIII should be equally valid and applicable to export concessions'. See, Qin (2012), Reforming WTO Disciplines on Export Duties, at 1161. Osakwe, Yu and Beslać appear to share this opinion. See, Osakwe, Chiedu, Yu, Dayong and Beslać, Petra (2015), Export Duty Commitments: The Treaty Dialogue and the Pattern of Commitments, in Dadush, Uri and Osakwe, Chiedu (eds) (2015), *WTO Accessions and Trade Multilateralism: Case Studies and Lessons from the WTO at Twenty*, Cambridge, Cambridge University Press, 741–63, at 747.

[160] Espa (2015), *Export Restrictions on Critical Minerals and Metals: Testing the Adequacy of WTO Disciplines*, at 163.

[161] WTO, Report of the Working Party on the Accession of the Republic of Tajikistan, WT/ACC/TJK/30, 6 November 2012, para. 169.

[162] WTO, Report of the Working Party on the Accession of the Republic of Kazakhstan, WT/ACC/KAZ/93, 23 June 2015, para. 540.

> The representative of Afghanistan confirmed that upon accession, Afghanistan would not introduce and would eliminate all duties, taxes, fees and charges applied to exports (with the exception of the 2% fixed tax on exports, which would be eliminated prior to 1 January 2021), unless specifically provided for in Annex 12 to this Report or applied in conformity with the provisions of Article VIII of the General Agreement on Tariffs and Trade 1994. Afghanistan would notify to the WTO any changes of its duties, taxes, fees and charges applied to exports on the day of their publication and in any case at least 30 days before any such changes enter into force. The Working Party took note of these commitments.[163]

Afghanistan was thus allowed to maintain an export tax of 2 per cent for 5 years following its accession, yet this is undoubtedly a WTO-Plus commitment in the sense that it will no longer be allowed to use export duties as a form of government revenue as of 2021. Moreover, recourse to Article XX of the GATT 1994 does not appear to be available to Afghanistan, considering the way in which the commitment paragraph has been drafted.

A reading of the different types of commitments relating to export duties reflects a wide diversity in the way working parties on accession have approached the issue. Table 6.1 summarizes the language used in paragraphs containing commitments in relation to export duties.

Table 6.1 Language used in commitments on export duties

Member	Paragraph	Scope	Language Used	(In)direct Reference to Article XX?
Bulgaria	38–9	All export taxes	'would minimize'	Application of export taxes 'in accordance with the provisions of the WTO Agreement'

[163] WTO, Report of the Working Party on the Accession of the Islamic Republic of Afghanistan to the World Trade Organization, WT/ACC/AFG/36, 13 November 2015, para. 145.

Member	Paragraph	Scope	Language Used	(In)direct Reference to Article XX?
Mongolia	24	'raw cashmere'	An export duty at the rate of not more than 30 per cent *ad valorem* 'would be introduced'. That export duty 'would be phased out' and 'eliminated' within ten years of the date of Mongolia's accession to the WTO	None
Latvia	69	Products listed in Annex 3	'abolish all' export duties listed in Annex 3 by 1 January 2000 with the exception of the duty on antiques	None
Estonia	80	All export taxes	'would minimize the use of export taxes'	Application of export taxes 'would be in accordance with the provisions of the WTO Agreement'
Georgia	82	All export taxes	'intended to minimize the use of export taxes'	Application of export taxes 'would be in accordance with the provisions of the WTO Agreement'
Croatia	101	All export taxes	'would apply export duties only'	Application of export taxes 'in accordance with the provisions of the WTO Agreement'

Table 6.1 (continued)

Member	Paragraph	Scope	Language Used	(In)direct Reference to Article XX?
China	11.3	All export taxes, unless provided for in Annex 6	'shall eliminate'	'or applied in conformity with the provisions of Article VIII of the GATT 1994'
Saudi Arabia	184	Iron and steel scrap	'would not impose'	None, 'Article XI of the GATT 1994 expressly permitted the imposition of export duties'
Viet Nam	260	Ferrous and non-ferrous scrap metal (Table 17)	'would apply' and 'would reduce'	Application of export taxes 'in conformity with the GATT 1994'
Ukraine	240	Only goods listed in Table 20(a)	'would reduce' and 'would not increase'	'unless justified under the exceptions of the GATT 1994'
Montenegro	132	All export taxes	'would not apply or reintroduce'	None
Russian Federation	638	Part V Schedule of Concessions and Commitments	'not to increase', 'to reduce' or 'to eliminate' export duties	'except in accordance with the provisions of the GATT 1994'
Tajikistan	169	All export taxes, unless provided for in Table 9	'shall eliminate'	'or applied in conformity with the provisions of Article VIII of the GATT 1994'

Member	Paragraph	Scope	Language Used	(In)direct Reference to Article XX?
Kazakhstan	540	Part V Schedule of Concessions and Commitments	'not to increase', 'to reduce' or 'to eliminate' export duties	'except in accordance with the provisions of the GATT 1994'
Afghanistan	145	All export taxes, unless provided in Annex 12	'not to increase', 'to reduce' or 'to eliminate' export duties	'or applied in conformity with the provisions of Article VIII of the GATT 1994'

Recall that the WTO Agreement in principle does not prohibit the use of export duties. However, when such duties are applied, their application has to be in conformity with the requirements of, for example, the MFN treatment obligation in Article I:1 of the GATT 1994 and Article XXIV:8 of the GATT 1994.[164] Interestingly, the commitments made by the Russian Federation and Kazakhstan also indicate that when these Members would apply export tariff rate quotas (TRQs), they would do so 'in a manner that is consistent with the WTO Agreement and in particular the GATT 1994'.[165] Since export duties are not a priori prohibited, any commitment not to introduce export duties exceeds the baseline obligation contained in the WTO Agreement. The extent to which the commitments made by the 15 acceding Members limit their regulatory freedom varies considerably (see Table 6.2). Croatia appears to have accepted the least stringent commitment by agreeing to 'apply export duties only in accordance with the provisions of the WTO Agreement'. This implies

[164] The commitments made by the Russian Federation and Kazakhstan contain explicit language to this effect: from the date of accession, Kazakhstan would apply export duties in conformity with the WTO Agreement, in particular with Article I of the GATT 1994. Accordingly, with respect to export duties and charges of any kind imposed on, or in connection with, exportation, any advantage, favour, privilege or immunity granted by Kazakhstan to any product destined for any other country shall be accorded immediately and unconditionally to the like product destined for the territories of all other WTO Members.

[165] WTO, Report of the Working Party on the Accession of the Russian Federation to the World Trade Organization, WT/ACC/RUS/70, 17 November 2011, para. 683; WTO, Report of the Working Party on the Accession of the Republic of Kazakhstan, WT/ACC/KAZ/93, 23 June 2015, para. 540.

that Croatia retains its freedom to impose export duties (no commitment). The only limitation arising from the commitment is that it would have to do so in a way that is consistent with, in particular, the MFN treatment obligation contained in Article I:1 GATT 1994. Bulgaria, Estonia and Georgia agreed to a commitment that requires them to 'minimize the use of export taxes' (soft commitments), and, when applying such taxes, 'to do so in accordance with the provisions of the WTO Agreement'. Much like Croatia's commitment, these commitments do not really restrict their regulatory freedom, but only require them to apply export duties on an MFN basis. More stringent commitments have been entered into by Mongolia (raw cashmere), Saudi Arabia (iron and steel scrap) and Viet Nam (ferrous and non-ferrous scrap metal). They all entered into a commitment that prohibits them from imposing export duties on particular products (positive listing). Viet Nam, moreover, signed a commitment to apply export taxes in a manner consistent with the GATT 1994, which implies that it would apply these taxes in an MFN-consistent manner. The wording of its commitment suggests that recourse to Article XX of the GATT 1994 may be available. Latvia, Ukraine and the Russian Federation all agreed to reduce, not to increase or eliminate export duties on a particular set of products listed in a table in their Protocol of Accession (Latvia and Ukraine) or in their Schedule of Concessions or Commitments (Russian Federation).[166] The most stringent commitments have been entered into by China, Montenegro and Tajikistan, who have all agreed to eliminate, not apply or reintroduce export taxes. In China and Tajikistan's case, a select number of products have been excluded from this obligation (negative listing), whereas in the case of Montenegro the commitment applies to all products. Interestingly, whereas some of the less strict commitments would leave open the possibility to resort to the general exceptions contained in Article XX of the GATT 1994, this option is not available in the case of China and Tajikistan (following the Appellate Body's reasoning in *China – Raw Materials* and *China – Rare Earths*) and Montenegro (because of the lack of any reference to the WTO Agreement or the GATT 1994) in the paragraph containing the commitment.

---

[166] In Latvia's case the bindings relate to wood and wood products, printed materials, iron and steel scrap and antiques. Ukraine's bindings deal with oilseeds, live cattle and hides and iron and steel scrap. Both cases illustrate a commitment to reduce export duties, not to eliminate them altogether. In the example of the Russian Federation, the commitment to reduce export duties was incorporated in its Schedule of Concessions or Commitments and refers to over 700 products in 26 HS [Harmonized System] chapters.

Table 6.2 Type of export duty commitment and availability of Article XX of the GATT 1994

Type of Commitment	Recourse to Article XX GATT 1994?
No commitment	Croatia
'Soft' commitment	Yes: Bulgaria, Estonia and Georgia
Positive listing	No: Mongolia, Saudi Arabia and Latvia Yes (in conformity with GATT 1994): Viet Nam Yes (unless justified under the exceptions of the GATT 1994): Ukraine Yes (incorporation in Schedules of Concessions or Commitments): Russian Federation and Kazakhstan
Negative listing	No: China, Montenegro, Tajikistan and Afghanistan

6.4.4 State-Owned Enterprises (SOEs)

See section 5.4.3.4.

6.4.5 Technical Barriers to Trade (TBT)

The Agreement on Technical Barriers to Trade (TBT Agreement) was negotiated in the context of the Uruguay Round and builds on the Tokyo Round Standards Code.[167] It contains disciplines on the application of technical regulations and standards as well as conformity assessment procedures.[168] Its provisions have been invoked in WTO dispute settlement proceedings on a number of occasions.[169] Typically commitments in protocols of accession stipulate that the TBT Agreement would be applied 'from the date of accession without recourse to any transition

[167] Agreement on Technical Barriers to Trade, 1868 U.N.T.S. 120, entered into force 1 January 1995 (TBT Agreement). The plurilateral Agreement on Technical Barriers to Trade was also known as the 'Standards Code'. For a more detailed overview of the negotiating history of the TBT Agreement, see Lester, Simon and Stemberg, William (2014), 'The GATT Origins of TBT Agreement Articles 2.1 and 2.2', *Journal of International Economic Law* (17) (1), pp. 215–32, at 217–21.

[168] See Articles 2.1, 2.2, 2.4 and Annex 1 of the TBT Agreement.

[169] Panel Report, *EC – Asbestos*; Panel Report, *US – Clove Cigarettes*; Panel Report, *US – Tuna II (Mexico)*; and Panel Report, *US – COOL*.

period'.[170] Some LDCs and developing-country Members were nevertheless able to obtain some kind of transition period, outlining the date by which they would fully implement the TBT Agreement.[171] Some LDCs, such as Cape Verde, merely committed to 'seek out all available technical assistance to ensure that its capacity to eventually implement the Agreement is assured'.[172] In some instances, the commitment made in the working party report also confirms the basic non-discrimination disciplines of the TBT Agreement, noting that the applicant 'would ensure that its technical regulations, standards, certification and labelling requirements are not applied to imports in an arbitrary manner, in a way that discriminates between supplier countries where the same conditions apply or as a disguised restriction on international trade'.[173] Some Members made rather specific commitments on the replacement of mandatory standards with voluntary standards.[174] Other Members that acceded to the WTO through the procedure laid down by Article XII of the WTO Agreement made detailed commitments on the application of transparency and notification requirements as stipulated by the TBT Agreement.[175] Some commitments made in working party reports reflect the concern of (some) members of the working party with regard to a particular product.[176] In some instances a commitment was made not to 'enforce voluntary standards contained in private sector Agreements or other commercial contracts'.[177] The Russian Federation and Kazakhstan both made extensive rules commitments in the area of technical barriers to trade, for example in the field of the use and application of mandatory and voluntary standards, as well as the application of conformity assessment procedures.[178] In general most commitments made under this heading fall within the scope of categories 2 and 3 of the typology outlined in section 5.4. Commitments made in respect of transitional periods can be characterized in category 1. Where LDCs or developing countries have had no access to a transitional period because of a

---

170 Bulgaria, Latvia, Estonia, Jordan, Georgia, Albania, Oman, Croatia, Lithuania, China, Chinese Taipei, Armenia, FYR Macedonia, Saudi Arabia, Viet Nam, Montenegro, Russian Federation, Vanuatu and Kazakhstan.

171 Nepal, Cambodia, Lao PDR, Tajikistan, Yemen and Seychelles.

172 Cape Verde and Samoa.

173 Kyrgyz Republic and Ukraine.

174 Jordan, Georgia, Oman and Moldova.

175 China, Saudi Arabia and Tonga.

176 Chinese Taipei (whisky) and Viet Nam (motorvehicles).

177 Cape Verde.

178 Russian Federation and Kazakhstan.

working party report commitment to that effect, these commitments may constitute more stringent commitments than the baseline obligation since Article 12 of the TBT Agreement provides for special and differential treatment of developing country Members. In some respects one could argue that some of the disciplines negotiated in the context of the accession process of some acceded Members serve as building blocks for the discussions on what is nowadays referred to as regulatory cooperation. Whereas the WTO itself does not, as such, provide for disciplines that should cater for enhanced forms of regulatory cooperation as envisaged, for example, in the context of the TTIP negotiations, some of the accession protocol commitments can be considered as enabling – to an extent – regulatory cooperation. Even though they do not refer to the setting of common standards, they do seek to ensure that barriers to trade arising from regulatory divergences or legal uncertainty are minimized and that costs for business are limited. Commitments relating to the establishment of enquiry points and notification authorities, and the conclusion of mutual recognition agreements with conformity assessment bodies of other Members can both be seen in this light. Having said so, these commitments fall short of the far-reaching proposals relating to the establishment of regulatory cooperation councils that have been part of the TTIP negotiations.

6.4.6 Sanitary and Phytosanitary Measures (SPS)

Similar to the TBT Agreement, the Agreement on the Application of Sanitary and Phytosanitary Measures (SPS Agreement) deals with the trade restrictive effects of certain NTBs. Sanitary and phytosanitary measures are defined in Annex A of the SPS Agreement. The Agreement builds on the GATT 1994, in particular on Article XX(b) of that Agreement.[179] It contains disciplines that govern how Members can apply SPS measures and which principles have to be adhered to in the process of doing so. In addition to laying down basic obligations relating to the right to adopt SPS measures, the need to ensure that these measures are only applied to the extent necessary and to ensure that they do not constitute arbitrary or unjustifiable discrimination, Article 2 of the SPS Agreement further provides that SPS measures that are consistent with the provisions of the SPS Agreement shall also be presumed to be

[179] The final recital of the preamble to the SPS Agreement provides: 'Desiring therefore to elaborate rules for the application of the provisions of GATT 1994 which relate to the use of sanitary or phytosanitary measures, in particular the provisions of Article XX(b)'.

consistent with the provisions of the GATT 1994. Article 3 of the SPS Agreement contains disciplines on the harmonization of SPS measures, whereas Article 4 deals with the equivalence of SPS measures in different WTO Members. Article 5 of the SPS Agreement lays down disciplines relating to risk assessments and risk management, inter alia by requiring Members to 'take into account the objective of minimizing negative trade effects'. Other articles of the SPS Agreement deal with transparency, technical assistance, and special and differential treatment.[180] As part of their accession process, acceding governments have to provide information on the SPS measures that are applied in their country. The following baseline protocol commitment for sanitary and phytosanitary measures has been identified:

> The representative of [X] confirmed that [X] would apply all obligations under the WTO Agreement on Sanitary and Phytosanitary Measures from the date of accession without recourse to any transition period.[181]

This baseline commitment was first used in the Working Party Report on the accession of Bulgaria, but it has been repeated on many occasions since. The first commitment that was somewhat more elaborate in nature can be found in the Working Party Report on the accession of the Kyrgyz Republic. Its commitment inter alia stipulates that the Kyrgyz government 'would be willing to consult with WTO Members concerning the effect of these [sanitary and certification] requirements on their trade with a view to resolving specific problems'. This can be seen as an indication of a 'notice-and-comment' procedure that is designed to reduce the trade restrictive effects of SPS measures. Stringent commitments in the field of SPS measures were undertaken by Jordan. Members of the Working Party raised the issue of unnecessary inspections of meat products, which prompted Jordan to make a commitment to 'implement the least trade restrictive requirements possible to prevent deceptive practices vis-à-vis consumers of meat, taking into account the national treatment requirements of Article III of GATT 1994'. Moreover:

> [t]he representative of Jordan confirmed that Jordan's sanitary and phytosanitary standards system would be in compliance with WTO provisions under the Agreement on the Application of Sanitary and Phytosanitary Measures as of the date of accession to the WTO, and that Jordan would apply all measures of the Agreement on the Application of Sanitary and

[180] See Articles 7, 9 and 10 of the SPS Agreement.
[181] Williams (2008), *A Handbook on Accession to the WTO*, at 96.

> Phytosanitary Measures *in a least trade distortive manner* from the date of accession without recourse to any transition period.[182]

This commitment goes significantly further than the baseline obligations found in the SPS Agreement since no such obligation can be found there. Considering the fact that commitments in working party reports can be enforced in WTO dispute settlement proceedings, the question arises whether other Members could challenge any Jordanian SPS measure, alleging that it is not the 'least trade distortive manner' to address a particular SPS-related problem. It should be noted that this particular commitment is exceptional in nature, and no other acceded Members have undertaken a similar commitment. Some LDCs were able to obtain a transition period that grants them a longer period of time to fully implement the obligations laid down by the SPS Agreement.[183] Countries such as Saudi Arabia, Ukraine, the Russian Federation and Kazakhstan all made extensive commitments in the area of SPS measures.

6.5 FOREIGN DIRECT INVESTMENT

Commitments made in relation to foreign direct investment (FDI) can be found in several sections of protocols of accession. These commitments have been made in three sections: i) Investment Regime, ii) Trading Rights, and iii) Trade-Related Investment Measures (TRIMS).[184] The fact that commitments have been made is interesting in and of itself since the WTO does not currently regulate FDI, leaving aside the disciplines contained in the TRIMS Agreement and the GATS. Six Members have made commitments under the heading 'Investment Regime' as part of their protocol of accession, 31 acceded Members have made commitments under the heading 'Trading Rights' and all acceded Members have made commitments under the heading 'Trade-Related Investment Measures'.

---

[182] WTO, Report of the Working Party on the Accession of the Hashemite Kingdom of Jordan to the World Trade Organization, WT/ACC/JOR/33, WT/MIN(99)/9, 3 December 1999, para. 151 (emphasis added).

[183] See, for example, Nepal, Cambodia, Cape Verde, Lao PDR, Yemen and Seychelles.

[184] Commitments made in the context of services may, to the extent that they relate to the third Mode of Supply (commercial presence) also relate to FDI. However, for the purposes of this monograph, these commitments have been listed under section 6.7 (Services).

6.5.1 Investment Regime

China, Estonia, Kazakhstan, Samoa, Saudi Arabia, Tonga and Liberia have all made commitments under this heading.[185] These commitments are rather diverse in nature and range from confirmations to apply national treatment to direct taxation to accepting that domestic investment laws and their implementation would be in full conformity with the WTO Agreement.[186]

6.5.2 Trading Rights

Trading rights commitments relate to domestic legislation that determines which enterprises are allowed to import and export. Twenty-nine acceded Members have made commitments that, in essence, confirm the right to trade in goods on a non-discriminatory basis. In some instances these commitments also clarify that any enterprise shall be permitted to register as importer or exporter. Moreover, some commitments entail the elimination of requirements for physical presence or investment in the acceding Member. As has been noted in the context of an examination of China's accession protocol commitments, '[t]hese provisions address national treatment of foreign persons with respect to their business and trading

---

[185] WTO, Report of the Working Party on the Accession of China, WT/ACC/CHN/49 and Corr. 1, 1 October 2001, para. 42; WTO, Report of the Working Party on the Accession of Estonia to the World Trade Organization, WT/ACC/EST/28, 9 April 1999, para. 15; WTO, Report of the Working Party on the Accession of the Republic of Kazakhstan, WT/ACC/KAZ/93, 23 June 2015, para. 87; WTO, Report of the Working Party on the Accession of Samoa to the World Trade Organization, WT/ACC/SAM/30, WT/MIN(11)/1, 1 November 2011, para. 22; WTO, Report of the Working Party on the Accession of the Kingdom of Saudi Arabia to the World Trade Organization, WT/ACC/SAU/61, 1 November 2005, para. 69; WTO, Report of the Working Party on the Accession of Tonga to the World Trade Organization, WTO/ACC/TON/17, WT/MIN(05)/4, 2 December 2005, para. 24; WTO, Report of the Working Party on the Accession of Liberia to the World Trade Organization, WTO/ACC/LBR/23, 9 October 2015, para. 38.

[186] Osakwe, Chiedu (2015), Contributions and Lessons from WTO Accessions: The Present and Future of the Rules-Based Multilateral Trading System, in Dadush, Uri and Osakwe, Chiedu (eds) (2015), *WTO Accessions and Trade Multilateralism: Case Studies and Lessons from the WTO at Twenty*, Cambridge, Cambridge University Press, 219–308, at 252. See the working party reports on the accessions of Estonia, China and Tonga.

opportunities in China, not the treatment of imported goods, and therefore are beyond the scope of GATT Article III and TRIMs'.[187] Moreover, China made a commitment to 'provide the same treatment to Chinese enterprises, including foreign-funded enterprises, and foreign enterprises and individuals in China'.[188]

6.5.3 Trade-Related Investment Measures (TRIMS)

A typical standard commitment in this sector confirms that the Member in question shall not maintain any measures inconsistent with the TRIMS Agreement and shall apply that agreement from the date of accession, without having recourse to a transition period.[189] In some instances Members have been able to secure a transition period, however. This type of commitment is more stringent than the baseline obligation since, for most original Members, TRIMS that existed at the time of the inception of their membership often still exist.[190]

6.6 TRADE-RELATED INTELLECTUAL PROPERTY REGIME

The Agreement on the Trade-Related Aspects of Intellectual Property Rights (TRIPS Agreement) 'recognizes the underlying public policy objectives of systems to protect intellectual property, lays down derailed

---

[187] Qin, Julia Ya (2003), '"WTO-Plus" Obligations and Their Implications for the World Trade Organization Legal System: An Appraisal of the China Accession Protocol', *Journal of World Trade* (37) (3), pp. 483–522, at 501.

[188] WTO, Report of the Working Party on the Accession of China, WT/ACC/CHN/49 and Corr. 1, 1 October 2001, paragraph 18; and Qin (2003), 'WTO-Plus' Obligations and Their Implications for the World Trade Organization Legal System, at 502.

[189] See, for example, Paragraph 300 in the Working Party Report on the Accession of Seychelles: 'The representative of Seychelles confirmed that from the date of accession, Seychelles would apply its investment regime in compliance with the WTO Agreement, including the WTO Agreement on Trade-Related Investment Measures (TRIMs Agreement), and would apply the TRIMs Agreement from the date of accession without recourse to any transition period in a non-discriminatory manner – to imports from all WTO Members and to domestically-produced goods. The Working Party took note of this commitment.' WTO, Report of the Working Party on the Accession of Seychelles, WT/ACC/SYC/64, 5 November 2014.

[190] Osakwe (2015), Contributions and Lessons from WTO Accessions, at 269.

minimum standards Members must adopt to protect the private rights of intellectual property holders and provides means that Members must make available under their law to enforce those rights'.[191] All Members that acceded under the procedure as laid down by Article XII of the WTO Agreement have accepted commitments in the field of Trade-Related Aspects of Intellectual Property Rights (TRIPs).[192] In most instances these commitments reflect the intention to apply the provisions of the TRIPS Agreement no later than the date of accession. Moreover, often these commitments reaffirm the non-discrimination provisions of the TRIPS Agreement. A typical standard commitment, such as the one included in the Working Party Report on the accession of Tajikistan, reads as follows:

> The representative of Tajikistan stated that Tajikistan would apply the provisions of the WTO Agreement on Trade-Related Aspects of Intellectual Property Rights no later than the date of its accession to the WTO, without recourse to any transitional periods.[193]

As was noted in section 5.4.3.3, in some instances commitments made in the field of TRIPs concern the accession of the applicant state to a particular international agreement. Seychelles, for example, agreed to the following commitment:

> The representative of Seychelles confirmed that Seychelles would accede to the International Union for the Protection of New Varieties of Plants (UPOV). He confirmed that his Government would notify, no later than the end of 2015, the accession to the Convention of International Union for the Protection of New Varieties of Plants.[194]

Other commitments under the heading 'Trade-Related Intellectual Property Regime' mainly relate to specific aspects of the laws and regulations of the acceding state in question. Commitments have been made, inter alia, to open a 'one-stop shop' for the coordination of the promotion and simplification of the registration of patents, trademarks and copyrights, to

---

[191] Williams (2008), *A Handbook on Accession to the WTO*, at 107.

[192] See for an overview of the commitments made by the Russian Federation, Lane, William P. (2013), 'Trapped in China's Shadow? Intellectual Property Protection in Post-WTO-Accession Russia', *Boston College International & Comparative Law Review* (36), pp. 183–217.

[193] WTO, Report of the Working Party on the Accession of Tajikistan, WT/ACC/TJK/30, 6 November 2012, para. 326.

[194] WTO, Report of the Working Party on the Accession of Seychelles, WT/ACC/SYC/64, 5 November 2014, para. 372.

amend the civil code to exclude domain names from a particular provision of the Civil Code so as to allow for the registration of the trademark of such names, and to clarify that all commercial scale trademark counterfeiting and copyright piracy was subject to criminal prosecution and that competent authorities had seizure and destruction authority in criminal cases.[195]

Some LDCs that acceded to the WTO have been granted a transitional period of a few years in order to grant them time to ensure the consistency of their domestic intellectual property legislation with their WTO obligations. Such a commitment can, for example, be found in the Protocol of Accession of Lao PDR, which acceded in 2012:

> The representative of Lao PDR confirmed that Lao PDR would apply fully the TRIPS Agreement no later than 31 December 2016 with the understanding that the protections for intellectual property rights as provided for in paragraphs 225 and 226 would be applied by Lao PDR by the dates specified in those paragraphs. The representative of Lao PDR also confirmed that Lao PDR would avail itself of special and differential treatment for Least-Developed Countries under the TRIPS Agreement and various Ministerial Conference Declarations including the Hong Kong Ministerial Declaration (paragraph 47), TRIPS Council Decision (IP/C/40), and the Eighth Ministerial Conference Decisions.[196]

Lao PDR is one example of several LDCs which have also accepted commitments in the area of intellectual property rights. As has been explained, some of these commitments that relate to the TRIPS Agreement might even constitute WTO-Plus commitments.[197] However, they also note that these commitments could enhance the predictability and

---

[195] WTO, Report of the Working Party on the Accession of Seychelles, WT/ACC/SYC/64, 5 November 2014, para. 345; WTO, Report of the Working Party on the Accession of the Russian Federation to the World Trade Organization, WT/ACC/RUS/70, WT/MIN(11)/2, 17 November 2011, para. 1253; and WTO, Report of the Working Party on the Accession of Viet Nam, WT/ACC/VNM/48, 27 October 2006, para. 465.

[196] WTO, Report of the Working Party on the Accession of Lao PDR to the World Trade Organization, WTO/ACC/LAO/45, 1 October 2012, para. 227.

[197] Bhattacharya, Alexandra and Laker Apecu, Joan (2015), Intellectual Property Rights Protection: The Plus/Minus Debate from a Least-Developed Country Perspective – Sense and Nonsense, in Dadush, Uri and Osakwe, Chiedu (eds) (2015), *WTO Accessions and Trade Multilateralism: Case Studies and Lessons from the WTO at Twenty*, Cambridge, Cambridge University Press, pp. 795–817, at 815.

transparency of the multilateral trading system in this respect.[198] Ultimately, although the obligations 'might appear more stringent or "plus" compared with the requirements of the TRIPS Agreement and the obligations on original LDC Members', 'the implications of these commitments must be assessed in a broader context, bearing in mind implications at both the multilateral and domestic levels'.[199]

6.7 POLICIES AFFECTING TRADE IN SERVICES

Trade in services is becoming increasingly important as a share of global GDP.[200] Services are an integral part of GVCs and the development of connecting the production of goods with services such as retail, marketing and transportation is known as the 'servicification of manufacturing'.[201] In the context of the WTO, the General Agreement on Trade in Services (GATS) lays down general rules that apply to all Members as well as specific commitments which have been negotiated by each Member individually.[202] Countries or customs territories seeking accession to the WTO have to provide information on their legislative

---

[198] Bhattacharya and Laker Apecu (2015), Intellectual Property Rights Protection, at 815. Moreover, they argue that the commitments undertaken in the context of WTO accession might be considered complementary to the commitments undertaken as part of other (regional) integration processes.

[199] Bhattacharya and Laker Apecu (2015), Intellectual Property Rights Protection, at 816.

[200] WTO, Trade in Services Brochure. Available at https://www.wto.org/english/thewto_e/20y_e/services_brochure2015_e.pdf (last accessed at 1 June 2017). The brochure notes that in 2014: 'trade in services totalled USD 4,800 billion, representing 21 per cent of world trade in goods and services. However, this total does not cover services delivered via foreign affiliates (i.e. essentially mode 3). The total trade in services is therefore estimated to be much larger, even twice as large, as mode 3 represents 55 per cent of total services trade.'

[201] See, inter alia, Lanz, Rainer and Maurer, Andreas (2015), Services and Global Value Chains: Some Evidence on Servicification of Manufacturing and Services Network, WTO Working Paper ERSD-2015-03, February 2015; and Lodefalk, Magnus (2015), Servicification of Manufacturing Firms Makes Divides in Trade-Policy Making Antiquated, Örebro University, School of Business Working Paper, 01/2015, January 2015.

[202] General Agreement on Trade in Services, 1869 U.N.T.S. 183, entered into force 1 January 1995 (GATS). Part II of the GATS contains the general obligations and disciplines whereas Part III contains the disciplines that govern the specific commitments made by Members.

framework governing trade in services. In principle accession negotiations have mainly focused on the specific – market access – commitments that the applicant would have to make.[203] However, some applicants have also made commitments under the section 'Services' of their working party report. Commitments under the heading 'Policies Affecting Trade in Services' have been made by 12 Members.[204] These commitments have mainly been made in respect of Article VI of the GATS, which deals with domestic regulation.[205] The applicants that undertook a relatively large number of protocol commitments 'were dynamic economies that were continuing the process of transition to a full market economy'.[206] After China with its 12 commitment-containing paragraphs, Saudi Arabia was the next country to include four lengthy rule commitments in the Working Party Report on its accession. These commitments mainly related to foreign financial institutions such as banks and insurance suppliers.[207] Viet Nam made 17 commitments under this heading, whereas Ukraine made 8 commitments.[208] In more recent working party reports a more or less standard commitment has been developed in respect of licensing procedures and conditions for services

---

203 During early accessions no commitments under this particular heading were made. Indeed, Croatia was the first Member that acceded under the procedure laid down by Article XII of the WTO Agreement to make an additional rule commitment under this heading. The commitment obligated Croatia to 'accord national treatment to foreign persons who have acquired assets on whatever legal basis in respect of their ownership rights and obligations, in accordance with GATS Article XVII'. As such, this commitment is a mere confirmation of the basic obligation already provided for in Article XII of the GATS. WTO, Report of the Working Party on the Accession of Croatia to the World Trade Organization, WT/ACC/HRV/59, 29 June 2000, para. 204. China was the first country to agree to the inclusion of no less than 12 commitment-containing paragraphs in its Working Party Report.

204 Croatia, China, Montenegro, Russia, Chinese Taipei, Saudi Arabia, Ukraine, Vanuatu, Viet Nam, Tajikistan, Seychelles and Kazakhstan.

205 Osakwe (2015), Contributions and Lessons from WTO Accessions, at 275.

206 Williams (2008), *A Handbook on Accession to the WTO*, at 110.

207 WTO, Report of the Working Party on the Accession of the Kingdom of Saudi Arabia to the World Trade Organization, WT/ACC/SAU/61, 1 November 2005, paras. 276, 296, 298 and 299.

208 WTO, Report of the Working Party on the Accession of Viet Nam, WT/ACC/VNM/48, 27 October 2006, paras. 479, 480, 483–5, 488, 489, 491, 494, 496, 498, 499, 502, 503 and 506–8; WTO, Report of the Working Party on the Accession of Ukraine to the World Trade Organization, WT/ACC/UKR/152, 25 January 2008, paras. 482–6 and 489–91.

and service suppliers.[209] The commitment reads as follows (using the Working Party Report on the accession of Montenegro as an example):

> Responding to specific requests of a Member, the representative of Montenegro confirmed that for the services included in Montenegro's Schedule of Specific Commitments Montenegro would ensure that its licensing procedures and conditions would not act as independent barriers to market access. She further confirmed, in particular that, from the date of accession: (i) Montenegro's licensing procedures and conditions would be published prior to becoming effective; (ii) Montenegro would specify reasonable timeframes for the review and decision by all relevant authorities in Montenegro's licensing procedures and conditions; (iii) applicants would be able to request licensing without individual invitation; (iv) any fees charged, which were not deemed to include fees determined through auction or a tendering process, would be commensurate with the administrative cost of processing an application; (v) the competent authorities of Montenegro would, after the receipt of an application, inform the applicant whether the application was considered complete under Montenegro's domestic laws and regulations and in the case of incomplete applications, would identify the additional information required to complete the application and provide an opportunity to rectify deficiencies; (vi) decisions would be taken promptly on all applications; (vii) if an application was terminated or denied, the applicant would be informed in writing and without delay of the reasons for such action. The applicant would have the possibility to resubmit, at his/her discretion, a new application addressing the reasons for termination or denial; and (viii) in case examinations were held for the licensing of professionals, such examinations would be scheduled at reasonable intervals.[210]

As noted, however, it appears that the amount of additional rules commitments made under this heading is relatively limited. Indeed, acceding countries which could be categorized as NMEs have accepted

---

[209] Similar commitments can be found in the working party reports on the accessions of the Russian Federation, Ukraine, Viet Nam, Tajikistan and Kazakhstan. See WTO, Report of the Working Party on the Accession of the Russian Federation to the World Trade Organization, WT/ACC/RUS/70, WT/MIN(11)/2, 17 November 2011, para. 1405; WTO, Report of the Working Party on the Accession of Ukraine to the World Trade Organization, WT/ACC/UKR/152, 25 January 2008, para. 498; WTO, Report of the Working Party on the Accession of Viet Nam, WT/ACC/VNM/48, 27 October 2006, para. 507; WTO, Report of the Working Party on the Accession of Tajikistan, WT/ACC/TJK/30, 6 November 2012, para. 335; and WTO, Report of the Working Party on the Accession of the Republic of Kazakhstan, WT/ACC/KAZ/93, 23 June 2015, para. 1132.

[210] WTO, Report of the Working Party on the Accession of Montenegro to the World Trade Organization, WT/ACC/CGR/38, WT/MIN(11)/7, 5 December 2011, para. 264.

commitments that specify the way in which they are supposed to give effect to the obligations laid down in the GATS. Moreover, these commitments often relate to licensing procedures which, in and of themselves, potentially can operate as barriers to trade in services. However, of greater importance for the services sector are the Member-specific market access commitments that have been scheduled upon accession. Considering the positive listing approach adopted in the context of the GATS framework, Members are already to a large extent able to determine the extent by which they want to liberalize their own services markets. Arguably this approach has resulted in a reduced need for additional rules obligations in the working party report, barring some exceptions in the case of NMEs.

6.8 TRANSPARENCY

See sections 5.4.3.2 and 6.3.

6.9 TRADE AGREEMENTS

Most of the 36 Members that acceded under the procedure laid down by Article XII of the WTO Agreement have made commitments under the heading 'Trade Agreements'. Applicants have to submit a full list of international agreements to which they are party as part of the process of accession.[211] The WTO is mainly interested in obtaining information on non-MFN agreements, that is, in bilateral or regional agreements that would have to be consistent with the regional economic integration exception as laid down in Article XXIV of the GATT 1994.[212] A standard commitment has been included in most protocols of accession. Ecuador's commitment (1995) reads as follows:

> The representative of Ecuador stated that his Government would use its best efforts to ensure that the WTO provisions for notification, consultation, and other requirements concerning preferential trading systems, free trade areas, and customs unions of which Ecuador is a member are met e.g., Article XXIV of the GATT 1994, Article V of GATS and paragraph 3 of the Enabling Clause. The Working Party took note of this commitment.[213]

---

[211] Williams (2008), *A Handbook on Accession to the WTO*, at 113.

[212] Williams (2008), *A Handbook on Accession to the WTO*, at 113.

[213] WTO, Report of the Working Party on the Accession of Ecuador, WT/L/77, 14 July 1995, para. 70.

The most recent commitment, made by Kazakhstan, stipulates:

> The representative of Kazakhstan confirmed that from the date of accession to the WTO Kazakhstan would observe relevant WTO provisions, including but not limited to Article XXIV of the WTO General Agreement on Tariffs and Trade 1994 and Article V of the WTO General Agreement on Trade in Services, in its participation in preferential trade agreements, and would ensure that the provisions of the WTO Agreements for notification, consultation and other requirements concerning free trade areas and customs unions were met from the date of accession. She confirmed that Kazakhstan would, upon accession, submit notifications and copies of its Free Trade Agreements, the EAEU Treaty and its sub-agreements to the WTO Committee on Regional Trade Agreements (CRTA). The Working Party took note of these commitments.[214]

In light of the ongoing proliferation of regional trade agreements (RTAs), it is evident that the WTO seeks to maintain the centrality of the multilateral trading system.[215] Thereto, review of the consistency of these RTAs by the Committee on Regional Trade Agreements is demanded in the standard commitment as outlined above. It is noteworthy that many of the other commitment paragraphs in working party reports also contain references to trade agreements that the applicant Member in question is party to.[216] In most cases these paragraphs explain the relationship between the commitment undertaken in the context of the WTO accession and the commitment undertaken as part of the relevant 'other'

---

[214] WTO, Report of the Working Party on the Accession of the Republic of Kazakhstan, WT/ACC/KAZ/93, 23 June 2015, para. 1174.

[215] Altemöller, Frank (2015), 'A Future for Multilateralism? New Regionalism, Counter-Multilateralism and Perspectives for the World Trade System after the Bali Ministerial Conference', *Global Trade and Customs Journal* (10) (1), pp. 42–53. It should be noted that regional arrangements may also lead to broader, MFN-based liberalization through so-called 'multilateralization'. See, in this context, Toohey, Lisa (2008), Stepping Stones and Stumbling Blocks: Vietnam's Regional Trade Arrangements and WTO Accession, in Buckley, Ross P., Lo, Vai Io and Boulle, Laurence (eds), *Challenges to Multilateral Trade: The Impact of Bilateral, Preferential and Regional Agreements*, Alphen aan den Rijn, Kluwer Law International, 65–84.

[216] See, for example, the Working Party Report on the Accession of the Russian Federation, in particular with respect to the commitments relating to technical barriers to trade included therein: WTO, Report of the Working Party on the Accession of the Russian Federation to the World Trade Organization, WT/ACC/RUS/70, WT/MIN(11)/2, 17 November 2011, paras. 712, 715, 728, 738, 745, 761, 773, 787, 789 and 803.

agreement on the same subject.[217] The most recent protocol of accession that was examined in the context of this mapping exercise contains more than 60 commitment-containing paragraphs in which reference is made to one and the same RTA.[218] In principle these commitments fall within the second category in that they seek to ensure the conformity of the acceding Member's trade policy with the obligations contained in Article XXIV of the GATT 1994, paragraph 3 of the Enabling Clause and Article V of the GATS.

Kazakhstan's commitment in the field of trade agreements deserves special attention. The commitment, contained in paragraph 313 of its Working Party Report, reads:

> To reflect the results of these negotiations, the CET and the Accession Schedule will be modified. For goods subject to negotiation according to paragraph 309 Kazakhstan confirmed that it would not have recourse to Articles XXIV:6 or XXVIII of the GATT 1994 and will continue to apply the commitments contained in the Accession Schedule from the date of its accession until such time as the adjusted tariff rates are negotiated and agreed by consensus with the affected Members have been bound in the modified schedule of Kazakhstan and been implemented by the EAEU. In case the EAEU does not implement the adjusted rates, the commitments contained in the Accession Schedule would prevail. The Working Party took note of these commitments.[219]

Because of Kazakhstan's trade negotiations in the context of the EAEU, the Members of the Working Party deemed it necessary to prevent Kazakhstan from having recourse to the provisions that govern the renegotiation of tariff concessions.[220] This commitment is a good illustration of the complexities that arise from the negotiation of additional rules commitments in protocols of accession. Recall the Panel's finding in *US – Shrimp II (Viet Nam)* that paragraphs of working party reports

---

[217] In the case of Kazakhstan and the Russian Federation, most references are made to their membership of the Eurasian Economic Union (referred to as the Eurasian Economic Community in the context of Russia's Protocol of Accession) or EAEU.

[218] WTO, Report of the Working Party on the Accession of the Republic of Kazakhstan, WT/ACC/KAZ/93, 23 June 2015. The Working Party Report contains 118 paragraphs that contain a commitment.

[219] WTO, Report of the Working Party on the Accession of the Republic of Kazakhstan, WT/ACC/KAZ/93, 23 June 2015, para. 313.

[220] Hoda, Anwarul (2001), *Tariff Negotiations and Renegotiations under the GATT and the WTO: Procedures and Practices*, Cambridge, Cambridge University Press.

that are not referenced in the concluding paragraph of that report do not constitute treaty text as they have not been integrated into the WTO Agreement (section 4.2.2.2.2). Paragraph 313 refers back to paragraph 309, which are both referenced in paragraph 1175 and which, hence, constitute treaty text. However, paragraph 309 subsequently refers back to paragraph 305, which stipulates (in relevant part) that:

> [t]he representative of Kazakhstan confirmed that, as a result of negotiations with those WTO Members with whom it had concluded bilateral goods market access protocols, upon accession:
>
> (a) for those goods for which the final bound tariff rate agreed in bilateral negotiations with WTO Members was lower than the final bound tariff rate of the Russian Federation as set out in its Protocol of Accession, Kazakhstan would bind its final bound tariff rate at the lower rate;
> (b) for those goods for which the final bound tariff rate of the Russian Federation as set out in its Protocol of Accession was lower than the final bound tariff rate agreed in Kazakhstan's bilateral tariff negotiations, Kazakhstan would bind its relevant final bound tariff rate at the lower final bound tariff rate of the Russian Federation;
> (c) for goods identified under subparagraph (b), Kazakhstan would adjust its bindings to reflect the staging of reductions that result from the Protocol of Accession of the Russian Federation; and,
> (d) for those goods for which the current bound tariff rate of the Russian Federation as set out in its Protocol of Accession was lower than the initial or current bound tariff agreed in Kazakhstan's bilateral tariff negotiations, Kazakhstan would bind its relevant initial or current bound tariff rate at the lower current bound tariff rate of the Russian Federation at every stage of implementation.
>
> The results of the bilateral market access negotiations and the commitments undertaken in subparagraphs (a) through (d) are contained in the Schedule of Concessions and Commitments on Goods number CLXXII and form Annex 1 to the Protocol of Accession (hereafter: 'the Accession Schedule').

This paragraph is, however, not referenced in paragraph 1175 and thus, following the Panel Report in *US – Shrimp II (Viet Nam)*, does not constitute treaty text. This construction poses several questions as to the way in which these commitments would eventually be interpreted in WTO dispute settlement should a case ever arise. The implications of this approach are not quite clear, but in any event this constitutes further evidence of the pragmatic approach that working parties have taken in negotiating accession commitments. For further analysis on the issue of waivers, see section 4.3.2.3.

6.10 CONCLUSION

Having examined the commitments contained in 36 protocols of accession and their corresponding working party reports, what can be said about the results of this mapping exercise? Has, as some authors have suggested, the WTO accession process become more burdensome and more difficult for acceding countries and customs territories in terms of the negotiation of rules commitments? Has the number of WTO-Plus, or more stringent, and WTO-Minus, or less stringent, commitments increased over time? Have recently acceded states such as Seychelles, Lao PDR, Afghanistan, Liberia and Kazakhstan had to drive a much harder bargain in order to be granted access to the WTO than, say, Ecuador, Panama or Mongolia? The evidence would suggest that, although the amount of commitments that are contained in working party reports has on average slightly increased, this is not the case.

First, in terms of the *type* of commitments that have been negotiated it appears that there is only one type of commitment that restricts the regulatory autonomy of the acceded Member by prohibiting conduct that other, original, WTO Members may still perform. These commitments relate to the elimination of export duties as discussed in section 6.4.3. However, even for those commitments a distinction can be made between far-reaching commitments such as those entered into by China, Tajikistan and Montenegro and more flexible 'best-efforts' type commitments such as those negotiated by, for example, Croatia. The commitments in this sector are a first illustration of the need on the part of developing countries and LDCs to obtain adequate legal advice during the entire length of the accession process, from the initial request for observer status to the conclusion of the accession package. In this sense it deserves to be mentioned that in respect of the working party reports of two recently acceded LDCs, no reference is made to Article XX of the GATT 1994 in respect of the export duty commitments. However, many of the commitments that have been negotiated merely confirm the acceding Member's intention to adhere to the baseline obligations provided by the WTO Agreement. Similarly, although many of the commitments are relatively specific in the sense that they prescribe a particular method of giving effect to these baseline obligations, this does not confirm the existence of increased hurdles for outsiders to join the organization. Rather, these specific commitments are aimed to ensure that the trade policy framework prevalent in the acceding Member can be adjusted along concrete guidelines, so as to ensure its conformity with the obligations the state or customs territory in question is about to undertake. The commitments undertaken by China, Viet Nam and Tajikistan to allow other WTO Members to apply a different type of methodology in the course of anti-dumping investigations are to be seen as more stringent commitments. They reflect a concern that a large degree of state influence in the economic affairs of these countries could lead to a situation in which no accurate domestic price can be identified in anti-dumping investigations. Another type of commitment that warrants attention is one in which a new Member relinquishes its right to make use of a certain provision of one of the covered agreements. Although this type of commitment is extremely rare – only Kazakhstan appears to have made such a commitment – this is a development that deserves attention.

Second, in terms of *the amount* of commitments that have been agreed to in protocols of accession it should be noted that, although there is a slight increase in the average amount of commitment-containing paragraphs, in general it is fair to say that the amount of commitments is mainly influenced by the type of economy in the acceding state or customs territory. This is illustrated by two examples discussed at length in this chapter. The first example is that of the NMEs. In general, this group of acceding states has had to accept more and more far-reaching commitments than any other type of Member. Regardless of whether the state or customs territory could be characterized as a developing country, if the WTO considered that the economic structure resembles that of an NME – mainly as characterized by the degree of state influence – the acceding state has been required to accept provisions that seek to curtail the negative effects of such state influence. This is most prominent in the field of WTO-Minus commitments that allow for special, NME-designated, anti-dumping methodologies. However, these commitments also reflect concern about the influence of SOEs, as evidenced by the commitments made by China, Viet Nam and Tajikistan. The second example is that of the group of LDCs that acceded to the WTO. These LDCs have, on average, had to accept far fewer and less stringent commitments than other acceding states. This is not to say that in some instances, such as where there is a requirement to implement the provisions of a certain agreement without having recourse to a transitional period, the commitments may be burdensome. However, considering that so far no LDC has been subject to WTO dispute settlement proceedings this may not appear to lead to any problems in practice.

Ultimately it appears that the WTO accession process and the commitments contained in protocols of accession are designed not to make life for acceding states deliberately complicated, but rather to ensure that they are in the best position to reap the benefits of their membership of the WTO. The accession process offers an opportunity for a critical examination of the applicant's trade policy prior to that policy becoming subject to the international legal norms of the WTO. In seeking to ensure that a new Member's trade policy is as WTO-compliant as realistically possible upon accession, the WTO also seeks to prevent that Member from being challenged in WTO dispute settlement proceedings.[221] It would be neither in the interest of the acceding state or customs territory nor in that of the WTO if the accession process amounted to nothing more than a box-ticking exercise. Considering indeed that the WTO features one of the most effective international dispute settlement systems, allowing states to enter without their trade policies being thoroughly scrutinized beforehand would merely mean that they would be challenged in a far more adversarial context upon accession.

---

[221] Toohey, Lisa (2014), 'Accession as Dialogue: Epistemic Communities and the World Trade Organization', *Leiden Journal of International Law* (27) (2), pp. 397–418.

PART IV

Conclusion

7. Concluding remarks

7.1 INTRODUCTION

This concluding chapter summarizes the main findings of this book. There are different categories of WTO Members with different levels of commitments made as part of their accession process. This is inherent in Article XII of the WTO Agreement, which refers to 'terms to be agreed'.[1] The concerns that have been raised in respect of the length and scope of the accession process have not resulted in a reduction in the applications for membership or a reduction in the use that has been made of the dispute settlement system. The WTO is on the road to achieve universal membership. However, although the membership has increased incrementally in the past decade, there are still some 30 states and customs territories that have either not yet applied for membership or that are currently in the process of accession. In this particular context, it cannot be denied that WTO accession is often a challenging process for developing countries and LDCs. After considering the experience of the 36 Members that have acceded under Article XII of the WTO Agreement,

[1] Qin has argued that this phrase should merely be understood as referring to the criteria for original membership, as in Article XI of the WTO Agreement. According to her, '[t]he Appellate Body, therefore, appears to agree that the absence of an express limit on the "terms of accession" authorizes the making of any country-specific rules via accession protocols'. Consequently, Qin argues that, taking into account the context and object and purpose of the WTO Agreement, the substantive conditions for the original membership as found in Article XI of the WTO Agreement 'should also be the substantive conditions for accession'. See Qin (2017), Mind the Gap: Navigating Between the WTO Agreement and Its Accession Protocols, at 234. However, this argument does not seem to be supported by the text of both articles, when read in conjunction. Qin agrees with this observation as she points out that the way in which WTO Members have approached Article XII of the WTO Agreement and its 'terms to be agreed' constitutes 'subsequent practice' in the sense of the Vienna Convention. Nevertheless, in her opinion this practice has 'grave implications for the WTO legal system as it results in "the dismantling of the uniformity of WTO rules", creates "a new exception to the non-discrimination principle" and "damages the legitimacy of the WTO"'.

it seems appropriate to propose some general recommendations to take into account when submitting a WTO accession bid.

7.2 DOES THE WTO HAVE A MULTI-TIERED MEMBERSHIP?

In Chapter 3, the term 'multi-tiered membership', as used in the context of this contribution, was defined as 'the situation in which different Members of the same organization are under different types of rules obligations that determine the way in which they can conduct their trade policy'.[2] In any event, the WTO has a two-tiered membership, composed of original Members and of Members that joined the organization by completing the accession process under Article XII of the WTO Agreement. However, in addition to this preliminary distinction, it is also warranted to conclude that certain groups of acceded Members can be identified based on the amount and type of rules commitments they accepted in their protocols of accession. This does not mean that acceded Members per definition have fewer rights than original Members, nor that they are under more stringent obligations. It does, however, mean that they have accepted tailor-made obligations that seek to address particular aspects of their economic and trade policy at the time of accession. The answer to the question whether the WTO has a multi-tiered membership should therefore be answered affirmatively. Since the inception of the multilateral trading system with the creation of the GATT 1947, the institutional set-up was designed to facilitate the accession of all states and customs territories regardless of their internal economic structure. Chapter 1 concluded that economic considerations have been the main driver behind most accession bids. Nevertheless, incumbent Contracting Parties, and later WTO Members, have always been conscious of the risk that free-riders pose to the system. Therefore, although universalism was always prevalent as an objective, it was never to be achieved regardless of the cost. This is reflected by the slow but steady increase in the number of Contracting Parties to the GATT 1947 and the number of Members of the WTO. The development of the membership of the multilateral trading system was explored in Chapter 2. The incremental growth of the membership can partially be explained by the fact that the concept of reciprocity always has played, and always will play, an extremely important role in the context of any trade negotiation. In order to avoid

---

[2] Section 3.1.

new Members to the system from piggybacking on earlier tariff concessions made by the original Members, the provisions governing the accession of new Members explicitly enabled the negotiations on tariff commitments with the state or customs territory interested in becoming part of the system: the famous 'terms to be agreed'. However, with the increased scope of the multilateral trading system, and the introduction of topics such as subsidies, standards and other non-tariff barriers, the content of the notion 'terms' also broadened exponentially. This topic was further explored in Chapter 3. GATT accession negotiations mainly focused on tariff commitments. However, in the GATT era, Contracting Parties also contemplated the non-application of the entire agreement in respect of certain new Members.[3] Moreover, in some instances, new Contracting Parties made 'import commitments', rather than tariff concessions.[4] These instances indicate that the distinction between market access commitments and rules commitments is crucial. It is submitted that the multi-tieredness of the WTO's membership and the length of the accession negotiations would, to some extent at least, appear to originate more from the fact that in some instances Members seek extensive market access commitments rather than that they originate from unrealistic and unfair rules commitments being imposed. Although several WTO-Plus commitments were identified in Chapter 6, it seems that the perceived lack of balance between original and some non-original Members arises mainly from the demands that are put on the table to obtain improved market access conditions, both in the field of trade in goods and trade in services.

7.3 LAWMAKING IN PROTOCOLS OF ACCESSION

In Chapter 5 the methodology of the mapping exercise was set out. This methodology includes the typology of the commitments contained in protocols of accession that were the subject of the actual exercise conducted in Chapter 6. The overall conclusions from the mapping

---

[3] Wang, Lei (1994), 'Non-Application Issues in the GATT and the WTO', *Journal of World Trade* (28) (2), pp. 49–74, at 58. Noting that '[w]hen Romania acceded to the GATT in 1971, the United States, for domestic law reasons, invoked Article XXXV and did not take part in negotiations on the Romanian import commitments. The condition of non-application in such circumstances went beyond the requirement of the lack of tariff negotiations and extended to the lack of accession negotiations.'

[4] Wang (1994), Non-Application Issues in the GATT and the WTO', at 58.

exercise conducted in Part III of this monograph were that two groups of non-original Members stand out from the average non-original Member. The first group consists of what have been termed 'Non-Market Economies'. Members that belong to this group have had to accept more commitment-containing paragraphs in their protocols of accession and, in general, a part of the commitments they have undertaken go beyond the baseline commitments that are applicable to the rest of the membership. The second group that was identified was the group of LDCs that acceded through the procedure laid down by Article XII of the WTO Agreement. In general the members of this group have had to accept fewer commitments than the average and, barring certain exceptions, their commitments do not appear to go significantly beyond the baseline commitments. The text of Article XII of the WTO Agreement does not place any limits on the type of 'terms' that may be agreed between the WTO and the acceding Member. In acceding to the WTO a state or customs territory exercises its sovereignty at the international level. It submits an accession bid, which is then considered by the WTO. The outcome of the negotiations, the accession package, can thus be assumed to have the support of both the acceded Member and the WTO. The amount and type of WTO-Plus obligations in protocols of accession appears to be limited. Nevertheless, the question can be raised whether these commitments amount to lawmaking conducted outside of the appropriate fora that the WTO provides for this type of activity. Have members of working parties attempted to introduce new disciplines into the WTO framework that are not part of the WTO Agreement itself? Have they used the accession process as a 'rule-making laboratory'? If this is so, how do these new disciplines contained in protocols of accession potentially impact the incumbent Members that are under no such disciplines? The first of these two questions can be answered with a moderate 'yes'. The commitments that have been undertaken on the elimination or reduction of export duties constitute the most prominent example of such lawmaking activity. Regardless of the way in which the commitment has been undertaken, any commitment in this area adds to the obligations contained in the WTO Agreement since that agreement does not contain a prohibition on the use of export duties. Consequently, where Members have attempted to introduce such commitments in working party reports, they have engaged in lawmaking. However, a finding that the accession process has served as a rule-making laboratory does not seem warranted based on the results of the mapping exercise. Nevertheless, the practice of negotiating member-specific commitments is further evidence of the pragmatic approach adopted by the WTO. This in turn gives rise to the second question: can such new disciplines influence the rights and obligations that the other Members of the WTO are under? Typically commitments contained in protocols of accession appear to be directed solely at the Member in question. Nevertheless, as evidenced by the statement contained in the Working Party Report on the Accession of Ukraine, incumbent Members have been aware of the potential implications that the inclusion of such commitments could have on their own rights and obligations:

> The Working Party agreed that these commitments do not constitute a reinterpretation of GATT 1994, *nor affect the rights and obligations of other members* in respect of provisions on the application of export duties, that are measures in accordance with GATT 1994.[5]

Another example relates to the language used in commitments on state-owned enterprises, or state-trading enterprises (see above, section 5.4.3.4). It cannot be excluded that the evolution of the language used in these protocol commitments might – in the long term – have an impact on the interpretation of similar provisions in the context of WTO dispute settlement. Although the commitments are member-specific, some have argued that the language used might serve as relevant context in future disputes. Whether this approach endangers the single undertaking approach that was adopted in the Uruguay Round is questionable. Leaving aside the question of whether this approach is useful in 21st century trade negotiations, it is not warranted to conclude that the commitments contained in protocols of accession would undermine the single undertaking. Although, indeed, there are commitments that deviate from the baseline obligations that are found in the WTO Agreement, in general these commitments are *based on* these very obligations. In some instances they may provide more detailed guidance on how a particular obligation should be implemented in the domestic legislation of the acceding Member, but overall this approach reveals a desire to ensure the correct implementation of the obligations that form part of the single undertaking. As such, it would seem that the accession process, if anything, strengthens, rather than weakens, the single undertaking.[6]

---

[5] WTO, Report of the Working Party on the Accession of Ukraine to the World Trade Organization, WT/ACC/UKR/152, 25 January 2008, para. 240 (emphasis added).

[6] Kireyev, Alexei and Sekkate, Mustapha (2015), WTO Accessions: What Does the Academic Literature Say?, in Dadush, Uri and Osakwe, Chiedu (eds) (2015), *WTO Accessions and Trade Multilateralism: Case Studies and Lessons from the WTO at Twenty*, Cambridge, Cambridge University Press, pp. 198–216, at 213. Kireyev and Sekkate argue that '[e]ven when trade negotiations stall,

Moreover, this argument assumes that the concept of a single undertaking is a goal in itself that should be maintained throughout all negotiations that take place in the context of the WTO. Whether this approach is desirable at all is subject to debate.[7] The fact that the accession package reflects the common desire of both the acceded Member and the WTO is a sufficient ground to assume that this is, indeed, what both parties wanted. The foregoing serves as further confirmation of the idea that trade lawmakers do not consider the WTO Agreement as a constitution, but rather regard the system much from a private contract law perspective.[8] This finding is supported by accession practice. In the first place, the language of Article XII of the WTO Agreement – 'terms to be agreed' – exemplifies this focus on treating the accession commitments as a sort of contract. It should be noted that when drafting the WTO Agreement in the course of the Uruguay Round, GATT Contracting

---

accession negotiations continue and contribute to rule-making, eliminating legal ambiguities and, overall, upgrading the multilateral trading system'.

[7] See, in particular, Rolland, Sonia E. (2010), 'Redesigning the Negotiation Process at the WTO', *Journal of International Economic Law* (13) (1), pp. 65–110. Rolland concludes that '[i]n normative terms, the strive for consistency in trade rules, which has been a major underpinning to the single undertaking approach, should not trump consideration of other values and objectives of the trading system that are included in the Marrakesh Agreement'. Lanoszka, Anna (2008), 'The Promises of Multilateralism and the Hazards of "Single Undertaking": The Breakdown of Decision Making within the WTO', *Michigan State Journal of International Law* (16) (2), pp. 655–75; VanGrasstek, Craig and Sauvé, Pierre (2006), 'The Consistency of WTO Rules: Can The Single Undertaking Be Squared with Variable Geometry?', *Journal of International Economic Law* (9) (4), pp. 837–64; Wolfe, Robert (2009), 'The WTO Single Undertaking as Negotiating Technique and Constitutive Metaphor', *Journal of International Economic Law* (12) (4), pp. 835–58.

[8] Lamp, Nicolas (2013), 'Lawmaking in the Multilateral Trading System', PhD thesis, Department of Law, London School of Economics and Political Science, September. Lamp submits that '[f]ollowing in the footsteps of John Jackson, it is commonplace for academics to regard the trading system as in some way a constitutional entity, a view that has gained particular currency in light of the exclusive and compulsory jurisdiction of the WTO's dispute settlement organs, and of the possibility to enforce their rulings through officially authorised and supervised trade sanctions. *There is little to no evidence, however that this view of the trading system is shared by the participants in trade lawmaking; instead, the model that has been consistently invoked by trade negotiators, particularly those from developed countries, is that of the private law contract.*'

Parties had the opportunity to change the text of this article.[9] Recall further the finding in section 2.3.2.3 that similar language has been included in the provision in the text of the Trans-Pacific Partnership (TPP) that governs accession to that agreement.[10] Second, the actual content of the commitments is further evidence of this approach. The commitments are, to a large extent, tailor-made. They reflect the concerns that the WTO has in respect of the prevailing trade policy and economic structure of the acceding state in question.

7.4 PROTOCOLS OF ACCESSION IN WTO DISPUTE SETTLEMENT

In only 5.3 per cent of all requests for consultations the violation of an accession protocol commitment was alleged by the complaining Member. This indicates that WTO Members appear to exercise due restraint in respect of the commitments that have been entered into by acceding Members. This finding is further confirmed by the fact that, so far, only alleged violations of commitments made by two non-original Members have been challenged.[11] Clearly one should exercise caution in using these statistics as support for the argument that WTO-Plus commitments should not be overstated. However, what these numbers indicate is that there is little evidence of WTO Members using the dispute settlement system to enforce allegedly strict accession protocol commitments vis-à-vis non-original Members. Nevertheless, where measures allegedly violating the commitments contained in protocols of accession have been

---

[9] Qin, Julia Ya (2015), 'The Conundrum of WTO Accession Protocols: In Search of Legality and Legitimacy', *Virginia Journal of International Law* (55) (2), pp. 370–450, at 443. Qin has suggested that the drafters should have included a phrase such as 'such terms shall be based on principles consistent with those applied to the Original Members of the WTO' to Article XII in order to emphasize that there shall be no discrimination between original and acceding Members. She appoints the failure to do so to oversight, as 'the adoption of such a provision would not have been controversial at the time the WTO Agreement was drafted'. Qin, however, acknowledges that because 'the WTO accession practice has developed in the opposite direction' it 'has become politically infeasible to reinstate this principled position'.

[10] That provision even explicitly includes the word 'conditions' in addition to the word 'terms'.

[11] China and Viet Nam have been the only two non-original Members who have been challenged in WTO dispute settlement proceedings based on an alleged violation of one or more of their accession protocol commitments.

challenged, complainants have mostly been successful.[12] The interpretation of the language used in protocol commitments has led panels and the Appellate Body to decide that – in the absence of an explicit cross-reference – the general exceptions contained in another covered agreement were not available to remedy a measure that was allegedly inconsistent with such a commitment. These decisions have been criticized but, ultimately, the decisions do not appear to have eroded the trust WTO Members have in the dispute settlement system. Therefore, although the interpretative approach that has been adopted might have resulted in outcomes that might appear unjust to certain scholars in the case of some disputes, in general this approach seems to ensure the coherence of the system as a whole. Moreover, it is to be expected that the Appellate Body took into account protocols of accession of other acceded Members in its interpretative exercise, in order to preclude any further disruption of the balance between old and new Members. Although this is not directly evident from the reports in question, it would appear unlikely for the Appellate Body not to have at least considered the commitments on the elimination and reduction of export duties made by other acceded Members. Perhaps this serves as evidence for the statement that the legitimizing function of the reports should be taken more seriously, and that the Appellate Body should be even more detailed in its reasoning. However, stating explicitly that other protocols of accession had been taken into account would have amounted to suggesting that these constitute relevant context in the sense of Article 31 of the Vienna Convention. In the absence of any arguments to this effect, it may have been considered unnecessary to explicitly state that commitments made by other acceded Members were indeed analysed. Considering that only a few Members have adopted a commitment that would appear to preclude recourse to Article XX of the GATT 1994 in respect of alleged violations of these commitments, the Appellate Body seems to have adopted an approach that is aimed at maintaining the integrity of the system as a whole. In general Members seem to have accepted this interpretative approach, presumably because they agree that it contributes to the overall stability and predictability of the rules-based multilateral trading system. Were the Appellate Body to have adopted a more activist

[12] It should be noted that this corresponds with the general trend in WTO dispute settlement: over 85% of disputes that reach the 'panel stage' result in a finding of at least one inconsistency with the respondent's WTO obligations. This is the result of the organizational structure of the dispute settlement system that, because of its emphasis on holding consultations prior to moving to litigation, filters out unsuccessful complaints at an early stage.

approach, by holding that, even in the absence of an explicit reference, the general exceptions contained in Article XX of the GATT 1994 would be applicable, this would have created a precedent that might have had unforeseeable consequences.[13] Finding that this provision could be available to justify violations of a protocol of accession could have opened the door for claims that Article XX of the GATT 1994 should also be available to justify violations of other non-GATT agreements such as the SCM Agreement.[14] It appears that WTO Members, generally speaking, appreciate the predictable, yet allegedly textualist, approach that prevails in WTO dispute settlement proceedings. The belief and confidence in the dispute settlement system of the WTO appears to be stronger than ever. WTO Members still bring their disputes to Geneva even if there are RTA dispute settlement provisions available. This finding is testament to the faith and trust that Members put in the Geneva-based system. While some consider that the Appellate Body's approach amounts to lawmaking and exceeding its mandate, others criticize the Appellate Body for not going far enough.[15]

---

[13] Unterhalter, David (2015), The Appellate Body under Review, in Marceau, Gabrielle (ed.) (2015), *A History of Law and Lawyers in the GATT/WTO: The Development of the Rule of Law in the Multilateral Trading System*, Cambridge, Cambridge University Press, pp. 466–75. Unterhalter notes that '[a]n interpretation that deviates from what a WTO member considers to have been negotiated is not likely to be taken as an interpretation that is reasonable but wrong. [...] It is for this reason that the Appellate Body has so deliberately avoided interpretations that are not rooted in the strictures of the Vienna Convention on the Law of Treaties, even at the risk of a certain mechanistic formalism.'

[14] Although it should be noted that the different natures of protocols of accession and covered agreements would also suggest that this argument might not be as easy to make as it might seem at the outset.

[15] Compare the approaches proposed by Steger and Qin respectively: see Steger, Debra P. (2005), The Challenges to the Legitimacy of the WTO, in Charnovitz, Steve, Steger, Debra P. and Van den Bossche, Peter (eds), *Law in the Service of Human Dignity: Essays in Honour of Florentino Feliciano*, Cambridge, Cambridge University Press, pp. 202–21 at 203–4; and Qin (2015), The Conundrum of WTO Accession Protocols: In Search of Legality and Legitimacy, at 445.

7.5 LESSONS FOR THE FUTURE – TOWARDS UNIVERSAL MEMBERSHIP

The political nature of the accession process clearly poses a number of problems that particularly affect capacity-constrained developing countries and Least-Developed Countries that wish to join the organization. Indeed, it is true that WTO accessions can be extremely lengthy and burdensome on the applicant state. However, it should be noted that the WTO is acutely aware of this problem and several initiatives have been employed to address it. One of these initiatives is the WTO's Least-Developed Countries and Accessions Programme which is also known as the 'China Programme'. This programme was launched under the Aid for Trade initiative in 2011 and 'aims to help least-developed countries (LDCs) integrate more effectively into the global economy by strengthening their participation in WTO activities and by helping those not yet members to join the Organization'.[16] The programme encompasses the WTO accessions internship programme, accessions round table meetings, and the participation of LDCs in various WTO meetings.[17] These initiatives, organized or initiated by WTO Members who have gone through the process of accession themselves can play an important role in trying to enlarge the membership of the organization by sharing experiences with LDCs. Other examples of initiatives aimed at sharing experiences of acceded Members with countries that have yet to accede include the publication of case studies on the WTO website, the interactive e-training course on the accession process, the publication of an edited volume on WTO accessions and trade multilateralism, and other accession-related technical assistance activities.[18] Currently there are 21 states that have applied for WTO membership and who are involved in the WTO accession process. Although the accession process of Azerbaijan appears to be relatively well advanced, the other accessions do not appear to be moving along swiftly. In at least five instances this can be explained by the fact that the countries in question are currently, or have

[16] WTO (2015), President Kenyatta Calls for Successful MC10 at China Round Table on LDC Accessions. Available at https://www.wto.org/english/news_e/news15_e/tech_14dec15_e.htm (last accessed at 20 October 2017).

[17] WTO (2015), President Kenyatta Calls for Successful MC10 at China Round Table on LDC Accessions. Available at https://www.wto.org/english/news_e/news15_e/tech_14dec15_e.htm (last accessed at 20 October 2017).

[18] WTO, Accession-Related Technical Assistance Activities. Available at https://www.wto.org/english/thewto_e/acc_e/acc_ta_e.htm (last accessed at 20 October 2017).

recently been, involved in military conflict. As a result, the priorities of their respective governments undoubtedly are in different areas. Other states face capacity-related problems which hampers progress in the accession process. It is difficult to estimate when the accessions of these 19 countries can reasonably be expected to be completed.[19] Even more difficult is estimating if and when the remaining non-observer states will submit an accession bid to the WTO.[20] States such as Eritrea, Somalia and South Sudan do not appear to be in a position to apply for accession in the short term. The same applies to North Korea, which is isolated in the international sphere. It also appears unlikely that Monaco and San Marino would apply for accession any time soon, considering that their economies are small and their share in global trade is minimal as well. With the accession of the Russian Federation in 2011, all major economies have now joined the multilateral trading system. Nevertheless, considering that there is still some way to go before the WTO can truly claim to have universal membership, what should acceding states, and states that might consider submitting a membership application in the future, be aware of?[21] What are the pitfalls for states that enter the WTO accession process? What should they take into account during their accession negotiations? Two main recommendations for states seeking to become a part of the multilateral trading system seem to be in order.[22] First, in terms of the general process of accession, it is essential that states have a clear idea of what they intend to obtain from WTO membership and what the price is that they are willing to pay for these benefits.[23] Consequently, it is advisable that acceding states and entities seek (legal) advice from either the private sector or from institutions such

---

[19] Toohey, Lisa (2012), 'Barriers to Universal Membership of the World Trade Organization', *Australian International Law Journal* (19), pp. 97–115.

[20] Eritrea, Federated States of Micronesia, Kiribati, Marshall Islands, North Korea, Monaco, Nauru, Palau, San Marino, Somalia, South Sudan, Timor-Leste, Turkmenistan and Tuvalu.

[21] Drabek, Zdenek and Woo, Wing Thye (2010), Who Should Join the WTO and Why? A Cost-Benefit Analysis of WTO Membership, in Drabek, Zdenek (ed.) (2010), *Is the World Trade Organization Attractive Enough for Emerging Economies? Critical Essays on the Multilateral Trading System*, Basingstoke, Palgrave Macmillan, pp. 249–93.

[22] See also Kireyev and Sekkate (2015), WTO Accessions: What Does the Academic Literature Say?, at 212.

[23] Kavass, Igor I. (2007), 'WTO Accession: Procedure, Requirements and Costs', *Journal of World Trade* (41) (3), pp. 453–74.

as the Geneva-based Advisory Centre on WTO Law (ACWL).[24] States such as Seychelles, which became a Member of the WTO in 2015, acceded to the ACWL in 2003. The ACWL also notes that LDCs that are Members of the WTO or in the process of acceding to the WTO are entitled to its legal services without becoming a Member of the Centre.[25] Second, in terms of concrete legal advice on particular issues to be negotiated as part of the accession process, it is extremely important to be conscious of the fact that the commitment-containing paragraphs of working party reports on the accession of a particular state constitute treaty text and are, as such, enforceable in WTO dispute settlement proceedings. Therefore it is vital for acceding entities to be aware that the language used in particular commitments matters. The absence of cross-references to particular provisions in the WTO Agreement may have as a consequence that such provisions cannot be relied upon to justify an alleged violation of a protocol commitment. Considering the controversy that arose because of the lack of such cross-references in China's Protocol of Accession in respect of its commitments on the elimination of export duties it is surprising that some of the more recently made commitments also do not contain such a cross-reference. At the same time it should be noted that the approach adopted by the working parties dealing with the accessions of the Russian Federation and Kazakhstan would appear to guarantee the availability of the general exceptions contained in Article XX of the GATT 1994 by incorporating the export duty commitments in the schedule of concessions. More generally it is important that the WTO itself maintains the focus on accessions that it has developed in recent years. In order to ensure that the objective of universal membership is kept in mind, the WTO should remain focused on providing trade-related technical assistance and capacity-building.[26] Such assistance should not just be provided to its Members, but also to countries that have requested observer status and even to countries that

---

[24] Bown, Chad P. and McCulloch, Rachel (2010), 'Developing Countries, Dispute Settlement and the Advisory Centre on WTO Law', *The Journal of International Trade & Economic Development: An International and Comparative Review* (19) (1), pp. 33–63.

[25] ACWL, Members. Available at http://www.acwl.ch/members-introduction/ (last accessed at 20 October 2017).

[26] Primo Braga, Carlos A. and Cattaneo, Olivier (eds) (2009), *The WTO and Accession Countries*, vols I and II, Cheltenham, UK and Northampton, MA, USA, Edward Elgar, at 559; Martin, Will (2010), Development Implications of WTO Accession Procedures, in Drabek, Zdenek (ed.) (2010), *Is the World Trade Organization Attractive Enough for Emerging Economies? Critical Essays on the Multilateral Trading System*, Basingstoke, Palgrave Macmillan, pp. 13–36.

have not yet requested such status. Of course, in the case of the latter, this should be subject to the country in question being open to receive such assistance when it is offered. Spreading knowledge of the multilateral trading system and building capacity in developing countries and LDCs is crucial for the continued legitimacy of the system.[27] The developmental dimension is clearly embedded in the objectives and functions of the WTO and as such should also be at the forefront of any discussions dealing with WTO accession. In this respect the continued contribution of the WTO to initiatives such as the European Law Students' Association (ELSA) Moot Court Competition on WTO Law (ELSA EMC) can only be applauded. In particular the creation of an African Regional Round in which teams from the African continent compete for a place in the global final in Geneva is to be welcomed. By enabling students from countries that are not yet WTO Members, such as Ethiopia, to take part in the competition, the WTO seeks to ensure that a new generation of trade lawyers is raised.

The concern that the accession process is becoming ever more burdensome and that increasingly stringent commitments are demanded from applicant states appears to be somewhat overstated in light of the findings presented in this monograph. Although it is undeniable that acceded Members have had to accept a substantial amount of commitment-containing paragraphs in the working party reports on their respective accessions, the amount of WTO-Plus rules obligations is relatively limited. Moreover, where additional commitments have been required, this has mostly been a reflection of particular concerns regarding the economic structure and trade policy of the acceding state in question. Returning to some of the observations presented earlier, it appears that the constraints faced by acceded developing and Least-Developed Countries in the actual implementation of the commitments are far more important than the amount of such commitments. In that respect it can only be hoped that the WTO as an organization, as well as its individual Members, will continue to contribute to and invest in accession-related capacity-building projects.

It is regrettable that the Doha Development Agenda appears to have died a slow death, notwithstanding the agreements that have been reached on certain individual issues. However, it should be mentioned that, in order to remain relevant, the WTO has to adapt to the changed circumstances in the world of international trade. The emergence of global value chains, the

---

[27] Bienen, Derk (2014), What Can Least Developed Countries Acceding to the World Trade Organization Learn from Other Acceded Countries?, BKP Development Research & Consulting, Trade and Development Discussion Paper No. 1/2014.

digital economy, e-commerce and the increase in cross-border investment are issues that cannot be ignored. Any future negotiating agenda in the WTO should reflect these new realities. However, it deserves mentioning that in times of an increase in regionalism, the corresponding fragmentation of international (economic) law and the emergence of a multi-polar world order, the WTO and the rules-based multilateral trading system constitute a relative safe-haven for developing and Least-Developed Countries. Where large economies have the ability and strength to conclude *inter se* agreements that reflect their interests, smaller economies largely depend on the Geneva-based system to make their interests heard. Therefore, the issue of WTO accession remains relevant, at least until the organization can truly claim universal membership.

Nevertheless, one can validly ask the question what a country such as Afghanistan – with a small share of trade as a percentage of GDP – has to gain by seeking WTO membership. Do the opportunity costs associated with having delegates in Geneva not outweigh the benefits that can be obtained in the short, or even the medium, term? It is submitted that completing the accession process brings about at least one major benefit in addition to the membership of the WTO itself. During the accession process emphasis is placed on developing a system of good governance and the creation of the rule of law. Several of the commitments in protocols of accession reflect this. Rule of law and good governance are prerequisites for increasing trade and investment. However, on a broader scale, the emphasis placed by the WTO – during the accession process – on creating independent tribunals that can hear complaints concerning matters relating to the WTO Agreement may lead to an increased awareness of the importance of the rule of law in developing countries. In later stages, the establishment of the rule of law in domestic proceedings relating to international trade may lead to the creation of a legal culture in which the rule of law is implemented on a larger scale. In this sense, WTO accession may represent a small, yet important step in the creation of a system of good governance in states where such a system was previously absent. It is submitted that future research could focus on the question whether the implementation of the commitments contained in protocols of accession may indeed lead to a better rule of law and good governance in non-original Members.

7.6 CONCLUSION

WTO accession is an intensive and often time-consuming exercise that requires commitment and preparation on behalf of the acceding state or customs territory. The outcome of this exercise may be summarized as the entry fee to the World Trade Organization, the multilateral trading system. This entry fee may include certain additional commitments that the new Member has promised to undertake. The WTO accession process has led to a situation in which there are different categories of Members which are under partially different obligations. In this sense, the membership of the WTO can indeed be characterized as multi-tiered. However, in general, the amount of commitments that are agreed upon in the course of the process of accession has not increased over time. Moreover, there is limited evidence that points at a situation in which these commitments have become more stringent over time. Rather, as has always been the intention of the drafters of the article that governs accession, the commitments are often country-specific, taking into account the peculiarities of the applicant's trade policy. The accession process appears to be aimed at ensuring that states and customs territories that wish to join the WTO are, from the date of accession, in compliance with as many as possible of the obligations that WTO Members have agreed to. Indeed, this may pose different burdens on different applicants, depending on their stage of economic development. However, it has been found that the number of commitments made by Least-Developed Countries (LDCs) is significantly lower than, for example, the number of commitments made by non-market economies (NMEs). This is, however, not to say that the WTO should not be cautious of the negative aspects that also form part of the accession process. There is still progress to be made in assisting capacity-constrained states and customs territories in making a successful accession bid. Moreover, although the membership of the WTO has increased steadily, there is still quite a way to go until it can claim universal membership. Since there are a number of applicants whose accession process is 'on hold' the WTO should think about ways that would ensure that the ongoing accessions are concluded as swiftly as possible. However, one should not forget that in this respect the acceding states and customs territories bear an equal degree of responsibility. There is no such thing as a free lunch in the context of the WTO. Hopefully, with increased technical assistance and trade-related capacity-building the WTO can sooner rather than later claim to have universal membership, as it can only be desired that the remaining non-Members can soon enjoy the benefits that the multilateral trading system undoubtedly brings.

Selected bibliography

Aaronson, Susan Ariel and Abouharb, M. Rodwan (2011), 'Unexpected Bedfellows: The GATT, the WTO and *Some* Democratic Rights', *International Studies Quarterly* (55) (2), pp. 379–408.

Aaronson, Susan Ariel and Abouharb, M. Rodwan (2013), 'Does the WTO Help Member States Improve Governance?', *World Trade Review* (13) (3), pp. 547–82.

Ala'i, Padideh and D'Orsi, Matthew (2011), Transparency in International Economic Relations and the Role of the WTO, in Ala'i, Padideh and Vaughn, Robert G. (eds) (2011), *Research Handbook on Transparency*, Cheltenham, UK and Northampton, MA, USA, Edward Elgar, pp. 368–99.

Allee, Todd L. and Scalera, Jamie E. (2012), 'The Divergent Effects of Joining International Organizations: Trade Gains and the Rigors of WTO Accession', *International Organization* (66) (2), pp. 243–76.

Andersen, Scott and Lau, Christian (2002), 'Hedging Hopes with Fears in China's Accession to the World Trade Organization: The Transitional Special-Product Safeguard for Chinese Exports', *The Journal of World Intellectual Property* (5) (3), pp. 405–76.

Anderson, Kym (2014), 'Contributions of the GATT/WTO to Global Economic Welfare: Empirical Evidence', *Journal of Economic Surveys* (30) (1), pp. 56–92.

Au, Thomas H. (2013), 'Reconciling WTO General Exceptions with China's Accession Protocol', *Tsinghua China Law Review* (5) (2), pp. 95–125.

Bagwell, Kyle and Staiger, Robert W. (1999), 'An Economic Theory of GATT', *The American Economic Review* (89) (1), pp. 215–48.

Baldwin, Richard (2014), 'WTO 2.0: Governance of 21st Century Trade', *The Review of International Organizations* (9) (2), pp. 261–83.

Baroncini, Elisa (2013), 'The Applicability of GATT Article XX to China's WTO Accession Protocol in the Appellate Body Report of the China – Raw Materials Case: Suggestions for a Different Interpretative Approach', *China-EU Law Journal* (1) (3–4), pp. 1–34.

Basra, Hardeep (2012), 'Increased Legalization or Politicalization? A Comparison of Accession under the GATT and WTO', *Journal of World Trade* (46) (4), pp. 937–60.

Beslać, Petra and Osakwe, Chiedu (2015), The Evolution of the GATT/WTO Accession Protocol: Legal Tightening and Domestic Ratification, in Dadush, Uri and Osakwe, Chiedu (eds) (2015), *WTO Accessions and Trade Multilateralism: Case Studies and Lessons from the WTO at Twenty*, Cambridge, Cambridge University Press, pp. 348–93.

Benedek, Wolfgang and Ginther, Konrad (1988), Planned-Economy Countries and GATT: Legal Issues of Accession, in *German Yearbook of International Law/Jahrbuch für Internationales Recht* (31), pp. 70–106.

Bhattacharya, Alexandra and Laker Apecu, Joan (2015), Intellectual Property Rights Protection: The Plus/Minus Debate from a Least-Developed Country Perspective – Sense and Nonsense, in Dadush, Uri and Osakwe, Chiedu (eds) (2015), *WTO Accessions and Trade Multilateralism: Case Studies and Lessons from the WTO at Twenty*, Cambridge, Cambridge University Press, pp. 795–817.

Bown, Chad P. and Crowley, Meredith A. (2010), 'China's Export Growth and the China Safeguard: Threats to the World Trading System?', *Canadian Journal of Economics* (43) (4), pp. 1353–88.

Bratanov, Dimitar (2015), Disciplining State Trading Practices: Lessons from WTO Accession Negotiations, in Dadush, Uri and Osakwe, Chiedu (eds) (2015), *WTO Accessions and Trade Multilateralism: Case Studies and Lessons from the WTO at Twenty*, Cambridge, Cambridge University Press, pp. 764–94.

Brazys, Samuel (2014), 'Outside Looking In: Non-Accession to the WTO', *Cambridge Review of International Affairs* (27) (4), pp. 644–65.

Bronckers, Marco and Maskus, Keith A. (2014), 'China – Raw Materials: A Controversial Step Towards Evenhanded Exploitation of Natural Resources', *World Trade Review* (13) (2), pp. 393–408.

Butkeviciene, Jolita, Hayashi, Michiko, Ognivtsev, Victor and Yamaoka, Tokio (2001), 'Terms of WTO Accession' in United Nations Conference on Trade and Development (2001), *WTO Accessions and Development Policies*, Geneva, United Nations, UNCTAD/DITC/TNCD/11, pp. 155–76.

Carroll, Peter (2014), 'Policy Transfer and Accession: A Comparison of Three International Governmental Organizations', *Journal of Comparative Policy Analysis: Research and Practice* (16) (3), pp. 280–96.

Chang, Pao-Li and Lee, Myoung-Jae (2011), 'The WTO Trade Effect', *Journal of International Economics* (85), pp. 53–71.

Charnovitz, Steve (2008), Mapping the Law of WTO Accession, in Janow, Merit E., Donaldson, Victoria and Yanovich, Alan (eds), *The WTO: Governance, Dispute Settlement and Developing Countries*, Huntington, NY, Juris Publishing, pp. 855–920.

Charnovitz, Steve and Hoekman, Bernard (2013), '*US – Tyres*: Upholding a WTO Accession Contract – Imposing Pain for Little Gain', *World Trade Review* (12) (2), pp. 273–96.

Cossy, Mireille (2012), Energy Trade and WTO Rules: Reflexions on Sovereignty over Natural Resources, Export Restrictions and Freedom of Transit, in Herrmann, Christoph and Terhechte, Jörg Philipp (eds) (2012), *European Yearbook of International Economic Law*, vol. 3, Heidelberg, Springer, pp. 281–306.

Curzon, Gerard (1965), *Multilateral Commercial Diplomacy: The General Agreement on Tariffs and Trade and Its Impact on National Commercial Politics and Techniques*, London, Joseph.

Curzon, Gerard and Curzon, Victoria (1989), 'Non-Discrimination and the Rise of "Material" Reciprocity', *The World Economy* (12) (4), pp. 481–500.

Dadush, Uri and Osakwe, Chiedu (eds) (2015), *WTO Accessions and Trade Multilateralism: Case Studies and Lessons from the WTO at Twenty*, Cambridge, Cambridge University Press.

Davis, Christina L. and Wilf, Meredith (2013), 'Joining the Club: Accession to the GATT/WTO', *The Journal of Politics* (79) (3), pp. 964–78.

Davis, Christina and Wilf, Meredith (2015), WTO Membership, in Martin, Lisa L. (ed.), *The Oxford Handbook of the Political Economy of International Trade*, New York, Oxford University Press.

Desta, Melaku Geboye (2009), 'Accession for What? An Examination of Ethiopia's Decision to Join the WTO', *Journal of World Trade* (43) (2), pp. 339–62.

Drabek, Zdenek and Woo, Wing Thye (2010), Who Should Join the WTO and Why? A Cost-Benefit Analysis of WTO Membership, in Drabek, Zdenek (ed.), *Is the World Trade Organization Attractive Enough for Emerging Economies? Critical Essays on the Multilateral Trading System*, Basingstoke, Palgrave Macmillan, pp. 249–93.

Du, Michael Ming (2012), 'Letter to the Editors: Has the WTO Appellate Body Pushed the Limits of Global Governance in the China-Publications Case? A Reply to Julia Qin', *Chinese Journal of International Law* (11), pp. 227–34.

Ehring, Lothar (2013), Nature and Status of WTO Accession Commitments: 'WTO-Plus' Obligations and Their Relationship to Other Parts of the WTO Agreement, in Cremona, Marise, Hilpold, Peter, Lavranos, Nikos, Schneider, Stefan Staiger and Ziegler, Andreas R. (eds), *Reflections on the Constitutionalisation of International Economic Law: Liber Amicorum for Ernst-Ulrich Petersmann*, Leiden, Martinus Nijhoff Publishers, pp. 337–61.

Espa, Ilaria (2012), 'The Appellate Body Approach to the Applicability of Article XX GATT in the Light of China – Raw Materials: A Missed Opportunity?', *Journal of World Trade* (46) (6), pp. 1399–424.

Espa, Ilaria (2015), *Export Restrictions on Critical Minerals and Metals: Testing the Adequacy of WTO Disciplines*, Cambridge, Cambridge University Press.

Fabri, Hélène Ruiz (2014), 'Is There a Case – Legally and Politically – for Direct Effect of WTO Obligations?', *European Journal of International Law* (25) (1), pp. 151–73.

Graafsma, Folkert and Kumashova, Elena (2014), 'In re China's Protocol of Accession and the Anti-Dumping Agreement: Temporary Derogation or Permanent Modification?', *Global Trade and Customs Journal* (9) (4), pp. 154–9.

Grant, Jason H. and Boys, Kathryn A. (2012), 'Agricultural Trade and the GATT/WTO: Does Membership Make a Difference?', *American Journal of Agricultural Economics* (94) (1), pp. 1–24.

Grynberg, Roman and Joy, Roy Mickey (2000), 'The Accession of Vanuatu to the WTO: Lessons for the Multilateral Trading System', *Journal of World Trade* (34) (6), pp. 159–73.

Hoda, Anwarul (2001), *Tariff Negotiations and Renegotiations under the GATT and the WTO: Procedures and Practices*, Cambridge, Cambridge University Press.

Huang, Chieh (2009), 'Non-Market Economies' Accessions to the WTO: Evolution of the Approach and Implications for the Organization', *The Hague Journal of Diplomacy* (4), pp. 61–81.

Huang, Dongli (2006), 'Legal Interpretation of Paragraph 242 of the Report of the Working Party on the Accession of China under the World Trade Organization Legal Framework', *Journal of World Trade* (40) (1), pp. 137–52.

Hufbauer, Gary Clyde and Cimino-Isaacs, Cathleen (2015), 'How Will TPP and TTIP Change the WTO System?', *Journal of International Economic Law* (18) (3), pp. 679–96.

Irwin, Douglas A. and Weiler, Joseph (2008), 'Measures Affecting the Cross-Border Supply of Gambling and Betting Services (DS285)', *World Trade Review* (7) (1), pp. 71–113.

Irwin, Douglas A., Mavroidis, Petros C. and Sykes, Alan O. (2008), *The Genesis of the GATT*, New York, Cambridge University Press.

Jackson, John H. (1969), *World Trade Law and the Law of GATT: A Legal Analysis of the General Agreement on Tariffs and Trade*, Charlottesville, VA, The Michie Company/Bobbs Merill.

Jackson, John H. (1997), *The World Trading System: Law and Policy of International Economic Relations*, Second Edition, Cambridge, MA, MIT Press.

Jackson, John H. (2000), *The Jurisprudence of GATT & the WTO*, Cambridge, Cambridge University Press.

Jones, Kent (2009), 'The Political Economy of WTO Accession: The Unfinished Business of Universal Membership', *World Trade Review* (8) (2), pp. 279–314.

Jones, Kent (2010), *The Doha Blues: Institutional Crisis and Reform in the WTO*, Oxford, Oxford University Press.

Karapinar, Baris (2012), 'Defining the Legal Boundaries of Export Restrictions: A Case Law Analysis', *Journal of International Economic Law* (15) (2), pp. 443–79.

Kennedy, Kevin C. (1987), 'The Accession of the Soviet Union to GATT', *Journal of World Trade* (21), pp. 23–39.

Kennedy, Matthew (2011), 'Two Single-Undertakings: Can the WTO Implement the Results of a Round?', *Journal of International Economic Law* (14) (1), pp. 77–120.

Kennedy, Matthew (2012), 'China's Role in WTO Dispute Settlement', *World Trade Review* (11) (4), pp. 555–89.

Kennedy, Matthew (2013), 'The Integration of Accession Protocols into the WTO Agreement', *Journal of World Trade* (47) (1), pp. 45–76.

Kim, Myeong Hwan (2010), 'Does the WTO Promote Trade? Further Evidence', *The Journal of International Trade & Economic Development: An International and Comparative Review* (19) (3), pp. 421–37.

Kireyev, Alexei and Sekkate, Mustapha (2015), WTO Accessions: What Does the Academic Literature Say?, in Dadush, Uri and Osakwe, Chiedu (eds) (2015), *WTO Accessions and Trade Multilateralism: Case Studies and Lessons from the WTO at Twenty*, Cambridge, Cambridge University Press, pp. 198–216.

Kong, Qingjiang (2000), 'China's WTO Accession: Commitments and Implications', *Journal of International Economic Law* (3) (4), pp. 655–90.

Laczkowski, Bohdan (1971), 'Poland's Accession to GATT', *Journal of World Trade* (5) (1), pp. 110–19.

Lane, William P. (2013), 'Trapped in China's Shadow? Intellectual Property Protection in Post-WTO-Accession Russia', *Boston College International & Comparative Law Review* (36), pp. 183–217.

Lanoszka, Anna (2001), 'The World Trade Organization Accession Process: Negotiating Participation in a Globalizing Economy', *Journal of World Trade* (35) (4), pp. 575–602.

Lee, Yong-Shik (2012), 'First WTO Case on Transitional Product-Safeguard Measure under Section 16 of the Protocol of China's Accession to the WTO: Affirming Discriminatory Safeguard Measure by the WTO?', *Journal of World Trade* (46) (4), pp. 913–36.

Lester, Simon, Mercurio, Bryan and Davies, Arwel (2012), *World Trade Law: Text, Materials and Commentary*, Oxford, Hart Publishing.

Liu, Han-Wei and Maughan, John (2012), 'China's Rare Earths Export Quotas: Out of the China – Raw Materials Gate, but Past the WTO's Finish Line?, *Journal of International Economic Law* (15) (4), pp. 971–1005.

Lücke, Matthias (1995), 'The Impact of Accession to GATT on the Trade-Related Policies of CIS Countries', *Journal of World Trade* (29) (4), pp. 165–92.

Marceau, Gabrielle (2001), 'Conflicts of Norms and Conflicts of Jurisdictions: The Relationship Between the WTO Agreement and MEAs and Other Treaties', *Journal of World Trade* (35) (6), pp. 1081–131.

Marceau, Gabrielle and Pedersen, Peter N. (1999), 'Is the WTO Open and Transparent? A Discussion of the Relationship of the WTO with Non-Governmental Organizations and Civil Society's Claims for More Transparency and Public Participation', *Journal of World Trade* (33) (1), pp. 5–49.

Martin, Will (2010), Development Implications of WTO Accession Procedures, in Drabek, Zdenek (ed.), *Is the World Trade Organization Attractive Enough for Emerging Economies? Critical Essays on the Multilateral Trading System*, Basingstoke, Palgrave Macmillan, pp. 13–36.

Matsushita, Mitsuo (2011), 'Export Control of Natural Resources: WTO Panel Ruling on the Chinese Export Restrictions of Natural Resources', *Trade, Law and Development* (3) (2), pp. 267–95.

Matsushita, Mitsuo (2012), 'A Note on the Appellate Body Report in the Chinese Minerals Export Restrictions Case', *Trade, Law and Development* (4) (2), pp. 400–420.

Mattoo, Aaditya (2003), 'China's Accession to the WTO: The Services Dimension', *Journal of International Economic Law* (6) (2), pp. 299–339.

Messerlin, Patrick A. (2004), 'China in the World Trade Organization: Antidumping and Safeguards', *World Bank Economic Review* (18) (1), pp. 105–30.

Milthorp, Peter (2009), 'WTO Accessions: The Story so Far', *The Hague Journal of Diplomacy* (4) (1), pp. 103–12.

Milthorp, Peter and Christy, David (2011), Energy Issues in Selected WTO Accessions, in Selivanova, Yulia (ed.), *Regulation of Energy in International Trade Law, WTO, NAFTA and Energy Charter*, Alphen aan den Rijn, Kluwer Law International, pp. 259–302.

Miranda, Jorge (2014), 'Interpreting Paragraph 15 of China's Protocol of Accession', *Global Trade and Customs Journal* (9) (3), pp. 94–103.

Náray, Péter (2001), *Russia and the World Trade Organization*, Basingstoke, Palgrave.

Nguyen, Nhan (2008), 'WTO Accession at Any Cost? Examining the Use of WTO-Plus and WTO-Minus Obligations for Least-Developed Country Applicants', *Temple International & Comparative Law Journal* (22), pp. 243–77.

O'Connor, Bernard (2015), Constructing Normal Value in WTO Anti-Dumping Law: Giving Meaning to the Phrase Open, Market Oriented Policies in the Preamble to the Marrakesh Declaration, paper, Nctm Studio Legale, Italy, February.

O'Connor, Bernard (2015), 'Much Ado about "Nothing": 2016, China and Market Economy Status', *Global Trade and Customs Journal* (10) (5), pp. 176–80.

Osakwe, Chiedu (2015), Contributions and Lessons from WTO Accessions: The Present and Future of the Rules-Based Multilateral Trading System, in Dadush, Uri and Osakwe, Chiedu (eds) (2015), *WTO Accessions and Trade Multilateralism: Case Studies and Lessons from the WTO at Twenty*, Cambridge, Cambridge University Press, pp. 219–308.

Parenti, Antonio (2000), 'Accession to the World Trade Organization: A Legal Analysis', *Legal Issues of Economic Integration* (27) (2), pp. 141–57.

Pauwelyn, Joost (2003), *Conflict of Norms in Public International Law: How WTO Law Relates to Other Rules of International Law*, Cambridge, Cambridge University Press.

Pauwelyn, Joost (2010), 'Case Note: Squaring Free Trade in Culture with Chinese Censorship: The WTO Appellate Body Report on China – Audiovisuals', *Melbourne Journal of International Law* (11) (1), pp. 119–40.

Pelc, Krzysztof J. (2011), 'Why Do Some Countries Get Better WTO Accession Terms than Others?', *International Organization* (65) (4), pp. 639–72.

Pham, Thi Hong Hanh (2011), 'Does WTO Accession Matter for the Dynamics of Foreign Investment and Trade? Vietnam's New Evidence', *Economics of Transition* (19) (2), pp. 255–85.

Piérola, Fernando (2010), 'The Availability of a GATT Article XX Defence with Respect to a Non-GATT Claim: Changing the Rules of the Game? Comments on the Appellate Body Report in China – Measures Affecting Trading Rights and Distribution Services for Certain Publications and Audiovisual Entertainment Products', *Global Trade and Customs Journal* (5) (4), pp. 172–5.

Pogoretskyy, Vitaliy (2013), 'Freedom of Transit and the Principles of Effective Right and Economic Cooperation: Can Systemic Interpretation of GATT Article V Promote Energy Security and the Development of an International Gas Market?', *Journal of International Economic Law* (16) (2), pp. 313–52.

Polouektov, Alexander (2002), 'Non-Market Economy Issues in the WTO Anti-Dumping Law and Accession Negotiations: Revival of a Two-Tier Membership', *Journal of World Trade* (36) (1), pp. 1–37.

Primo Braga, Carlos A. and Cattaneo, Olivier (eds) (2009), *The WTO and Accession Countries*, vols I and II, Cheltenham, UK and Northampton, MA, USA, Edward Elgar.

Qin, Julia Ya (1993), 'China and GATT: Accession Instead of Resumption', *Journal of World Trade* (27) (2), pp. 77–98.

Qin, Julia Ya (2003), '"WTO-Plus" Obligations and Their Implications for the World Trade Organization Legal System: An Appraisal of the China Accession Protocol', *Journal of World Trade* (37) (3), pp. 483–522.

Qin, Julia Ya (2004), 'WTO Regulation of Subsidies to State-Owned Enterprises (SOEs): A Critical Appraisal of the China Accession Protocol', *Journal of International Economic Law* (7) (4), pp. 863–919.

Qin, Julia Ya (2010), 'Challenges of Interpreting "WTO-Plus" Provisions', *Journal of World Trade* (44) (1), pp. 127–72.

Qin, Julia Ya (2011), 'Pushing the Limits of Global Governance: Trading Rights, Censorship and WTO Jurisprudence – A Commentary on the China-Publications Case', *Chinese Journal of International Law* (10), pp. 271–322.

Qin, Julia Ya (2012), 'Reforming WTO Discipline on Export Duties: Sovereignty over Natural Resources, Economic Development and Environmental Protection', *Journal of World Trade* (46) (5), pp. 1147–90.

Qin, Julia Ya (2012), 'The Predicament of China's "WTO-Plus" Obligation to Eliminate Export Duties: A Commentary on the China – Raw Materials Case', *Chinese Journal of International Law* (11) (2), pp. 237–46.

Qin, Julia Ya (2014), 'Judicial Authority in WTO Law: A Commentary on the Appellate Body's Decision in China – Rare Earths', *Chinese Journal of International Law* (13) (4), pp. 639–51.

Qin, Julia Ya (2015), 'The Conundrum of WTO Accession Protocols: In Search of Legality and Legitimacy', *Virginia Journal of International Law* (55) (2), pp. 370–450.

Qin, Julia Ya (2017), Mind the Gap: Navigating Between the WTO Agreement and Its Accession Protocols, in Elsig, Manfred, Hoekman, Bernard and Pauwelyn, Joost (2017), *Assessing the World Trade*

Organization: Fit for Purpose?, Cambridge, Cambridge University Press, pp. 223–75.
Rao, Weijia (2013), 'China's Market Economy Status under WTO Antidumping Law after 2016', *Tsinghua China Law Review* (5), pp. 151–68.
Roessler, Frieder (1975), 'GATT and Access to Supplies', *Journal of World Trade* (9) (1), pp. 25–40.
Rose, Andrew K. (2004), 'Do We Really Know That the WTO Increases Trade?', *The American Economic Review* (94) (1), pp. 98–113.
Sachs, Jeffrey D. and Woo, Wing Thye (2003), 'China's Economic Growth after WTO Membership', *Journal of Chinese Economic and Business Studies* (1) (1), pp. 1–31.
Shaffer, Gregory (2015), 'How the World Trade Organization Shapes Regulatory Governance', *Regulation and Governance* (9) (1), pp. 1–15.
Spadi, Fabio (2002), 'Discriminatory Safeguards in the Light of the Admission of the People's Republic of China to the World Trade Organization', *Journal of International Economic Law* (5) (2), pp. 421–43.
Steger, Debra P. (2005), The Challenges to the Legitimacy of the WTO, in Charnovitz, Steve, Steger, Debra P. and Van den Bossche, Peter (eds), *Law in the Service of Human Dignity: Essays in Honour of Florentino Feliciano*, Cambridge, Cambridge University Press, pp. 202–21.
Stern, Brigitte (2010), Interpretation in International Trade Law, in Fitzmaurice, Malgosia, Elias, Olufemi and Merkouris, Panos (eds) (2010), *Treaty Interpretation and the Vienna Convention on the Law of Treaties: 30 Years On*, Leiden, Nijhoff, pp. 111–28.
Subramanian, Arvind and Wei, Shang-Jin (2007), 'The WTO Promotes Trade, Strongly but Unevenly', *Journal of International Economics* (72), pp. 151–75.
Toohey, Lisa (2012), 'Barriers to Universal Membership of the World Trade Organization', *Australian International Law Journal* (19), pp. 97–115.
Toohey, Lisa (2014), 'Accession as Dialogue: Epistemic Communities and the World Trade Organization', *Leiden Journal of International Law* (27) (2), pp. 397–418.
Tyagi, Mitali (2012), 'Flesh on a Legal Fiction: Early Practice in the WTO on Accession Protocols', *Journal of International Economic Law* (15) (2), pp. 391–441.
Unterhalter, David (2015), The Appellate Body under Review, in Marceau, Gabrielle (ed.) (2015), *A History of Law and Lawyers in the GATT/WTO: The Development of the Rule of Law in the Multilateral Trading System*, Cambridge, Cambridge University Press, pp. 466–75.

Valles, Cherise (2015), 'Appellate Body Report in China: Rare Earths – Addressing Violations of WTO-Plus Obligations', *Global Trade and Customs Journal* (10) (4), pp. 130–35.

Van Damme, Isabelle (2009), *Treaty Interpretation by the WTO Appellate Body*, Oxford, Oxford University Press.

Van Damme, Isabelle (2010), 'Treaty Interpretation by the WTO Appellate Body', *European Journal of International Law* (21) (3), pp. 605–48.

Van den Bossche, Peter and Zdouc, Werner (2013), *The Law and Policy of the World Trade Organization*, Third Edition, Cambridge, Cambridge University Press

Villiger, Mark E. (2009), *Commentary on the 1969 Vienna Convention on the Law of Treaties*, Leiden, Martinus Nijhoff.

Wang, Heng (2010), Enhancing Business Participation in Trade Policy-Making: Lessons from China, in Steger, Debra P. (ed.) (2010), *Redesigning the World Trade Organization for the Twenty-First Century*, Ottawa, Centre for International Governance Innovation, pp. 257–84.

Wang, Lei (1994), 'Non-Application Issues in the GATT and the WTO', *Journal of World Trade* (28) (2), pp. 49–74.

Watson, Keith William (2012), Interpreting WTO Accession Commitments According to Their Functional Relationship with Provisions of the WTO Agreements, Thesis submitted in partial satisfaction of the requirements for the degree of Master of Laws, Faculty of the George Washington University Law School, 20 May.

Willemyns, Ines (2016), 'Disciplines on State-Owned Enterprises in International Economic Law: Are We Moving in the Right Direction?', *Journal of International Economic Law* (19) (3), pp. 657–80.

Williams, Peter John (2008), *A Handbook on Accession to the WTO*, Cambridge, Cambridge University Press.

Wouters, Jan and De Meester, Bart (2007), *The World Trade Organization: A Legal and Institutional Analysis*, Antwerp, Intersentia.

Wouters, Jan, Coppens, D. and Geraets, D. (2012), The Influence of General Principles of Law, in Gaines, Sanford E., Olsen, Britte Egelund and Sørensen, Karsten Engsig (eds), *Liberalizing Trade – in the EU and the WTO – a Legal Comparison*, Cambridge, Cambridge University Press, pp. 43–74.

Yamaoka, Tokio (2013), 'Analysis of China's Accession Commitments in the WTO: New Taxonomy of More and Less Stringent Commitments, and the Struggle for Mitigation by China', *Journal of World Trade* (47) (1), pp. 105–58.

Index

accession commitments
  Accession Commitments Database (ACDB) 206–7
  additional 62
  anti-dumping 249–53
  'best-efforts' type 301
  categorization of
    anti-dumping investigations, allowing methodologies of other WTO Members 224–7
    conformity, ensuring 214–15
    efforts to categorize in protocols of accession 205–7
    implementing WTO obligations and bringing measures into conformity with 215–23
    'prohibitions' 227–8
    transitional periods and special and differential treatment 213–14
  China 112, 113, 173, 222, 272, 276, 284, 290, 301, 302
  establishing 17–18
  GATT 1947 17–18
  goods 90–92
  incorporation by reference into protocols of accession 118
  interpretation in protocols of accession 4
  Kazakhstan 233, 236, 237–8, 283, 286, 289, 298
  legal basis for rules commitments 138–40
  legal status in Working Party reports 116–18
  non-market economies (NMEs) 248–9
  relationship between commitments in protocols of accession and WTO Agreement 132, 138–97
    Article XX of GATT 1994 140–91
    relevance of protocols of accession for the interpretation of other agreements 195–7
    rights for other WTO Members in protocols of accession 191–3
    waivers in protocols of accession 193–5
  rules *see* rules commitments
  Russian Federation 223, 236, 237, 283, 286, 289
  services 92, 94, 223
  Tajikistan 225, 238, 272, 284, 301, 302
  typology 204, 212–28
  Ukraine 232, 236, 289, 295
  Viet Nam 225, 236–7, 272, 277, 284, 295, 302
'accession package' 3–4, 70, 71, 312
  contents 62, 87
  negotiations 97
  protocols of accession 87–9
  Schedules of Concessions 90
  Working Party Reports (WPRs) 62, 88, 89
ACDB (Accession Commitments Database) 206–7
acquiescence doctrine 137
ADA *see* Anti-Dumping Agreement (ADA)
Ad-Hoc Tariff Procedures Sub-committee 37, 38
Advisory Centre on WTO Law (ACWL) 317–18

Afghanistan 7, 207, 213, 280, 320
African countries, accession to GATT 45
Aggregate Measurement of Support (AMS) 91
Agreement Establishing the World Trade Organization *see* WTO Agreement (Agreement Establishing the World Trade Organization (15 April 1994)
Agreement on Customs Valuation 213, 218, 235
Agreement on Government Procurement (GPA) 81, 219
Agreement on Implementation of Article VI of the General Agreement on Tariffs and Trade 1994 (Anti-Dumping Agreement) *see* Anti-Dumping Agreement (ADA)
Agreement on Import Licensing Procedures 148
Agreement on Preshipment Inspection 148
Agreement on Rules of Origin 31
Agreement on Subsidies and Countervailing Measures *see* SCM Agreement (Agreement on Subsidies and Countervailing Measures) 91–2
Agreement on the Trade-Related Aspects of Intellectual Property Rights *see* TRIPs Agreement (Agreement on the Trade-Related Aspects of Intellectual Property Rights)
Agreement on Trade Facilitation (TFA) 149
Agreement on Trade in Civil Aircraft 219–20
Agreement on Trade-Related Investment Measures *see* TRIMs (Trade-Related Investment Measures) Agreement
agricultural support and export subsidies 91–92
Annecy Protocol, GATT 1947 37
Antidumping Manual of the United States Department of Commerce (USDOC) 254, 265
Antidumping (AD) Code 1967 76
Anti-Dumping Agreement (ADA) 193, 215, 224–5
  see also Antidumping (AD) Code 1967; anti-dumping investigations/proceedings; NMEs and anti-dumping investigations
  alleged infringement 272
  and non-market economies 249–50, 259, 261–2, 263, 265, 269, 270
anti-dumping investigations/proceedings
  see also Anti-Dumping Agreement (ADA)
  accession commitments 249–53
  Basic Anti-Dumping Regulation (EU) 253–4, 255, 258, 261–3
  economic characterization of a state 50
  individual margins of dumping 225
  and NMEs *see* NMEs and anti-dumping investigations
  other WTO Members, allowing different methodology 224–7
  price comparability in determining subsidies and dumping 225–6
  in United States 254–5
Antigua 45
Appellate Body (WTO) 5, 97, 109, 130, 137
  see also dispute settlement system (of WTO); *Table of Cases*; WTO (World Trade Organization); WTO Agreement (Agreement Establishing the World Trade Organization (15 April 1994)
  and Article XX of GATT 1994 142, 143, 145, 169–72, 174–6, 178, 180–84, 188–9
  characterization of protocols of accession as integral parts of WTO Agreement 99, 113, 116, 120, 122–3, 129

criticism of 98, 119, 129, 174, 199, 315
interpretative approach 5, 118, 174, 190–91, 199, 203
and membership of the WTO 59, 64
on non-market economies (NMEs) 256–7, 265, 271
pragmatic approach of 120, 310
relationship between commitments in protocols of accession and WTO Agreement 142, 143, 145
and relevance of protocols of accession for interpretation of other instruments 195–6
subsequent agreement concept 134, 135
applicable law, dispute settlement 108–9
Argentina 43
Armenia 216, 220, 247
Article XX of GATT 1994 5, 99, 137, 199, 287, 314, 315
see also GATT 1994 (General Agreement on Tariffs and Trade 1994)
balancing rights and obligations arising from protocols of accession with covered agreements 186–91
export duties 275, 276, 278
general exceptions *see* general exceptions, Article XX of GATT 1994
Panel reports 141–2, 144, 168–9, 173, 174, 176–7, 180
protocols of accession
balancing rights and obligations with covered agreements 186–91
references to Article XX in 150–68
relationship between commitments in and WTO Agreement 139, 140–91
and WTO dispute settlement 168–85
references to 151–67
in protocols of accession 150–68
in WTO agreements 148–9
relationship between commitments in protocols of accession and WTO Agreement 139, 140–91
discrimination test 145–6
exhaustible natural resources concept 143, 144
two-tier test 145
three-tier test 143, 144
scope of application 99, 146–68
substance of 99, 140–46
Asia-Pacific Economic Cooperation (APEC) 60

Bali Ministerial Conference (2013) 65, 67, 81
Barbuda 45
baseline obligations in WTO Agreement 6, 74–5, 311
mapping exercise 204, 211, 212–13, 264
Belize 45
Botswana 45
Bretton Woods Conference (July, 1944)/framework 11, 12
Brexit (vote for UK leaving the EU), 2016 1
Buenos Aires Ministerial Conference (December 2017) 65
Bulgaria 222, 274, 275, 284

Cambodia 248
Cancún Ministerial Conference (September 2003) 65, 66
Cape Verde 223, 286
categorization of acceding countries
GATT 1947 47–52
former colonies 37, 47, 72
non-market economies (NMEs) 47–52
NMEs (non-market economies) 296–7
Central and Eastern European countries 49, 51
Chile 41
China
accession bid to WTO (2001) 29

agricultural sector, benefits of WTO accession on 28
bilateral agreements with US 64
commitments 112, 113, 173, 222, 272, 276, 284, 290, 301, 302
disputes involving 110–11, 112, 118, 121
foreign direct investment (FDI) 290
as NME 247
protocol of accession 88, 89, 111, 112, 118, 128, 195, 199, 209, 223, 226
anti-dumping measures 225, 250, 251, 252, 272
export duties 276
non-market economies (NMEs) 256, 257–8
quest for market economy status 267, 268
relationship between commitments in protocols of accession and WTO Agreement 150, 169, 170, 173, 174, 177–9, 183–5
status 192
Transitional Product-Specific Safeguard Mechanism (TPSSM) 245, 248
transitional safeguards 191–2, 240
WTO-Plus obligations 205
quest for market economy status 267–73
state-owned enterprises (SOEs) 222
transitional safeguards 240, 243
and United States 64, 113, 244, 266–7
Working Party Report 113, 150, 193, 222, 276
WTO challenge against anti-dumping practices in December 2016 266–7
Colombia 45, 141–2
colonies, former 37, 47, 72
commitments *see* accession commitments
Committee on Regional Trade Agreements (CRTA) 298
Convention of International Union for the Protection of New Varieties of Plants 220
'Copenhagen Criteria' 49
'covered' agreements 107–8, 109
balancing rights and obligations with 186–91
critical mass agreements 33, 35
Croatia 276, 277, 284, 301
Cuba 51
customs valuation 6, 213, 218, 235
Czechoslovakia 50, 51

developing country Members 79, 209
see also LDCs (Least-Developed Countries)
capacity issues 316, 319
technical barriers to trade (TBTs) 286–7
differential export tax (DET) 271
discrimination test
arbitrary discrimination 145, 146
Article XX of GATT 1994 145–6
non-discrimination principle 14–20, 22, 27
unjustifiable discrimination 145–6
dispute settlement system (of WTO)
see also Appellate Body (WTO); WTO Agreement (Agreement Establishing the World Trade Organization) (15 April 1994)
conflict, notion of 130–31
Dispute Settlement Body *see* DSB (Dispute Settlement Body), WTO
Dispute Settlement Understanding *see* DSU (Understanding on Rules and Procedures Governing the Settlement of Disputes)
enforceability of protocols of accession under 98, 105–38, 313–15
absence of enforceability arguments 112–16
interim conclusions 118–19
judicial activism issues 105–6

legal status of commitments in Working Party Reports 116–18
legal theory of enforceability 119–38
involving protocols of accession 110–19
multilateral nature 137
Panel reports 97, 111, 113–18, 120, 122, 137
as quasi-judicial system 81
'reversed-consensus' rule 21
and Vienna Convention 98, 109, 115, 121, 127, 128
Working Party Reports (WPRs) 112–14, 116–18
Dispute Settlement Understanding *see* DSU (Understanding on Rules and Procedures Governing the Settlement of Disputes)
Doha Development Agenda 319–20
Doha Development Round (2001) 32–34, 80, 81
Doha Ministerial Conference (November 2001) 65, 66, 80
Doha Ministerial Decision on Implementation-Related Issues and Concerns 135
Draft Annecy Protocol of Terms of Accession to the General Agreement on Tariffs and Trade 37
DSB (Dispute Settlement Body), WTO 4, 5, 21, 79
jurisdiction 86, 121
DSU (Understanding on Rules and Procedures Governing the Settlement of Disputes)
see also dispute settlement system (of WTO)
Article 1.1 86, 126
Article 3.2 105, 108, 189
Article 11 108, 119
Article 19.2 106, 189
as Annex 2 to WTO Agreement 107
Appendix 1 86–87, 107–8, 109, 134, 180
applicable law 108–9
'covered' agreements 107–8, 109
functions provided in 79
jurisdiction 107–8
references to protocols of accession in 86–7
and Vienna Convention 109

EAEU *see* Eurasian Economic Union (EAEU)
Eastern European countries 51
see also specific countries, such as Russian Federation; Ukraine
economic motives for WTO accession 23–8
country- and sector-specific impacts 27–8
foreign direct investment (FDI) 26–7, 33
non-discrimination 27
trade increases 23–6
economic policies 231–4
Ecuador 87, 297
embedded liberalism 248
enforceability of protocols of accession 100–138
see also accession commitments
under GATT regime 100–105
judicial activism issues 105–6
legal theory 98, 119–38
acquiescence doctrine 137
Article XII of WTO Agreement, under 126–7
interim conclusion 136–8
protocols of accession as an amendment or modification of WTO Agreement 123–5
protocols of accession as an integral part of WTO Agreement 99, 120–23
protocols of accession as subsequent practice or agreement 121, 132–6
protocols of accession as successive treaty relating to same subject matter 127–32
under WTO dispute settlement system 105–38

absence of enforceability arguments 112–16
DSU 107–9
interim conclusions 118–19
involving protocols of accession 110–19
legal status of commitments in Working Party Reports 116–18
legal theory 119–38
Estonia 275, 276, 277, 284, 290
Eurasian Economic Union (EAEU) 237, 238, 299
European Commission 49
European Councils 49
European Law Students' Association (ELSA) 319
European Union (EU)
accession process 48–9
Basic Anti-Dumping Regulation 253–4, 255, 258, 261–3
challenges against the treatment of NMEs, in anti-dumping investigations 255–64
China's quest for market economy status in 267–73
China's WTO challenge against anti-dumping practices in December 2016 266–7
trade defence instruments reform 267–73
existing legislation exception ('grandfather clause'), GATT regime 100–105, 198
export duties 273–85
export subsidies 91–2
externalities of WTO accession 29–32

foreign direct investment (FDI) 289–91
investment regime 290
as motive for WTO accession 26–7, 33
trading rights 290–91
TRIMs 291
and WTO accession 26
founding parties *see under* GATT 1947 (General Agreement on Tariffs and Trade 1947)
future developments 316–20
trade defence instruments reform 267–73
universal membership 316–20
WTO accession process reform 65–9

GATS (General Agreement on Trade in Services) 73, 148, 218, 222, 297, 299
framework for making and enforcing policies 235, 236
policies affecting trade in services 294, 297
Schedule of Specific Commitments annexed to 89
GATT 1947 (General Agreement on Tariffs and Trade 1947)
Annecy Protocol 37
Article I 16, 17
Article I(1) 15
Article II 14–15, 16, 17
Article III 15, 16, 17
Article VI, Article VI:1 263
Article XI 103, 104
Article XXIII 37
Article XXIV:2 37
Article XXV 37
Article XXV:5 101
Article XXVI 37
Article XXVI:5(c) 37, 40, 42–5, 47, 69, 72, 97
Article XXXIII 21, 37–40, 41, 42, 51, 69, 72, 97, 246
Preamble 14, 16
Part I 14
Part II 14
Part III 14
becoming a Contracting Party to 37–52
beginnings 41–6
categorization of acceding countries 47–52
joining GATT as accession or succession 37–40

categorization of acceding countries 47–52
former colonies 37, 47, 72
non-market economies (NMEs) 47–52
commitments, establishing 17–18
Contracting Parties 1, 2, 4, 37–52, 308
and multilateral trading system 13, 14, 15
original 14, 39, 51, 69, 72
and WTO 20, 21
creation 19, 22
drafting of 37, 51
early multilateral trading system 13–20
entry into force 13
foreign policy objectives 18–20
founding of 2
'grandfather clause' (existing legislation exception) 100–105, 198
growth in membership
in 1950s 42
in 1960s 43–4
in 1970s 44–5
in 1980s 45
in 1990s 46–7
and the ITO 12–13, 75
limitations of 83
Most-Favoured-Nation (MFN) treatment 15, 17
National Treatment principle 15–16
negotiations 2, 13, 37, 50, 73
New York Conference 1947 37
non-discrimination principle 14, 14–20
non-market economies (NMEs) 245–7
'open-door' policy 69–70
original Contracting Parties 41
Panel reports 2, 20, 100–105
Preamble 246
Protocol of Provisional Application (PPA) 13–14, 41, 102–3
rationale underpinning 14–20
reciprocity principle 14–20
relationship with GATT 1994 20, 146–7
rules 20
signature of Final Act 41
tariff reduction agreement, perceived as 2
terms-of-trade losses, avoiding 16–17
text 146–7
Working Party on Accession 37
World Trade Organization succeeding 1, 20
GATT 1994 (General Agreement on Tariffs and Trade 1994)
Ad Note to Article VI:1 50, 51, 256, 259, 260, 262, 263, 266
Article I 147, 191, 278
Article I:1 283, 284
Article I(a) 20–21
Article II 191
Article III 112, 140, 191, 217, 288, 291
Article V 233
Article VI 249, 250, 252, 264
Article VI:1 50, 256, 259, 260, 262, 263, 269
Article VI:2 193
Article VIII 276, 280
Article X 217, 218, 236
Article X:1 31
Article X:2 235
Article XI 274
Article XI:2(a) 275
Article XIX 240
Article XVII 221, 222–3
Article XVII:1(b) 222
Article XX *see* Article XX of GATT 1994
Article XXIV 299
Article XXIV:8 283
Article XXVIII 279
Article XXXIII 3, 70
Introductory Text 85–6
references to protocols of accession in 84–6
relationship with GATT 1947 20, 146–7

Schedule of Concessions and Commitments annexed to 89
GATT regime
see also GATT 1947 (General Agreement on Tariffs and Trade 1947); GATT 1994 (General Agreement on Tariffs and Trade 1994)
enforceability of protocols of accession under 100–105
Harmonized System 195–6
impact on trade 24, 25
General Agreement on Tariffs and Trade 1947 *see* GATT 1947 (General Agreement on Tariffs and Trade 1947)
General Agreement on Trade in Services (GATS) *see* GATS (General Agreement on Trade in Services)
General Council of WTO 62, 79, 80
general exceptions, Article XX of GATT 1994 99, 137, 171, 198, 199, 314, 315, 318
see also Article XX of GATT 1994; existing legislation exception ('grandfather clause'), GATT regime; GATT 1994 (General Agreement on Tariffs and Trade 1994); protocols of accession
export duties 276, 278–9, 284
relationship between commitments in protocols of accession and WTO Agreement 140, 141
balancing rights and obligations with covered agreements 187, 188, 190
protocols of accession and WTO dispute settlement 174, 177, 178, 184
scope of application of Article XX 148, 149
Geneva Ministerial Conference (December 2009) 65, 67
Geneva Ministerial Conference (December 2011) 65, 67
Geneva Ministerial Conference (May 1998) 65
Georgia 216, 247, 276, 277, 284
Germany 100–101
Ghana 42
global value chains (GVCs) 244, 319
goods, policies affecting trade in 240–89
see also services
export duties 273–85
NMEs, and anti-dumping investigations 245–73
SPS Agreement 287–9
TBT Agreement 285–7
transitional safeguards 240–45
goods commitments 90–92
governance, improved 27, 32, 33, 34, 320
'grandfather clause' (existing legislation exception), GATT regime 100–105, 198
gross domestic product (GDP) 24

Haiti 42
Havana Charter, ITO 12, 14, 49–50
historical institutionalism 62
Hong Kong 45
Hong Kong Ministerial Conference (December 2005) 65, 66–7
Hungary 27
Contracting Party, becoming 51, 52, 70

Iceland 43
Indonesia 40, 42
information technology, liberalization 80–81
institutional structure of the WTO 5, 79–80
interface principle 248
International Law Commission (ILC) 133
International Monetary Fund (IMF)
accession to 69
creation 11
goals 11–12
International Trade Organization (ITO) 2, 37, 75

and GATT 1947 12–13, 75
Havana Charter 12, 14, 49–50
International Union for the Protection of New Varieties of Plants (UPOV) 220, 221
interpretative approach
as all-purpose response 120–21
of Appellate Body 5, 118, 174, 190–91, 199, 203, 314
'textualist' 188, 190
interventionist policy 270, 272
Ireland 43
Israel 43
ITO *see* International Trade Organization (ITO)

Jordan 289
judicial activism 105–6
jurisdiction, and dispute settlement 107–8
and DSB 86, 121

Kazakhstan 7, 168, 207, 238, 248, 290, 318
commitments 233, 236, 237–8, 283, 286, 289, 298
economic policies 231–2
waivers in protocols of accession 193, 194, 195
Working Party Report 231, 233, 238, 279, 299
Kennedy Round 76, 83
Korea 43

Lao PDR 223, 293
Latvia 275, 284
lawmaking, in protocols of accession 309–13
LDCs (Least-Developed Countries) 26, 78, 209, 316, 318, 319, 321
accession difficulties 68–71
Guidelines for the Accession of LDCs 68, 71
Least-Developed Countries and Accessions Programme 316
technical barriers to trade (TBTs) 286–7
transitional periods 68, 214, 289
legal theory
enforceability of protocols of accession 98, 119–38
acquiescence doctrine 137
Article XII of WTO Agreement, under 126–7
interim conclusion 136–8
protocols of accession as an amendment or modification of WTO Agreement 123–5
protocols of accession as an integral part of WTO Agreement 99, 120–23, 129
protocols of accession as subsequent practice or agreement 121, 132–6
protocols of accession as successive treaty relating to same subject matter 127–32
legality, versus legitimacy 4
legalization of multilateral trading system 72–5
Lesotho 45
liberalization of trade 2, 4, 32, 49, 139, 239
multilateral trading system 73, 75
NMEs and GATT 1947 245–6, 247
Liberia 7, 207, 290

Malaysia 42
Maldives 45
mapping exercise 6–7, 203–29
categorization of commitments
anti-dumping investigations, allowing methodologies of other WTO Members 224–7
conformity, ensuring 214–15
implementing WTO obligations and bringing measures into conformity with 215–23
'prohibitions' 227–8
transitional periods and special and differential treatment 213–14
implementing WTO obligations and bringing measures into conformity with 215–23
internal taxes 216–17

international agreements 219–21
state-owned enterprises 221–3
transparency 217–19
numbers 207–11
protocols of accession, efforts to categorize commitments in 205–7
results 230–303
economic policies 231–4
foreign direct investment (FDI) 289–91
framework for making/enforcing policies 234–40
goods, policies affecting trade in 240–89
protocols of accession, rules commitments in 230
services, policies affecting trade in 294–7
trade agreements 297–300
TRIPs Agreement 291–4
scope 207–12
substance of 211–12
typology of accession protocol commitments 204, 212–28
market economy
China's quest for market economy status 267–73
missing terminology in GATT 1947 and WTO Agreement 49, 246
Marrakesh Agreement *see* WTO Agreement (Agreement Establishing the World Trade Organization (15 April 1994)
Mauritius 44
membership of GATT 2, 3
see also GATT 1947 (General Agreement on Tariffs and Trade 1947)
evolution of 33, 36, 42–7
countries joining in 1950s 42
countries joining in 1960s 43–4
countries joining in 1970s 44–5
countries joining in 1980s 45
countries joining in 1990s 46–7
First Admission Case 47–8
impact on trade 24, 25
original Contracting Parties 33, 97
membership of the WTO 3, 4, 6
see also WTO (World Trade Organization); WTO accession; WTO Agreement (Agreement Establishing the World Trade Organization (15 April 1994)
development 52–3
new WTO members in the 2000s 53
new WTO members in the 2010s and beyond 54–5
new WTO members the 1990s 53
growth in membership from 1995 to 2016 3
impact on trade 24, 25
multi-tiered 4, 6, 74, 75, 308–9
non-original Members 60, 68, 77, 82, 84, 97, 98, 99, 121, 139, 185, 210, 276, 308, 309, 310, 313
original Members 59–60, 61, 74, 82, 84, 99, 291, 307, 308, 309
two-tiered 73, 93, 139
WTO Agreement 82
Mexico 45
MFN *see* Most-Favoured-Nation (MFN) treatment
Mill, John Stuart 19
Ministerial Conferences of the WTO 62, 65–9, 79, 124, 125
Bali (2013) 65, 67, 81
Buenos Aires (December 2017) 65
Cancún (September 2003) 65, 66
Doha (November 2001) 65, 66
Geneva (December 2009) 65, 67
Geneva (December 2011) 65, 67
Geneva (May 1998) 65
Hong Kong (December 2005) 65, 66–7
Nairobi (2015) 67–9
Seattle (November–December 1999) 65
Singapore (December 1996) 65
Mongolia 275
Montenegro 232, 278, 284, 296, 301
Morocco 45
Most-Favoured-Nation (MFN) treatment 15, 17, 239, 284

rationales for WTO accession 23, 27
Multilateral Trade Agreements (annexed to WTO Agreement) 17, 21, 198, 246
see also trade agreements; WTO Agreement (Agreement Establishing the World Trade Organization (15 April 1994)
commitments in protocols and WTO Agreement, relationship between 177–80
and DSU 107–8, 115
joining the WTO 56–60, 68
mapping exercise 214, 227
and protocols of accession 136
relationship between commitments in protocols of accession and WTO Agreement 182, 183, 184, 185, 187, 189
and WTO Agreement 82, 83
multilateral trading system 72–94, 75, 308
see also GATT 1947 (General Agreement on Tariffs and Trade 1947); GATT 1994 (General Agreement on Tariffs and Trade 1994); WTO (World Trade Organization)
'accession package' *see* 'Accession Package'
Annex I Agreements 3
commitments *see* accession commitments
creation 11, 18
early period 11–20, 39
'entry fee' to 97, 114, 204, 321
as forum 25–6
institutional features 36
International Trade Organization 12–13
legalization 72–5
liberalization of trade 73, 75
motivations for joining 28
see also rationales for WTO accession
participation of NMEs in 50
Punta del Este Declaration 1986 76–7
reasons for establishing 19
recommendations for states seeking to become part of 317–18
rules-based 1
single undertaking, WTO built upon 3, 75–93
unique nature of accession to 69
WTO Agreement *see* WTO Agreement (Agreement Establishing the World Trade Organization (15 April 1994)
WTO study 207
multi-tiered membership, of WTO 4, 6, 308–9

Nairobi Ministerial Conference (2015) 67–9
National Treatment principle 15–16, 27
negotiations
GATT 1947 2, 13, 37, 50, 73
trade agreements 299–300
trust-building 26
WTO accession 35, 73
WTO Agreement 80–81
Nepal 216
New York Conference (1947) 37
NMEs (non-market economies) 27, 231
see also WTO accession
and anti-dumping *see* NMEs and anti-dumping investigations
categorization of acceding countries 296–7
commitments of 248–9, 321
and GATT 1947 47–52, 245–7
imports from 50, 225, 253, 254, 257, 265
methodologies 145–73, 264, 269
participation in multilateral trading system 50, 52
as planned-economy countries 50
in the WTO 247–73
NMEs and anti-dumping investigations 245–73

see also anti-dumping investigations/proceedings
accession commitments on anti-dumping 249–53
challenges against the treatment of NMEs 253–66
against the EU 255–64
against the US 265–6
China's WTO challenge against anti-dumping practices in December 2016 266–7
non-discrimination principle
benefits of non-discrimination 27
energy sector 232
GATT 1947 14–20, 22
non-market economies (NMEs) *see* NMEs (non-market economies)
non-observer states (non-accessions) 55–6
non-tariff barriers (NTBs) 2, 73, 83, 239
Norway 103
notice-and-comment procedures 236, 239, 288
NTBs (non-tariff barriers) 2, 73, 239

Oman 220, 222

planned-economy countries (PECs), terminology 50
see also non-market economies (NMEs)
plurilateral trade agreements (PTAs) 22, 33, 35, 230
Poland 27, 40
Contracting Party, becoming 43, 51, 52
policies
domestic framework 6
economic 231–4
framework for making and enforcing 234–40
goods, affecting trade in 240–89
market-oriented 27
services, affecting trade in 294–7
trade, prior to Second World War 2
political motives for WTO accession 28–9
Portugal 43
preferential trade agreements (PTAs) 22
pre-shipment inspection 6
Principles of Political Economy (Mill) 19
production networks, international 33
'prohibitions,' accession commitments 227–8
protectionism 2, 234
Protocol of Provisional Application (PPA), GATT 1947 13–14, 41
dispute settlement 102–3
protocols of accession 97–199
see also accession commitments; WTO accession; WTO Agreement and protocols of accession
'accession package'/process 62, 87–9
as amendment or modification of the WTO Agreement 123–5
China 88, 89, 111, 112, 118, 128, 195, 199, 226
anti-dumping measures 225, 250, 251, 252, 272
export duties 276
mapping exercise 209, 223
non-market economies (NMEs) 256, 257–8
quest for market economy status 267, 268
relationship between commitments in protocols of accession and WTO Agreement 150, 169, 170, 173, 174, 177–9, 183–5
status 192
Transitional Product-Specific Safeguard Mechanism (TPSSM) 245, 248
transitional safeguards 191–2, 240
WTO-Plus obligations 205
efforts to categorize commitments in 205–7
enforceability *see* enforceability of protocols of accession

as integral part of WTO Agreement 99, 113, 116, 120–23, 129, 192, 198
interpretation of commitments in 4
lawmaking in 309–13
non-market economies (NMEs) 193
references to
in the DSU 86–7
in the GATT 1994 84–6, 150–68
in the WTO Agreement 83–4
relevance for the interpretation of other agreements 195–7
rights for other WTO Members in NME methodologies 193
transitional safeguards 191–3
Russian Federation 278, 300
Spain 101–2
structure 88, 89
as subsequent practice or agreement 132–6
as a successive treaty relating to same subject matter 127–32
transitional safeguards 191–3
waivers in 193–5
in WTO dispute settlement *see* dispute settlement system (of WTO)
PTAs *see* plurilateral trade agreements (PTAs)
Punta del Este Declaration 1986 76–7

quantitative restrictions 6

rationales for WTO accession 22–34
economic motives 23–8
externalities 29–32
governance, improved 27
market-oriented policies 27
political motives 28–9
reciprocity principle, GATT 1947 14–20
reform proposals, WTO accession process 65–9
Regional Comprehensive Economic Partnership 23
regional trade agreements (RTAs) 22, 32–4, 60, 81, 298, 315
regionalization, accession in times of 32–4
regulatory cooperation 239
'reversed-consensus' rule 21
Romania 27, 309
Contracting Party, becoming 51, 52, 70
RTAs *see* regional trade agreements (RTAs)
rule of law 6, 320
dispute settlement system (of WTO) 121, 125
mapping exercise 198, 234–5, 247
rationales for WTO accession 26, 31
rules commitments 4, 73, 92–3, 205, 230, 286
legal basis for 138–40
see also accession commitments
Russian Federation 137, 181, 317, 318
commitments 223, 236, 237, 283, 286, 289
export duties 278, 284
protocol of accession 209–10, 278, 300
Schedule of Concessions and Commitments 278

Samoa 290
sanitary and phytosanitary measures (SPS) 6, 287–9
see also SPS Agreement (Agreement on the Application of Sanitary and Phytosanitary Measures)
Saudi Arabia 167, 181, 289, 290, 295
export duties 276–7, 284
Schedules of Commitments 62, 89
Schedules of Concessions 62, 89, 90
SCM Agreement (Agreement on Subsidies and Countervailing Measures) 112, 172, 315
and Article XX of GATT 1994 147, 171, 189
mapping exercise 214, 215, 223, 225, 250–52

Seattle Ministerial Conference (November–December 1999) 65
services
  see also GATS (General Agreement on Trade in Services); goods, policies affecting trade in
  liberalization of trade in 73
  policies affecting trade in 294–7
  Punta del Este Declaration 77
  trade in 80
services commitments 92, 94, 223
Seychelles 218, 220
Singapore 44
Singapore Ministerial Conference (December 1996) 65
single undertaking, WTO built upon 3, 75–93, 311
  dispute settlement 81
  institutional structure of the WTO 79–80
  membership of the WTO 82
    see also membership of the WTO
  negotiations 80–81
  Punta del Este Declaration 1986 76–7
  references to protocols of accession 83–7
    in the DSU 86–7
    in GATT 1994 84–6
    in WTO Agreement 83–4
  scope of the WTO 83
  WTO Agreement 77–87
    see also WTO Agreement (Agreement Establishing the World Trade Organization (15 April 1994)
Spain 43, 101–2
special and differential treatment 213–14
SPS Agreement (Agreement on the Application of Sanitary and Phytosanitary Measures) 93, 287–9
  see also sanitary and phytosanitary measures (SPS)
  and Article XX of GATT 1994 147, 148, 171
  Committee 81
standardization of accession process 73
state interventionism 270, 272
state-owned enterprises (SOEs) 6, 221–3
subsequent agreement concept, protocols of accession 121, 132–6
subsidies 91–2
supply-chain trade 33, 35
Suriname 44
Switzerland 43, 100–101

Tajikistan 218, 220, 248, 250
  commitments 225, 238, 272, 284, 301, 302
  as market economy 253
  Working Party Report 193, 223, 226, 251, 253, 292
Tariff Agreement Committee 37
tariffs
  barriers, reducing 73, 78, 83
  concessions 40, 62, 73, 91, 194
  GATT 1947 perceived as a tariff reduction agreement 2
  Most-Favoured-Nation (MFN) treatment 239
  non-tariff barriers (NTBs) 2, 73, 83, 239
  Non-Tariff Measures 52
  renegotiations 194
  tariff rate quotas (TRQs) 6, 283
taxation
  differential export tax (DET) 271
  export duties 273–85
  internal 216–17
TBT Agreement (Agreement on Technical Barriers to Trade) 3, 135, 285, 285–7
  see also technical barriers to trade (TBTs)
  Committee 81
  rules commitments 92–3
technical barriers to trade (TBTs) 6
  see also TBT Agreement (Agreement on Technical Barriers to Trade)
Thailand 45, 104

Tokyo Round 52, 76, 83, 285
Tonga 290
TPP *see* Trans-Pacific Partnership (TPP)
TPSSM *see* Transitional Product-Specific Safeguard Mechanism (TPSSM)
trade
  see also TRIMs (Trade-Related Investment Measures); TRIPs Agreement (Agreement on the Trade-Related Aspects of Intellectual Property Rights)
  agreements *see* trade agreements
  agricultural 27–8
  foreign direct investment (FDI) 290–91
  impact of GATT/WTO on 24, 25
  liberalization of *see* liberalization of trade
  as motive for WTO accession 23–6
  policies affecting, in goods 240–89
  pre-Second World War policy 2
  relative to GDP 24
  remedies 215
  in services 80
  supply-chain 33, 35
  terms-of-trade losses, avoiding 16–17
  Transatlantic Trade and Investment Partnership (TTIP) 22
trade agreements 68, 297–300
  see also Multilateral Trade Agreements (annexed to WTO Agreement)
  and joining the WTO 59, 60
  plurilateral trade agreements (PTAs) 22, 33, 35, 230
  preferential trade agreements (PTAs) 22
  regional trade agreements (RTAs) 22, 32–4, 60, 81, 298, 315
  21st Century Trade Agreements 239
Trade in Services Agreement (TISA) 23
trade-related aspects of intellectual property rights (TRIPs) 6
  see also TRIPs Agreement (Agreement on the Trade-Related Aspects of Intellectual Property Rights)
Transatlantic Trade and Investment Partnership (TTIP) 22, 223, 230, 239, 287
Transitional Product-Specific Safeguard Mechanism (TPSSM) 242–5
  and China 245, 248
transitional safeguards
  goods, policies affecting trade in 240–45
  protocols of accession 191–3
Trans-Pacific Partnership (TPP) 23, 60, 223, 230, 239
transparency obligations 6, 217–19
Treaty on the European Union (TEU) 48–9
TRIMs (Trade-Related Investment Measures) Agreement 112, 148, 213
  foreign direct investment (FDI) 289, 291
TRIPs Agreement (Agreement on the Trade-Related Aspects of Intellectual Property Rights) 31, 93, 291–4
  mapping exercise 213–14, 218, 221, 235
TRQs (tariff rate quotas) 6, 283
Truman, Harry S. 19
trust-building 26
TTIP *see* Transatlantic Trade and Investment Partnership (TTIP)

Ukraine 220, 311
  commitments 232, 236, 289, 295
  export duties 277, 284
  Working Party Report 167, 168, 232, 237, 277, 311
UN Conference on Trade and Development (UNCTAD) 205
UN Conference on Trade and Employment 37

Second Session of the Preparatory Committee (1947) 41
Understanding on Rules and Procedures Governing the Settlement of Disputes *see* DSU (Understanding on Rules and Procedures Governing the Settlement of Disputes)
United Nations
accession to 69
Charter 47, 48
establishment (October, 1945) 12
UN Conference on Trade and Development 205
UN Conference on Trade and Employment 12, 41
United States 11, 309
anti-dumping legislation 254–5
challenges against the treatment of NMEs, in anti-dumping investigations 265–6
and China 64, 113, 244, 266–7
Uruguay 100–101
Uruguay Round of Multilateral Trade Negotiations (Uruguay Round) 2–3, 20, 21, 33, 36, 195
Agreements Act 266
completion 1, 46, 52, 56, 72, 146
impetus for 83
outcome 76–7
Punta del Este Declaration 1986 formally launching 76

Vanuatu 216, 217, 223
Vienna Convention on the Law of Treaties (1969)
Article 2 128
Article 30 127, 128, 130, 132, 135, 136, 180, 185, 187
Article 31 130, 132–3, 135, 144, 195, 196–7
Article 32 130
dispute settlement 98, 109, 115, 121, 127, 128
later-in-time rule 185
rules on treaty interpretation 132
Viet Nam 26, 216, 223, 225
commitments 225, 236–7, 272, 277, 284, 295, 302
NMEs and anti-dumping investigations 248, 250, 252, 272
protocols of accession, status 117–18, 121, 193
Working Party Report 193, 226, 237, 251, 252, 265

Wilcox, Clair 18–19, 50
Working Party Reports (WPRs)
'accession package' 62, 88, 89
accession process 62
Bulgaria 274
China 113, 117, 150, 174, 193, 222, 276
commitment paragraphs 208–9
GATT protocols of accession 104
Kazakhstan 231, 233, 238, 279, 299
Kyrgyz Republic 222
legal status of commitments in 116–18
Tajikistan 193, 223, 226, 251, 253, 292
taxation 217
transparency obligations 218
Ukraine 167, 168, 232, 237, 277, 311
Viet Nam 193, 226, 237, 251, 252, 265
WTO dispute settlement process 112–14, 116–18
Yemen 167
World Bank (WB)
accession to 69
creation 11
goals 11–12
World Trade Organization *see* WTO (World Trade Organization)
WPRs *see* Working Party Reports (WPRs)
WTO (World Trade Organization)
see also WTO accession
accession *see* WTO accession
Appellate Body *see* Appellate Body (WTO)

Committee on Regional Trade Agreements (CRTA) 298
countries not yet GATT Contracting Parties at time of establishment 57
dispute settlement *see* dispute settlement system (of WTO)
founding of (1995) 1, 20, 33, 52, 72, 76
functions 78–9
General Council 62, 79, 80
impact on trade 24, 25
institutional structure 5, 79–80
joining process 56–69
four-step 59–65
reform proposals 65–9
WTO Agreement 56–9
Least-Developed Countries and Accessions Programme 316
membership *see* membership of the WTO
Ministerial Conferences *see* Ministerial Conferences of the WTO
negotiations 80–81
NMEs in 247–73
objectives 77–8
Panel reports 97, 111, 113–18, 120, 122, 137, 299–300
protocols of accession *see* protocols of accession
references to Article XX of the GATT 1994 in agreements 148–9
scope 83
Secretariat 73
single undertaken, built upon 3, 75–93
succeeding of GATT 1947 1, 20
WTO accession
see also protocols of accession
'accession package' 3–4, 70, 71, 312
contents 62, 87
negotiations 97
protocols of accession 87–89
Schedules of Concessions 90
Working Party Reports (WPRs) 62, 88, 89
accession process
four-step 59–65
informality of 36, 60
reform proposals 65–69
standardization 73
tabular format 63
and agricultural sector 28
commitments *see* accession commitments
country- and sector-specific impacts 27–8
Doha Development Round (2001) 32–4, 80, 81
foreign direct investment (FDI) 26
impacts *see* impacts of accession
joining process 56–69
LDCs (Least-Developed Countries) *see* LDCs (Least-Developed Countries)
market access 73
negotiations 35, 73
non-GATT Contracting Parties 97
non-observer states (non-accessions) 55–6
in numbers 52–6
rationales for *see* rationales for WTO accession
regionalization, in times of 32–4
rules commitments 205
statistics 52–6
train track analogy 62
WTO Agreement (Agreement Establishing the World Trade Organization (15 April 1994) 77–87
Article II
Article II:1 78
Article II:2 83
Article II:4 85
Article III 78–9
Article III:2 80
Article III:3 81
Article IV
Article IV:2 79
Article IV:3 79
Article X 123–4, 125

Article XI 56–7, 82
Article XII 3, 5, 21, 56, 72, 82, 83, 84, 121, 124, 203–4, 221, 240, 246, 286, 292, 307, 310, 312
Article XII:1 57–60
Article XII:3 219
joining process 57–9, 61, 64, 70
as legal basis for enforcement 126–7
wording 70
Article XVI, Article XVI:4 235
Annex 2 107
Annex 4 219
accession conditions 69
Preamble 77–8, 246
baseline obligations *see* baseline obligations in WTO Agreement
creation 20
DSU as Annex 2 107
Ministerial Decision on Acceptance of and Accession to 84
objectives of the WTO in Preamble 77–8
obligations, implementing and bringing measures into conformity with 215–23
internal taxes 216–17
international agreements 219–21
state-owned enterprises 221–3
transparency 217–19
and protocols of accession *see* WTO Agreement and protocols of accession
scope 105, 138
signature in Marrakesh 77
terms 82
Trade Negotiations Committee, Marrakesh 84
as an umbrella agreement 3, 83
World Trade Organization based on 4
WTO Agreement and protocols of accession
commitments, relationship between 132, 138–97
Article XX of GATT 1994, under 140–90
issues 140–97
legal basis for rules commitments 138–40
relevance of protocols of accession for the interpretation of other agreements 195–7
rights for other WTO Members in protocols of accession 191–3
waivers in protocols of accession 193–5
dispute settlement 168–85
integration clause 123
petitio principii fallacy 122
protocols of accession as an amendment or modification of WTO Agreement 123–5
protocols of accession as integral part of WTO Agreement 99, 112, 114, 116, 120–23, 129, 192, 198
references to protocols of accession in WTO Agreement 83–4
WTO-Minus obligations 6, 206, 228, 245, 302
see also WTO-Plus obligations
WTO-Plus obligations 6, 7, 58, 293, 301, 309
see also WTO-Minus obligations
export duties 279
mapping exercise 205, 212, 218, 234, 245
protocols of accession, status 187, 188, 199

Yemen 167, 223
Yugoslavia 27, 43, 51
Contracting Party, becoming 70

Zambia 45